The Definitive Guide to Modern Java Clients with JavaFX 17

Cross-Platform Mobile and Cloud Development

Second Edition

Stephen Chin
Johan Vos
James Weaver

With Contributions by:
Gail Anderson, Paul Anderson, Bruno Borges, Anton Epple,
Weiqi Gao, Jonathan Giles, José Pereda, Sven Reimers,
Eugene Ryzhikov, and William Antônio Siqueira

Apress®

The Definitive Guide to Modern Java Clients with JavaFX 17: Cross-Platform Mobile and Cloud Development

Stephen Chin
Belmont, CA, USA

Johan Vos, PhD
Gluon, Leuven, Belgium

James Weaver
Marion, IN, USA

ISBN-13 (pbk): 978-1-4842- 7267-1
https://doi.org/10.1007/978-1-4842-7268-8

ISBN-13 (electronic): 978-1-4842- 7268-8

Managing Director, Apress Media LLC: Welmoed Spahr
Acquisitions Editor: Steve Anglin
Development Editor: Matthew Moodie
Coordinating Editor: Mark Powers

Cover designed by eStudioCalamar

Cover image by Janko Ferlic on Unsplash (www.unsplash.com)

Distributed to the book trade worldwide by Apress Media, LLC, 1 New York Plaza, New York, NY 10004, U.S.A. Phone 1-800-SPRINGER, fax (201) 348-4505, e-mail orders-ny@springer-sbm.com, or visit www. springeronline.com. Apress Media, LLC is a California LLC and the sole member (owner) is Springer Science + Business Media Finance Inc (SSBM Finance Inc). SSBM Finance Inc is a **Delaware** corporation.

For information on translations, please e-mail booktranslations@springernature.com; for reprint, paperback, or audio rights, please e-mail bookpermissions@springernature.com.

Apress titles may be purchased in bulk for academic, corporate, or promotional use. eBook versions and licenses are also available for most titles. For more information, reference our Print and eBook Bulk Sales web page at http://www.apress.com/bulk-sales.

Any source code or other supplementary material referenced by the author in this book is available to readers on GitHub via the book's product page, located at www.apress.com/9781484272671. For more detailed information, please visit http://www.apress.com/source-code.

Printed on acid-free paper

Table of Contents

About the Authors

Stephen Chin is Head of Developer Relations at JFrog and a Java Champion. He has keynoted numerous Java conferences around the world including Devoxx, JNation, JavaOne, Joker, and Open Source India. Stephen is an avid motorcyclist who has done evangelism tours in Europe, Japan, and Brazil, interviewing hackers in their natural habitat. When he is not traveling, he enjoys teaching kids how to do embedded and robot programming together with his teenage daughter. You can follow his hacking adventures at `http://steveonjava.com/`.

Johan Vos started to work with Java in 1995. He was part of the Blackdown team, porting Java to Linux. His main focus is on end-to-end Java, combining backend systems and mobile/embedded devices. He received a Duke's Choice Award in 2014 for his work on JavaFX on mobile.

In 2015, he cofounded Gluon, which allows enterprises to create (mobile) Java client applications leveraging their existing backend infrastructure. Gluon received a Duke's Choice Award in 2015.

Johan is a Java Champion, a member of the BeJUG and Devoxx steering groups, and a JCP member. He is one of the lead authors of the *Pro JavaFX* books (published by Apress) and the author of *Quantum Computing for Java Developers* (Manning), and he has been a speaker at numerous conferences on Java.

Johan contributes to a number of projects, including OpenJFX, OpenJDK, and GraalVM, and is the project lead for OpenJDK Mobile and the co-lead for OpenJFX.

James Weaver is a developer, author, and speaker with a passion for quantum computing and JavaFX. He is a Java Champion and a JavaOne Rockstar. James has written books including *Inside Java, Beginning J2EE*, the *Pro JavaFX* series, and *Raspberry Pi with Java*. As an IBM quantum developer advocate, James speaks internationally at quantum and classical computing conferences. He tweets as @JavaFXpert and blogs at `http://JavaFXpert.com` and `http://CulturedEar.com`.

About the Contributors

Gail C. Anderson is a Java Champion, Oracle Groundbreaker Ambassador, and past member of the NetBeans Dream Team. She is the director of research and founding member of the Anderson Software Group, a leading provider of training courses in Java, JavaFX, Python, Go, Modern C++, and other programming languages.

Gail enjoys researching and writing about leading-edge Java technologies. She is the co-author of eight textbooks on software programming, including *JavaFX Rich Client Programming on the NetBeans Platform*.

Gail has conducted technical sessions and hands-on labs at Oracle Code One and NetBeans Day conferences in San Francisco, Europe, and Latin America. Gail has also presented sessions at Devoxx and Devnexus.

For more information about Gail, visit asgteach.com, the Anderson Software Group on Facebook, and @gail_asgteach on Twitter.

Paul L. Anderson is a Java Champion, Oracle Groundbreaker Ambassador, and past member of the NetBeans Dream Team. He is the director of training and founding member of the Anderson Software Group, a leading provider of training courses in Java, JavaFX, Python, Go, Modern C++, and other programming languages.

Paul is an experienced speaker and specializes in making the technical aspects of software engineering fun and understandable. He is the co-author of eight textbooks on software programming, including *JavaFX Rich Client Programming on the NetBeans Platform*.

Paul has conducted technical sessions and hands-on labs at Oracle Code One and NetBeans Day conferences in San Francisco, Europe, and Latin America. Paul has also presented sessions at Devoxx and Devnexus and is the author of LiveLesson videos on JavaFX programming and Java Reflection.

For more information about Paul, visit asgteach.com, the Anderson Software Group on Facebook, and @paul_asgteach on Twitter.

Bruno Borges has been developing applications with the Java platform since 2000. Throughout his career, Bruno has developed desktop applications with Swing and JavaFX platforms, as well as dozens of large web systems with Java EE standards and third-party libraries like Spring Framework, Apache projects, and others. His experience building systems for corporations and government agencies led him to join big vendors like Oracle and Microsoft in the fields of product management and developer relations to foster investment in tools and runtimes for Java developers across different industries. Bruno is an active participant of the Java community at large and a recognized conference speaker and influencer and was recently named a Java Champion. Some of his most well-known public projects are the JavaFX port of the game *2048*, the Twitter component for Apache Camel, his work with Oracle to initiate the donation of NetBeans to the Apache Software Foundation, the Docker images for Oracle products, and the Java EE platform account on Twitter to foster the community. You can learn more about his work at https://brunoborges.io.

Anton Epple is a consultant for a wide variety of companies worldwide, ranging from startups to Fortune 500 companies, in many areas, including financial institutions and aerospace. Anton is a member of the NetBeans Dream Team and the organizer of the JayDay developer conference in Munich. In 2013, he joined the Java Champions and received a JavaOne Rockstar Award. In 2014, he received a Duke's Choice Award for his work on DukeScript.

Weiqi Gao is a partner and principal software engineer at Object Computing, Inc. in St. Louis, Missouri, USA. He has decades of software development experience and has been using Java technology since 1998. He is interested in programming languages, object-oriented systems, distributed and cloud computing, and graphical user interfaces. He is part of the original author team that produced the *Pro JavaFX* series for Apress. He is a member of the steering committee of the St. Louis Java Users Group. Weiqi holds a PhD in mathematics.

Jonathan Giles is a principal Java architect at Microsoft. Before this, he was a technical lead in the JavaFX team at Sun Microsystems and Oracle Corp. for 9 years, where he led the development of the JavaFX user interface (UI) controls library and other related libraries. With his considerable contributions to Java, he takes immense pride in having his code deployed on almost every computer on the planet. Jonathan is passionate about creating excellent developer experiences with considered API design, documentation, testing, and tooling. He has toured the world extensively to present and write on these topics, and as a result he is a Java Champion, a JavaOne Rockstar, and a Duke's Choice Award winner.

José Pereda, PhD, who specializes in structural engineering, works as a software engineer at Gluon Software. He is a Java Champion, Oracle Groundbreaker Ambassador, and JavaOne Rockstar. Having worked with Java since 1999, he is a JavaFX advocate, developing Java applications for mobile and embedded platforms connected to the cloud and enterprise systems. He also works on open source projects like OpenJFX and FXyz 3D (`https://github.com/jperedadnr`), co-authors JavaFX-related books (such as *JavaFX 8: Introduction by Example* and *JavaFX 9 by Example*, both published by Apress), blogs (`http://jperedadnr.blogspot.com.es/`), tweets (`@JPeredaDnr`), and speaks at JUGs and conferences (JavaOne, Devoxx, JAX, Jfokus, JavaLand, JCrete, JBCNConf, to name a few). José lives with his family in Valladolid, Spain.

Sven Reimers, based at Lake Constance in Southern Germany, works as a systems engineer at Airbus Defence and Space, creating next-generation ground segment software for space systems. He has more than 20 years of experience building complex software systems and more than 20 years of experience with Java, going back to its early days. In 2009, Reimers was the winner of the Duke's Choice Award in the Network Solutions category for ND SatCom Satellite Communication Management Software. He is part of the Apache NetBeans PMC, a contributor to OpenJFX, and the leader and founder of JUG Bodensee. For his long-term commitment to Java and the community, Reimers was named a Java Champion in 2014.

Eugene Ryzhikov is a software architect with more than 30 years of experience in software development and design. He has created software ranging from real-time maps for very specialized field units all the way to large energy trading systems. He has been using Java since the very beginning. His main interests are UI/UX, data visualization, advanced systems architecture/design, and serverless technology. Eugene is a cofounder of Gluon, an open source contributor, speaker at multiple conferences, and Java Rockstar.

In addition, his interests also include traditional Okinawan martial arts, jazz piano, and traveling with his lovely wife and daughter.

William Antônio Siqueira is a senior software engineer working at Red Hat and is a longtime JavaFX blogger and Java developer. He is also a local JUG contributor and has created and contributed to several Java and JavaFX projects. Previously, he contributed to Visage, a JavaFX DSL, and created the first JavaFX group in Portugal. His current interests include data visualization, machine learning, and process automation.

About the Technical Reviewer

 **Preethi Vasudev** earned an MS in Computer Information Systems and Cyber Security from Auburn University, Alabama. She is an Oracle-certified Java 8 programmer with more than 15 years of industry experience in investment banking, healthcare, and other areas. She is interested in Java and related technologies and enjoys participating in coding competitions.

Foreword

The early 1990s saw the introduction of several game-changing technologies, two of which were the Java programming language and the World Wide Web. Prior to that period, client-server architectures were all the rage. One of the big challenges of client-server was developing application user interfaces (UIs) for various client machines and operating systems.

While most of the application development world was content with adapting web-based technologies such as HTTP, HTML, and JavaScript to client application development, a remnant of developers envisioned an alternative future. This future is being realized today in the form of rich, responsive clients that execute on the nearly ubiquitous Java Virtual Machine (JVM). I have had the privilege of co-laboring with many of these talented and revolutionary developers, several of whom have contributed the content that you'll read in the following pages. These champions of JavaFX include Gail Anderson, Paul Anderson, Bruno Borges, Stephen Chin, Carl Dea, Toni Epple, Weiqi Gao, Jonathan Giles, José Pereda, Eugene Ryzhikov, Sven Reimers, William Antônio Siqueira, and Johan Vos.

Here's a sampling of the rich client treasures buried in this book: First, the groundwork is laid by showing how prevalent Java is in user interfaces that you may not have realized are written in Java. Then, the fundamentals of JavaFX are methodically revealed in a very approachable manner. After this treatment of foundational concepts, deep dives are taken in the important capabilities and libraries contained in JavaFX. Some of these capabilities are behind the scenes, such as JavaFX properties and binding, and some are visual, such as JavaFX controls and 3D graphics. After these JavaFX internal deep dives, several environments in which JavaFX can add much value are explored in depth. These environments include web, desktop, mobile, and embedded devices and the cloud. Finally, some leading-edge uses of JavaFX are discussed, including machine learning and scientific applications.

It is important to note that JavaFX is developed in the OpenJDK umbrella and has its own release vehicle. As such, there is only one JavaFX, and it works on desktop, mobile, and embedded platforms. JavaFX evolves with and leverages new features of Java, ensuring that it will continue to be a cutting-edge platform.

It is my pleasure and honor to recommend this book and the JavaFX technologies discussed and innovated by my dear friends and colleagues.

—James Weaver

CHAPTER 1

Getting Started with Client Java

Written by Stephen Chin

Client technologies are the basis for building any interface that users interact with. Because they are the first part of an application that a user sees, they also leave the greatest impact on your audience. Therefore, it is important that user interfaces look good and also are easy to use and intuitive.

Whether it be desktop, mobile, tablet, or embedded devices, Java client technologies provide a simple and elegant solution to building modern user experiences. Because the Java language is cross-platform, this reduces the effort to build and maintain your application for multiple screens and form factors. Also, as one of the most widely used programming languages, anyone can help maintain your code, making it a solid foundation for the future.

In this chapter, we will show some examples of Java client technology in action and guide you through building your own cross-platform client to demonstrate how easy it is to accomplish this.

Java Client Technology in Action

Java client technology has been used for decades for all sorts of applications from business applications to development tools and even games. Also, now that Java runs on mobile and embedded platforms, you also find Java applications on your phone, tablet, and Raspberry Pi devices. It is often hard to tell if you are using a Java application because it is packaged together with the required Java libraries, so it appears just like any other native application.

We will explore several different Java client applications that you may or may not have used to give you an idea of the potential of this technology.

© Stephen Chin, Johan Vos and James Weaver 2022
S. Chin et al., *The Definitive Guide to Modern Java Clients with JavaFX 17*,
https://doi.org/10.1007/978-1-4842-7268-8_1

Java Clients in Business

Java client technology is a staple in enterprise companies for internal applications. This is because it is great at building highly customized applications with complex controls like graphs, trees, tables, and Gantt charts. By building applications once and taking advantage of Java's cross-platform capabilities, enterprises save on initial implementation cost as well as maintenance.

Common use cases for Java client technology in the industry are high-speed trading, train monitoring and scheduling, supply chain management, medical imaging, and inventory management. MINT systems make a training and resource management system (TRMS) that has been adopted by numerous commercial airlines such as Emirates Airlines, JetBlue Airways, Azul Linhas Aéreas Brasileiras, FedEx Express, Lufthansa Group, and the Avianca-Taca Group.[1]

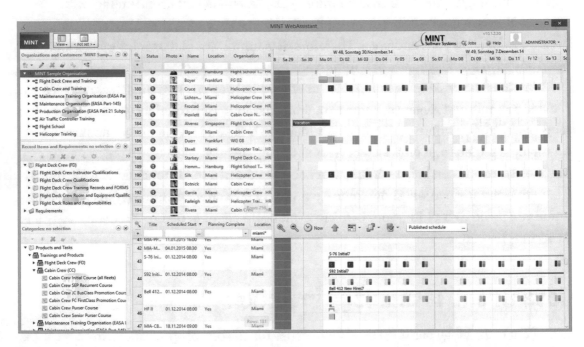

Figure 1-1. *MINT software system for airline training and resource management[2]*

---

[1] MINT Software Systems – European Airline Training Symposium (EATS). Retrieved from `www.eats-event.com/mint/`. July 19, 2019.

[2] Casall, Alexander. 20 JavaFX real-world applications. Retrieved from `https://jaxenter.com/20-javafx-real-world-applications-123653.html`. February 11, 2016.

Figure 1-1 shows one of the more complex user interface screens from MINT TRMS. It makes use of trees, tables, ribbons, and Gantt charts implemented using the latest Java client technology, JavaFX. JavaFX is a user interface toolkit that provides all of the layouts, controls, and charts that you need to build modern applications. This demonstrates a very complex view that would be challenging to implement in any other cross-platform technology.

To find out more about how you can easily build complex applications using pre-built JavaFX controls, check out Chapter 4, "JavaFX Controls Deep Dive."

Gaming and 3D

Java client technology is also great for building games. One of the most popular games of all time was built by a single person using Java technology. Markus Persson (aka Notch) released a development version of Minecraft in 2009.[3] All the initial development was done in his spare time until the alpha release made enough money so he could start his own company, Mojang, and focus on the game full time. It is now the world's second highest-grossing video game with 91 million monthly users.[4]

---

[3] Wikipedia. Minecraft. Retrieved from https://en.wikipedia.org/wiki/Minecraft. August 2019.

[4] Gilbert, Ben. "Minecraft" is still one of the biggest games in the world, with over 91 million people playing monthly. Retrieved from www.businessinsider.com/minecraft-has-74-million-monthly-players-2018-1. October 2018.

Figure 1-2. *Minecraft server example from Tingsterland created by @tingsterchin[5]*

Much of the success of Minecraft is through the large modding community who builds plugins that change the behavior of and enhance the game, taking it far beyond the original gameplay limitations. An example of a customer Minecraft server created by a young developer is shown in Figure 1-2. Java offers a great platform for building extensible applications through dynamic class loading and a secure sandbox model. Also with 12 million Java developers worldwide,[6] there is no shortage of development expertise and talent.

---

[5] Screenshot from a Minecraft server running at `https://tingsterland.com/`

[6] Oracle Makes Developers More Productive with Latest Java Release. Retrieved from `www.prnewswire.com/news-releases/oracle-makes-developers-more-productive-with-latest-java-release-300814269.html`. March 2019.

Minecraft is built entirely in Java using client technologies such as Swing and Java 2D and a Java gaming library called LWJGL. The high level of abstraction offered by Java and these libraries made it possible for Notch to develop Minecraft in a short period of time and support a variety of platforms without a large team of developers.

An even easier 3D library to get started with is the built-in 3D support in JavaFX. You can find out more about 3D graphics in Chapter 8, "JavaFX 3D."

Mobile Conference Apps

Java client technology is not just for the desktop. Using mobile JavaFX technology developed by Gluon,[7] you can run your Java client on phones, tablets, and embedded devices like Raspberry Pi. Existing JavaFX applications can be ported directly to mobile devices with small changes in styling of controls to make them work on different screen sizes. For handling mobile-specific APIs, Gluon offers Charm Down, which provides cross-platform integration with hardware features.

A great example of JavaFX mobile in action is the Devoxx conference application. This was originally built for the JavaOne conference in San Francisco and contributed to the open source community. The Devoxx conference picked it up and has done a great job extending it to be a general-purpose conference application that serves dozens of Devoxx and Voxxed conferences taking place around the world each year.

---

[7] Official website for Gluon: https://gluonhq.com/

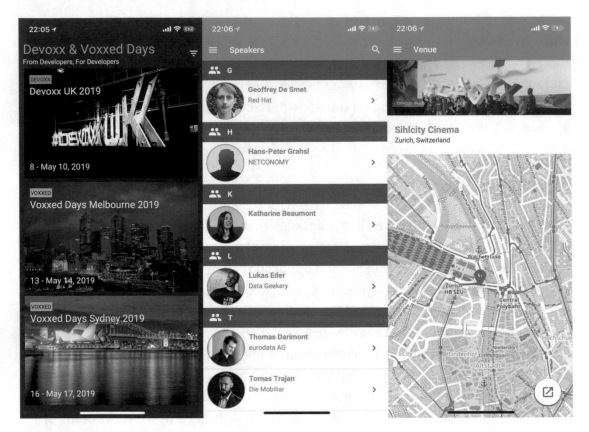

Figure 1-3. *Devoxx conference mobile application. From left to right: conference selection, speaker list, and venue navigation*[8]

Figure 1-3 shows several of the different screens within the conference application to select an event, showcase speakers, and navigate to the venue. According to Stephan Janssen, founder of the Devoxx conference family, "JavaFX mobile technology has helped us to streamline multiple native applications into a single cross-platform application that is well supported on iOS and Android devices. This is a better experience for conference attendees and much easier to keep up-to-date."

We have a simple mobile example coming up later in this chapter to show how easy it is to use this technology and a more thorough guide in Chapter 11, "Native Mobile Apps for iOS and Android."

---

[8] Screenshots from the Devoxx iOS conference application. Official conference website: `https://devoxx.com/`

A Modern Approach to Client Java

While client Java technology has been around for a long time, the development ecosystem has been under constant change. There have been significant advances in mobile, cloud computing, and app distribution that affect how you build and distribute your client applications. This book is focused on making you successful as a modern application developer by guiding you toward design and implementation best practices.

The three specific best practices that we are going to describe here and reinforce throughout the rest of the book are as follows:

1. Target mobile first.

2. Build for the cloud.

3. Package your platform.

Target Mobile First

The utilization of smartphones has been increasing steadily since iPhone and Android came out in 2007 and 2008, respectively. As of 2021, mobile smartphones and tablets have overtaken the desktop in web traffic, accounting for 54.8% of all web requests as shown in Figure 1-4. As a result, mobile is not just an option but a required interface for successful applications.

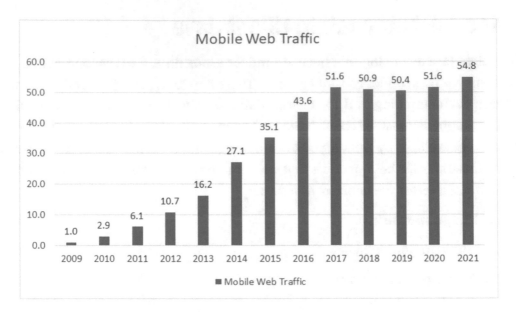

Figure 1-4. *Mobile usage since 2009 as a percentage of global web traffic*[9]

Smartphones have gotten to the point where they have the processing capability, memory, storage, and resolution to run full applications that were traditionally thought of as desktop-only. A tablet with a Bluetooth keyboard can easily be used as a desktop replacement for many use cases. Also, smartphones and tablets come with built-in wireless Internet, which makes it possible to use them even where broadband is not available.

As a result, there is a rising number of "smartphone-dependent" users who only have Internet access through a phone, but do not have broadband that could be used for a desktop or laptop to connect. As shown in Figure 1-5, 28% of US millennials (18–29 years old) are smartphone dependent. This demographic will only be able to use your application if it has a mobile version available!

---

[9] Percentage of all global web pages served to mobile phones from 2009 to 2021. Retrieved from https://gs.statcounter.com/platform-market-share/desktop-mobile-tablet/worldwide/#yearly-2009-2021. April 2021.

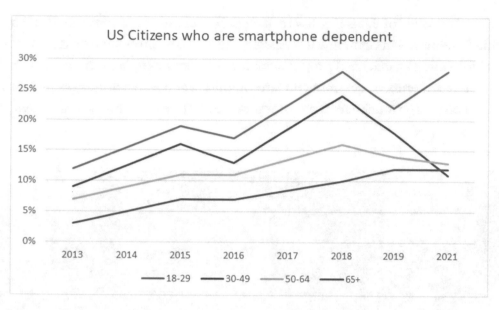

Figure 1-5. *Smartphone-dependent US citizens by age bracket according to the Pew Research Center[10]*

As discussed earlier, JavaFX has great mobile capabilities that are augmented by Gluon, who is an OpenJDK contributor. By using JavaFX mobile, you can write an application code base once and then target multiple screens including smartphones, tablets, and desktops. This gives your application a huge competitive advantage to desktop-only applications that do not allow users to take their work on the road with them. Find out more in Chapter 11, "Native Mobile Apps for iOS and Android"!

Build for the Cloud

The model for application backends has shifted from on-premise to the cloud. The reason for this is that there is an end user shift in expectations on how they interact with data. Historically, users would own and manage their data locally. With the rise of readily available high-speed connections, accessible encryption and security, and multiple screens per user, this expectation has changed. Now users expect data that is always online and available so it can be used from any device and easily shared and collaborated on.

---

[10] Mobile Fact Sheet. Retrieved from www.pewinternet.org/fact-sheet/mobile/. June 2021.

A good example of this is eteoBoard, a digital collaborative scrum board built by Saxonia Systems AG in Germany. It is designed to solve the problem with distributed teams by creating an extended project team room across multiple locations. This is done by using teleconference equipment on large monitors and an electronic project board displayed on a large touchscreen monitor powered by JavaFX technology as shown in Figure 1-6.

Figure 1-6. *Example of the eteoBoard being used to manage a project backlog[11]*

The eteoBoard application uses SynchronizeFX[12] for real-time synchronization of the user interface state between multiple clients. All of the project data gets loaded to and stored from either Atlassian Jira or Microsoft Team Foundation Server, both of which are cloud-based agile lifecycle management packages with REST interfaces. From an end user standpoint, all of this is transparent, and they get an always up-to-date view of the current project data so they can focus on the progress of the team.

---

[11] ETEO – One Team – One Office. Promotional video: www.youtube.com/watch?v=mX1SvXeUetQ
[12] Open source repo for SynchronizeFX: https://github.com/saxsys/SynchronizeFX

This demonstrates the user expectation shift that data is always online and available, which has necessitated the need for client applications to tightly integrate with cloud backends. For more information on how you can take advantage of the cloud in your client applications, check out the section "Building for the Cloud" in Chapter 9, "JavaFX, the Web, and Cloud Infrastructure."

Package Your Platform

Desktop computers and even mobile devices have scaled to where hard disk and network transfer concerns are secondary to user experience. This is demonstrated by the steady increase in the size of the top ten mobile applications as shown in Figure 1-7, which averages over 1 GB. This means that small optimizations like having a shared Java runtime for all applications are not worth the extra steps, complexity, and failure scenarios.

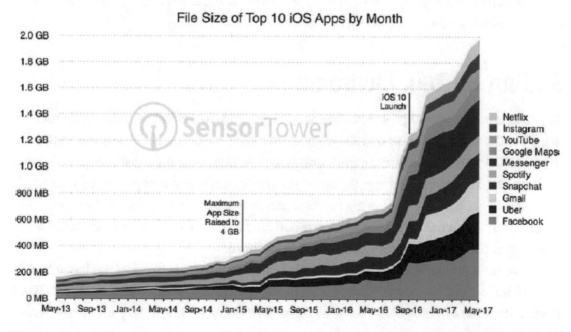

Figure 1-7. *File size of top ten iOS apps since 2013 as collected by Sensor Tower[13]*

---

[13] The Size of iPhone's Top Apps Has Increased by 1,000% in Four Years. Retrieved from https://sensortower.com/blog/ios-app-size-growth. June 2017.

Legacy technologies like Applets and Web Start are not recommended as a way to distribute your application. Since they rely on a shared Java runtime, a misconfigured system can easily result in the failure of an end user to run your application. Worse yet, these technologies introduce a security issue if not kept up-to-date. As a result, these are deprecated and should not be used.[14]

Instead, you should package everything your application needs as a single distribution. This includes the class files, libraries, and even the Java runtime required to run your application. While this may seem like a lot to include, it only costs an extra 20–30 MB on average and guarantees that your users will have a working Java runtime that is tested with the specific version of the application you are using.

Java 14 reintroduced a tool called jpackage that takes care of bundling the Java runtime together with your application for distribution. You can find out more about this and other packaging solutions in Chapter 10, "Packaging Apps for the Desktop." In addition, Chapter 11, "Native Mobile Apps for iOS and Android," builds on this with information on packaging your mobile apps and releasing them in the app stores on iOS and Android devices.

Setting Up Your Environment

To get started with client programming, we are going to do a small sample application using JavaFX technology. To do this, we need to have a modern Java version as well as the JavaFX libraries. Our recommendation is to always go with the most recent version of OpenJDK, because it provides the latest security patches and is supported for free by Oracle. Also, if you are following the best practice of packaging your application, it doesn't matter what version of Java your end user has installed because you will be bundling the latest Java runtime with your application.

You can download OpenJDK from `http://jdk.java.net`. Just select the latest "ready for use" build from the page shown in Figure 1-8, which was Java Development Kit (JDK) 17 as of the time of writing. The releases increment every 6 months, so your version will likely be different.

---

[14] Karakun has started a project to revive Java Web Start for Java 11+, which is a good option if you are heavily invested in web deployment: `https://openwebstart.com/`

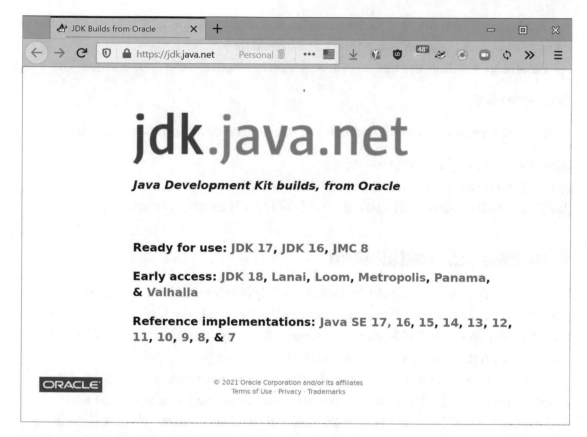

Figure 1-8. *OpenJDK download site on jdk.java.net*

OpenJDK does not come with an installer, but it is easy enough to install it from the command line. Here are the instructions per operating system on how to do this easily.

macOS JDK Installation

Open a terminal and go to the folder where you downloaded OpenJDK. You can unzip and untar it with the following command:

```
tar xf openjdk-17_osx-x64_bin.tar.gz
```

Make sure to substitute the right filename for the version of OpenJDK you downloaded. Then you need to move it into the JDK folder so it will be recognized:

```
sudo mv jdk-17.jdk /Library/Java/JavaVirtualMachines/
```

Again, substitute the right folder name for the version of OpenJDK you unzipped and enter your admin password since this is a protected folder.

Finally, to test that your new Java install is recognized, run the java command:

```
java -version
```

And you should see output as follows for the version of OpenJDK you installed:

```
openjdk version "17" 2021-09-16
OpenJDK Runtime Environment (build 17+??-????)
OpenJDK 64-Bit Server VM (build 17+??-????, mixed mode, sharing)
```

Windows JDK Installation

Windows JDK comes as a zip file. To install it, unzip it to a suitable file location, such as C:/Program Files/Java/. If you have not previously installed a JDK, this folder may not exist, but can be created with admin privileges. The copy operation to this folder will also require admin privileges, which Windows should prompt you to confirm.

Next, you need to create your JAVA_HOME environment variable that a lot of tools expect to be set. To do this, open the System Properties dialog where you can edit environment variables. This dialog is hidden fairly well on modern Windows operating systems, but can be reliably accessed via the Run dialog by pressing Windows+R and entering sysdm.cpl as shown in Figure 1-9.

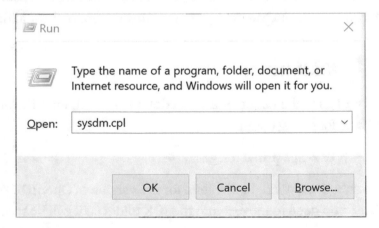

Figure 1-9. *Using the Run dialog to bring up System Properties*

Once the System Properties dialog is open, select the Advanced tab, and the dialog should be on the screen shown in Figure 1-10.

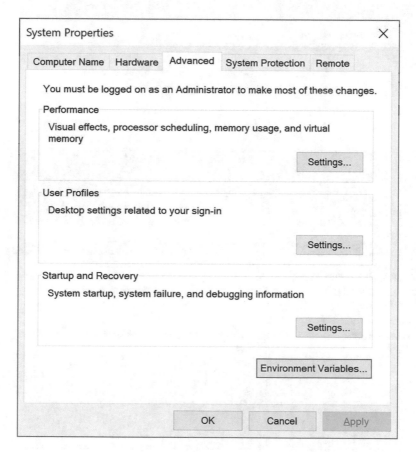

Figure 1-10. *System Properties dialog showing the Advanced tab*

On this tab, click the "Environment Variables…" button. This will bring up the dialog shown in Figure 1-11 that allows you to create and edit environment variables.

Figure 1-11. *Environment Variables dialog box*

In the Environment Variables dialog, we will create one new variable and modify the Path. To create a new variable, click the "New…" button under "System variables." Call this variable "JAVA_HOME" and give it a value that is the location of your newly unzipped OpenJDK distribution. To avoid mistyping, you can use the "Browse Directory…" button to select the folder you created earlier. The exact value will vary based on your JDK version, but mine was "C:\Program Files\Java\jdk-17".

Next, modify the Path environment variable to include a reference to the JDK bin folder. To do this, select the "Path" variable, which can be found under System variables, and click "Edit…" You will be presented with a dialog as shown in Figure 1-12.

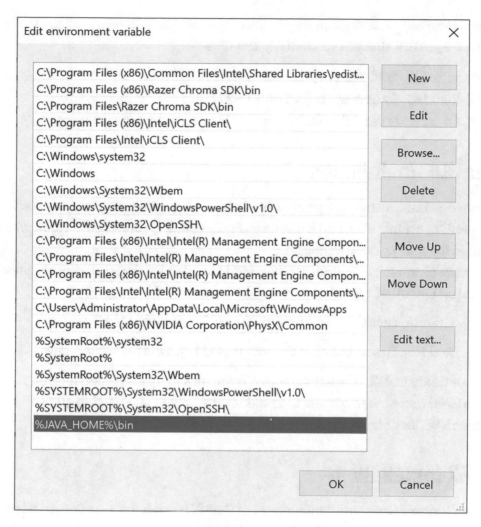

Figure 1-12. *Windows Path environment variable editing dialog*

Click the "New" button and enter "%JAVA_HOME%\bin" as the value. If you are on an earlier version of Windows, you may just have a simple text field with individual path elements separated by semicolons. If this is the case, just go to the end of the field and enter the JDK bin value preceded by a semicolon. If you have a previous installation of Java, you may need to find the Path entry for that and delete it so it doesn't override your new install. Once completed, click "OK" and exit the dialogs.

You can now test that the OpenJDK installation is working by opening a command prompt and typing the Java version command:

```
java -version
```

If it is installed correctly, you should get output like the following indicating the version of OpenJDK that you successfully installed:

```
openjdk version "17" 2021-09-16
OpenJDK Runtime Environment (build 17+??-????)
OpenJDK 64-Bit Server VM (build 17+??-????, mixed mode, sharing)
```

Linux JDK Installation

If you are on Linux, installing OpenJDK is a breeze. Most Linux distributions come with OpenJDK preinstalled, and it can be easily updated by running the appropriate command for your package managed.

Here are example commands for different Linux distributions (modify as appropriate for the latest OpenJDK version):

- Ubuntu, Debian: `sudo apt-get install openjdk-17-jdk`

- Red Hat, Oracle Linux: `sudo yum install java-17-openjdk-devel`

If your newly installed Java distribution is not picked up as the default, you can use the `update-alternatives` command to modify the default Java version and add in your new OpenJDK distribution if it does not show up in the list.

JavaFX Installation

JavaFX no longer comes as a standard part of OpenJDK, so it must be downloaded and configured separately. The JavaFX SDK is built and packaged by Gluon, an official OpenJFX contributor. Their builds can be downloaded from `https://gluonhq.com/ products/javafx/`, which is shown in Figure 1-13.

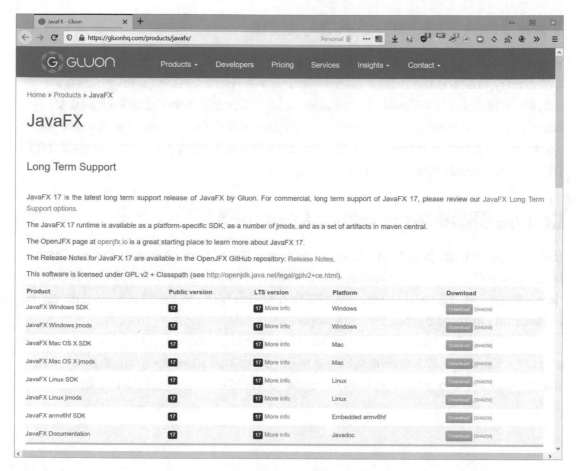

Figure 1-13. *JavaFX download site provided by Gluon*

Choose the matching version of JavaFX for the OpenJDK version you installed earlier, which was JavaFX 17 as of the time of writing. You may need to scroll down past the "Long Term Support" builds section and find the "Latest Release" farther down on the page. Download the SDK for your platform of choice.

Once downloaded, unzip the JavaFX SDK to a directory of your choice. For the purpose of this book, we will assume you left it in your Downloads folder, but feel free to move it to a more permanent location.

Now your Java and JavaFX installation is all prepared, and you are ready to create a modern client application. We will walk you through the steps for your first client application in the next section.

Your First Modern Java Client

We are going to guide you through creating your first client application using JavaFX technology, which is the most modern user interface platform available. There is a rich set of tools for Java development also building UIs with JavaFX, so for this first tutorial, you won't even need to write a single line of code. However, this will give you an appreciation for what is possible with modern client technology and lay a foundation for UI concepts introduced in subsequent chapters.

Coding Client Apps with IntelliJ IDEA

It is possible to code JavaFX applications with any IDE of your choice, including IntelliJ, NetBeans, Eclipse, or Visual Studio Code. However, we are going to introduce client development with IntelliJ Community Edition, which is the industry standard for coding in Java and entirely free for client development.

To download the latest version of IntelliJ, go to `https://www.jetbrains.com/idea/` and click "Download." This will take you to the download page shown in Figure 1-14 where you can choose to download the open source community edition for free.

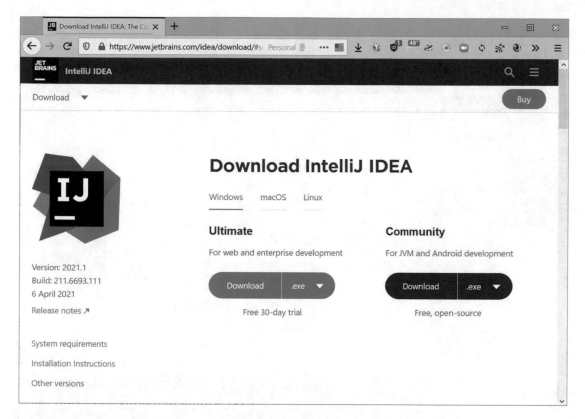

Figure 1-14. *IntelliJ Community Edition download*

After downloading, install IntelliJ and launch it. You will be given some options for configuring IntelliJ. Feel free to customize, but the defaults should be fine. Create a new project, and you will get the dialog shown in Figure 1-15.

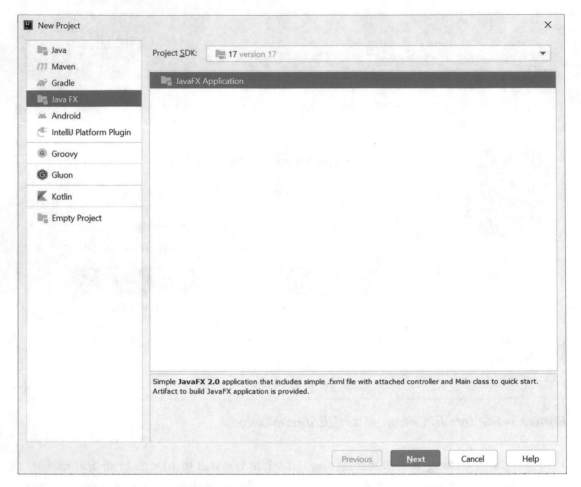

Figure 1-15. *New Project creation dialog in IntelliJ*

It should automatically pick up the system JDK that you configured earlier. Here you can select Java FX in the left pane, and it will give you a JavaFX Application template. Click "Next" and choose a project name like "HelloModernWorld" and click "Finish." This will open your project in a new window as shown in Figure 1-16.

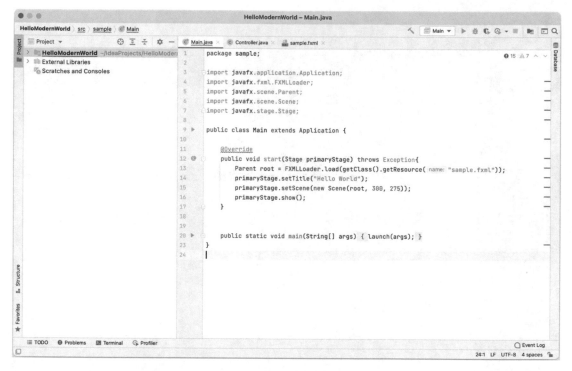

Figure 1-16. *Hello Modern World project created*

The standard project creates a minimal JavaFX application that contains a main class, a controller, and an FXML file for the user interface. This project is not runnable yet since it cannot find the JavaFX libraries that we downloaded earlier, which is obvious from the red highlighting. To fix this, we need to add a module dependency on the JavaFX libraries.

In the "File" menu, choose "Project Structure..." to open the Project Settings dialog. Here, select "Modules" on the left and choose the "Dependencies" tab to get to the screen shown in Figure 1-17.

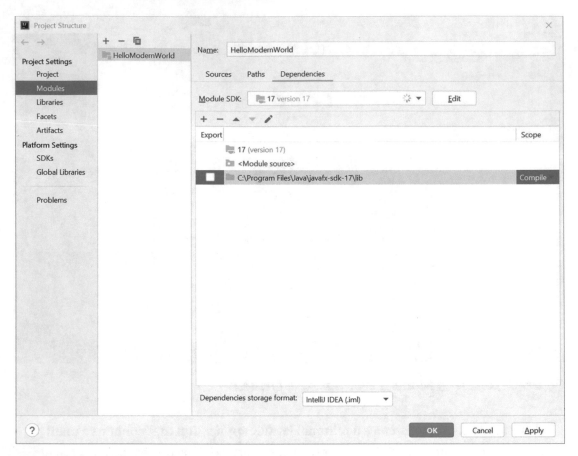

Figure 1-17. *Project Structure dialog in IntelliJ*

To add the JavaFX libraries, click the "+" symbol at the bottom of the pane and select "JARs or directories…" Then navigate to the OpenJFX JDK you downloaded and unzipped earlier and choose the "lib" folder. Click "OK," and this will complete the dependency, fixing the syntax highlighting.

You can try running the application by going to the "Run" menu and choosing "Run 'Main," but the configuration of JavaFX is not complete, and you will still get an error as shown in Figure 1-18.

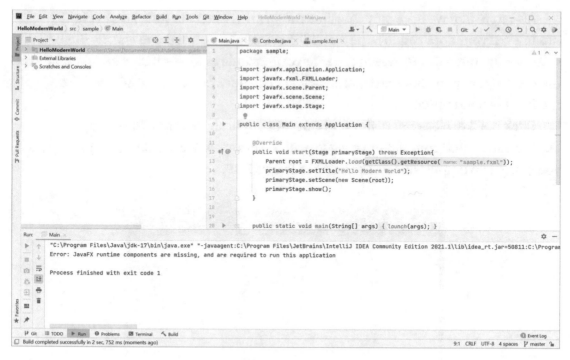

Figure 1-18. *Run error on missing JavaFX runtime components*

To add in the missing runtime components, open the configuration dialog by going to the "Run" menu and choosing "Edit Configurations…" This will open the Run/Debug Configurations dialog where you can enter VM options that get passed to the Java Virtual Machine.

To specify the JavaFX runtime library to use, pass in a VM option as follows:

```
--module-path /Users/schin/Downloads/javafx-sdk-17/lib --add-modules
javafx.controls,javafx.fxml
```

Be sure to modify the module path to the correct location for your user (it must be fully qualified), the right version of the JavaFX SDK, and the platform-specific path separators. An easy way to make sure you get this right is to right-click the field and choose "Insert Path" so you get a standard file system picker and IntelliJ will create the right path format for your operating system.

Also note that we have only specified the `javafx.controls` and `javafx.fxml` modules. If your application requires additional modules, be sure to specify them in this comma-separated list. However, you often can exclude modules if they are automatically included by an inter-module dependency, such as `javafx.base`, that all the other modules depend upon.

Click "OK" to close this dialog and run your application again. This time the application should compile and execute with no errors; however, since it is just a stub, you will get an empty window as shown in Figure 1-19.

Figure 1-19. *Empty Hello World application*

In the next section, we will show you how to modify this application to build a quick Hello Modern World application.

Rapid Application Development with Scene Builder

Scene Builder is a great tool to rapidly build modern client applications. It gives a WYSIWYG (what you see is what you get) visual representation of your application as you are building it with convenient palettes for layouts and controls and a properties editor for components you add to the scene graph. It also directly operates on FXML files as the intermediate format to declaratively specify your user interface without impacting your Java code.

The IntelliJ template already includes the boilerplate code to create a new application off of an FXML file, so we just need to edit the FXML file in Scene Builder to modify the user interface.

Scene Builder is also built, packaged, and distributed by Gluon, so we can download it from the same website where we got JavaFX. Go to `https://gluonhq.com/products/scene-builder/`, and you will see a download page similar to Figure 1-20 where you can get the right version of Scene Builder for your operating system.

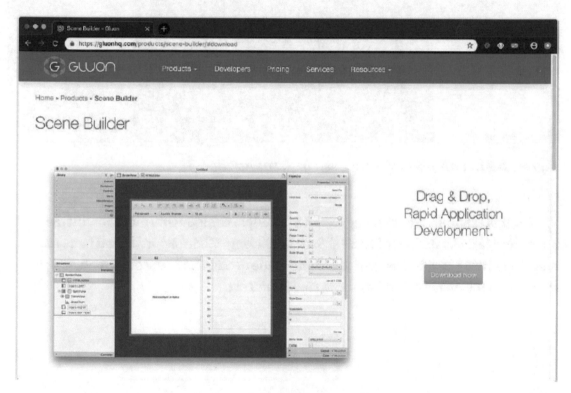

Figure 1-20. *Scene Builder download page provided by Gluon*

After installing and running Scene Builder, you will be presented with a welcome dialog where you can open an existing project. Navigate to your HelloModernWorld project folder, and choose the `sample.fxml` file that is in the `src/sample` directory.

This will open the basic Scene Builder user interface with your empty project as shown in Figure 1-21.

***Figure 1-21.** Sample project opened in Scene Builder*

For this example, we are going to add in a couple components that show off the image and text capabilities of JavaFX. Start by clicking "Controls" in the left pane and dragging a new "ImageView" into the center pane to add it to the scene graph, which should add the image control as shown in Figure 1-22.

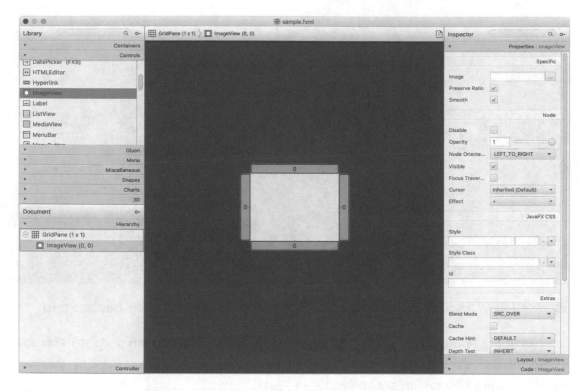

Figure 1-22. *ImageView control added to the scene graph*

For the background, we will use a Creative Commons–licensed image from NASA showing part of the RapidScat instrument used on the space station to measure ocean winds from space. You can download a 1024-pixel version of this from the following URL:

```
http://bit.ly/RapidScat1024
```

Place this file in the same folder as the FXML file and then select it in Scene Builder by updating the Image property in the right pane. To bring up the File Selection dialog, click the "…" button next to the text entry field.

To increase the size of the image, click "Layout" in the right field and delete the "Fit Width" and "Fit Height" values. This will change the layout to automatically scale to the size of the image that we imported rather than constraining it as shown in Figure 1-23.

Figure 1-23. *ImageView showing the RapidScat instrument[15] as a background*

Next, click "Containers" on the left and drag an AnchorPane as a child of the GridPane in the bottom-left "Hierarchy" pane. This will allow us to add additional controls that we can drag around Scene Builder and position freely.

Under the AnchorPane, you can add in a few different controls to write the text for your sample application. I recommend the Label control, which can be found under the Controls category in the top-left pane. To create the layout as shown in Figure 1-24, I added in three labels and modified the Font, Size, and Color as follows:

- Hello World: Font, Courier; Size, 96 px; Color, WHITE

- Java: Font, System; Size, 77 px; Color, #FFA518

- FX: Font, System; Size, 77 px; Color, #5382A1

[15] NASA. Special Purpose Dextrous Manipulator (SPDM), DEXTRE carrying the RapidScat instrument assembly. Retrieved from https://commons.wikimedia.org/wiki/File:ISS-RapidScat_nadir_adapter_removed_from_CRS-4_Dragon_trunk_(ISS041E049097).jpg. September 2014.

Figure 1-24. *Text overlay on the Hello Modern World application*

And finally, to make the text pop out a bit, you can add a visual effect. Select the AnchorPane element in the "Hierarchy" pane and go to the "Modify" menu and choose the "Set Effect" submenu. There are a selection of different effects you can apply to any element in the scene graph. Choose the "Bloom" effect, and you will get a distinct visual style.

Save your changes to the FXML file by going to the "File" menu and choosing "Save." This will automatically update the file in your project and should allow you to immediately run your application and see the changes.

Switch back to IntelliJ IDEA. Before running the project, we are going to make a few updates to the Main.java class:

- Delete the size constraints on the Scene. Simply erase the second and third parameters that specify a fixed size in the constructor.

- Change the window title. Simply update the setTitle call to name the window "Hello Modern World" to match the project name.

The updated Main.java code is shown in Listing 1-1.

Listing 1-1. Main class for Hello Modern World

```java
public class Main extends Application {
    @Override
    public void start(Stage primaryStage) throws Exception{
        Parent root = FXMLLoader.load(getClass().getResource("sample.fxml"));
        primaryStage.setTitle("Hello Modern World");
        primaryStage.setScene(new Scene(root));
        primaryStage.show();
    }
    public static void main(String[] args) {
        launch(args);
    }
}
```

Now try running your project again. With the updates you made to the FXML file and Main.java class, you should be greeted with a modern Hello World example as shown in Figure 1-25.

Figure 1-25. *Completed Hello Modern World application*

The Path to Modern Client Development

This chapter set the groundwork for understanding recent developments in client programming for Java with examples of applications used in the real world that you may not have even realized were written in this very powerful programming language. Also, you learned why you should approach building modern client applications with a mobile-first approach, building for the cloud and packaging your application for end users. You were also able to successfully complete building your first modern client application in JavaFX, which is the latest in Java client frameworks.

In the coming chapters, we are going to cover these topics in more detail, expanding on how you can go about packaging your application for multiple platforms, architecting your application for integration with REST and other cloud architectures, and showcasing the latest capabilities of Java client frameworks. We hope you are as eager to learn how to build modern UIs as we are to write and share this knowledge.

CHAPTER 2

JavaFX Fundamentals

Written by Gail Anderson and Paul Anderson

With the Java SDK and JavaFX installed on your system, let's create some applications and explore the fundamentals of JavaFX. First, we'll describe the basic structure of a JavaFX application along with selected features that make JavaFX a powerful choice for modern clients. We'll show you how to create UIs that are appealing and responsive. We'll look at FXML, the XML-based markup language that lets you define and configure your UI. We'll also introduce Scene Builder, a stand-alone drag-and-drop utility for designing and configuring a JavaFX UI.

To further refine or completely restyle your UI, JavaFX uses Cascading Style Sheets (CSS). We'll show you several ways to use CSS with JavaFX.

JavaFX properties provide a powerful binding mechanism. We'll introduce JavaFX properties and binding. We'll show why JavaFX observables and binding help create compact code that is less error-prone than bulky listeners. We'll also explore several layout controls and show you how easy it is to incorporate animation into your UI.

We'll finish the chapter with a sample application that implements a master-detail UI using JavaFX collections, an editable form, and buttons for typical database CRUD operations.

Throughout the chapter, we'll introduce topics that subsequent chapters cover in greater depth. This, then, is meant to give you a taste of what is possible with JavaFX and to provide the basics for exploring JavaFX even further throughout this book. Let's begin!

JavaFX Stage and Scene Graph

A JavaFX application is controlled by the JavaFX platform, a runtime system that builds your application object and constructs the JavaFX Application Thread. To build a JavaFX application, you must extend the JavaFX Application class. The JavaFX runtime system controls the application lifecycle and invokes the application `start()` method.

© Stephen Chin, Johan Vos and James Weaver 2022
S. Chin et al., *The Definitive Guide to Modern Java Clients with JavaFX 17*,
https://doi.org/10.1007/978-1-4842-7268-8_2

JavaFX uses a theater metaphor: the top-level container is the Stage and is constructed by the platform for you. In desktop applications, the Stage is the window. Its appearance depends on the host system and varies among macOS, Windows, and Linux platforms. Normally, the window is decorated with controls that resize, minimize, and quit your application. It's also possible to construct undecorated windows. You can specialize the Application class for other environments, too. For example, with the Gluon Mobile application framework, your program extends Mobile Application, an application class specifically written for mobile devices.

JavaFX Is Single-Threaded

You must always construct and modify the Stage and its Scene objects on the JavaFX Application Thread. Note that JavaFX (like Swing) is a single-threaded UI model. For the JavaFX developer, this is mostly a straightforward restriction. As you create UI elements, respond to event handlers, manage dynamic content with animation, or make changes in the scene graph, work continues to execute on the JavaFX Application Thread.

To keep the UI responsive, however, you should assign long-running work to background tasks in separate threads. In this case, work that modifies the UI must be separate from work being executed on a background thread. Fortunately, JavaFX has a well-developed concurrency API that helps developers assign long-running tasks to one or more separate threads. This keeps the UI thread responsive to user events. These topics are explored in Chapter 13, "Machine Learning and JavaFX."

Hierarchical Node Structure

Continuing with the theater metaphor, the Stage holds a scene. The scene consists of JavaFX elements such as the root, which is the top scene element and contains what is called the scene graph.

The scene graph is a strictly hierarchical structure of elements that visualize your application. These elements are called Nodes. A Node has exactly one parent (except the root node) and may contain other Nodes. Or a Node can be a leaf node with no children. Nodes must be added to the scene graph in order to participate in the rendering of that scene. Furthermore, a Node may be added only once to a scene, unless it is first removed and then added somewhere else.

Parent nodes in general manage their children by arranging them within the scene according to layout rules and any constraints you configure. JavaFX uses a two-dimensional coordinate system for 2D graphics with the origin at the upper-left corner of the scene, as shown in Figure 2-1. Coordinate values on the x-axis increase to the right, and y-axis values increase as you move down the scene.

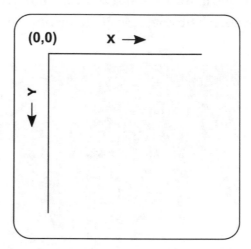

Figure 2-1. *JavaFX 2D coordinate system*

JavaFX also supports 3D graphics and represents the third dimension with z-axis values, providing depth. See Chapter 8, "JavaFX 3D," for an "in-depth" look at the three-dimensional capabilities of JavaFX.

JavaFX has an absolute coordinate system, in addition to local coordinate systems that are relative to the parent. In each case, the coordinate system's origin is the upper-left corner of the parent. In general, layout controls hide the complexities of component placement within the scene and manage the placement of its children for you. Component placement is based on the specific layout control and how you configure it.

It's also possible to nest layout controls. For example, you can place multiple VBox controls in an HBox or put an AnchorPane into one pane of a SplitPane control. Other parent nodes are more complex visual nodes, such as TextField, TextArea, and Button. These nodes have managed subparts. For example, Button includes a labeled text part and optional graphic. This graphic can be any node type but is typically an image or icon.

Recall that leaf nodes have no child nodes. Examples include Shape (such as Rectangle, Ellipse, Line, Path, and Text) and ImageView, a node for rendering an image.

A Simple Shape Example

Figure 2-2 shows a simple JavaFX application called MyShapes that displays an ellipse and a text element centered in an application window. The appearance of this window varies depending on the underlying platform. When you resize the window, the visible elements will remain centered in the resized space. Even though this is a simple program, there's much to learn here about JavaFX rendering, layout features, and nodes.

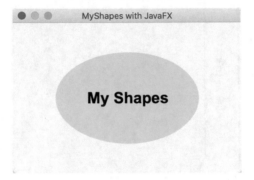

Figure 2-2. *MyShapes application*

Listing 2-1 shows the source for the MyShapes program. Class MyShapes is the main class and extends Application. The JavaFX runtime system instantiates MyShapes as well as the primary Stage, which it passes to the overridden start() method. The runtime system invokes the start() method for you.

Listing 2-1. MyShapes.java

```
package org.modernclient;
import javafx.application.Application;
import javafx.scene.Scene;
import javafx.scene.layout.StackPane;
import javafx.scene.paint.Color;
import javafx.scene.shape.Ellipse;
import javafx.scene.text.Font;
import javafx.scene.text.Text;
import javafx.stage.Stage;
public class MyShapes extends Application {
```

```
@Override
public void start(Stage stage) throws Exception {
    // Create an Ellipse and set fill color
    Ellipse ellipse = new Ellipse(110, 70);
    ellipse.setFill(Color.LIGHTBLUE);
    // Create a Text shape with font and size
    Text text = new Text("My Shapes");
    text.setFont(new Font("Arial Bold", 24));
    StackPane stackPane = new StackPane();
    stackPane.getChildren().addAll(ellipse, text);
    Scene scene = new Scene(stackPane, 350, 230,
                    Color.LIGHTYELLOW);
    stage.setTitle("MyShapes with JavaFX");
    stage.setScene(scene);
    stage.show();
}
public static void main(String[] args) {
    launch(args);
}
}
```

Note the import statements that reference packages in `javafx.application`, `javafx.scene`, and `javafx.stage`.

Note   Be sure to specify the correct package for any import statements. Some JavaFX classes, such as Rectangle, have the same class name as their AWT or Swing counterparts. All JavaFX classes are part of package `javafx`.

This program creates several nodes and adds them to a StackPane layout container. The program also creates the scene, configures the stage, and shows the stage. Let's look at these steps in detail.

First, we create an Ellipse shape, providing a width and height in pixels. Since Ellipse extends Shape, we can also configure any Shape property. This includes fill, which lets you specify an interior paint value.

Color

A Shape's fill property can be a JavaFX color, a linear gradient, a radial gradient, or an image. Let's briefly discuss color. You can specify colors in JavaFX in several ways. Here, we set the Ellipse fill property to Color.LIGHTBLUE. There are currently 147 predefined colors in the JavaFX Color class, named alphabetically from ALICEBLUE to YELLOWGREEN. However, you can also specify colors using web RGB values with either hexadecimal notation or decimal numbers. You can optionally provide an alpha value for transparency. Fully opaque is 1 and fully transparent is 0. A transparency of .5, for example, shows the color but lets the background color show through as well.

Here are a few examples that set a Shape's fill with color:

```
ellipse.setFill(Color.LIGHTBLUE);              // Light blue, fully opaque
ellipse.setFill(Color.web("#ADD8E6"));         // Light blue, fully opaque
ellipse.setFill(Color.web("#ADD8E680"));       // Light blue, .5 opaque
ellipse.setFill(Color.web("0xADD8E6"));        // Light blue, fully opaque
ellipse.setFill(Color.web("0xADD8E680"));      // Light blue, .5 opaque
ellipse.setFill(Color.rgb(173, 216, 230));     // Light blue, fully opaque
ellipse.setFill(Color.rgb(173, 216, 230, .5)); // Light blue, .5 opaque
```

Chapter 5, "Mastering Visual and CSS Design," shows you additional options for specifying colors, gradients, and images with CSS and JavaFX.

Notably, you can interpolate a color's values, and that is how JavaFX constructs gradients. We'll show you how to create a linear gradient shortly.

Text Is a Shape

We next create a Text object. Text is also a Shape with additional properties, such as font, text alignment, text, and wrapping width. The constructor provides the text, and the setFont() method sets its font.

The JavaFX Coordinate System

Note that we created the Ellipse and Text nodes, but they are not yet in our scene graph. Before we add them to the scene, we must put these nodes in some kind of layout container. Layout controls are extremely important in managing your scene graph.

These controls not only arrange components for you but also respond to events such as resizing, the addition or removal of elements, and any changes to the sizes of one or more nodes in the scene graph.

To show you just how important layout controls are, let's replace the StackPane in Listing 2-1 with a Group and specify the placement manually. Group is a parent node that manages its children but does not provide any layout capability. Here we create a group and add the ellipse and text elements with the constructor. We then specify group as the scene's root node:

```
Group group = new Group(ellipse, text);
...
Scene scene = new Scene(group, 350, 230, Color.LIGHTYELLOW);
```

Group uses default alignment settings for its children and places everything at the origin (0,0), the upper-left corner of the scene. For Text, the default placement is the bottom-left edge of the text element. In this case, the only visible portions will be the letters that extend below the bottom edge (the lowercase "y" and "p" letters of "My Shapes"). The Ellipse will be centered at the group origin (0,0), and therefore only the lower-right quadrant will be visible.

This arrangement is clearly not what we want. To fix this, let's manually center the shapes in the 350 × 230 scene, as follows:

```
Group group = new Group(ellipse, text);
// Manually placing components is tedious and error-prone
ellipse.setCenterX(175);
ellipse.setCenterY(115);
text.setX(175-(text.getLayoutBounds().getWidth()/2));
text.setY(115+(text.getLayoutBounds().getHeight()/2));
...
Scene scene = new Scene(group, 350, 230, Color.LIGHTYELLOW);
```

Now the shapes will be nicely centered in the scene. But this is still not ideal. The shapes will remain stuck in the scene at these coordinates when the window resizes (unless you write code that detects and reacts to window resizing). And you don't want to do that. Instead, use JavaFX layout controls!

Layout Controls

Let's take a slight detour now to discuss some common layout controls. To manage the nodes of a scene, you use one or more of these controls. Each control is designed for a particular layout configuration. Furthermore, you can nest layout controls to manage groups of nodes and specify how the layout should react to events, such as resizing or changes to the managed nodes. You can specify alignment settings as well as margin controls and padding.

There are several ways to add nodes to layout containers. You can add child nodes with the layout container's constructor. You can also use method `getChildren().add()` for a single node and method `getChildren().addAll()` for multiple nodes. In addition, some layout controls have specialized methods for adding nodes. Let's look at a few commonly used layout controls now to show you how JavaFX can compose a scene for you.

StackPane

A convenient and easy layout container is StackPane, which we used in Listing 2-1. This layout control stacks its children from back to front in the order that you add nodes. Note that we add the Ellipse first so that it appears behind the Text node. In the opposite order, the ellipse would obscure the text element.

By default, StackPane centers all of its children. You can provide a different alignment for the children or apply an alignment to a specific node in the StackPane. For example,

```
// align the text only
stackPane.setAlignment(text, Pos.BOTTOM_CENTER);
```

centers the Text node along the bottom edge of the StackPane. Now when you resize the window, the ellipse remains centered, and the text remains anchored to the bottom edge of the window. To specify the alignment of all managed nodes to the bottom edge, use

```
// align all managed nodes
stackPane.setAlignment(Pos.BOTTOM_CENTER);
```

Although both the ellipse and the text appear at the bottom of the window, they won't be centered relative to each other since they will be aligned at their respective bottom edges.

AnchorPane

AnchorPane manages its children according to configured anchor points, even when a container resizes. You specify an offset from the pane's edge for a component. Here, we add a Label to an AnchorPane and anchor it to the lower-left side of the pane with a 10-pixel offset:

```
AnchorPane anchorPane = new AnchorPane();
Label label = new Label("My Label");
anchorPane.getChildren().add(label);
AnchorPane.setLeftAnchor(label, 10.0);
AnchorPane.setBottomAnchor(label, 10.0);
```

AnchorPane is typically used as a top-level layout manager for controlling margins, even when the window is resized.

GridPane

GridPane lets you place child nodes in a flexibly sized two-dimensional grid. Components can span rows and/or columns, but the row size is consistent for all components in a given row. Similarly, the column's width is consistent for a given column. GridPane has specialized methods that add nodes to a particular cell designated by a column and row number. Optional arguments let you specify column and row span values. For example, the first label here is placed in the cell corresponding to column 0 and row 0. The second label goes into the cell corresponding to column 1 and row 0, and it spans two columns (the second and third columns). We must also provide a row span value (here it is set to 1):

```
GridPane gridPane = new GridPane();
gridPane.add(new Label("Label1"), 0, 0);
gridPane.add(new Label("Label2 is very long"), 1, 0, 2, 1);
```

GridPane is useful for laying out components in forms that accommodate columns or rows of various sizes. GridPane also allows nodes to span either multiple columns or rows. We use GridPane in our master-detail UI example (see "Putting It All Together" later in this chapter).

FlowPane and TilePane

FlowPane manages its children in either a horizontal or vertical flow. The default orientation is horizontal. You can specify the flow direction with the constructor or use method setOrientation(). Here, we specify a vertical orientation with the constructor:

```
FlowPane flowpane = new FlowPane(Orientation.VERTICAL);
```

FlowPane wraps child nodes according to a configurable boundary. If you resize a pane that contains a FlowPane, the layout will adjust the flow as needed. The size of the cells depends on the size of the nodes, and it will not be a uniform grid unless all the nodes are the same size. This layout is convenient for nodes whose sizes can vary, such as ImageView nodes or shapes. TilePane is similar to FlowPane, except TilePane uses equal-sized cells.

BorderPane

BorderPane is convenient for desktop applications with discrete sections, including a top toolbar (Top), a bottom status bar (Bottom), a center work area (Center), and two side areas (Right and Left). Any of the five sections can be empty. Here is an example of a BorderPane with a rectangle in the center and a label at the top:

```
BorderPane borderPane = new BorderPane();
Label colorLabel = new Label("Color: Lightblue");
colorLabel.setFont(new Font("Verdana", 18));
borderPane.setTop(colorLabel);
Rectangle rectangle = new Rectangle(100, 50, Color.LIGHTBLUE);
borderPane.setCenter(rectangle);
borderPane.setAlignment(colorLabel, Pos.CENTER);
borderPane.setMargin(colorLabel, new Insets(20,10,5,10));
```

Note that BorderPane uses a center alignment by default for the center area and a left alignment for the top. To keep the top area label centered, we configure its alignment with Pos.CENTER. We also set margins around the label with BorderPane static method setMargin(). The Insets constructor takes four values corresponding to the top, right, bottom, and left edges. Similar alignment and margin configurations apply to other layout components, too.

SplitPane

SplitPane divides the layout space into multiple horizontally or vertically configured areas. The divider is movable, and you typically use other layout controls in each of SplitPane's areas. We use SplitPane in our master-detail UI example (see "Putting It All Together" later in this chapter).

HBox, VBox, and ButtonBar

The HBox and VBox layout controls provide single horizontal or vertical placements for child nodes. You can nest HBox nodes inside a VBox for a grid-like effect or nest VBox nodes inside an HBox component. ButtonBar is convenient for placing a row of buttons of equal size in a horizontal container.

For detailed information on these and other layout controls, see Chapter 4, "JavaFX Controls Deep Dive."

Make a Scene

Returning to Listing 2-1, the Scene holds the scene graph, defined by its root node. First, we construct the Scene and provide `stackPane` as the root node. We then specify its width and height in pixels and supply an optional fill argument for the background (`Color.LIGHTYELLOW`).

What's left is to configure the Stage. We provide a title, set the scene, and show the stage. The JavaFX runtime renders our scene, as shown in Figure 2-2.

Figure 2-3 shows a hierarchical view of the scene graph for our MyShapes application. The root node is the StackPane, which contains its two child nodes, Ellipse and Text.

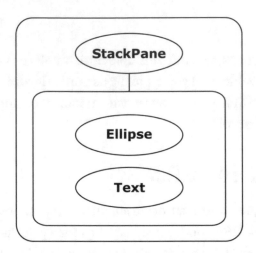

Figure 2-3. *MyShapes scene graph*

Enhancing the MyShapes Application

One of the advantages of JavaFX over older UI toolkits is the ease with which you can apply effects, gradients, and animation to nodes in your scene graph. We will return to the concept of scene graph nodes repeatedly, since that's how the JavaFX runtime efficiently renders the visual parts of your application. Let's apply some modifications to MyShapes now to show you some of these features. Because JavaFX is able to interpolate colors, you can use colors to define gradients. Gradients give depth to a shape and can be either radial or linear. Let's show you a linear gradient.

Linear Gradient

Linear gradients require two or more colors, called stops. A gradient stop consists of a color and an offset between 0 and 1. This offset specifies where to place the color along the gradient. The gradient calculates the proportional shading from one color stop to the next.

In our example, we'll use three color stops: `Color.DODGERBLUE`, `Color.LIGHTBLUE`, and `Color.GREEN`. The first stop will have offset 0, the second offset .5, and the third offset 1.0, as follows:

```
Stop[] stops = new Stop[] { new Stop(0, Color.DODGERBLUE),
        new Stop(0.5, Color.LIGHTBLUE),
        new Stop(1.0, Color.LIGHTGREEN)};
```

The LinearGradient constructor specifies the x-axis range followed by the y-axis range. The following linear gradient has a constant x-axis but varies its y-axis. This is called a vertical gradient. (We use this vertical gradient in program MyShapes2, shown in Figure 2-4.)

```
// startX=0, startY=0, endX=0, endY=1
LinearGradient gradient = new LinearGradient(0, 0, 0, 1, true,
        CycleMethod.NO_CYCLE, stops);
```

Boolean true indicates the gradient stretches through the shape (where 0 and 1 are proportional to the shape), and NO_CYCLE means the pattern does not repeat. Boolean false indicates the gradient's x and y values are instead relative to the local coordinate system of the parent.

To make a horizontal gradient, specify a range for the x-axis and make the y-axis constant, as follows:

```
// startX=0, startY=0, endX=1, endY=0
LinearGradient gradient = new LinearGradient(0, 0, 1, 0, true,
        CycleMethod.NO_CYCLE, stops);
```

Other combinations let you specify diagonal gradients or reverse gradients, where colors appear in the opposite order.

DropShadow

Next, let's add a drop shadow effect to the ellipse. You specify the color of the drop shadow, as well as a radius and x and y offsets. The larger the radius, the larger the shadow. The offsets represent the shadow placement relative to the outer edge of the shape. Here, we specify a radius of 30 pixels with an offset of 10 pixels to the right and below the shape:

```
ellipse.setEffect(new DropShadow(30, 10, 10, Color.GRAY));
```

These offsets simulate a light source emanating from the upper left of the scene. When the offsets are 0, the shadow surrounds the entire shape, as if the light source were shining directly above the scene.

Reflection

A reflection effect mirrors a component and fades to transparent, depending on how you configure its top and bottom opacities, fraction, and offset. Let's add a reflection effect to our Text node. We'll use .8 for the fraction, so that the reflection will be eight-tenths of the reflected component. The offset specifies how far below the bottom edge the reflection starts in pixels. We specify 1 pixel (the default is 0). The reflection starts at fully opaque (top opacity) and transitions to fully transparent (bottom opacity) unless you modify the top and bottom opacity values:

```
Reflection r = new Reflection();
r.setFraction(.8);
r.setTopOffset(1.0);
text.setEffect(r);
```

Figure 2-4 shows the enhanced MyShapes program running in a window. You see the linear gradient fill applied to the ellipse, a drop shadow on the ellipse, and the reflection effect applied to the text.

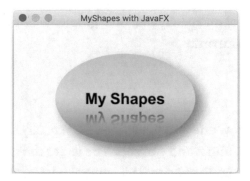

Figure 2-4. *Enhanced MyShapes application (MyShapes2)*

Configuring Actions

Now it's time to make our application do something. JavaFX defines various types of standard input events with the mouse, gestures, touch, or keys. These input event types each have specific handlers that process them.

Let's keep things simple for now. We'll show you how to write an event handler to process a single mouse click event. We'll create the handler and attach it to a node in our scene graph. The program's behavior will vary depending on which node acquires the handler. We can configure the mouse click handler on the Text, Ellipse, or StackPane node.

Here's the code to add an action event handler to the Text node:

```
text.setOnMouseClicked(mouseEvent -> {
    System.out.println(mouseEvent.getSource().getClass()
        + " clicked.");
});
```

When the user clicks inside the text, the program displays the line

```
class javafx.scene.text.Text clicked.
```

If the user clicks in the background area (the stack pane) or inside the ellipse, nothing happens. If we attach the same listener to the ellipse instead of the text, we see the line

```
class javafx.scene.shape.Ellipse clicked.
```

Note that because the Text object appears in front of the ellipse in the stack pane, clicking the Text object does not invoke the event handler. Even though these scene graph nodes appear on top of each other, they are separate nodes in the hierarchy. That is, one isn't inside the other; rather, they are both distinct leaf nodes managed by the stack pane. In this case, if you want both nodes to respond to a mouse click, you would attach the mouse event handler to both nodes. Or you could attach just one event handler to the StackPane node. Then, a mouse click anywhere inside the window triggers the handler with the following output line:

```
class javafx.scene.layout.StackPane clicked.
```

Let's do something a bit more exciting and apply an animation to the MyShapes program.

Animation

JavaFX makes animation very easy when you use the built-in transition APIs. Each JavaFX transition type controls one or more Node (or Shape) properties. For example, the FadeTransition controls a node's opacity, varying the property over time. To fade something out gradually, you change its opacity from fully opaque (1) to completely transparent (0). The TranslateTransition moves a node by modifying its translateX and translateY properties (or translateZ if you're working in 3D).

You can play multiple transitions in parallel with a ParallelTransition or sequentially with a SequentialTransition. To control timing between two sequential transitions, use PauseTransition or configure a delay before a transition begins with transition method setDelay(). You can also define an action when a transition completes using the transition action event handler property onFinished.

Transitions begin with method play() or playFromStart(). Method play() starts the transition at its current time; method playFromStart() always begins at time 0. Other methods include stop() and pause(). You can query a transition's status with getStatus(), which returns one of the Animation.Status enum values: RUNNING, PAUSED, or STOPPED.

All transitions support the common properties duration, autoReverse, cycleCount, onFinished, currentTime, and either node or shape (for Shape-specific transitions).

Let's define a RotateTransition now for our MyShapes program. The rotation begins when a user clicks inside the window. Figure 2-5 shows the program running during the rotate transition.

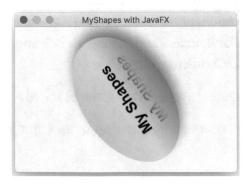

Figure 2-5. *MyShapes application with RotateTransition (MyShapes2)*

Listing 2-2 shows the animation code in the start() method of the MyShapes program.

Listing 2-2. Using RotateTransition

```
public class MyShapes extends Application {
    @Override
    public void start(Stage stage) throws Exception {
        ...
        // Define RotateTransition
        RotateTransition rotate = new RotateTransition(
                    Duration.millis(2500), stackPane);
        rotate.setToAngle(360);
        rotate.setFromAngle(0);
        rotate.setInterpolator(Interpolator.LINEAR);
        // configure mouse click handler
        stackPane.setOnMouseClicked(mouseEvent -> {
            if (rotate.getStatus().equals(Animation.Status.RUNNING)) {
                rotate.pause();
            } else {
                rotate.play();
            }
        });
        ...
    }
}
```

The RotateTransition constructor specifies a duration of 2500 milliseconds and applies the transition to the StackPane node. The rotation animation begins at angle 0 and proceeds linearly to angle 360, providing one full rotation. The animation starts when the user clicks anywhere inside the StackPane layout control.

There are a few interesting things to notice in this example. First, because we define the transition on the StackPane node, the rotation applies to all of the StackPane's children. This means that not only will the Ellipse and Text shapes rotate but the drop shadow and reflection effects rotate, too.

Second, the event handler checks the transition status. If the animation is in progress (running), the event handler pauses the transition. If it's not running, it starts it up with play(). Because play() starts at the transition's current time, a pause() followed by play() resumes the transition where it was paused.

JavaFX Properties

You control nodes by manipulating their properties. JavaFX properties are similar to regular JavaBean properties. They have setters and getters, generally hold values, and follow the same naming conventions. But JavaFX properties are more powerful because they are *observable*. In this section, we'll introduce the concept of JavaFX properties, listeners, and binding, which help you configure and control the nodes in your scene graph.

You've already seen how to configure nodes in your scene graph by manipulating properties associated with that node. For example, the fill property in the ellipse provides the shape's interior color. Likewise, the height and width properties define the size of an ellipse. The font property defines the text's font, and its text property holds the words "My Shapes."

Because JavaFX properties are observable, you can define listeners that are notified when a property value changes or becomes invalid. Furthermore, you can use a built-in binding mechanism to link the value of one or more properties to another property. You can specify unidirectional binding or bidirectional binding. You can even define your own JavaFX properties and include them in your programs as part of model objects or control objects.

In order to use bind expressions or attach listeners to JavaFX properties, you must access a property through its *property getter*. By convention, a property getter is the property name in lowercase letters followed by the word Property with an uppercase "P." For example, the property getter for the fill property is fillProperty(), and the property getter for a node's opacity property would be opacityProperty(). With any property getter, you can access property metadata (such as its name with property getter method getName() as well as its value with property getter method getValue()). Let's show you property listeners first.

Property Listeners

JavaFX property listeners that apply to object properties (not collections) come in two flavors: invalidation listeners and change listeners. Invalidation listeners fire when a property's value is no longer valid. For this example and the ones that follow, we'll discuss the MyShapesProperties program, which is based on the previous MyShapes application. In this new program, we've added a second Text object placed in a VBox layout control below the rotating StackPane. Figure 2-6 shows the updated scene graph with the top-level VBox.

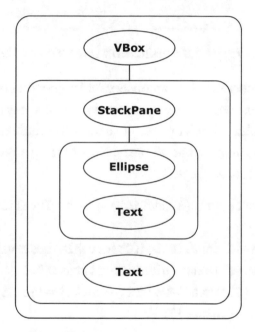

Figure 2-6. *MyShapesProperties scene graph*

Invalidation Listeners

Invalidation listeners have a single method that you override with lambda expressions. Let's show you the non-lambda expression first, so you can see the full method definition. When you click the StackPane, the mouse click handler rotates the StackPane control as before. The second Text object displays the status of the RotationTransition animation, which is managed by the read-only status property. You'll see either RUNNING, PAUSED, or STOPPED. Figure 2-7 shows the animation paused.

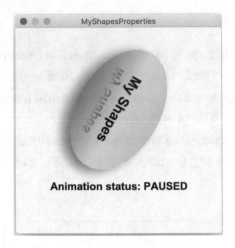

Figure 2-7. *MyShapesProperties application with an invalidation listener*

The invalidation listener includes an observable object that lets you access the property. Because the observable is nongeneric, you must apply an appropriate type cast to access the property value. Here's one way to access the value of the animation's status property in a listener attached to that property. Note that we attach the listener with the property getter method statusProperty():

```
rotate.statusProperty().addListener(new InvalidationListener() {
    @Override
    public  void invalidated(Observable observable) {
        text2.setText("Animation status: " +
            ((ObservableObjectValue<Animation.Status>)observable)
            .getValue());
    }
});
```

Here we implement the same listener with a lambda expression:

```
rotate.statusProperty().addListener(observable -> {
    text2.setText("Animation status: " +
        ((ObservableObjectValue<Animation.Status>)observable)
        .getValue());
});
```

Since we access just the status property value, we can bypass the observable with method getStatus(), which returns an enum. This avoids the casting expression:

```
rotate.statusProperty().addListener(observable -> {
    text2.setText("Animation status: " + rotate.getStatus());
});
```

Change Listeners

When you need access to the previous value of an observable as well as its current value, use a change listener. Change listeners provide the observable and the new and old values. Change listeners can be more expensive, since they must keep track of more information. Here's the non-lambda version of a change listener that displays both the old and new values. Note that you don't have to cast these parameters, since change listeners are generic:

```
rotate.statusProperty().addListener(
            new ChangeListener<Animation.Status>() {
    @Override
    public void changed(
        ObservableValue<? extends Animation.Status>
        observableValue,
          Animation.Status oldValue, Animation.Status newValue) {
            text2.setText("Was " + oldValue + ", Now " + newValue);
        }
});
```

Here's the version with a more compact lambda expression:

```
rotate.statusProperty().addListener(
            (observableValue, oldValue, newValue) -> {
    text2.setText("Was " + oldValue + ", Now " + newValue);
});
```

Figure 2-8 shows the MyShapesProperties running with a change listener attached to the animation's status property. Now we can display both the previous and current values.

Figure 2-8. *MyShapesProperties application with a change listener*

Binding

JavaFX binding is a flexible, API-rich mechanism that lets you avoid writing listeners in many situations. You use binding to link the value of a JavaFX property to one or more other JavaFX properties. Property bindings can be unidirectional or bidirectional. When properties are the same type, the unidirectional bind() method may be all you need. However, when properties have different types or you want to compute a value based on more than one property, then you'll need the fluent and bindings APIs. You can also create your own binding methods with custom binding.

Unidirectional Binding

The simplest form of binding links the value of one property to the value of another. Here, we bind text2's rotate property to stackPane's rotate property:

```
text2.rotateProperty().bind(stackPane.rotateProperty());
```

This means any changes to stackPane's rotation will immediately update text2's rotate property. When this binding is set in the MyShapesProperties program, any clicks inside the StackPane initiate a rotate transition. This makes both the StackPane and text2 components rotate together. The StackPane rotates because we start the RotateTransition defined for that node. The text2 node rotates because of the bind expression.

Note that when you bind a property, you cannot explicitly set its value unless you unbind the property first.

Bidirectional Binding

Bidirectional binding provides a two-way relationship between two properties. When one property updates, the other also updates. Here's an example with two text properties:

```
text2.textProperty().bindBidirectional(text.textProperty());
```

Both text controls initially display "My Shapes." When the user clicks inside the stackPane and the stackPane rotates, both text properties will now contain the animation status because of the change listener.

Bidirectional binding is not completely symmetrical; the initial value of both properties takes on the value of the property passed in the call to bindBidirectional(). Unlike bind(), you can explicitly set either property when using bidirectional binding.

Fluent API and Bindings API

The fluent and bindings APIs help you construct bind expressions when more than one property needs to participate in a binding or when it's necessary to perform some sort of calculation or conversion. For example, the following bind expression displays the rotation angle of the StackPane as it rotates from 0 to 360 degrees. The text property is a string, and the rotate property is a double. The binding method asString() converts the double to a string, formatting the number with a single digit to the right of the decimal point:

```
text2.textProperty().bind(stackPane.rotateProperty()
        .asString("%.1f"));
```

For a more complex example, let's update text2's stroke property (its color) depending on whether the animation is running or not. Here we construct a binding with When based on a ternary expression. This sets the stroke color to green when the animation is running and to red when the animation is stopped or paused:

```
text2.strokeProperty().bind(new When(rotate.statusProperty()
        .isEqualTo(Animation.Status.RUNNING))
        .then(Color.GREEN).otherwise(Color.RED));
```

The text2 text property is set in the change listener that is attached to the animation status property we showed earlier.

Figure 2-9 shows application MyShapesProperties with the complex bind expression attached to the `text2 strokeProperty`. Since the animation is running, the stroke property is set to `Color.GREEN`.

Figure 2-9. *MyShapesProperties application with the fluent and bindings APIs*

For additional examples of JavaFX properties and binding, see Chapter 3, "Properties and Bindings."

Using FXML

You've seen how JavaFX APIs create scene graph nodes and configure them for you. The MyShapes and MyShapesProperties programs use only JavaFX code to build and configure these objects. An alternative approach is to declare scene graph nodes with FXML, a markup notation based on XML. FXML lets you describe and configure your scene graph in a declarative format. This approach has several advantages:

- FXML markup structure is hierarchical, so it reflects the structure of your scene graph.

- FXML describes your view and supports a Model-View-Controller (MVC) architecture, providing better structure for larger applications.

- FXML reduces the JavaFX code you have to write to create and configure scene graph nodes.

- You can design your UI with Scene Builder. This drag-and-drop tool is a stand-alone application that provides a visual rendering of your scene. And Scene Builder generates the FXML markup for you.

- You can also edit your FXML markup with text and IDE editors.

FXML affects the structure of your program. The main application class now invokes an FXMLLoader. This loader parses your FXML markup, creates JavaFX objects, and inserts the scene graph into the scene at the root node. You can have multiple FXML files, and typically each one has a corresponding JavaFX controller class. This controller class may include event handlers or other statements that dynamically update the scene. The controller also includes business logic that manages a specific view.

Let's return to our MyShapes example (now called MyShapesFXML) and use an FXML file for the view and CSS for styling. Figure 2-10 shows the files in our program, arranged for use with build tools or IDEs.

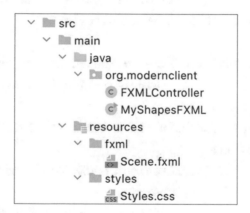

Figure 2-10. *MyShapesFXML with FXML and CSS*

The JavaFX source code appears under the **java** subdirectory. The **resources** subdirectory contains the FXML and CSS files (here **Scene.fxml** and **Styles.css**).

This program includes a rotating StackPane, VBox control, and second Text object. Listing 2-3 shows the FXML code that describes our scene graph: a top-level VBox that includes a StackPane and Text element. The StackPane includes the Ellipse and Text shapes.

Listing 2-3. Scene.fxml

```
<?xml version="1.0" encoding="UTF-8"?>
<?import javafx.scene.effect.DropShadow?>
<?import javafx.scene.effect.Reflection?>
<?import javafx.scene.layout.StackPane?>
<?import javafx.scene.layout.VBox?>
<?import javafx.scene.paint.LinearGradient?>
<?import javafx.scene.paint.Stop?>
<?import javafx.scene.shape.Ellipse?>
<?import javafx.scene.text.Font?>
<?import javafx.scene.text.Text?>
<VBox alignment="CENTER" prefHeight="350.0" prefWidth="350.0"
spacing="50.0"
 xmlns="http://javafx.com/javafx/10.0.1" xmlns:fx=http://javafx.com/fxml/1
 fx:controller="org.modernclient.FXMLController">
    <children>
        <StackPane fx:id="stackPane" onMouseClicked="#handleMouseClick"
                            prefHeight="150.0" prefWidth="200.0">
            <children>
                <Ellipse radiusX="110.0" radiusY="70.0">
                    <fill>
                        <LinearGradient endX="0.5" endY="1.0" startX="0.5">
                            <stops>
                                <Stop color="DODGERBLUE" />
                                <Stop color="LIGHTBLUE" offset="0.5" />
                                <Stop color="LIGHTGREEN" offset="1.0" />
                            </stops>
                        </LinearGradient>
                    </fill>
                    <effect>
                        <DropShadow color="GREY" offsetX="5.0"
                                            offsetY="5.0" />
                    </effect>
                </Ellipse>
```

```
            <Text text="My Shapes">
                <font>
                    <Font name="Arial Bold" size="24.0" />
                </font>
                <effect>
                    <Reflection fraction="0.8" topOffset="1.0" />
                </effect>
            </Text>
        </children>
    </StackPane>
    <Text fx:id="text2" text="Animation Status: ">
        <font>
            <Font name="Arial Bold" size="18.0" />
        </font>
    </Text>
  </children>
</VBox>
```

The top-level container includes the name of the JavaFX controller class with attribute fx:controller. The VBox specifies its alignment, preferred sizes, and spacing followed by its children: the StackPane and Text. Here, we configure the StackPane with preferred sizing. A special attribute fx:id specifies a variable name corresponding to this node. In the JavaFX controller class, you'll now see this variable name annotated with @FXML for the StackPane. This is how you access objects in the controller class that are declared in FXML files.

In addition, StackPane specifies an onMouseClicked event handler called #handleMouseClick. This event handler is also annotated with @FXML in the JavaFX controller class.

Here, the StackPane children, Ellipse and Text, are declared inside the Children FXML node. Neither has an associated fx:id attribute, since the controller class does not need to access these objects. You also see the linear gradient, drop shadow, and reflection effect configurations.

Note that the Text object with fx:id "text2" appears after the StackPane definition. This makes the second Text object appear under the StackPane in the VBox. We also specify an fx:id attribute to access this node from the JavaFX controller.

Controller Class

Let's show you the controller class now. You'll notice the code is more compact, since object instantiations and configuration code are no longer done with Java statements. All that is now specified in the FXML markup. Listing 2-4 shows the controller code for FXMLController.java.

Listing 2-4. FXMLController.java

```java
package org.modernclient;
import javafx.animation.Animation;
import javafx.animation.Interpolator;
import javafx.animation.RotateTransition;
import javafx.beans.binding.When;
import javafx.fxml.FXML;
import javafx.fxml.Initializable;
import javafx.scene.input.MouseEvent;
import javafx.scene.layout.StackPane;
import javafx.scene.paint.Color;
import javafx.scene.text.Text;
import javafx.util.Duration;
import java.net.URL;
import java.util.ResourceBundle;
public class FXMLController implements Initializable {
    @FXML
    private StackPane stackPane;
    @FXML
    private Text text2;
    private RotateTransition rotate;
    @Override
    public void initialize(URL url, ResourceBundle rb) {
        rotate = new RotateTransition(Duration.millis(2500), stackPane);
        rotate.setToAngle(360);
        rotate.setFromAngle(0);
        rotate.setInterpolator(Interpolator.LINEAR);
```

```
    rotate.statusProperty().addListener(
                    (observableValue, oldValue, newValue) -> {
        text2.setText("Was " + oldValue + ", Now " + newValue);
    });
    text2.strokeProperty().bind(new When(rotate.statusProperty()
            .isEqualTo(Animation.Status.RUNNING))
            .then(Color.GREEN).otherwise(Color.RED));
}
@FXML
private void handleMouseClick(MouseEvent mouseEvent) {
    if (rotate.getStatus().equals(Animation.Status.RUNNING)) {
        rotate.pause();
    } else {
        rotate.play();
    }
}
}
```

The controller class implements Initializable and overrides method `initialize()`, which is invoked for you at runtime. Importantly, the private class fields `stackPane` and `text2` are annotated with @FXML. The @FXML annotation associates variable names in the controller class to the objects described in the FXML file. There is no code in the controller class that creates these objects because the FXMLLoader does that for you.

The `initialize()` method does three things here. First, it creates and configures the RotateTransition and applies it to the `stackPane` node. Second, it adds a change listener to the transition's status property. And third, a bind expression for the `text2` stroke property specifies its color based on the rotate transition's status.

The @FXML annotation with `handleMouseClick()` indicates that the FXML file configures the event handler. This mouse click event handler starts and stops the rotate transition's animation.

JavaFX Application Class

The main application class, MyShapesFXML, now becomes very simple. Its job is to invoke the FXMLLoader, which parses the FXML (**Scene.fxml**), builds the scene graph, and returns the scene graph root. All you have to do is build the Scene object and configure the stage as before, as shown in Listing 2-5.

Listing 2-5. MyShapesFXML.java

```java
package org.modernclient;
import javafx.application.Application;
import javafx.fxml.FXMLLoader;
import javafx.scene.Parent;
import javafx.scene.Scene;
import javafx.scene.paint.Color;
import javafx.stage.Stage;
public class MyShapesFXML extends Application {
    @Override
    public void start(Stage stage) throws Exception {
        Parent root = FXMLLoader.load(getClass()
                            .getResource("/fxml/Scene.fxml"));
        Scene scene = new Scene(root, Color.LIGHTYELLOW);
        scene.getStylesheets().add(getClass()
            .getResource("/styles/Styles.css").toExternalForm());
        stage.setTitle("MyShapesApp with JavaFX");
        stage.setScene(scene);
        stage.show();
    }
    public static void main(String[] args) {
        launch(args);
    }
}
```

Adding CSS

Now let's show you how to incorporate your own styles with CSS. One advantage of JavaFX is its ability to style nodes with CSS. JavaFX comes bundled with a default stylesheet, **Modena.css**. You can augment these default styles or replace them with new ones. Our example CSS file found in file **Styles.css** is a single style class (mytext) that sets its font style to italic, as shown in Listing 2-6.

Listing 2-6. Styles.css

```
.mytext {
    -fx-font-style: italic;
}
```

To use this stylesheet, you must first load the file, either in the application's start() method or in the FXML file. Listing 2-5 shows how you load a stylesheet in MyShapesFXML.java. Once the file is added to the available stylesheets, you can apply the style classes to a node. To apply individually defined style classes to a specific node, for instance, use

```
text2.getStyleClass().add("mytext");
```

Here, "mytext" is the style class, and text2 is the second Text object in our program.

Alternatively, you can specify the stylesheet in the FXML file. The advantage of this approach is that styles are now available inside Scene Builder. Here is the modified **Scene.fxml** file that loads this customized CSS file and applies the customized CSS style class to the text2 Text node:

```
...
<VBox alignment="CENTER" prefHeight="350.0" prefWidth="350.0"
spacing="50.0"
        stylesheets="@../styles/Styles.css"
        xmlns="http://javafx.com/javafx/10.0.1"
        xmlns:fx="http://javafx.com/fxml/1"
        fx:controller="org.modernclient.FXMLController">
    <children>

<StackPane fx:id="stackPane" onMouseClicked="#handleMouseClick"
prefHeight="150.0" prefWidth="200.0">
        ... code removed ...
    </StackPane>
    <Text fx:id="text2" styleClass="mytext" text="Animation Status: ">
        <font>
            <Font name="Arial Bold" size="18.0" />
        </font>
    </Text>
    </children>
</VBox>
```

65

See Chapter 5, "Mastering Visual and CSS Design," for an in-depth discussion on how to use CSS in JavaFX applications.

Using Scene Builder

Scene Builder was originally developed at Oracle and is now open sourced. It is available for download from Gluon here: `https://gluonhq.com/products/scene-builder/`. Scene Builder is a stand-alone drag-and-drop tool for creating JavaFX UIs. Figure 2-11 shows the main Scene Builder window with file **Scene.fxml** from the MyShapesFXML program.

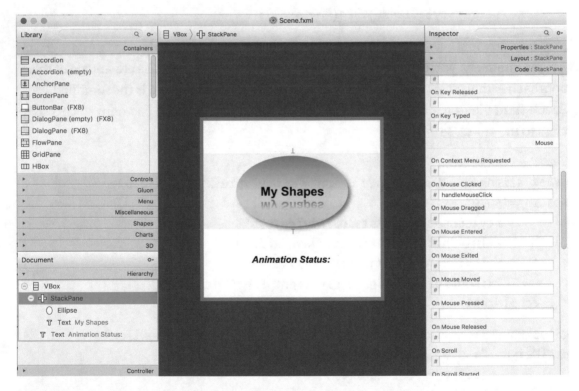

Figure 2-11. *FXML file with Scene Builder for MyShapesFXML*

The upper-left window shows the JavaFX component library. This library includes containers, controls, shapes, 3D, and more. From this window, you select components and drop them onto your scene in the middle visual view or onto the Document window shown in the lower-left area.

The Document window shows the scene graph hierarchy. You can select components and move them within the tree. The right window is an Inspector window that lets you configure each component, including its properties, layout settings, and code. In Figure 2-11, the StackPane is selected in the Document hierarchy window and appears in the center visual view. In the Inspector window, the OnMouseClicked property is set to `#handleMouseClick`, which is the name of the corresponding method in the JavaFX controller class.

Scene Builder is particularly helpful when building real-world form-based UIs. You can visualize your scene hierarchy and easily configure layout and alignment settings.

Putting It All Together

It's time to build a more interesting JavaFX application now, one that implements a master-detail view. As we show you this application, we'll explain several JavaFX features that help you control the UI and keep your data and the application consistent.

First, we use Scene Builder to construct and configure the UI. Our example includes a Person model class and an underlying ObservableList that holds data. The program lets users make changes, but we don't persist any data. JavaFX has ObservableLists that manage collections of data, and you can write listeners and bind expressions that respond to any data changes. The program uses a combination of event handlers and bind expressions to keep the application state consistent.

Master-Detail UI

For the UI, we use a JavaFX ListView control in the left window (the master view) and a Form on the right (the detail view). In Scene Builder, we select an AnchorPane as the top-level component and the scene graph root. A SplitPane layout pane divides the application view into two parts, and each part has AnchorPane as its main container. Figure 2-12 shows the Person UI application running.

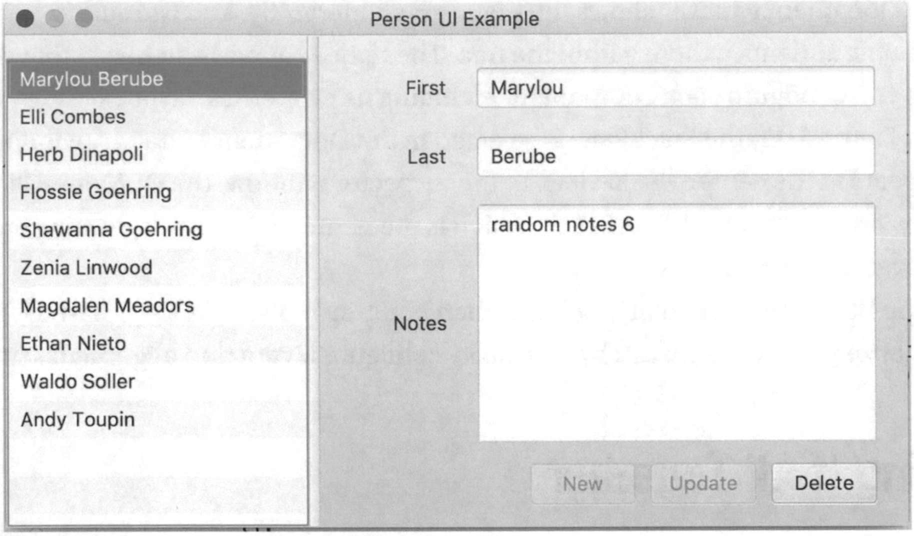

Figure 2-12. *Person UI application*

The ListView control lets you perform selections for a Person object. Here, the first Person is selected, and the details of that Person appear in the form control on the right. The form control has the following layout:

- The form contains a GridPane (two columns by four rows) that holds TextFields for the `firstname` and `lastname` fields of Person.

- A TextArea holds the `notes` field for Person. Labels in the first column mark each of these controls.

- The bottom row of the GridPane consists of a ButtonBar that spans both columns and aligns on the right side by default. The ButtonBar sizes all of its buttons to the width of the widest button label so the buttons have a uniform size.

- The buttons let you perform New (create a Person and add that Person to the list), Update (edit a selected Person), and Delete (remove a selected Person from the list).

- Bind expressions query the state of the application and enable or disable the buttons. Figure 2-12 shows the New and Update buttons disabled with the Delete button enabled.

Figure 2-13 shows a hierarchical view of our scene graph for the Person UI application.

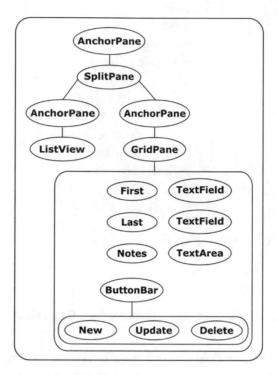

Figure 2-13. *Person UI scene graph hierarchy*

Figure 2-14 shows the file structure of the application. **Person.java** contains the Person model code, and **SampleData.java** provides the data to initialize the application. **FXMLController.java** is the JavaFX controller class, and **PersonUI.java** holds the main application class. Under resources, the FXML file **Scene.fxml** describes the UI.

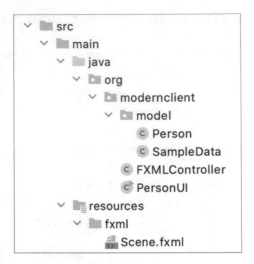

Figure 2-14. *Person UI application file structure*

The Model

Let's begin with the Person class shown in Listing 2-7. This is the "model" we use for this application.

Our Person class has three fields: `firstname`, `lastname`, and `notes`. These fields are implemented as JavaFX properties, making them observable. We follow the naming conventions described earlier to implement the getter, setter, and property getter. Fortunately, JavaFX provides convenience classes that help you create properties. Here we use `SimpleStringProperty()` to construct each field as a JavaFX string property.

Listing 2-7. model.Person.java

```
package org.modernclient.model;
import javafx.beans.Observable;
import javafx.beans.property.SimpleStringProperty;
import javafx.beans.property.StringProperty;
import javafx.util.Callback;
import java.util.Objects;
public class Person {
    private final StringProperty firstname = new SimpleStringProperty(
            this, "firstname", "");
    private final StringProperty lastname = new SimpleStringProperty(
            this, "lastname", "");
```

```java
private final StringProperty notes = new SimpleStringProperty(
        this, "notes", "sample notes");
public Person() {
}
public Person(String firstname, String lastname, String notes) {
    this.firstname.set(firstname);
    this.lastname.set(lastname);
    this.notes.set(notes);
}
public String getFirstname() {
    return firstname.get();
}
public StringProperty firstnameProperty() {
    return firstname;
}
public void setFirstname(String firstname) {
    this.firstname.set(firstname);
}
public String getLastname() {
    return lastname.get();
}
public StringProperty lastnameProperty() {
    return lastname;
}
public void setLastname(String lastname) {
    this.lastname.set(lastname);
}
public String getNotes() {
    return notes.get();
}
public StringProperty notesProperty() {
    return notes;
}
```

```java
    public void setNotes(String notes) {
        this.notes.set(notes);
    }
    @Override
    public String toString() {
        return firstname.get() + " " + lastname.get();
    }
    @Override
    public boolean equals(Object obj) {
        if (this == obj) return true;
        if (obj == null || getClass() != obj.getClass()) return false;
        Person person = (Person) obj;
        return Objects.equals(firstname, person.firstname) &&
                Objects.equals(lastname, person.lastname) &&
                Objects.equals(notes, person.notes);
    }
    @Override
    public int hashCode() {
        return Objects.hash(firstname, lastname, notes);
    }
}
```

Observable Lists

When working with JavaFX collections, you'll typically use ObservableLists that detect list changes with listeners. Furthermore, the JavaFX controls that display lists of data expect observable lists. These controls automatically update the UI in response to list modifications. We'll explain some of these intricacies as we walk you through our example program.

Implementing ListView Selection

A ListView control displays items in an observable list and lets you select one or possibly multiple items. To display a selected Person in the form fields in the right view, you use a change listener for the selectedItemProperty. This change listener is invoked each time the user either selects a different item from the ListView or deselects the selected item. You can use the mouse for selecting, as well as the arrow keys, Home (for the first item), and End (for the last item). On a Mac, use Fn+left arrow for Home and Fn+right arrow for End. For deselecting (either command+click for a Mac or Ctrl+click on Linux or Windows), the new value is null, and we clear all the form control fields. Listing 2-8 shows the ListView selection change listener.

Listing 2-8. ListView selection change listener

```
listView.getSelectionModel().selectedItemProperty().addListener(
        personChangeListener = (observable, oldValue, newValue) -> {
            // newValue can be null if nothing is selected
            selectedPerson = newValue;
            modifiedProperty.set(false);
            if (newValue != null) {
                // Populate controls with selected Person
                firstnameTextField.setText(selectedPerson.getFirstname());
                lastnameTextField.setText(selectedPerson.getLastname());
                notesTextArea.setText(selectedPerson.getNotes());
            } else {
                firstnameTextField.setText("");
                lastnameTextField.setText("");
                notesTextArea.setText("");
            }
        });
```

Boolean property `modifiedProperty` tracks whether the user has changed any of the three text controls in the form. We reset this flag after each ListView selection and use this property in a bind expression to control the Update button's disable property.

Using Multiple Selection

By default, a ListView control implements single selection so at most one item can be selected. ListView also provides multiple selection, which you enable by configuring the selection mode, as follows:

```
listView.getSelectionModel().setSelectionMode(SelectionMode.MULTIPLE);
```

With this setting, each time the user adds another item to the selection with Ctrl+click or command+click, the selectedItemProperty listener is invoked with the new selection. The getSelectedItems() method returns all of the currently selected items, and the newValue argument is the most recently selected value. For example, the following change listener collects multiple selected items and prints them:

```
listView.getSelectionModel().selectedItemProperty().addListener(
        personChangeListener = (observable, oldValue, newValue) -> {
    ObservableList<Person> selectedItems =
                    listView.getSelectionModel().getSelectedItems();
    // Do something with selectedItems
    System.out.println(selectedItems);
 });
```

Our Person UI application uses single selection mode for the ListView.

ListView and Sort

Suppose you want to sort the list of names by last name and then first name. JavaFX has several ways to sort lists. Since we need to keep names sorted, we'll wrap the underlying ObservableArrayList in a SortedList. To keep the list sorted in ListView, we invoke ListView's setItems() method with the sorted list. A comparator specifies the ordering. First, we compare each Person's last name for sorting and then the first names if necessary. To set the sorting, the setComparator() method uses an anonymous class or, more succinctly, a lambda expression:

```
// Use a sorted list; sort by lastname; then by firstname
SortedList<Person> sortedList = new SortedList(personList);
sortedList.setComparator((p1, p2) -> {
    int result = p1.getLastname().compareToIgnoreCase(p2.getLastname());
    if (result == 0) {
        result = p1.getFirstname().compareToIgnoreCase(p2.getFirstname());
    }
    return result;
});
listView.setItems(sortedList);
```

Note that the comparator arguments p1 and p2 are inferred as Person types since SortedList is generic.

For a more in-depth discussion of the ListView control, including advanced editing and display features using cells and cell factories, see Chapter 4, "JavaFX Controls Deep Dive."

Person UI Application Actions

Our Person UI application implements three actions: Delete (remove the selected Person object from the underlying list), New (create a Person object and add it to the underlying list), and Update (make changes to the selected Person object and update the underlying list). Let's go over each action in detail, with an eye toward learning more about the JavaFX features that help you build this type of application.

Delete a Person

The controller class includes an action event handler for the Delete button. Here's the FXML snippet that defines the Delete button:

```
<Button fx:id="removeButton" mnemonicParsing="false"
                onAction="#removeButtonAction" text="Delete" />
```

The fx:id attribute names the button so the JavaFX controller class can access it. The onAction attribute corresponds to the ActionEvent handler in the controller code. We're not using keyboard shortcuts in this application, so we set attribute mnemonicParsing to false.

Note   When mnemonic parsing is true, you can specify a keyboard shortcut to activate a labeled control, such as Alt+F to open a File menu. You define the keyboard shortcut by preceding the targeted letter with an underbar character in the label.

You cannot update a SortedList directly, but you can apply changes to its underlying list (ObservableList personList). The SortedList always keeps its elements sorted whenever you add or delete items.

Here is the event handler in the controller class:

```
@FXML
private void removeButtonAction(ActionEvent actionEvent) {
    personList.remove(selectedPerson);
}
```

This handler removes the selected Person object from the backing observable array list. The ListView control's selection change listener sets selectedPerson, as shown in Listing 2-8.

Note that we don't have to check selectedPerson against null here. Why not? You'll see that we disable the Delete button when the selectedItemProperty is null. This means the Delete button's action event handler can never be invoked when the user deselects an element in the ListView control. Here's the bind expression that controls the Delete button's disable property:

```
removeButton.disableProperty().bind(
    listView.getSelectionModel().selectedItemProperty().isNull());
```

This elegant statement makes the event handler more compact and subsequently less error-prone. Both the button disableProperty and the selection model selectedItemProperty are JavaFX observables. You can therefore use them in bind expressions. The property that invokes bind() automatically updates when the bind() arguments' values change.

Add a Person

The New button adds a Person to the list and subsequently updates the ListView control. A new item is always sorted because the list re-sorts when elements are added to the wrapped list. Here is the FXML that defines the New button. Similar to the Delete button, we define both the fx:id and onAction attributes:

```
<Button fx:id="createButton" mnemonicParsing="false"
        onAction="#createButtonAction" text="New" />
```

Under what circumstances should we disable the New button?

- When clicking New, no items in the ListView should be selected. Therefore, we disable the New button if the `selectedItemProperty` is not null. Note that you deselect the selected item with command+click or Ctrl+click.

- We should not create a new Person if either the first or last name field is empty. So we disable the New button if either of these fields is empty. We do allow the Notes field to be empty, however.

Here is the bind expression that implements these restrictions:

```
createButton.disableProperty().bind(
    listView.getSelectionModel().selectedItemProperty().isNotNull()
        .or(firstnameTextField.textProperty().isEmpty()
        .or(lastnameTextField.textProperty().isEmpty())));
```

Now let's show you the New button event handler:

```
@FXML
private void createButtonAction(ActionEvent actionEvent) {
    Person person = new Person(firstnameTextField.getText(),
            lastnameTextField.getText(), notesTextArea.getText());
    personList.add(person);
    // and select it
    listView.getSelectionModel().select(person);
}
```

First, we create a new Person object using the form's text controls and add this Person to the wrapped list (`ObservableList personList`). To make the Person's data visible and editable right away, we select the newly added Person.

Update a Person

An update of a Person is not as straightforward as the other operations. Before we delve into the details of why, let's first look at the Update button's FXML code, which is similar to the other buttons:

```
<Button fx:id="updateButton" mnemonicParsing="false"
        onAction="#updateButtonAction" text="Update" />
```

By default, a sorted list does not respond to individual array elements that change. For example, if Person "Ethan Nieto" changes to "Ethan Abraham," the list will not re-sort the way it does when items are added or removed. There are two ways to address this. First is to remove the item and add it back again with the new values.

The second way is to define an *extractor* for the underlying object. An extractor defines properties that should be observed when changes occur. Normally, changes to individual list elements are not observed. Observable objects returned by the extractor flag update changes in a list ChangeListener. Thus, to make a ListView control display a properly sorted list after changes to individual elements, you need to define an ObservableList with an extractor.

The benefit of extractors is that you only include the properties that affect sorting. In our example, properties `firstname` and `lastname` affect the list's order. These properties should go in the extractor.

An extractor is a static callback method in the model class. Here's the extractor for our Person class:

```
public class Person {
  ...
      public static Callback<Person, Observable[]> extractor =
          p-> new Observable[] {
              p.lastnameProperty(), p.firstnameProperty()
          };
}
```

Now the controller class can use this extractor to declare an ObservableList called `personList`, as follows:

```
private final ObservableList<Person> personList =
          FXCollections.observableArrayList(Person.extractor);
```

With the extractor set up, the sorted list detects changes in both `firstnameProperty` and `lastnameProperty` and re-sorts as needed.

Next, we define when the Update button is enabled. In our application, the Update button should be disabled if no items are selected or if either the firstname or lastname text field becomes empty. And finally, we disable Update if the user has not yet made changes to the form's text components. We track these changes with a JavaFX Boolean property called modifiedProperty, created with the JavaFX Boolean property helper class, SimpleBooleanProperty. We initialize this Boolean to false in the JavaFX controller class, as follows:

```
private final BooleanProperty modifiedProperty =
    new SimpleBooleanProperty(false);
```

We reset this Boolean property to false in the ListView selection change listener (Listing 2-8). The modifiedProperty is set to true when a keystroke occurs in any of the three fields that can change: the first name, last name, and notes controls. Here is the keystroke event handler, which is invoked when a keystroke is detected inside the focus for each of these three controls:

```
@FXML
private void handleKeyAction(KeyEvent keyEvent) {
    modifiedProperty.set(true);
}
```

Of course, the FXML markup must configure attribute onKeyReleased for all three text controls to invoke the keystroke event handler. Here is the FXML for the firstname TextField, which links the handleKeyAction event handler to a key release event for this control:

```
<TextField fx:id="firstnameTextField" onKeyReleased="#handleKeyAction"
    prefWidth="248.0"
    GridPane.columnIndex="1"
    GridPane.hgrow="ALWAYS" />
```

And here is the bind expression for the Update button, which is disabled if the selectedItemProperty is null, the modifiedProperty is false, or the text controls are empty:

```
updateButton.disableProperty().bind(
    listView.getSelectionModel().selectedItemProperty().isNull()
        .or(modifiedProperty.not())
        .or(firstnameTextField.textProperty().isEmpty()
        .or(lastnameTextField.textProperty().isEmpty())));
```

Now let's show you the Update button's action event handler. This handler is invoked when the user clicks the Update button after selecting an item in the ListView control and making at least one change to any of the text fields.

But there is one more housekeeping chore to do. Before starting the update of the selected item with the values from the form controls, we must remove the listener on the selectedItemProperty. Why? Recall that changes to the firstname or lastname property will affect the list dynamically and possibly re-sort it. Furthermore, this may change ListView's idea of the currently selected item and invoke the ChangeListener. To prevent this, we remove the listener during the update and add the listener back when the update finishes. During the update, the selected item remains unchanged (even if the list re-sorts). Thus, we clear the modifiedProperty flag to ensure the Update button gets disabled:

```
@FXML
private void updateButtonAction(ActionEvent actionEvent) {
    Person p = listView.getSelectionModel().getSelectedItem();
    listView.getSelectionModel().selectedItemProperty()
                .removeListener(personChangeListener);
    p.setFirstname(firstnameTextField.getText());
    p.setLastname(lastnameTextField.getText());
    p.setNotes(notesTextArea.getText());
    listView.getSelectionModel().selectedItemProperty()
                .addListener(personChangeListener);
    modifiedProperty.set(false);
}
```

Person UI with Records

One of the exciting new features in Java 16 is *records*. Records allow you to model classes that hold immutable data and describe state, often with a single line of code. Let's refactor our Person UI example to use Java records for the Person model class. We do this for several reasons.

- Modern Java clients with JavaFX will continue to evolve as applications leverage new Java features. After all, JavaFX is implemented with Java APIs and can certainly take advantage of new features as they become available.

- Our UI example is a good candidate for records, since using a Person record instead of a class is a straightforward approach.

- We originally implemented Person with JavaFX properties, which are observable and mutable. But, in the context of our application, is this mutability necessary or even desirable?

- Java records help make your code more readable, since often a single line defines the state of your model class.

Person Record

We declare a record with its name and its immutable components; each component has a name and type. These components are final instance fields in the generated class. Java generates accessor methods for the fields, a constructor, and default implementations for methods equals(), hashCode(), and toString().

Here's the new Person class, which is much shorter than the non-record version shown in Listing 2-7!

```
public record Person (String firstname, String lastname, String notes) {
    @Override
    public String toString() {
        return firstname + " " + lastname;
    }
}
```

Note that we supply our own toString() implementation to replace the auto-generated toString(), since ListView uses this to display each Person object. The generated accessor methods are firstname(), lastname(), and notes() to match the elements declared in the record header. We update our application to use these names instead of the conventional getter forms. This affects the selectedItemProperty change listener and the sorted list comparator.

No changes are necessary to the createButtonAction or removeButtonAction event handlers. There is also no change to the code that creates our sample list of Person objects (SampleData.java).

Records do require changes to the updateButtonAction event handler, however. Since a Person object is now immutable, we cannot update its fields. Therefore, to update a Person, we must create a new Person object, remove the old one, and add the new one to the backing list. The sorted list automatically updates with the new data. Here is the new updateButtonAction event handler:

```
@FXML
  private void updateButtonAction(ActionEvent actionEvent) {
      Person person = new Person(firstnameTextField.getText(),
      lastnameTextField.getText(),
                  notesTextArea.getText());
      personList.remove(listView.getSelectionModel().getSelectedItem());
      personList.add(person);
      listView.getSelectionModel().select(person);
      modifiedProperty.set(false);
  }
```

By removing and adding a Person, the update process becomes simpler. The extractor to detect changes is no longer necessary, nor do we need to temporarily remove the selectedItemProperty change listener during updates.

By restricting Person to be an immutable container, we greatly simplify Person and the readability of our program. However, JavaFX properties and binding are still ideal features to maintain the state of the UI.

Key Point Summary

This chapter has covered a lot of ground. Let's review the key points:

- JavaFX is a modern UI toolkit that runs efficiently in desktop, mobile, and embedded environments.

- JavaFX uses a theater metaphor. The runtime system creates the primary stage and invokes the start() method of your application.

- You create a hierarchical scene graph and install the root node in the scene.

- The JavaFX runtime system performs all UI updates and scene graph modifications on the JavaFX Application Thread. Any long-running work should be relegated to background tasks in separate threads to keep the UI responsive. JavaFX has a well-developed concurrency library that helps you keep UI code separate from background code.

- JavaFX supports both 2D and 3D graphics. The origin in 2D graphics is the upper-left corner of the scene.

- JavaFX includes a rich set of layout controls that let you arrange components in a scene. You can nest layout controls and specify resizing criteria.

- JavaFX defines a scene graph as a hierarchical collection of Nodes. Nodes are described by their properties.

- JavaFX properties are observable. You can attach listeners and use the rich bindings APIs to link properties to each other and detect changes.

- JavaFX lets you define high-level animations called transitions.

- The hierarchical nature of the scene graph means parent nodes can delegate rendering work to their children.

- JavaFX supports a wide range of events that let you react to user inputs and changes to a scene graph.

- While you can write JavaFX applications completely in Java, a better approach is to write visual descriptions in FXML, a markup language for specifying UI content. FXML helps separate visual code from model and controller code.

- Each FXML file typically describes a scene and configures a controller.

- Scene Builder is a handy drag-and-drop tool for defining and configuring components in a scene.

- You can customize the style of JavaFX controls and forms with CSS files that you load in FXML or in Java code.

- ObservableLists let you listen for changes in a list.

- JavaFX has several controls for displaying lists of data. You configure these controls with ObservableLists so that changes are automatically detected by the control.

- You can react to individual element changes by defining an extractor in the model class. The extractor specifies the properties that should signal change events.

- Wrapping an ObservableList with SortedList keeps a list sorted. A comparator lets you customize the sort criteria.

- Consider implementing immutable model classes with Java records. Records are a new Java feature available since Java 16.

CHAPTER 3

Properties and Bindings

Written by Weiqi Gao

Heaven acts with vitality and persistence.

In correspondence with this

The superior person keeps himself vital without ceasing.

—I Ching

The first two chapters introduced you to the big picture of client-side Java and the fundamentals of JavaFX. In this chapter, we delve deeper into the bindings and properties framework, the part of JavaFX that, together with the declarative UI language FXML and the visual UI designer Scene Builder, makes JavaFX desktop and mobile client applications elegant and enjoyable to write.

The `javafx.base` module is the home of the JavaFX properties and bindings framework. It exports the following packages:

- `javafx.beans`
- `javafx.beans.binding`
- `javafx.beans.property`
- `javafx.beans.property.adapter`
- `javafx.beans.value`
- `javafx.collections`
- `javafx.collections.transformation`
- `javafx.event`

© Stephen Chin, Johan Vos and James Weaver 2022
S. Chin et al., *The Definitive Guide to Modern Java Clients with JavaFX 17*,
https://doi.org/10.1007/978-1-4842-7268-8_3

- `javafx.util`

- `javafx.util.converter`

We will focus on the `javafx.beans` and `javafx.collections` packages and their subpackages.

Key Concepts

At the core of the properties and bindings API is a set of interfaces that give life to the two concepts central to our discussion: *property* and *binding*. Figure 3-1 shows these interfaces.

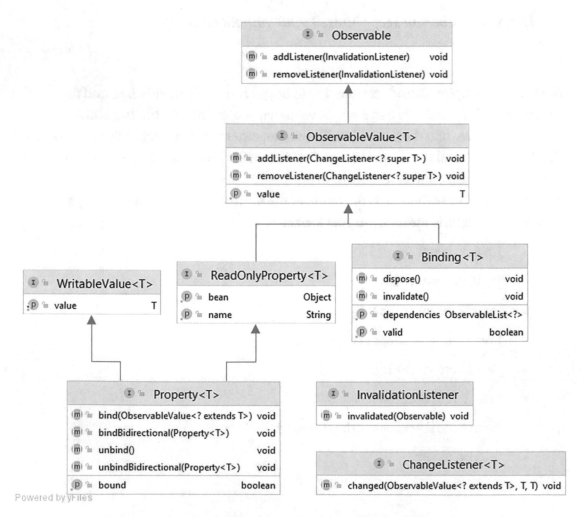

Figure 3-1. *Key interfaces of the JavaFX properties and bindings framework*

Observable and InvalidationListener

The Observable interface allows you to register InvalidationListeners to a Property or a Binding so that you will receive a notification when the Property or Binding becomes *invalidated*. A Property becomes invalidated if its set() or setValue() method is called with a value different from its currently held value. A Binding becomes invalidated when its invalidate() method is called or when its dependencies become invalidated. The callback method in InvalidationListener has the following signature, giving you access to a reference to the Observable object:

```
void invalidated(Observable observable);
```

> **Note**   An invalidation event is fired only once by the properties in JavaFX if you call the setters with the same value several times in a row.

ObservableValue and ChangeListener

The ObservableValue interface allows you to register ChangeListeners with a Property or a Binding so that you will receive a notification when the value of the Property or Binding changes from one value to a different value. The notification comes in the form of a callback method in ChangeListener with the following signature, giving you access to a reference to the property or binding whose value has changed, as well as the old and the new values:

```
void changed(ObservableValue<? extends T> observable,
             T oldValue, T newValue)
```

> **Note**   Weak versions of the InvalidationListener and the ChangeListener, and some other listeners introduced later in this chapter, exist to help avoid memory leaks.

WritableValue and ReadOnlyProperty

The WritableValue interface provides the setValue() method to a Property. The ReadOnlyProperty interface injects two methods to a Property: a getBean() method that returns the holder of the property and a getName() method that returns a descriptive name of the property. Both methods may return null if the property is not part of a bigger object or if a descriptive name is not important.

JavaFX Properties

With all preliminaries out of the way, we can finally look at the Property interface. It provides five methods:

```
void bind(ObservableValue<? extends T> observable);
void unbind();
boolean isBound();
void bindBidirectional(Property<T> other);
void unbindBidirectional(Property<T> other);
```

The bind() method establishes a *unidirectional binding* between the Property and the ObservableValue. The unbind() method releases the binding. And the isBound() method reports whether a unidirectional binding is in effect. Once in effect, the unidirectional binding establishes a *dependency* of the former onto the latter. The set() or setValue() method on the Property will throw a RuntimeException, and the get() or getValue() method will return the value of the ObservableValue.

The bindBidirectional() method establishes a *bidirectional binding* between the two Property objects. The unbindBidirectional() method releases it. Once in effect, calling set() or setValue() on either property will cause both objects' values to be updated.

Caution   Each Property may have at most one active unidirectional binding at a time. It may have as many bidirectional bindings as you want. The isBound() method pertains only to unidirectional bindings. Calling bind() a second time with a different ObservableValue will unbind the previous one and replace it with the new one.

To summarize what we covered so far, we see that a Property can hold a value, can notify others when its value changes, and can be bound to others to reflect the bound objects' values. Listing 3-1 shows a silly program that exercises these functionalities.

Listing 3-1. PropertiesExample.java

```java
package org.modernclients.propertiesandbindings;
import javafx.beans.InvalidationListener;
import javafx.beans.property.IntegerProperty;
import javafx.beans.property.SimpleIntegerProperty;
import javafx.beans.value.ChangeListener;
public class PropertiesExample {
    private static IntegerProperty i1;
    public static void main(String[] args) {
        createProperty();
        addAndRemoveInvalidationListener();
        addAndRemoveChangeListener();
        bindAndUnbindOnePropertyToAnother();
    }
    private static void createProperty() {
        System.out.println();
        i1 = new SimpleIntegerProperty(1024);
        System.out.println("i1 = " + i1);
        System.out.println("i1.get() = " + i1.get());
        System.out.println("i1.getValue() = "
                + i1.getValue());
    }
    private static void addAndRemoveInvalidationListener() {
        System.out.println();
        final InvalidationListener invalidationListener =
                observable -> {
                    System.out.println(
                            "The observable has been " +
                                    "invalidated: " +
                                    observable + ".");
                };
```

```java
        i1.addListener(invalidationListener);
        System.out.println("Added invalidation listener.");
        System.out.println("Calling i1.set(2048).");
        i1.set(2048);
        System.out.println("Calling i1.setValue(3072).");
        i1.setValue(3072);
        i1.removeListener(invalidationListener);
        System.out.println("Removed invalidation listener.");
        System.out.println("Calling i1.set(4096).");
        i1.set(4096);
    }
    private static void addAndRemoveChangeListener() {
        System.out.println();
        final ChangeListener<Number> changeListener =
                (observableValue,
                 oldValue,
                 newValue) -> {
                    System.out.println(
                            "The observableValue has " +
                                    "changed: oldValue = " +
                                    oldValue +
                                    ", newValue = " +
                                    newValue);
                };
        i1.addListener(changeListener);
        System.out.println("Added change listener.");
        System.out.println("Calling i1.set(5120).");
        i1.set(5120);
        i1.removeListener(changeListener);
        System.out.println("Removed change listener.");
        System.out.println("Calling i1.set(6144).");
        i1.set(6144);
    }
    private static void bindAndUnbindOnePropertyToAnother() {
        System.out.println();
```

```java
        IntegerProperty i2 = new SimpleIntegerProperty(0);
        System.out.println("i2.get() = " + i2.get());
        System.out.println("Binding i2 to i1.");
        i2.bind(i1);
        System.out.println("i2.get() = " + i2.get());
        System.out.println("Calling i1.set(7168).");
        i1.set(7168);
        System.out.println("i2.get() = " + i2.get());
        System.out.println("Unbinding i2 from i1.");
        i2.unbind();
        System.out.println("i2.get() = " + i2.get());
        System.out.println("Calling i1.set(8192).");
        i1.set(8192);
        System.out.println("i2.get() = " + i2.get());
    }
}
```

Note   The source code for this section can be found under chapter3 in the source bundle accompanying the book. It is organized as a Gradle project with subprojects, one for each example.

This program is self-explanatory, and you can almost visualize in your mind how it executes. We used an abstract class `IntegerProperty` and its concrete implementation `SimpleIntegerProperty` in the program. It holds a primitive `int` value.

Listing 3-2 shows bidirectional binding at work.

Listing 3-2. BidirectionalBindingExample.java

```java
package org.modernclients.propertiesandbindings;

import javafx.beans.property.SimpleStringProperty;
import javafx.beans.property.StringProperty;
public class BidirectionalBindingExample {
    public static void main(String[] args) {
        System.out.println("Constructing two StringProperty" +
                " objects.");
```

```
        StringProperty prop1 = new SimpleStringProperty("");
        StringProperty prop2 = new SimpleStringProperty("");
        System.out.println("Calling bindBidirectional.");
        prop2.bindBidirectional(prop1);
        System.out.println("prop1.isBound() = " +
                prop1.isBound());
        System.out.println("prop2.isBound() = " +
                prop2.isBound());
        System.out.println("Calling prop1.set(\"prop1" +
                " says: Hi!\")");
        prop1.set("prop1 says: Hi!");
        System.out.println("prop2.get() returned:");
        System.out.println(prop2.get());
        System.out.println("Calling prop2.set(prop2.get()" +
                " + \"\\nprop2 says: Bye!\")");
        prop2.set(prop2.get() + "\nprop2 says: Bye!");
        System.out.println("prop1.get() returned:");
        System.out.println(prop1.get());
    }
}
```

Creating Bindings

We explored the key interfaces of the JavaFX properties and bindings framework in the last section. And we learned the fundamentals about Property objects as well. In this section, we pick up the other half of the framework and examine Bindings.

JavaFX Bindings

The Binding interface provides four methods:

```
boolean isValid();
void invalidate();
ObservableList<?> getDependencies();
void dispose();
```

A Binding's *validity* can be queried with the isValid() method and set with the invalidate() method. It has a list of *dependencies* that can be obtained with the getDependencies() method. And finally, the dispose() method signals that the Binding will not be used anymore and resources used by it can be cleaned up.

Therefore, a Binding represents a *unidirectional binding with multiple dependencies.* Each dependency can send invalidation events to the Binding, making it invalidated. When the value of the Binding is queried through the get() or getValue() call, if it is invalidated, its value is recalculated based on the dependencies' values. This value will be cached and used in subsequent value queries, until the Binding becomes invalidated again. This lazy value evaluation is what makes the JavaFX properties and bindings framework efficient. Attaching a ChangeListener forces eager evaluation.

As one binding can be used as a dependency of another binding, complex binding trees can be constructed. This is another source of the great power of the JavaFX properties and bindings framework.

Caution   As with any complex structures, care must be taken to avoid performance degradations and behavior mistakes, especially under high-load scenarios.

Unlike with properties, the framework provides no concrete binding classes. Therefore, all bindings are custom bindings, and there are several ways to create them:

- Extending an abstract base class, such as DoubleBinding
- Using factory methods in the utility class Bindings
- Using fluent API methods in the property and binding classes

Create Bindings by Direct Extension

Listing 3-3 shows a program that creates a binding by directly extending DoubleBinding and using it to calculate the area of a rectangle.

Listing 3-3. DirectExtensionExample.java

```
package org.modernclients.propertiesandbindings;
import javafx.beans.binding.DoubleBinding;
import javafx.beans.property.DoubleProperty;
import javafx.beans.property.SimpleDoubleProperty;
```

```java
public class DirectExtensionExample {
    public static void main(String[] args) {
        System.out.println("Constructing x with value 2.0.");
        final DoubleProperty x =
                new SimpleDoubleProperty(null, "x", 2.0);
        System.out.println("Constructing y with value 3.0.");
        final DoubleProperty y =
                new SimpleDoubleProperty(null, "y", 3.0);
        System.out.println("Creating binding area" +
                " with dependencies x and y.");
        DoubleBinding area = new DoubleBinding() {
            {
                super.bind(x, y);
            }
            @Override
            protected double computeValue() {
                System.out.println("computeValue()" +
                        " is called.");
                return x.get() * y.get();
            }
        };
        System.out.println("area.get() = " + area.get());
        System.out.println("area.get() = " + area.get());
        System.out.println("Setting x to 5");
        x.set(5);
        System.out.println("Setting y to 7");
        y.set(7);
        System.out.println("area.get() = " + area.get());
    }
}
```

Here, we extend the DoubleBinding class by overriding its only abstract method computeValue() to calculate the area of a rectangle with sides x and y. We also call the superclass's bind() method to make the properties x and y our dependencies.

Running this program prints the following to the console:

```
Constructing x with value 2.0.
Constructing y with value 3.0.
Creating binding area with dependencies x and y.
computeValue() is called.
area.get() = 6.0
area.get() = 6.0
Setting x to 5
Setting y to 7
computeValue() is called.
area.get() = 35.0
```

Notice that `computeValue()` is called only once when we call `area.get()` twice in a row.

Type-Specific Specializations

Before we move on to the next method of creating bindings, we need to fill you in on some details about the generic nature of the key interfaces and their type-specific specializations.

The previous examples in the chapter included classes like `IntegerProperty`, `StringProperty`, and `DoubleBinding`. These are specialized classes of the generic types `Property<T>` and `Bindings<T>`. Because of Java's primitive type and reference type dichotomy, direct use of generic types, such as `Property<Integer>`, while dealing with primitive values incurs boxing and unboxing inefficiencies. To alleviate this cost, type-specific specializations of the generic types are constructed for primitive `boolean`, `int`, `long`, `float`, and `double` values in such a way that when their `get()` or `set()` methods are called, and when doing internal calculations, the primitive types are never boxed and unboxed. Similar specializations are also constructed for the `String` and `Object` reference types for uniformity reasons. This accounts for the existence of the `BooleanProperty`, `IntegerProperty`, `LongProperty`, `FloatProperty`, `DoubleProperty`, `StringProperty`, and `ObjectProperty` classes.

Caution   Don't be fooled by the name `IntegerProperty` into thinking that it is
a container of an `Integer` object. It really is not. It is a container of primitive `int`
values. The same is true for the other primitive-based classes.

Another aspect of these type-specific specializations is that the specializations for the
numeric primitive types are derived using `Number` as the type parameter. And a practical
consequence is that any numeric property can call `bind()` on any other numeric
property or binding. Listing 3-4 shows a program that illustrates this.

Listing 3-4. NumericPropertiesExample.java

```
package org.modernclients.propertiesandbindings;
import javafx.beans.property.DoubleProperty;
import javafx.beans.property.FloatProperty;
import javafx.beans.property.IntegerProperty;
import javafx.beans.property.LongProperty;
import javafx.beans.property.SimpleDoubleProperty;
import javafx.beans.property.SimpleFloatProperty;
import javafx.beans.property.SimpleIntegerProperty;
import javafx.beans.property.SimpleLongProperty;
public class NumericPropertiesExample {
    public static void main(String[] args) {
        IntegerProperty i =
                new SimpleIntegerProperty(null, "i", 1024);
        LongProperty l =
                new SimpleLongProperty(null, "l", 0L);
        FloatProperty f =
                new SimpleFloatProperty(null, "f", 0.0F);
        DoubleProperty d =
                new SimpleDoubleProperty(null, "d", 0.0);
        System.out.println("Constructed numerical" +
                " properties i, l, f, d.");
        System.out.println("i.get() = " + i.get());
        System.out.println("l.get() = " + l.get());
        System.out.println("f.get() = " + f.get());
        System.out.println("d.get() = " + d.get());
```

```
        l.bind(i);
        f.bind(l);
        d.bind(f);
        System.out.println("Bound l to i, f to l, d to f.");
        System.out.println("i.get() = " + i.get());
        System.out.println("l.get() = " + l.get());
        System.out.println("f.get() = " + f.get());
        System.out.println("d.get() = " + d.get());
        System.out.println("Calling i.set(2048).");
        i.set(2048);
        System.out.println("i.get() = " + i.get());
        System.out.println("l.get() = " + l.get());
        System.out.println("f.get() = " + f.get());
        System.out.println("d.get() = " + d.get());
        d.unbind();
        f.unbind();
        l.unbind();
        System.out.println("Unbound l to i, f to l, d to f.");
        f.bind(d);
        l.bind(f);
        i.bind(l);
        System.out.println("Bound f to d, l to f, i to l.");
        System.out.println("Calling d.set(10000000000L).");
        d.set(10000000000L);
        System.out.println("d.get() = " + d.get());
        System.out.println("f.get() = " + f.get());
        System.out.println("l.get() = " + l.get());
        System.out.println("i.get() = " + i.get());
    }
}
```

Running this application gives the following output:

```
Constructed numerical properties i, l, f, d.
i.get() = 1024
l.get() = 0
f.get() = 0.0
```

```
d.get() = 0.0
Bound l to i, f to l, d to f.
i.get() = 1024
l.get() = 1024
f.get() = 1024.0
d.get() = 1024.0
Calling i.set(2048).
i.get() = 2048
l.get() = 2048
f.get() = 2048.0
d.get() = 2048.0
Unbound l to i, f to l, d to f.
Bound f to d, l to f, i to l.
Calling d.set(10000000000L).
d.get() = 1.0E10
f.get() = 1.0E10
l.get() = 10000000000
i.get() = 1410065408
```

Factory Methods in Bindings

The Bindings class contains more than 200 factory methods that make new bindings out of existing observable values and regular values. The methods are overloaded to account for the myriads of combinations of parameter types.

The add(), subtract(), multiply(), and divide() methods do the obvious, creating a new numeric binding out of two numeric values, at least one of which is an observable value. The program in Listing 3-5 illustrates their use. It calculates the area of a triangle with vertices (x1,y1), (x2,y2), and (x3,y3) using the formula

$$area = (x1*y2 + x2*y3 + x3*y1 - x1*y3 - x2*y1 - x3*y2)/2$$

Listing 3-5. TriangleAreaExample.java

```
package org.modernclients.propertiesandbindings;
import javafx.beans.binding.Bindings;
import javafx.beans.binding.NumberBinding;
import javafx.beans.property.IntegerProperty;
```

```java
import javafx.beans.property.SimpleIntegerProperty;
public class TriangleAreaExample {
    public static void main(String[] args) {
        IntegerProperty x1 = new SimpleIntegerProperty(0);
        IntegerProperty y1 = new SimpleIntegerProperty(0);
        IntegerProperty x2 = new SimpleIntegerProperty(0);
        IntegerProperty y2 = new SimpleIntegerProperty(0);
        IntegerProperty x3 = new SimpleIntegerProperty(0);
        IntegerProperty y3 = new SimpleIntegerProperty(0);
        final NumberBinding x1y2 = Bindings.multiply(x1, y2);
        final NumberBinding x2y3 = Bindings.multiply(x2, y3);
        final NumberBinding x3y1 = Bindings.multiply(x3, y1);
        final NumberBinding x1y3 = Bindings.multiply(x1, y3);
        final NumberBinding x2y1 = Bindings.multiply(x2, y1);
        final NumberBinding x3y2 = Bindings.multiply(x3, y2);
        final NumberBinding sum1 = Bindings.add(x1y2, x2y3);
        final NumberBinding sum2 = Bindings.add(sum1, x3y1);
        final NumberBinding diff1 =
                Bindings.subtract(sum2, x1y3);
        final NumberBinding diff2 =
                Bindings.subtract(diff1, x2y1);
        final NumberBinding determinant =
                Bindings.subtract(diff2, x3y2);
        final NumberBinding area =
                Bindings.divide(determinant, 2.0D);
        x1.set(0); y1.set(0);
        x2.set(6); y2.set(0);
        x3.set(4); y3.set(3);
        printResult(x1, y1, x2, y2, x3, y3, area);
        x1.set(1); y1.set(0);
        x2.set(2); y2.set(2);
        x3.set(0); y3.set(1);
        printResult(x1, y1, x2, y2, x3, y3, area);
    }
```

```
        private static void printResult(IntegerProperty x1,
                                        IntegerProperty y1,
                                        IntegerProperty x2,
                                        IntegerProperty y2,
                                        IntegerProperty x3,
                                        IntegerProperty y3,
                                        NumberBinding area) {
        System.out.println("For A(" +
                x1.get() + "," + y1.get() + "), B(" +
                x2.get() + "," + y2.get() + "), C(" +
                x3.get() + "," + y3.get() +
                "), the area of triangle ABC is " +
                area.getValue());
    }
}
```

Running this program prints the following to the console:

```
For A(0,0), B(6,0), C(4,3), the area of triangle ABC is 9.0
For A(1,0), B(2,2), C(0,1), the area of triangle ABC is 1.5
```

Other factory methods in Bindings include the logical operators and(), or(), and not(); numeric operators min(), max(), and negate(); null testing operators isNull() and isNotNull(); string operators length(), isEmpty(), and isNotEmpty(); and relational operators equal(), equalIgnoreCase(), greaterThan(), graterThanOrEqual(), lessThan(), lessThanOrEqual(), notEqual(), and notEqualIgnoreCase(). The names of those methods are self-describing, and they all do what you think they do. For example, to make sure that the send money button is enabled only when a recipient is selected and the amount entered is greater than zero, we can write

```
sendBtn.disableProperty().bind(Bindings.not(
    Bindings.and(recipientSelected,
        Bindings.greaterThan(amount, 0.0))));
```

There are a set of factory methods named createDoubleBinding() and so on that allow you to create a binding from a Callable and a set of dependencies. The DoubleBinding that we created in Listing 3-3 can be simplified as

```
DoubleBinding area = Bindings.createDoubleBinding(() -> {
    return x.get() * y.get();
}, x, y);
```

The convert(), concat(), and a couple of overloaded format() methods can be used to convert non-string observable values into observable string values, concatenate several observable string values together, and format an observable numeric value or a date value into an observable string value. To display a temperature value in a Label, we can use the following binding:

```
tempLbl.textProperty().bind(Bindings.format("%2.1f \u00b0C", temperature));
```

As the value of the temperature property changes, the formatted string representation of the temperature changes with it. For example, when temperature is 37.5, the label will display 37.5 °C.

There are a set of factory methods named select() and selectInteger() and so on that work on *JavaFX Beans*, Java classes that conform to the JavaFX Bean convention. There are also methods that work on *observable collections*, observables that contain not a single value, but a List, a Map, a Set, or an array of elements. We cover them in later sections of this chapter.

Create Bindings with the Fluent API

Fluent APIs consist of a set of coordinating classes whose methods are designed to be chained together in such a way that the method chains, when read out aloud, describe what they do in prose-like sentences. The fluent API for creating bindings is embodied in the IntegerExpression series of classes. These expression classes are superclasses of both the property classes and the binding classes. Thus, the fluent API methods are readily available from the familiar property and binding classes. You can get a feel for these methods by browsing through the Javadocs of the expression classes. And in general, they reflect what the Bindings class has to offer. The following are a few example bindings built using the fluent API:

```
recipientSelected.and(amount.greaterThan(0.0)).not()
temperature.asString("%2.1f \u00b0C")
```

They are equivalent to the bindings that we constructed in the last section using factory methods from the Bindings class.

One fact that is worth pointing out here is that all the methods for the type-specific numeric expressions are defined in the NumberExpression base interface with a return type of NumberBinding and are overridden in the type-specific expression classes with an identical parameter signature but a more specific return type. This is called *covariant return-type overriding* and has been a Java language feature since Java 5. One of the consequences of this fact is that numeric bindings built with the fluent API have more specific types than those built with factory methods in the Bindings class.

Listing 3-6 shows a fluent API version of the triangle area example in Listing 3-5.

Listing 3-6. TriangleAreaFluentExample.java

```
package org.modernclients.propertiesandbindings;
import javafx.beans.binding.Bindings;
import javafx.beans.binding.NumberBinding;
import javafx.beans.binding.StringExpression;
import javafx.beans.property.IntegerProperty;
import javafx.beans.property.SimpleIntegerProperty;
public class TriangleAreaFluentExample {
    public static void main(String[] args) {
        IntegerProperty x1 = new SimpleIntegerProperty(0);
        IntegerProperty y1 = new SimpleIntegerProperty(0);
        IntegerProperty x2 = new SimpleIntegerProperty(0);
        IntegerProperty y2 = new SimpleIntegerProperty(0);
        IntegerProperty x3 = new SimpleIntegerProperty(0);
        IntegerProperty y3 = new SimpleIntegerProperty(0);
        final NumberBinding area = x1.multiply(y2)
                .add(x2.multiply(y3))
                .add(x3.multiply(y1))
```

```
            .subtract(x1.multiply(y3))
            .subtract(x2.multiply(y1))
            .subtract(x3.multiply(y2))
            .divide(2.0D);
    StringExpression output = Bindings.format(
            "For A(%d,%d), B(%d,%d), C(%d,%d)," +
                    " the area of triangle ABC is %3.1f",
            x1, y1, x2, y2, x3, y3, area);
    x1.set(0); y1.set(0);
    x2.set(6); y2.set(0);
    x3.set(4); y3.set(3);
    System.out.println(output.get());
    x1.set(1); y1.set(0);
    x2.set(2); y2.set(2);
    x3.set(0); y3.set(1);
    System.out.println(output.get());
    }
}
```

Running this program prints the following to the console:

```
For A(0,0), B(6,0), C(4,3), the area of triangle ABC is 9.0
For A(1,0), B(2,2), C(0,1), the area of triangle ABC is 1.5
```

The class When allows you to express if/then/else logic in a fluent API. You can construct an object of this class using either the constructor or the when() factory method in the Bindings class, passing in an ObservableBooleanValue. Overloaded then() methods on the When object return an object of a nested condition builder class, which in turn has overloaded otherwise() methods that return a binding object. This allows you to build up a binding this way:

```
new When(condition).then(result).otherwise(alternative)
```

Here, condition is an ObservableBooleanValue, and result and alternative are of similar types and can be either observable or non-observable. The resulting binding's type is similar to that of result and alternative.

Listing 3-7 shows an example of the use of this API. Here, we calculate the area of a triangle with sides a, b, and c, using Heron's formula

```
area = sqrt(s * (s - a) * (s - b) * (s - c))
```

where s = (a + b + c) / 2 is the semiperimeter. Recall that in a triangle, the sum of any two sides is greater than the third side.

Listing 3-7. HeronsFormulaExample.java

```java
package org.modernclients.propertiesandbindings;
import javafx.beans.binding.DoubleBinding;
import javafx.beans.binding.When;
import javafx.beans.property.DoubleProperty;
import javafx.beans.property.SimpleDoubleProperty;
public class HeronsFormulaExample {
    public static void main(String[] args) {
        DoubleProperty a = new SimpleDoubleProperty(0);
        DoubleProperty b = new SimpleDoubleProperty(0);
        DoubleProperty c = new SimpleDoubleProperty(0);
        DoubleBinding s = a.add(b).add(c).divide(2.0d);
        final DoubleBinding areaSquared = new When(
                a.add(b).greaterThan(c)
                        .and(b.add(c).greaterThan(a))
                        .and(c.add(a).greaterThan(b)))
                .then(s.multiply(s.subtract(a))
                        .multiply(s.subtract(b))
                        .multiply(s.subtract(c)))
                .otherwise(0.0D);
        a.set(3);
        b.set(4);
        c.set(5);
        System.out.printf("Given sides a = %1.0f," +
                    " b = %1.0f, and c = %1.0f," +
                    " the area of the triangle is" +
                    " %3.2f\n", a.get(), b.get(), c.get(),
                Math.sqrt(areaSquared.get())));
```

```
        a.set(2);
        b.set(2);
        c.set(2);
        System.out.printf("Given sides a = %1.0f," +
                    " b = %1.0f, and c = %1.0f," +
                    " the area of the triangle is" +
                    " %3.2f\n", a.get(), b.get(), c.get(),
                Math.sqrt(areaSquared.get()));
    }
}
```

Running this program prints the following to the console:

```
Given sides a = 3, b = 4, and c = 5, the area of the triangle is 6.00
Given sides a = 2, b = 2, and c = 2, the area of the triangle is 1.73
```

It should be noted that the fluent API has its limitations. As the relationship becomes more complicated or goes beyond the available operators, the direct extension method is preferred. Listing 3-8 shows just such a program that solves the same problem as Listing 3-7.

Listing 3-8. HeronsFormulaDirectExtensionExample.java

```
package org.modernclients.propertiesandbindings;
import javafx.beans.binding.DoubleBinding;
import javafx.beans.property.DoubleProperty;
import javafx.beans.property.SimpleDoubleProperty;
public class HeronsFormulaDirectExtensionExample {
    public static void main(String[] args) {
        final DoubleProperty a = new SimpleDoubleProperty(0);
        final DoubleProperty b = new SimpleDoubleProperty(0);
        final DoubleProperty c = new SimpleDoubleProperty(0);
        DoubleBinding area = new DoubleBinding() {
            {
                super.bind(a, b, c);
            }
```

```
            @Override
            protected double computeValue() {
                double a0 = a.get();
                double b0 = b.get();
                double c0 = c.get();
                if ((a0 + b0 > c0) && (b0 + c0 > a0) &&
                        (c0 + a0 > b0)) {
                    double s = (a0 + b0 + c0) / 2.0D;
                    return Math.sqrt(s * (s - a0) *
                            (s - b0) * (s - c0));
                } else {
                    return 0.0D;
                }
            }
        };
        a.set(3);
        b.set(4);
        c.set(5);
        System.out.printf("Given sides a = %1.0f," +
                    " b = %1.0f, and c = %1.0f," +
                    " the area of the triangle" +
                    " is %3.2f\n", a.get(), b.get(),
                c.get(), area.get());
        a.set(2);
        b.set(2);
        c.set(2);
        System.out.printf("Given sides a = %1.0f," +
                    " b = %1.0f, and c = %1.0f," +
                    " the area of the triangle" +
                    " is %3.2f\n", a.get(), b.get(),
                c.get(), area.get());
    }
}
```

Observable Collections

JavaFX provides support for observable collections in the packages `javafx.collections` and `javafx.collections.transformation`.

They introduce four more subinterfaces of `Observable` to go along with the `ObservableValue` interface that we studied in earlier sections of this chapter. They are `ObservableList`, `ObservableMap`, `ObservableSet`, and `ObservableArray`. The observable list, map, and set also extend the `List`, `Map`, and `Set` Java collections' framework interfaces, respectively, and therefore can be used just like normal collections. Since they hold only boxed primitive values, there is no need for type-specific specializations. The observable array, on the other hand, holds an array internally and has type-specific specializations for `int` and `float` types. They are used in the JavaFX 3D API.

The main purpose of these interfaces is to allow you to register and unregister change listeners. Aside from that, the `ObservableList` interface has additional methods that manipulate the observable list in a more efficient way. The `ObservableMap` and `ObservableSet` interfaces have no additional methods. The `ObservableArray` interface with its `ObservableIntegerArray` and `ObservableFloatArray` subinterfaces has methods that manipulate the observable array.

Factory and Utility Methods in FXCollections

The `FXCollections` utility class contains factory methods for creating observable collections and arrays. They resemble the factory methods in `java.util.Collections` except that they return observable collections and arrays. They are the only means through which instances of system-provided observable collections and arrays are created.

The `FXCollections` utility class also provides a few methods for manipulating the `ObservableList` objects it creates. These include the `copy()`, `fill()`, `replaceAll()`, `reverse()`, `rotate()`, `shuffle()`, and `sort()` methods. They perform the same functionality as their `java.util.Collections` counterparts, except that they pay attention to minimize the number of list change notifications generated.

Listing 3-9 shows usages of FXCollections methods.

Listing 3-9. FXCollectionsExample.java

```java
package org.modernclients.propertiesandbindings;
import javafx.collections.FXCollections;
import javafx.collections.ListChangeListener;
import javafx.collections.MapChangeListener;
import javafx.collections.ObservableFloatArray;
import javafx.collections.ObservableList;
import javafx.collections.ObservableMap;
import javafx.collections.ObservableSet;
import javafx.collections.SetChangeListener;
import java.util.Arrays;
import java.util.Comparator;
import java.util.Random;
public class FXCollectionsExample {
    public static void main(String[] args) {
        ObservableList<String> list =
                FXCollections.observableArrayList();
        ObservableMap<String, String> map =
                FXCollections.observableHashMap();
        ObservableSet<Integer> set =
                FXCollections.observableSet();
        ObservableFloatArray array =
                FXCollections.observableFloatArray();
        list.addListener((ListChangeListener<String>) c -> {
            System.out.println("\tlist = " +
                    c.getList());
        });
        map.addListener((MapChangeListener<String, String>) c -> {
            System.out.println("\tmap = " +
                    c.getMap());
        });
```

```
    set.addListener((SetChangeListener<Integer>) c -> {
        System.out.println("\tset = " +
                c.getSet());
    });
    array.addListener((observableArray,
                        sizeChanged, from, to) -> {
        System.out.println("\tarray = " +
                observableArray);
    });
    manipulateList(list);
    manipulateMap(map);
    manipulateSet(set);
    manipulateArray(array);
}
private static void manipulateList(
        ObservableList<String> list) {
    System.out.println("Calling list.addAll(\"Zero\"," +
            " \"One\", \"Two\", \"Three\"):");
    list.addAll("Zero", "One", "Two", "Three");
    System.out.println("Calling copy(list," +
            " Arrays.asList(\"Four\", \"Five\")):");
    FXCollections.copy(list,
            Arrays.asList("Four", "Five"));
    System.out.println("Calling replaceAll(list," +
            " \"Two\", \"Two_1\"):");
    FXCollections.replaceAll(list, "Two", "Two_1");
    System.out.println("Calling reverse(list):");
    FXCollections.reverse(list);
    System.out.println("Calling rotate(list, 2):");
    FXCollections.rotate(list, 2);
    System.out.println("Calling shuffle(list):");
    FXCollections.shuffle(list);
    System.out.println("Calling shuffle(list," +
            " new Random(OL)):");
    FXCollections.shuffle(list, new Random(OL));
```

```java
        System.out.println("Calling sort(list):");
        FXCollections.sort(list);
        System.out.println("Calling sort(list, c)" +
                " with custom comparator: ");
        FXCollections.sort(list, new Comparator<String>() {
            @Override
            public int compare(String lhs, String rhs) {
                // Reverse the order
                return rhs.compareTo(lhs);
            }
        });
        System.out.println("Calling fill(list," +
                " \"Ten\"): ");
        FXCollections.fill(list, "Ten");
    }
    private static void manipulateMap(
            ObservableMap<String, String> map) {
        System.out.println("Calling map.put(\"Key\"," +
                " \"Value\"):");
        map.put("Key", "Value");
    }
    private static void manipulateSet(
            ObservableSet<Integer> set) {
        System.out.println("Calling set.add(1024):");
        set.add(1024);
    }
    private static void manipulateArray(
            ObservableFloatArray array) {
        System.out.println("Calling  array.addAll(3.14159f," +
                " 2.71828f):");
        array.addAll(3.14159f, 2.71828f);
    }
}
```

Here, we created an observable list, an observable map, an observable set, and an observable array using FXCollections factory methods, attached listeners to them, and manipulated them in some way, including using FXCollections utility methods for the list and ObservableFloatArray methods for the array.

Running this program prints the following to the console:

```
Calling list.addAll("Zero", "One", "Two", "Three"):
        list = [Zero, One, Two, Three]
Calling copy(list, Arrays.asList("Four", "Five")):
        list = [Four, Five, Two, Three]
Calling replaceAll(list, "Two", "Two_1"):
        list = [Four, Five, Two_1, Three]
Calling reverse(list):
        list = [Three, Two_1, Five, Four]
Calling rotate(list, 2):
        list = [Five, Four, Three, Two_1]
Calling shuffle(list):
        list = [Five, Four, Two_1, Three]
Calling shuffle(list, new Random(0L)):
        list = [Three, Five, Four, Two_1]
Calling sort(list):
        list = [Five, Four, Three, Two_1]
Calling sort(list, c) with custom comparator:
        list = [Two_1, Three, Four, Five]
Calling fill(list, "Ten"):
        list = [Ten, Ten, Ten, Ten]
Calling map.put("Key", "Value"):
        map = {Key=Value}
Calling set.add(1024):
        set = [1024]
Calling  array.addAll(3.14159f, 2.71828f):
        array = [3.14159, 2.71828]
```

Change Listeners for Observable Collections

The ObservableList, ObservableMap, ObservableSet, and ObservableArray
interfaces provide addListener() and removeListener() methods to register and
unregister listeners to be notified of changes to the underlying collection or array. The
corresponding ListChangeListener, MapChangeListener, and SetChangeListener
interfaces each have an onChanged() callback method whose parameter is a nested
Change class. And the ArrayChangeListener interface has an onChanged() callback
method with explicit parameters.

Listing 3-10 shows a program where an ObservableList<String> is manipulated
and the corresponding Change object is queried in an attached ListChangeListener
implemented as a lambda.

Listing 3-10. ObservableListExample.java

```
package org.modernclient.propertiesandbindings;

import javafx.beans.Observable;
import javafx.collections.FXCollections;
import javafx.collections.ObservableList;

import java.util.Arrays;
import java.util.Iterator;
import java.util.List;
import static javafx.collections.ListChangeListener.Change;
public class ObservableListExample {
    public static void main(String[] args) {
        ObservableList<String> strings =
                FXCollections.observableArrayList();
        strings.addListener((Observable observable) -> {
            System.out.println("\tlist invalidated");
        });
        strings.addListener((Change<? extends String> change) -> {
            System.out.println("\tstrings = " +
                    change.getList());
        });
```

```
        System.out.println("Calling add(\"First\"): ");
        strings.add("First");
        System.out.println("Calling add(0, \"Zeroth\"): ");
        strings.add(0, "Zeroth");
        System.out.println("Calling addAll(\"Second\"," +
                " \"Third\"): ");
        strings.addAll("Second", "Third");
        System.out.println("Calling set(1," +
                " \"New First\"): ");
        strings.set(1, "New First");
        final List<String> list =
                Arrays.asList("Second_1", "Second_2");
        System.out.println("Calling addAll(3, list): ");
        strings.addAll(3, list);
        System.out.println("Calling remove(2, 4): ");
        strings.remove(2, 4);
        final Iterator<String> iterator =
                strings.iterator();
        while (iterator.hasNext()) {
            final String next = iterator.next();
            if (next.contains("t")) {
                System.out.println("Calling remove()" +
                        " on iterator: ");
                iterator.remove();
            }
        }
        System.out.println("Calling removeAll(" +
                "\"Third\", \"Fourth\"): ");
        strings.removeAll("Third", "Fourth");
    }
}
```

Running this program prints the following to the console:

```
Calling add("First"):
        list invalidated
        strings = [First]
Calling add(0, "Zeroth"):
        list invalidated
        strings = [Zeroth, First]
Calling addAll("Second", "Third"):
        list invalidated
        strings = [Zeroth, First, Second, Third]
Calling set(1, "New First"):
        list invalidated
        strings = [Zeroth, New First, Second, Third]
Calling addAll(3, list):
        list invalidated
        strings = [Zeroth, New First, Second, Second_1, Second_2, Third]
Calling remove(2, 4):
        list invalidated
        strings = [Zeroth, New First, Second_2, Third]
Calling remove() on iterator:
        list invalidated
        strings = [New First, Second_2, Third]
Calling remove() on iterator:
        list invalidated
        strings = [Second_2, Third]
Calling removeAll("Third", "Fourth"):
        list invalidated
        strings = [Second_2]
```

Change Events in ListChangeListener

In the last section, we queried the ListChangeListener.Change object only for its list property, which references the list being observed. This object holds much more information about the changes to the underlying list. It represents one or more discrete changes, each of which can be elements added, elements removed, elements replaced, or elements permuted. The change interface provides methods for you to query every aspect of the changes.

The next() and reset() methods control a cursor that iterates through the discrete changes. The cursor is positioned before the first discrete change when onChanged() is called. Once the cursor is on a valid discrete change, the wasAdded(), wasRemoved(), wasReplaced(), and wasPermuted() methods tell you what kind of discrete change it is.

Once you know what discrete change the cursor is positioned on, you can call the other methods to get more details about the discrete change. For element added, you can get at the from (inclusive) and to (exclusive) indices, the addedSize, and the addedSubList. For element removed, you can get at the from and to (same as from) indices where elements were removed, the removedSize, and the removed list. For element replaced, which can be thought of as a removal followed by an addition, the information pertinent to both addition and removal should be examined. For element permuted, the getPermutation(int i) method maps the before index to the after index.

Listing 3-11 shows a program with a pretty printing implementation of ListChangeListener that prints out the details of the Change object when a change event is fired.

Listing 3-11. ListChangeEventExample.java

```java
package org.modernclients.propertiesandbindings;
import javafx.collections.FXCollections;
import javafx.collections.ListChangeListener;
import javafx.collections.ObservableList;
public class ListChangeEventExample {
    public static void main(String[] args) {
        ObservableList<String> strings =
                FXCollections.observableArrayList();
        strings.addListener(new MyListener());
        System.out.println("Calling addAll(\"Zero\"," +
                " \"One\", \"Two\", \"Three\"): ");
        strings.addAll("Zero", "One", "Two", "Three");
        System.out.println("Calling" +
                " FXCollections.sort(strings): ");
        FXCollections.sort(strings);
```

```
        System.out.println("Calling set(1, \"Three_1\"): ");
        strings.set(1, "Three_1");
        System.out.println("Calling setAll(\"One_1\"," +
                " \"Three_1\", \"Two_1\", \"Zero_1\"): ");
        strings.setAll("One_1", "Three_1", "Two_1", "Zero_1");
        System.out.println("Calling removeAll(\"One_1\"," +
                " \"Two_1\", \"Zero_1\"): ");
        strings.removeAll("One_1", "Two_1", "Zero_1");
    }
    private static class MyListener implements
            ListChangeListener<String> {
        @Override
        public void onChanged(
                Change<? extends String> change) {
            System.out.println("\tlist = " +
                    change.getList());
            System.out.println(prettyPrint(change));
        }
        private String prettyPrint(
                Change<? extends String> change) {
            StringBuilder sb =
                    new StringBuilder("\tChange event data:\n");
            int i = 0;
            while (change.next()) {
                sb.append("\t\tcursor = ")
                        .append(i++)
                        .append("\n");
                final String kind =
                        change.wasPermutated() ? "permutated" :
                        change.wasReplaced() ? "replaced" :
                        change.wasRemoved() ? "removed" :
                        change.wasAdded() ? "added" :
                        "none";
                sb.append("\t\tKind of change: ")
                        .append(kind)
                        .append("\n");
```

```
sb.append("\t\tAffected range: [")
        .append(change.getFrom())
        .append(", ")
        .append(change.getTo())
        .append("]\n");
if (kind.equals("added") ||
        kind.equals("replaced")) {
    sb.append("\t\tAdded size: ")
            .append(change.getAddedSize())
            .append("\n");
    sb.append("\t\tAdded sublist: ")
            .append(change.getAddedSubList())
            .append("\n");
}
if (kind.equals("removed") ||
        kind.equals("replaced")) {
    sb.append("\t\tRemoved size: ")
            .append(change.getRemovedSize())
            .append("\n");
    sb.append("\t\tRemoved: ")
            .append(change.getRemoved())
            .append("\n");
}
if (kind.equals("permutated")) {
    StringBuilder permutationSB =
            new StringBuilder("[");
    int from = change.getFrom();
    int to = change.getTo();
    for (int k = from; k < to; k++) {
        int permutation =
                change.getPermutation(k);
        permutationSB.append(k)
                .append("->")
                .append(permutation);
```

```
                        if (k < change.getTo() - 1) {
                            permutationSB.append(", ");
                        }
                    }
                    permutationSB.append("]");
                    String permutation =
                            permutationSB.toString();
                    sb.append("\t\tPermutation: ")
                            .append(permutation).append("\n");
                }
            }
            return sb.toString();
        }
    }
}
```

Running this program prints the following to the console:

```
Calling addAll("Zero", "One", "Two", "Three"):
        list = [Zero, One, Two, Three]
        Change event data:
                cursor = 0
                Kind of change: added
                Affected range: [0, 4]
                Added size: 4
                Added sublist: [Zero, One, Two, Three]
Calling FXCollections.sort(strings):
        list = [One, Three, Two, Zero]
        Change event data:
                cursor = 0
                Kind of change: permutated
                Affected range: [0, 4]
                Permutation: [0->3, 1->0, 2->2, 3->1]
```

```
Calling set(1, "Three_1"):
        list = [One, Three_1, Two, Zero]
        Change event data:
                cursor = 0
                Kind of change: replaced
                Affected range: [1, 2]
                Added size: 1
                Added sublist: [Three_1]
                Removed size: 1
                Removed: [Three]
Calling setAll("One_1", "Three_1", "Two_1", "Zero_1"):
        list = [One_1, Three_1, Two_1, Zero_1]
        Change event data:
                cursor = 0
                Kind of change: replaced
                Affected range: [0, 4]
                Added size: 4
                Added sublist: [One_1, Three_1, Two_1, Zero_1]
                Removed size: 4
                Removed: [One, Three_1, Two, Zero]
Calling removeAll("One_1", "Two_1", "Zero_1"):
        list = [Three_1]
        Change event data:
                cursor = 0
                Kind of change: removed
                Affected range: [0, 0]
                Removed size: 1
                Removed: [One_1]
                cursor = 1
                Kind of change: removed
                Affected range: [1, 1]
                Removed size: 2
                Removed: [Two_1, Zero_1]
```

Change Events in MapChangeListener

The MapChangeListener.Change event is much simpler than its observable list counterpart in that it reflects the change in one key only. Therefore, no next() nor reset() method is necessary. If multiple keys are affected, multiple change events will be fired.

The wasAdded() and wasRemoved() methods indicate whether a key is added or removed. You can always get at the key that is affected by the change. And if a key is added, you can get at the valueAdded; and if a key is removed, you can get at the valueRemoved.

Listing 3-12 shows a program that manipulates an observable map and records the change events generated.

Listing 3-12. MapChangeEventExample.java

```java
package org.modernclients.propertiesandbindings;
import javafx.collections.FXCollections;
import javafx.collections.MapChangeListener;
import javafx.collections.ObservableMap;
import java.util.HashMap;
import java.util.Iterator;
import java.util.Map;
public class MapChangeEventExample {
    public static void main(String[] args) {
        ObservableMap<String, Integer> map =
                FXCollections.observableHashMap();
        map.addListener(new MyListener());
        System.out.println("Calling put(\"First\", 1): ");
        map.put("First", 1);
        System.out.println("Calling put(\"First\", 100): ");
        map.put("First", 100);
        Map<String, Integer> anotherMap = new HashMap<>();
        anotherMap.put("Second", 2);
        anotherMap.put("Third", 3);
        System.out.println("Calling putAll(anotherMap): ");
        map.putAll(anotherMap);
```

```
        Iterator<Map.Entry<String, Integer>> entryIterator =
                map.entrySet().iterator();
        while (entryIterator.hasNext()) {
            final Map.Entry<String, Integer> next =
                    entryIterator.next();
            if (next.getKey().equals("Second")) {
                System.out.println("Calling remove on" +
                        " entryIterator: ");
                entryIterator.remove();
            }
        }
        final Iterator<Integer> valueIterator =
                map.values().iterator();
        while (valueIterator.hasNext()) {
            final Integer next = valueIterator.next();
            if (next == 3) {
                System.out.println("Calling remove on" +
                        " valueIterator: ");
                valueIterator.remove();
            }
        }
    }
}
private static class MyListener implements
        MapChangeListener<String, Integer> {
    @Override
    public void onChanged(
            Change<? extends String, ? extends Integer>
                    change) {
        System.out.println("\tmap = " + change.getMap());
        System.out.println(prettyPrint(change));
    }
    private String prettyPrint(
            Change<? extends String, ? extends Integer>
                    change) {
        StringBuilder sb =
```

```
                    new StringBuilder("\tChange event" +
                            " data:\n");
        sb.append("\t\tWas added: ")
                .append(change.wasAdded())
                .append("\n");
        sb.append("\t\tWas removed: ")
                .append(change.wasRemoved())
                .append("\n");
        sb.append("\t\tKey: ")
                .append(change.getKey())
                .append("\n");
        sb.append("\t\tValue added: ")
                .append(change.getValueAdded())
                .append("\n");
        sb.append("\t\tValue removed: ")
                .append(change.getValueRemoved())
                .append("\n");
        return sb.toString();
    }
  }
}
```

Change Events in SetChangeListener

The SetChangeListener.Change event is even simpler than that of the observable map because no values are involved when an observable set is modified.

Listing 3-13 shows a program that manipulates an observable set and records the change events generated.

Listing 3-13. SetChangeEventExample.java

```
package org.modernclients.propertiesandbindings;
import javafx.collections.FXCollections;
import javafx.collections.ObservableSet;
import javafx.collections.SetChangeListener;
import java.util.Arrays;
```

```java
public class SetChangeEventExample {
    public static void main(String[] args) {
        ObservableSet<String> set =
                FXCollections.observableSet();
        set.addListener(new MyListener());
        System.out.println("Calling add(\"First\"): ");
        set.add("First");
        System.out.println("Calling addAll(" +
                "Arrays.asList(\"Second\", \"Third\")): ");
        set.addAll(Arrays.asList("Second", "Third"));
        System.out.println("Calling remove(" +
                "\"Third\"): ");
        set.remove("Third");
    }
    private static class MyListener
            implements SetChangeListener<String> {
        @Override
        public void onChanged(Change<? extends String>
                                        change) {
            System.out.println("\tset = " +
                    change.getSet());
            System.out.println(prettyPrint(change));
        }
        private String prettyPrint(
                Change<? extends String> change) {
            StringBuilder sb =
                    new StringBuilder("\tChange" +
                            " event data:\n");
            sb.append("\t\tWas added: ")
                    .append(change.wasAdded())
                    .append("\n");
            sb.append("\t\tWas removed: ")
                    .append(change.wasRemoved())
                    .append("\n");
```

```
            sb.append("\t\tElement added: ")
                    .append(change.getElementAdded())
                    .append("\n");
            sb.append("\t\tElement removed: ")
                    .append(change.getElementRemoved())
                    .append("\n");
            return sb.toString();
        }
    }
}
```

Change Events in ArrayChangeListener

The onChanged() method in ArrayChangeListener has the following signature:

```
public void onChanged(T observableArray,
    boolean sizeChanged, int from, int to);
```

As is true for many manager classes of arrays, the ObservableArray has a *capacity* and a *size*. The capacity is the length of the underlying backing array, and the size is the number of elements that contain application data. The size is always less than or equal to the capacity. The ensureCapacity() method sets the capacity to a specified value and reallocates the underlying array if necessary. The resize() method changes the size. If the new size is greater than the old capacity, the capacity is increased. If the new size is greater than the old size, the extra elements are filled with zero. If the new size is less than the old size, the backing array does not shrink, but the lost elements are filled with zeroes. The trimToSize() method shrinks the capacity down to the size. The clear() method resizes the observable array to size zero. The size() method returns the current size of the observable array.

The type-specific specializations of the ObservableArray, the Observable IntegerArray, and the ObservableFloatArray have overloaded methods that manipulate the underlying array in a type-specific way. The get() method gets the value at a specified index. The set() method sets a value or an array of values at a specified index. The addAll() method appends additional elements to the observable array. The setAll() method replaces the elements in the observable array. The toArray() method returns a primitive array filled with the content of the observable array. The get() and set() methods may throw ArrayIndexOutOfBoundsException.

Listing 3-14 shows a program that manipulates an ObservableIntegerArray and displays the change notifications.

Listing 3-14. ArrayChangeEventExample.java

```java
package org.modernclients.propertiesandbindings;
import javafx.collections.FXCollections;
import javafx.collections.ObservableIntegerArray;
public class ArrayChangeEventExample {
    public static void main(String[] args) {
        final ObservableIntegerArray ints =
                FXCollections.observableIntegerArray(10, 20);
        ints.addListener((array,
                        sizeChanged, from, to) -> {
            StringBuilder sb =
                    new StringBuilder("\tObservable Array = ")
                            .append(array)
                            .append("\n")
                            .append("\t\tsizeChanged = ")
                            .append(sizeChanged).append("\n")
                            .append("\t\tfrom = ")
                            .append(from).append("\n")
                            .append("\t\tto = ")
                            .append(to)
                            .append("\n");
            System.out.println(sb.toString());
        });
        ints.ensureCapacity(20);
        System.out.println("Calling addAll(30, 40):");
        ints.addAll(30, 40);
        final int[] src = {50, 60, 70};
        System.out.println("Calling addAll(src, 1, 2):");
        ints.addAll(src, 1, 2);
        System.out.println("Calling set(0, src, 0, 1):");
        ints.set(0, src, 0, 1);
        System.out.println("Calling setAll(src):");
```

```
        ints.setAll(src);
        ints.trimToSize();
        final ObservableIntegerArray ints2 =
                FXCollections.observableIntegerArray();
        ints2.resize(ints.size());
        System.out.println("Calling copyTo(0, ints2," +
                " 0, ints.size()):");
        ints.copyTo(0, ints2, 0, ints.size());
        System.out.println("\tDestination = " + ints2);
    }
}
```

The output of this application is shown here:

```
Calling addAll(30, 40):
        Observable Array = [10, 20, 30, 40]
                sizeChanged = true
                from = 2
                to = 4
Calling addAll(src, 1, 2):
        Observable Array = [10, 20, 30, 40, 60, 70]
                sizeChanged = true
                from = 4
                to = 6
Calling set(0, src, 0, 1):
        Observable Array = [50, 20, 30, 40, 60, 70]
                sizeChanged = false
                from = 0
                to = 1
Calling setAll(src):
        Observable Array = [50, 60, 70]
                sizeChanged = true
                from = 0
                to = 3
Calling copyTo(0, ints2, 0, ints.size()):
        Destination = [50, 60, 70]
```

Create Bindings for Observable Collections

The Bindings utility class includes factory methods for creating bindings out of observable collections.

The overloaded methods valueAt(), booleanValueAt(), integerValueAt(), longValueAt(), floatValueAt(), doubleValueAt(), and stringValueAt() create a binding of the appropriate type out of an observable collection of the same type and an index or a key of the appropriate type, either observable or non-observable.

For example, if authorizations is an ObservableMap<Person, Boolean> that represents the authorization status of Person objects and user is an ObjectProperty<Person> object, then booleanValueAt(authorizations, user) is a BooleanBinding that represents the authorization status of the user.

The overloaded bindContent() method binds a non-observable collection to an observable collection of the same kind, making sure the non-observable collection has the same content as the observable collection. The unbindContent() method removes such a content binding. The overloaded bindContentBidirectional() method binds two observable collections of the same kind, making sure they have the same content. The unbindContentBidirectional() method removes such a bidirectional content binding.

JavaFX Beans

In previous sections, we studied individual JavaFX properties and observable collections. Now we study how to group them together in larger units to form more meaningful software components.

The Java Beans concept existed almost from the beginning. It introduces three architectural concepts: *properties*, *events*, and *methods*. Methods are straightforward in Java. Events are provided through listener interfaces and event objects, which JavaFX controls still use. Properties are provided using the now very familiar public getter and setter methods.

JavaFX introduces the *JavaFX Bean* concept where in addition to the getter and the setter, a JavaFX Bean property also has a *property getter*. For a property named height of type double, the three methods are as follows:

```
public final double getHeight();
public final void setHeight(double height);
public DoubleProperty heightProperty();
```

127

Just as traditional properties are usually implemented with a backing field of the same type, JavaFX Bean properties are usually implemented with a backing field of the appropriate Property type. Since these properties are reference types, for a JavaFX Bean with many properties, potentially many extra objects will be created. Depending on the usage pattern, different strategies can be used to implement these properties.

Note   Read-only JavaFX Bean properties can be defined with a getter and a property getter that returns a read-only version of a JavaFX property.

Eagerly Instantiated Property

The simplest strategy for implementing JavaFX Bean properties is the *eagerly instantiated property* strategy. Each property is backed by an appropriate property type that is instantiated at construction time. The getter and setter simply call the backing property's get() and set() methods. The property getter returns the backing property itself. Listing 3-15 shows a JavaFX Bean with int, String, and Color properties.

Listing 3-15. JavaFXBeanModelExample.java

```
package org.modernclients.propertiesandbindings;
import javafx.beans.property.*;
import javafx.scene.paint.Color;
public class JavaFXBeanModelExample {
    private IntegerProperty i =
            new SimpleIntegerProperty(this, "i", 0);
    private StringProperty str =
            new SimpleStringProperty(this, "str", "Hello");
    private ObjectProperty<Color> color =
            new SimpleObjectProperty<Color>(this, "color",
                    Color.BLACK);
    public final int getI() {
        return i.get();
    }
```

```java
    public final void setI(int i) {
        this.i.set(i);
    }
    public IntegerProperty iProperty() {
        return i;
    }
    public final String getStr() {
        return str.get();
    }
    public final void setStr(String str) {
        this.str.set(str);
    }
    public StringProperty strProperty() {
        return str;
    }
    public final Color getColor() {
        return color.get();
    }
    public final void setColor(Color color) {
        this.color.set(color);
    }
    public ObjectProperty<Color> colorProperty() {
        return color;
    }
}
```

Notice that we used the property constructor with full context, including the bean, the property's name, and the initial value to initialize the properties.

Half-Lazily Instantiated Property

If the setter and the property getter are never called, the getter will always return the default value of a property; and you don't need a property instance to know that. This is the basis of the *half-lazy instantiation* strategy. In this strategy, the property is instantiated only if the setter is called with a value different from the default value or if the property getter is called. This strategy works best for JavaFX Beans with many properties, only a few of which are set.

Listing 3-16 shows an example of this strategy.

Listing 3-16. JavaFXBeanModelHalfLazyExample.java

```java
package org.modernclients.propertiesandbindings;
import javafx.beans.property.SimpleStringProperty;
import javafx.beans.property.StringProperty;
public class JavaFXBeanModelHalfLazyExample {
    private static final String DEFAULT_STR = "Hello";
    private StringProperty str;
    public final String getStr() {
        if (str != null) {
            return str.get();
        } else {
            return DEFAULT_STR;
        }
    }
    public final void setStr(String str) {
        if ((this.str != null) ||
                !(str.equals(DEFAULT_STR))) {
            strProperty().set(str);
        }
    }
    public StringProperty strProperty() {
        if (str == null) {
            str = new SimpleStringProperty(this,
                    "str", DEFAULT_STR);
        }
        return str;
    }
}
```

Fully Lazily Instantiated Property

Thinking a little deeper about the half-lazy instantiation strategy, we ask ourselves, "Do we really need to instantiate the property when the setter is called?" The answer, of course, is no, if we have a place to put it, just like in the old days. This gives rise to the *full-lazy instantiation* strategy. In this strategy, the property is instantiated only if the property getter is called. The getter and setter go through the property object only if it is already instantiated; otherwise, they go through a separate backing field.

Listing 3-17 shows an example of this strategy.

Listing 3-17. JavaFXBeanModelFullLazyExample.java

```
package org.modernclients.propertiesandbindings;
import javafx.beans.property.SimpleStringProperty;
import javafx.beans.property.StringProperty;
public class JavaFXBeanModelFullLazyExample {
    private static final String DEFAULT_STR = "Hello";
    private StringProperty str;
    private String _str = DEFAULT_STR;
    public final String getStr() {
        if (str != null) {
            return str.get();
        } else {
            return _str;
        }
    }
    public final void setStr(String str) {
        if (this.str != null) {
            this.str.set(str);
        } else {
            _str = str;
        }
    }
```

```
    }
    public StringProperty strProperty() {
        if (str == null) {
            str = new SimpleStringProperty(this,
                    "str", DEFAULT_STR);
        }
        return str;
    }
}
```

Selection Bindings

Now that we understand the JavaFX Bean concept, we can go back to the `Bindings` utility class and learn about the `select()` and `selectInteger()` methods and so on. They have signatures like the following:

```
selectInteger(Object root, String... steps);
```

These selection operators allow you to create bindings that observe deeply nested JavaFX Bean properties. Here, `root` is an object reference in scope, and each `step` is a property of the object at hand that points to the next object and so on.

It's best to illustrate the concept with an example. Consider the class `Lighting` (in `javafx.scene.effect`). It has a property named `light` of type `Light`. And `Light` has a property named `color` of type `Color` (in `javafx.scene.paint`). Listing 3-18 shows a program that constructs a select binding that reaches into the `color` of the `light` of the root object.

Listing 3-18. SelectBindingExample.java

```
package org.modernclients.propertiesandbindings;
import javafx.beans.binding.Bindings;
import javafx.beans.binding.ObjectBinding;
import javafx.beans.property.ObjectProperty;
import javafx.beans.property.SimpleObjectProperty;
import javafx.scene.effect.Light;
import javafx.scene.effect.Lighting;
import javafx.scene.paint.Color;
```

```java
public class SelectBindingExample {
    public static void main(String[] args) {
        ObjectProperty<Lighting> root =
                new SimpleObjectProperty<>();
        final ObjectBinding<Color> colorBinding =
                Bindings.select(root, "light", "color");
        colorBinding.addListener((o, oldValue, newValue) ->
                System.out.println("\tThe color changed:\n" +
                        "\t\told color = " + oldValue +
                        ",\n\t\tnew color = " + newValue));
        System.out.println("firstLight is black.");
        Light firstLight = new Light.Point();
        firstLight.setColor(Color.BLACK);
        System.out.println("secondLight is white.");
        Light secondLight = new Light.Point();
        secondLight.setColor(Color.WHITE);
        System.out.println("firstLighting has firstLight.");
        Lighting firstLighting = new Lighting();
        firstLighting.setLight(firstLight);
        System.out.println("secondLighting has secondLight.");
        Lighting secondLighting = new Lighting();
        secondLighting.setLight(secondLight);
        System.out.println("Making root observe" +
                " firstLighting.");
        root.set(firstLighting);
        System.out.println("Making root observe" +
                " secondLighting.");
        root.set(secondLighting);
        System.out.println("Changing secondLighting's" +
                " light to firstLight");
        secondLighting.setLight(firstLight);
        System.out.println("Changing firstLight's" +
                " color to red");
        firstLight.setColor(Color.RED);
    }
}
```

Running this program prints the following to the console:

```
firstLight is black.
secondLight is white.
firstLighting has firstLight.
secondLighting has secondLight.
Making root observe firstLighting.
        The color changed:
                old color = null,
                new color = 0x000000ff
Making root observe secondLighting.
        The color changed:
                old color = 0x000000ff,
                new color = 0xffffffff
Changing secondLighting's light to firstLight
        The color changed:
                old color = 0xffffffff,
                new color = 0x000000ff
Changing firstLight's color to red
        The color changed:
                old color = 0x000000ff,
                new color = 0xff0000ff
```

Adapting Java Beans

For the many old-fashioned Java Beans written over the years, JavaFX provides a set of adapter classes in the `javafx.beans.property.adapter` package that turn Java Bean properties into JavaFX properties.

Recall that a Java Bean property is a *bound property* if a `PropertyChange` event is fired when the property is changed. It is a *constrained property* if a `VetoableChange` event is fired when it is changed. And if a registered listener throws a `PropertyVetoException`, the change does not take effect.

Listing 3-19 shows a `Person` bean with a plain property `name`, a bound property `address`, and a constrained property `phoneNumber`.

Listing 3-19. Person.java

```java
package org.modernclients.propertiesandbindings;
import java.beans.PropertyChangeListener;
import java.beans.PropertyChangeSupport;
import java.beans.PropertyVetoException;
import java.beans.VetoableChangeListener;
import java.beans.VetoableChangeSupport;
public class Person {
    private PropertyChangeSupport propertyChangeSupport;
    private VetoableChangeSupport vetoableChangeSupport;
    private String name;
    private String address;
    private String phoneNumber;
    public Person() {
        propertyChangeSupport =
                new PropertyChangeSupport(this);
        vetoableChangeSupport =
                new VetoableChangeSupport(this);
    }
    public String getName() {
        return name;
    }
    public void setName(String name) {
        this.name = name;
    }
    public String getAddress() {
        return address;
    }
    public void setAddress(String address) {
        String oldAddress = this.address;
        this.address = address;
        propertyChangeSupport.firePropertyChange("address",
                oldAddress, this.address);
    }
```

```java
    public String getPhoneNumber() {
        return phoneNumber;
    }
    public void setPhoneNumber(String phoneNumber)
            throws PropertyVetoException {
        String oldPhoneNumber = this.phoneNumber;
        vetoableChangeSupport.fireVetoableChange("phoneNumber",
                oldPhoneNumber, phoneNumber);
        this.phoneNumber = phoneNumber;
        propertyChangeSupport.firePropertyChange("phoneNumber",
                oldPhoneNumber, this.phoneNumber);
    }
    public void addPropertyChangeListener(PropertyChangeListener l) {
        propertyChangeSupport.addPropertyChangeListener(l);
    }
    public void removePropertyChangeListener(PropertyChangeListener l) {
        propertyChangeSupport.removePropertyChangeListener(l);
    }
    public PropertyChangeListener[] getPropertyChangeListeners() {
        return propertyChangeSupport.getPropertyChangeListeners();
    }
    public void addVetoableChangeListener(VetoableChangeListener l) {
        vetoableChangeSupport.addVetoableChangeListener(l);
    }
    public void removeVetoableChangeListener(VetoableChangeListener l) {
        vetoableChangeSupport.removeVetoableChangeListener(l);
    }
    public VetoableChangeListener[] getVetoableChangeListeners() {
        return vetoableChangeSupport.getVetoableChangeListeners();
    }
}
```

A Java Bean property of type String can be adapted into a JavaBeanStringProperty using the JavaBeanStringPropertyBuilder:

```
JavaBeanStringPropertyBuilder.create()
        .bean(person)
        .name("name")
        .build();
```

This follows the familiar builder pattern: you call the static create() method to get an instance of the builder and then call the bean() and name() methods on the builder instance to configure the builder, telling it which bean and which property to adapt. Finally, you call the build() method on the builder to get the adapted JavaFX property.

The builder class has more methods that can be used to deal with more esoteric situations, for example, when the getter or setter does not follow the familiar naming convention but was specified using metadata.

Listing 3-20 shows a program that adapts the three Java Bean properties of the Person class into JavaBeanStringProperty objects.

Listing 3-20. JavaBeanPropertiesExample.java

```
package org.modernclients.propertiesandbindings;
import javafx.beans.property.SimpleStringProperty;
import javafx.beans.property.adapter.JavaBeanStringProperty;
import javafx.beans.property.adapter.JavaBeanStringPropertyBuilder;
import java.beans.PropertyVetoException;
public class JavaBeanPropertiesExample {
    public static void main(String[] args)
            throws NoSuchMethodException {
        adaptJavaBeansProperty();
        adaptBoundProperty();
        adaptConstrainedProperty();
    }
    private static void adaptJavaBeansProperty()
            throws NoSuchMethodException {
        Person person = new Person();
        JavaBeanStringProperty nameProperty =
                JavaBeanStringPropertyBuilder.create()
```

```
                            .bean(person)
                            .name("name")
                            .build();
        nameProperty.addListener((observable, oldValue, newValue) -> {
            System.out.println("JavaFX property " +
                    observable + " changed:");
            System.out.println("\toldValue = " +
                    oldValue + ", newValue = " + newValue);
        });
        System.out.println("Setting name on the" +
                " JavaBeans property");
        person.setName("Weiqi Gao");
        System.out.println("Calling fireValueChange");
        nameProperty.fireValueChangedEvent();
        System.out.println("nameProperty.get() = " +
                nameProperty.get());
        System.out.println("Setting value on the" +
                " JavaFX property");
        nameProperty.set("Johan Vos");
        System.out.println("person.getName() = " +
                person.getName());
    }
    private static void adaptBoundProperty()
            throws NoSuchMethodException {
        System.out.println();
        Person person = new Person();
        JavaBeanStringProperty addressProperty =
                JavaBeanStringPropertyBuilder.create()
                        .bean(person)
                        .name("address")
                        .build();
        addressProperty.addListener((observable, oldValue, newValue) -> {
            System.out.println("JavaFX property " +
                    observable + " changed:");
```

```
        System.out.println("\toldValue = " +
                oldValue + ", newValue = " + newValue);
    });
    System.out.println("Setting address on the" +
            " JavaBeans property");
    person.setAddress("12345 main Street");
}
private static void adaptConstrainedProperty()
        throws NoSuchMethodException {
    System.out.println();
    Person person = new Person();
    JavaBeanStringProperty phoneNumberProperty =
            JavaBeanStringPropertyBuilder.create()
                    .bean(person)
                    .name("phoneNumber")
                    .build();
    phoneNumberProperty.addListener((observable,
                                oldValue, newValue) -> {
        System.out.println("JavaFX property " +
                observable + " changed:");
        System.out.println("\toldValue = " +
                oldValue + ", newValue = " + newValue);
    });
    System.out.println("Setting phoneNumber on the" +
            " JavaBeans property");
    try {
        person.setPhoneNumber("800-555-1212");
    } catch (PropertyVetoException e) {
        System.out.println("A JavaBeans property" +
                " change is vetoed.");
    }
    System.out.println("Bind phoneNumberProperty" +
            " to another property");
    SimpleStringProperty stringProperty =
            new SimpleStringProperty("866-555-1212");
```

```
        phoneNumberProperty.bind(stringProperty);
        System.out.println("Setting phoneNumber on the" +
                " JavaBeans property");
        try {
            person.setPhoneNumber("888-555-1212");
        } catch (PropertyVetoException e) {
            System.out.println("A JavaBeans property" +
                    " change is vetoed.");
        }
        System.out.println("person.getPhoneNumber() = " +
                person.getPhoneNumber());
    }
}
```

Notice that since name is not a bound property, calling person.setName() does not automatically propagate the new value to the adapted nameProperty. We must call fireValueChangedEvent() on nameProperty to make that happen. For the bound property address, calling person.setAddress() propagates the new value to addressProperty automatically. For the constrained property phoneNumber, after we bound the adapted phoneNumberProperty to another stringProperty, calling person.setPhoneNumber() throws a PropertyVetoException, and the new value is rejected.

Running this program prints the following to the console:

```
Setting name on the JavaBeans property
Calling fireValueChange
JavaFX property StringProperty [bean: org.modernclients.propertiesand
bindings.Person@5a8e6209, name: name, value: Weiqi Gao] changed:
        oldValue = null, newValue = Weiqi Gao
nameProperty.get() = Weiqi Gao
Setting value on the JavaFX property
JavaFX property StringProperty [bean: org.modernclients.propertiesand
bindings.Person@5a8e6209, name: name, value: Johan Vos] changed:
        oldValue = Weiqi Gao, newValue = Johan Vos
person.getName() = Johan Vos
Setting address on the JavaBeans property
JavaFX property StringProperty [bean: org.modernclients.propertiesand
```

```
bindings.Person@1f36e637, name: address, value: 12345 main Street] changed:
        oldValue = null, newValue = 12345 main Street
Setting phoneNumber on the JavaBeans property
JavaFX property StringProperty [bean: org.modernclients.propertiesand
bindings.Person@35d176f7, name: phoneNumber, value: 800-555-1212] changed:
        oldValue = null, newValue = 800-555-1212
Bind phoneNumberProperty to another property
JavaFX property StringProperty [bean: org.modernclients.propertiesand
bindings.Person@35d176f7, name: phoneNumber, value: 866-555-1212] changed:
        oldValue = 800-555-1212, newValue = 866-555-1212
Setting phoneNumber on the JavaBeans property
A JavaBeans property change is vetoed.
person.getPhoneNumber() = 866-555-1212
```

Summary

In this chapter, you learned the fundamentals of the JavaFX properties and bindings framework. You should now understand the following important principles:

- JavaFX properties and bindings hold values and fire events to attached listeners.

- An invalidation event is fired when the value becomes invalid. And a change event is fired when the value is recomputed, potentially lazily.

- Type-specific specializations of the generic key interfaces exist for boolean, int, long, float, double, String, and Object types. For primitive types, they avoid boxing and unboxing.

- Attaching ChangeListener to a property forces eager evaluation.

- New bindings can be created through direct extension, using factory methods in Bindings, or using the fluent API.

- Observable collections exist for List, Map, Set, and int and float arrays. Their change event is more complicated than observable values.

- Observable collections and arrays are created using factory methods in the FXCollections utility class.

- The JavaFX Bean properties are defined by a getter, a setter, and a property getter.

- JavaFX Bean properties can be implemented through the eager instantiation, half-lazy instantiation, and full-lazy instantiation strategies.

- Old-style Java Bean properties can be adapted easily to JavaFX properties.

Resources

The following are useful resources for working with the content of this chapter:

- Martin Fowler's write-up on fluent interface APIs: www.martinfowler.com/bliki/FluentInterface.html.

- The Javadoc of the JavaFX framework hosted at https://openjfx. io/javadoc/17/.

- We used Gradle to build the source. Here's its documentation site: https://docs.gradle.org/current/userguide/userguide.html.

- The JavaFX Gradle plugin helps a lot in managing JavaFX dependencies: https://github.com/openjfx/javafx-gradle-plugin.

- We use the Gradle module plugins to organize the source into Java modules: https://github.com/java9-modularity/gradle-modules-plugin.

CHAPTER 4

JavaFX Controls Deep Dive

Written by Jonathan Giles

When JavaFX first shipped back in 2007, it did not have any user interface controls available for users to put into their user interfaces. Developers had to settle for either creating their own rudimentary UI controls or importing UI components from the Swing toolkit that also ships with Java. Starting with JavaFX 1.2, this situation started to improve, with the introduction of a number of critically important UI controls, such as `Button`, `ProgressBar`, and `ListView`. In subsequent releases, JavaFX began to attain a complete and well-regarded set of UI controls, providing the ability to construct user interfaces for applications that one would find inside a corporate environment.

This chapter will introduce most of the UI controls that exist in the core JavaFX 17 release. Due to the limited number of pages available in this chapter, the code samples are kept intentionally brief. Rest assured that the code repository for this book includes a comprehensive demo application that covers all JavaFX UI controls, with code that can be copied/pasted into your own applications.

The UI Controls Module

Beginning with JavaFX 9, almost all UI controls are now encapsulated within the `javafx.controls` module.[1] This module is split into four exported packages, as shown in the following:

---

[1] There exists one exception: HTMLEditor is in the javafx.web module, given its dependence on the WebView component. This will be discussed more later in this chapter.

- javafx.scene.chart: This package houses the charting components for building charts such as line, bar, area, pie, bubble, and scatter charts. These will not be covered as part of this chapter.

- javafx.scene.control: This package houses the APIs for almost all user interface controls in JavaFX. This is the primary package we will cover in this chapter.

- javafx.scene.control.cell: This package houses the APIs for a large number of pre-built "cell factories," which we will cover in more depth when we get to the "Advanced Controls" section later in this chapter.

- javafx.scene.control.skin: This package houses the "skins," or the visual components, for each UI control. We won't be covering this package in this chapter as it is beyond the scope of this book.

What Is a UI Control?

A valid question to ask in the context of JavaFX is: **What exactly is a UI control?** A simple definition might be that it is a visual component that forms a small part of a user interface and that is often interactive (but not always). In the strictest sense, a UI control extends from the Control class, but a more relaxed definition would allow for any component that extends from Node to be considered a UI control. For the sake of this chapter, most of the UI controls being discussed extend from the Control class.

This inevitably leads to the next question: **What is the Control class?** Control is a class that extends from Parent, which itself extends from Node. In the commonly referenced MVC[2] nomenclature, a Control can be thought of as the model. In any user interface built using JavaFX UI controls, a developer should only ever interact with the Control classes, as these are where all API exists for manipulating and reading the state of the control.

---

[2] MVC stands for "Model-View-Controller." Essentially, it is a way of separating cleanly the three pillars of a user interface: API (Model), visuals (View), and the way in which the view impacts the model (the Controller).

144

Because the `Control` class extends from `Node`, it is afforded all abilities that `Node` has. This means a UI control can have effects, rotation, scaling, and numerous other properties modified, as necessary. Event handlers for mouse, swipe, drag, touch, key input, and more can also be added in the standard fashion. Adding UI controls to a scene graph is also handled in the same fashion as any `Node` – by adding it to a layout container with the relevant sizing information, layout constraints, and so on.

As of JavaFX 9, and as noted previously, the visuals of all UI controls, known as the skins, have also become public API in the `javafx.scene.control.skin` package. The reason the skins are public API is to enable developers to subclass them and to therefore override the default visuals of a UI control.

JavaFX Basic Controls

There exist a subset of UI controls in JavaFX that can be considered critical to almost all user interfaces, but are basic in the sense that they are simplistic to use, both from an end user perspective and a UI developer perspective. This section will introduce each of these basic controls in turn. As of JavaFX 17, the basic UI controls can be broken down into three subgroups:

1. "Labeled" controls: `Button`, `CheckBox`, `Hyperlink`, `Label`, `RadioButton`, and `ToggleButton`

2. "Text input" controls: `TextField`, `TextArea`, and `PasswordField`

3. "Other" simple controls: `ProgressBar`, `ProgressIndicator`, and `Slider`

Labeled Controls

Most controls that display read-only text extend from a common abstract superclass known as `Labeled`. This class specifies a common set of properties for handling alignment, fonts, graphic (and graphic positioning), wrapping, and so on, as well as, of course, for the text to be displayed itself. Because `Labeled` is abstract, it is not commonly used directly, but many of the actual UI controls extend from it, including `Button`, `CheckBox`, `Hyperlink`, `Label`, `RadioButton`, and `ToggleButton`. In addition to these basic controls, other more advanced controls (to be covered later in this chapter) also benefit from `Labeled`, including `MenuButton`, `TitledPane`, and `Cell`.

The most important properties[3] for `Labeled` are shown in Table 4-1.

Table 4-1. *Properties of the Labeled class*

1Property	Type	Description
alignment	ObjectProperty<Pos>	Specifies how the text and graphic should be aligned.
contentDisplay	ObjectProperty<ContentDisplay>	Specifies the positioning of the graphic relative to the text.
font	ObjectProperty<Font>	The default font to use for text.
graphic	ObjectProperty<Node>	An optional icon for the Labeled.
textAlignment	ObjectProperty<TextAlignment>	Specifies the behavior for lines of text when text is multiline.
text	StringProperty	The text to display in the label.
wrapText	BooleanProperty	Specifies whether text should wrap into multiple lines when width is exceeded.

As noted, because the `Labeled` class is abstract, most developers do not use this class directly. Instead, they use one of the concrete subclasses that ship with JavaFX, which will be detailed in more depth now.

Label

Because `Labeled` is so comprehensive, the concrete `Label` class is extremely simple – it only adds one additional piece of API. This is called `labelFor` and is used to make keyboard navigation into UI controls using mnemonics simpler, as well as to improve text-to-speech output for people who are blind and partially sighted. It is best practice, when using a `Label` to describe another control (e.g., a `Slider`), to associate the `Label`

---

[3] This chapter covers a lot of UI controls, and to save some pages, not all properties will be included for each UI control. In this chapter, we will pick out the most critical properties for highlighting, but you are encouraged to refer to the Javadoc materials for relevant classes to see the complete set of properties.

instance with the Slider instance by saying label.labelFor(slider), for example. This means that when focus is given to the Slider control, the screen reading software for people with full or partial blindness can read out the text of the Label to help describe to users what the Slider is used for.

Button

The Button class enables users to execute some action by giving a visual affordance that can be clicked. When a user clicks a button, it becomes "armed," and when the mouse is released, it "fires," before becoming "disarmed." The most important properties for Button are shown in Table 4-2.

Table 4-2. *Properties of the Button (and ButtonBase) class*

Property	Type	Description
armed	ReadOnlyBooleanProperty[4]	Indicates whether the user is currently clicking the button.
cancelButton	BooleanProperty	If true, the button will handle Escape key presses.
defaultButton	BooleanProperty	If true, the button will handle Enter key presses.
onAction	ObjectProperty<EventHandler< ActionEvent>>	A callback that is executed when a Button is fired.

There is only one method of relevance, and that is the fire() method. This method can be called to programmatically fire the Button, resulting in the associated onAction event being called. The more common case is when a user directly clicks the button, and this has the same result – to fire the button and to cause whatever onAction event handler is installed to be called. The code to handle action events is shown in Listing 4-1.

---

[4] As the name implies, a ReadOnlyBooleanProperty is a property that can be observed for changes, but cannot be modified by the user directly. In the case of the armed property on Button, it can only become armed through user interaction by pressing and holding their mouse button. At this point, the armed read-only Boolean property will be modified to represent the new armed state.

Listing 4-1. Creating a JavaFX Button instance that handles clicks by printing to the console

```
var button = new Button("Click Me!");
button.setOnAction(event -> System.out.println("Button was clicked"));
```

CheckBox

Typically, a CheckBox enables a user to specify whether something is true or false. In JavaFX this is possible, but there is also the ability to show a third state: indeterminate. By default, the JavaFX CheckBox will toggle between checked and unchecked states only (and this is reflected in the selected property). To support toggling through the indeterminate state, developers must set the allowIndeterminate property to true. When this is enabled, the indeterminate property can be read, in conjunction with the selected property, to determine the state of the CheckBox.

Because CheckBox is a Labeled control, it supports displaying text and graphic adjacent to the checkbox. There are only a few additional properties of high importance, as shown in Table 4-3. A typical usage of CheckBox is shown in Listing 4-2.

Table 4-3. *Properties of the CheckBox class*

Property	Type	Description
allowIndeterminate	BooleanProperty	Determines if the CheckBox should toggle into the indeterminate state.
indeterminate	BooleanProperty	Specifies whether the CheckBox is currently indeterminate.
selected	BooleanProperty	Specifies whether the CheckBox is currently selected.

Listing 4-2. Creating a CheckBox instance that is determinate (i.e., only toggles between selected and unselected)

```
CheckBox cb = new CheckBox("Enable Power Plant");
cb.setIndeterminate(false);
cb.setOnAction(e -> log("Action event fired"));
cb.selectedProperty()
    .addListener(i -> log("Selected state change to " + cb.isSelected()));
```

Hyperlink

The Hyperlink control is essentially a Button control that is presented in the form of a hyperlink – text with an underline – much as one would expect to see on a web site. The API for Hyperlink therefore is equivalent to the Button class, with one small addition: a visited property to indicate whether the user has clicked the link, as shown in Table 4-4. If visited is true, a developer may choose to style the Hyperlink differently. A typical usage of Hyperlink is shown in Listing 4-3.

Table 4-4. *Properties of the Hyperlink class*

Property	Type	Description
visited	BooleanProperty	Toggles to true when the hyperlink has been fired for the first time by the user.

Listing 4-3. Creating a Hyperlink instance and listening for it to be clicked

```
var hyperlink = new Hyperlink("Click Me!");
hyperlink.setOnAction(event -> log("Hyperlink was clicked"));
```

ToggleButton

ToggleButton is a Button (meaning that it can still fire action events), but generally this is not the best approach to take. This is because the intent of a ToggleButton is to toggle its selected property state between being selected and unselected, once per click. When a ToggleButton is selected, its visual appearance is different, appearing to be "pushed in." ToggleButton instances may be added to a ToggleGroup to control selection.

What Is a ToggleGroup?

ToggleGroup is a class that simply contains a list of Toggle instances whose selected state it manages. ToggleGroup ensures that at most only one Toggle can be selected at a time.

Toggle is an interface with two properties – selected and toggleGroup. Classes that implement this interface include ToggleButton, RadioButton, and RadioMenuItem.

How Do I Use ToggleButton and ToggleGroup?

What this all boils down to then is that a ToggleButton may be associated with a ToggleGroup by instantiating a ToggleGroup instance, and multiple ToggleButton instances, and setting the toggleGroup property on each ToggleButton to be the single ToggleGroup instance. This is shown in Listing 4-4.

In doing this, the ToggleButton instances in this group have an additional constraint placed on them: there can only be one ToggleButton selected at any one time. Should a user select a new ToggleButton, the previously selected ToggleButton will become unselected. When ToggleButtons are placed in a ToggleGroup, it is valid for there to be no selected ToggleButton instances (i.e., the selected ToggleButton can be unselected). The main properties of ToggleButton are shown in Table 4-5.

Table 4-5. *Properties of the ToggleButton class*

Property	Type	Description
selected	BooleanProperty	Indicates whether the toggle is selected.
toggleGroup	ObjectProperty<ToggleGroup>	The ToggleGroup to which this ToggleButton belongs.

Listing 4-4. Creating three ToggleButtons and adding them to a single ToggleGroup and listening to selection changes

```
// create a few toggle buttons
ToggleButton tb1 = new ToggleButton("Toggle button 1");
ToggleButton tb2 = new ToggleButton("Toggle button 2");
ToggleButton tb3 = new ToggleButton("Toggle button 3");

// create a toggle group and add all the toggle buttons to it
ToggleGroup group = new ToggleGroup();
group.getToggles().addAll(tb1, tb2, tb3);
// it is possible to add an onAction listener for each button
tb1.setOnAction(e -> log("ToggleButton 1 was clicked on!"));
// but it is better to add a listener to the toggle group  selectedToggle
property
group.selectedToggleProperty()
    .addListener(i -> log("Selected toggle is " + group.
    getSelectedToggle()));
```

RadioButton

RadioButton is a ToggleButton, with a different styling applied and a slightly different behavior when placed in a ToggleGroup. Whereas ToggleButtons in a ToggleGroup can be all unselected, in the case of RadioButtons in a ToggleGroup, there is no way for a user to unselect all RadioButtons. This is because, visually, a RadioButton can only be clicked to enter the selected state. Subsequent clicks have no effect (certainly it does not result in unselection). Therefore, the only way to unselect a RadioButton is to select a different RadioButton in the same ToggleGroup.

Because the API for RadioButton is essentially equivalent to ToggleButton, please refer to Listing 4-4 for the ToggleButton code sample. The only difference is to replace ToggleButton instances with RadioButton instances.

Text Input Controls

The next set of controls to cover, after the simple Labeled controls, are the three controls primarily used for text input, namely, TextArea, TextField, and PasswordField. TextField is designed to receive single-line input from users, whereas TextArea is designed to receive multiline input. PasswordField extends from TextField, enabling users to enter sensitive information by masking user input. In all three cases, these controls do not accept rich text input (see the HTMLEditor control later in this chapter for one option for rich text input).

TextArea and TextField extend from an abstract class called TextInputControl, which offers a base set of functionality, as well as a number of properties and methods that are applicable to both classes (the most important of which are shown in Table 4-6). For example, TextInputControl enables caret positioning (caret is the blinking cursor that indicates where text input will appear), text selection and formatting, and of course editing.

Table 4-6. *Properties of the TextInputControl class*

Property	Type	Description
anchor	ReadOnlyIntegerProperty	The anchor of the text selection. The range between anchor and caret represents the text selection range.
caretPosition	ReadOnlyIntegerProperty	The current position of the caret within the text.
editable	BooleanProperty	Whether the user can edit the text in the control.
font	ObjectProperty<Font>	The font to use to render the text.
length	ReadOnlyIntegerProperty	The number of characters entered in the control.
promptText	StringProperty	Text to display when there is no user input.
selectedText	ReadOnlyStringProperty	The text that has been selected in the control, via mouse or keyboard or programmatically.
textFormatter	ObjectProperty<TextFormatter<?>>	See section "TextFormatter."
text	StringProperty	The textual content of this control.

TextFormatter

Before we dive into the concrete controls, we will first take a quick diversion to cover the TextFormatter API mentioned in the preceding text. A TextFormatter has two distinct mechanisms that enable it to influence what is accepted and displayed within text input controls:

1. A filter that can intercept and modify user input. This helps to keep the text in the desired format. A default text supplier can be used to provide the initial text.

2. A value converter and value can be used to provide special format that represents a value of type V. If the control is editable and the text is changed by the user, the value is then updated to correspond to the text.

It's possible to have a formatter with just a filter or value converter. If a value converter is not provided however, setting a value will result in an IllegalStateException, and the value is always null.

TextField, PasswordField, and TextArea

As already noted, the TextField control is used to receive a single line of unformatted text from a user. This is ideal for forms requesting username, email address, and so on. The two key properties are text and onAction. The text property has already been discussed as it is inherited from TextInputControl, and onAction functions as expected given we have already covered Button and similar classes: when the Enter key is pressed, an ActionEvent is fired from the TextField, alerting the developer that the user has chosen to "submit" their input. Listing 4-5 demonstrates the standard way to use a TextField control.

Listing 4-5. Creating and using a TextField control

```
TextField textField = new TextField();
textField.setPromptText("Enter name here");

// this is fired when the user hits the Enter key
textField.setOnAction(e -> log("Entered text is: " + textField.getText()));

// we can also observe input in real time
textField.textProperty()
    .addListener((o, oldValue, newValue) -> log("current text input is " +
    newValue));
```

PasswordField functions in exactly the same way as TextField, except that it obscures the user input so that there is some degree of security from prying eyes behind the user. In addition, for security reasons, the PasswordField does not support cut and copy operations (paste is still valid however). There are no additional properties or API on PasswordField.

The TextArea control is designed for multiple lines of user input, but again only supports unformatted text. The TextArea control is best used in situations where a single line of input is not desirable. For example, if you wish to ask your user for feedback (which may span multiple sentences or paragraphs), a TextArea is the best option. Because TextArea is designed for multiple lines of input, there are a few useful properties worth becoming acquainted with, as shown in Table 4-7.

Table 4-7. *Properties of the TextArea class*

Property	Type	Description
prefColumnCount	IntegerProperty	Preferred number of text columns.
prefRowCount	IntegerProperty	Preferred number of text rows.
wrapText	BooleanProperty	Whether to wrap text or let the TextArea scroll horizontally when a line exceeds the width available.

Other Simple Controls

Beyond the Labeled controls and the text input controls, there are three other controls that can be considered "simple": ProgressBar, ProgressIndicator, and Slider.

ProgressBar and ProgressIndicator

JavaFX offers two UI controls for displaying progress to users: ProgressBar and ProgressIndicator. They are very closely related in terms of API, as ProgressBar extends ProgressIndicator and adds no additional API. The most important properties for ProgressIndicator are shown in Table 4-8.

Both controls can be used to display progress or can be set into an indeterminate state to indicate to the user that work is proceeding, but that the progress is unknown at this point in time.

To show progress, developers should set the progress property to a value between 0.0 and 1.0. This at first may appear counterintuitive – why use a range between 0.0 and 1.0, instead of a range of 0–100? The answer isn't clear that this was a conscious design choice throughout the entire JavaFX UI toolkit whenever dealing with percentages. To make the progress controls switch to their indeterminate form, simply set the progress property value to –1. When this is done, the indeterminate property will change from false to true.

A simple usage example is shown in Listing 4-6.

Table 4-8. *Properties of the ProgressIndicator class*

Property	Type	Description
indeterminate	ReadOnlyBooleanProperty	A Boolean flag indicating if the indeterminate progress animation is playing.
progress	DoubleProperty	The actual progress (between 0.0 and 1.0), or can be set to −1 for indeterminate.

Listing 4-6. Creating a ProgressBar that will show 25% progress

```
ProgressBar p2 = new ProgressBar();
p2.setProgress(0.25F);
```

Slider

The Slider control is used to enable users to specify a value within a certain min/max range. This is made possible by displaying to the user a "track" and a "thumb." The thumb can be dragged by the user to change the value. It is therefore no surprise that the three most critical properties of a Slider control are its min, max, and value properties, shown in Table 4-9. A simple example of using a slider is shown in Listing 4-7.

Table 4-9. *Properties of the Slider class*

Property	Type	Description
blockIncrement	DoubleProperty	How much the Slider moves if the track is clicked.
max	DoubleProperty	The maximum value represented by the Slider.
min	DoubleProperty	The minimum value represented by the Slider.
orientation	ObjectProperty<Orientation>	Whether the Slider is horizontal or vertical.
value	DoubleProperty	The current value represented by the Slider.

Listing 4-7. Creating a slider that will have a range between 0.0 and 1.0

```
Slider slider = new Slider(0.0f, 1.0f, 0.5f);
slider.valueProperty()
    .addListener((o, oldValue, newValue) -> log("Slider value is " + newValue));
```

Container Controls

Now that we have worked through the simple UI controls, we can move on to some more exciting controls. This section will be covering "container" controls, or controls that are used to contain and display other user interface elements. These container controls provide some additional functionality, be it the ability to collapse their content, offer a tabbed interface to change views, or something else.

Accordion and TitledPane

TitledPane is a container that displays a title area and a content area and has the ability to expand and collapse the content area by clicking the title area. This is useful for side panels and the like in a user interface in that it allows for information to be displayed but optionally collapsed by users, such that they only see what they need to see.

TitledPane extends from Labeled, so as we discussed earlier, there is a large array of properties to customize the display. One should note however that these Labeled properties are applied only to the title area of the TitledPane and not the content area. The primary properties of TitledPane are shown in Table 4-10.

Table 4-10. *Properties of the TitledPane class*

Property	Type	Description
animated	BooleanProperty	Whether the TitledPane animates as it expands and collapses.
collapsible	BooleanProperty	Whether the TitledPane can be collapsed by the user.
content	ObjectProperty<Node>	The Node to display in the content area of the TitledPane.
expanded	BooleanProperty	Whether the TitledPane is currently expanded or not.
text	StringProperty	The text to show in the header area of the TitledPane.

With TitledPane introduced, we can move on to Accordion, which is a control that is simply a container of zero or more TitledPanes. When an Accordion is displayed to the user, it only allows for one TitledPane to be expanded at any time. Expanding a different TitledPane will result in the currently expanded TitledPane being collapsed.

There is only one notable property – expandedPane – which is an
ObjectProperty<TitledPane> that represents the currently expanded TitledPane, as
noted in Table 4-11.

Table 4-11. *Properties of the Accordion class*

Property	Type	Description
expandedPane	ObjectProperty<TitledPane>	The currently expanded TitledPane in the Accordion.

To add TitledPanes to the Accordion, we use the getPanes() method to retrieve the
ObservableList of TitledPanes, and we add the applicable TitledPanes into this list. The
result of doing this will be that the TitledPanes will be displayed stacked vertically in the
order that they appear within this list. A code example of this is shown in Listing 4-8.

Listing 4-8. Creating three TitledPanes and adding them all to a single
Accordion

```
TitledPane t1 = new TitledPane("TitledPane 1", new Button("Button 1"));
TitledPane t2 = new TitledPane("TitledPane 2", new Button("Button 2"));
TitledPane t3 = new TitledPane("TitledPane 3", new Button("Button 3"));
Accordion accordion = new Accordion();
accordion.getPanes().addAll(t1, t2, t3);
```

ButtonBar

The ButtonBar control was added in the JavaFX 8u40 release, so it is relatively new
and relatively unknown. ButtonBar can be thought of as being essentially an HBox for
Button controls (although it works with any Node), with the added functionality of
placing the provided buttons in the correct order for the operating system on which the
user interface is running. This is extremely useful for dialogs, for example, as Windows,
macOS, and Linux all have different button orderings. There are a small number of useful
properties, as shown in Table 4-12, and Listing 4-9 demonstrates how to create and
populate a ButtonBar instance.

Table 4-12. *Properties of the ButtonBar class*

Property	Type	Description
buttonMinWidth	DoubleProperty	The minimum width of all buttons placed in the ButtonBar.
buttonOrder	StringProperty	The ordering of buttons in the ButtonBar.

Listing 4-9. Creating a ButtonBar with "Yes" and "No" buttons. Ordering will depend on the operating system that this code is executed on

```
// Create the ButtonBar instance
ButtonBar buttonBar = new ButtonBar();

// Create the buttons to go into the ButtonBar
Button yesButton = new Button("Yes");
ButtonBar.setButtonData(yesButton, ButtonData.YES);

Button noButton = new Button("No");
ButtonBar.setButtonData(noButton, ButtonData.NO);

// Add buttons to the ButtonBar
buttonBar.getButtons().addAll(yesButton, noButton);
```

ScrollPane

ScrollPane is a control that is crucial to almost every user interface – the ability to scroll horizontally and vertically when content extends beyond the bounds of the user interface. For example, imagine an image manipulation program such as Adobe Photoshop. In this user interface, you may zoom in to work on a tiny section of your drawing, and the horizontal and vertical scrollbars allow for you to move this section around to see adjoining sections.

Unlike some other UI toolkits, it is not necessary to wrap UI controls such as ListView, TableView, and the like with a ScrollPane, as they have built-in scrolling and handle it for the developer. Therefore, a ScrollPane is typically used by developers in instances where they are doing something relatively custom. An example is shown in Listing 4-10, and the properties of ScrollPane are shown in Table 4-13.

Table 4-13. *Properties of the ScrollPane class*

Property	Type	Description
content	ObjectProperty<Node>	The Node to be displayed.
fitToHeight	BooleanProperty	Will attempt to keep content resized to match height of viewport.
fitToWidth	BooleanProperty	Will attempt to keep content resized to match width of viewport.
hbarPolicy	ObjectProperty<Scroll BarPolicy>	Sets policy for when to show horizontal scrollbars.
hmax	DoubleProperty	The maximum allowed hvalue.
hmin	DoubleProperty	The minimum allowed hvalue.
hvalue	DoubleProperty	The current horizontal position of the ScrollPane.
vbarPolicy	ObjectProperty<Scroll BarPolicy>	Sets policy for when to show vertical scrollbars. This can be one of the enum constants in ScrollPane.ScrollBarPolicy: ALWAYS, AS_NEEDED, or NEVER.
vmax	DoubleProperty	The maximum allowed vvalue.
vmin	DoubleProperty	The minimum allowed vvalue.
vvalue	DoubleProperty	The current vertical position of the ScrollPane.

Listing 4-10. Creating a ScrollPane instance

```
// in this sample we create a linear gradient to make the scrolling visible
Stop[] stops = new Stop[] { new Stop(0, Color.BLACK), new Stop(1, Color.
RED)};
LinearGradient gradient = new LinearGradient(0, 0, 1500, 1000, false,
CycleMethod.NO_CYCLE, stops);
// we place the linear gradient inside a big rectangle
Rectangle rect = new Rectangle(2000, 2000, gradient);
// which is placed inside a scrollpane that is quite small in comparison
ScrollPane scrollPane = new ScrollPane();
scrollPane.setPrefSize(120, 120);
```

```
scrollPane.setContent(rect);
// and we then listen (and log) when the user is scrolling vertically or
horizontally
ChangeListener<? super Number> o = (obs, oldValue, newValue) -> {
    log("x / y values are: (" + scrollPane.getHvalue() + ", " + scrollPane.
    getVvalue() + ")");
};
scrollPane.hvalueProperty().addListener(o);
scrollPane.vvalueProperty().addListener(o);
```

SplitPane

The SplitPane control accepts two or more children and draws them with a draggable divider between them. The user is then able to use this divider to give more space to one child, at the cost of taking space away from the other child. A SplitPane control is great for user interfaces where there is a main content area, and then an area on the left/right/ bottom of the content area is used to display more context-specific information. In this scenario, the user may give additional space to the main content area or the context-specific area as necessary.

Historically, UI toolkits have only supported two children (i.e., a "left" and a "right" or a "top" and a "bottom"), but JavaFX removed this restriction and allows for an unlimited number of children, with one restriction: all children must have the same divider orientation. This means that a SplitPane only has one orientation property for all dividers (as shown in Table 4-14). There is however a way around this: simply embed SplitPane instances inside each other, such that the end result consists of dividers operating both horizontally and vertically in the desired order.

The SplitPane control observes the minimum and maximum size properties of its children. It will never reduce the size of a node below its minimum size and will never give it more size than its maximum size. For this reason, it is recommended that all nodes added to a SplitPane be wrapped inside a separate layout container, such that the layout container may handle the sizing of the node, without impacting the SplitPane's ability to function.

A divider's position ranges from 0 to 1.0 (inclusive). A position of 0 will place the divider at the left-/topmost edge of the SplitPane plus the minimum size of the node. A position of 1.0 will place the divider at the right-/bottommost edge of the SplitPane minus the minimum size of the node. A divider position of 0.5 will place the divider in the middle of the SplitPane. Setting the divider position greater than the node's maximum size position will result in the divider being set at the node's maximum size position. Setting the divider position less than the node's minimum size position will result in the divider being set at the node's minimum size position.

An example of creating a SplitPane is shown in Listing 4-11.

Table 4-14. *Properties of the SplitPane class*

Property	Type	Description
orientation	ObjectProperty<Orientation>	The orientation of the SplitPane.

Listing 4-11. Creating a SplitPane instance with three children (and therefore two dividers)

```
final StackPane sp1 = new StackPane();
sp1.getChildren().add(new Button("Button One"));

final StackPane sp2 = new StackPane();
sp2.getChildren().add(new Button("Button Two"));

final StackPane sp3 = new StackPane();
sp3.getChildren().add(new Button("Button Three"));

SplitPane splitPane = new SplitPane();
splitPane.getItems().addAll(sp1, sp2, sp3);
splitPane.setDividerPositions(0.3f, 0.6f, 0.9f);
```

TabPane

TabPane is a UI control that enables for tabbed interfaces to be displayed to users. For example, most of you will be familiar with the tabbed interface in your preferred web browser, so that you do not need to have multiple windows open – one for each page that you wish to have open.

Table 4-15 outlines the most important properties, but the two most useful properties are the side property and the tabClosingPolicy property. The side property is for specifying on which side of the TabPane the tabs will be displayed (by default this is Side.TOP, which means that the tabs will be at the top of the TabPane). The tabClosingPolicy is for specifying whether tabs can be closed by the user – there is a TabClosingPolicy enum, with three valid values:

1. UNAVAILABLE: Tabs cannot be closed by the user.

2. SELECTED_TAB: The currently selected tab will have a small close button in the tab area (shown as a small "x"). When a different tab is selected, the close button will disappear from the previously selected tab and instead be shown on the newly selected tab.

3. ALL_TABS: All tabs visible in the TabPane will have the small close button visible.

The JavaFX TabPane functions by exposing an ObservableList of Tab instances. Each Tab instance consists of a title property and a content property. When a Tab is added to the tabs list, it will be displayed in the user interface in the order in which it appears in the list. This is demonstrated in Listing 4-12.

Table 4-15. *Properties of the TabPane class*

Property	Type	Description
rotateGraphic	BooleanProperty	Whether graphics should rotate to display appropriately when tabs are placed on the left/right side.
selectionModel	ObjectProperty<SingleS electionModel>	The selection model being used in the TabPane.[5]
side	ObjectProperty<Side>	The location at which tabs will be displayed.
tabClosingPolicy	ObjectProperty<TabClos ingPolicy>	Described in the preceding text.

---

[5] Selection models are discussed later in this chapter.

Listing 4-12. How to instantiate and use a TabPane

```
TabPane tabPane = new TabPane();
tabPane.setTabClosingPolicy(TabPane.TabClosingPolicy.UNAVAILABLE);

for (int i = 0; i < 5; i++) {
    Tab tab = new Tab("Tab " + I, new Rectangle(200, 200, randomColor()));
    tabPane.getTabs().add(tab);
}
```

ToolBar

The ToolBar control is a very simple UI control. In its most common permutation, it can be thought of as a stylized HBox – that is, it presents whatever nodes are added to it horizontally, with a background gradient. The most common elements to add to a ToolBar are other UI controls such as Button, ToggleButton, and Separator, but there is no restriction on what can be placed within a ToolBar, as long as it is a Node.

The ToolBar control does offer one useful piece of functionality – it supports the concept of overflow, so that if there are more elements to be displayed than there is space to display them all, it removes the "overflowing" elements from the ToolBar and instead shows an overflow button that when clicked pops up a menu containing all overflowing elements of the ToolBar.

As noted in Table 4-16, ToolBar offers a vertical orientation, so that it may be placed on the left- or right-hand side of an application user interface, although this is not as common as being placed at the top of the user interface, typically just below the menu bar.

An example of creating a ToolBar is shown in Listing 4-13.

Table 4-16. *Properties of the ToolBar class*

Property	Type	Description
orientation	ObjectProperty\<Orientation\>	Whether the ToolBar should be horizontal or vertical.

Listing 4-13. Instantiating a ToolBar with multiple Button and Separator
instances

```
ToolBar toolBar = new ToolBar();
toolBar.getItems().addAll(
    new Button("New"),
    new Button("Open"),
    new Button("Save"),
    new Separator(),
    new Button("Clean"),
    new Button("Compile"),
    new Button("Run"),
    new Separator(),
    new Button("Debug"),
    new Button("Profile")
);
```

Other Controls

HTMLEditor

The HTMLEditor control enables users to create rich text input that is internally formatted
as HTML content. The control provides a number of UI controls to specify font size,
color, and type, as well as alignment and so on.

One point to note about the HTMLEditor control is that, because it is dependent on
the JavaFX WebView component for rendering the user input, this control does not ship in
the javafx.controls module, but rather the javafx.web module, and within that it can
be found in the javafx.scene.web package.

Despite the large amount of functionality offered to the end user, there is surprisingly
little API available to the developer using HTMLEditor. There are no relevant properties,
and the only relevant methods are the getter and setter methods for htmlText. These
methods operate with a String, and it is expected that this String consists of valid HTML.[6]

---

[6] Note that if the contentEditable property on the <body> tag of the provided HTML is not set to
true, the HTMLEditor will become read-only. You can ensure that the text remains editable by
ensuring the body element contains contentEditable="true".

Pagination

The simplest way to understand the Pagination control is to think of the Google search results page, with the "Goooooooogle" text at the bottom and the numbers "1, 2, 3,...10." Each of these numbers represents a page of results, and the user may click these to be taken to that page. Of importance is the fact that Google doesn't predetermine the elements to place on any page other than the current page – the rest of the pages are only determined when they are requested.

This is precisely the functionality that Pagination offers in JavaFX. The key properties of the Pagination class are shown in Table 4-17. Pagination is an abstract way of representing multiple pages, where only the currently showing page actually exists in the scene graph and all other pages are only generated upon request.

This is the first time in this chapter we have encountered a situation where we make use of the "callback" functionality used in a number of JavaFX UI controls. This is made use of in the pageFactory, to allow for on-demand generation of pages, as requested by the user. As this chapter progresses, we will encounter this approach a number of more times, so it is worth your time to ensure you understand what happens in Listing 4-14, especially where the pageFactory is set.

Table 4-17. *Properties of the Pagination class*

Property	Type	Description
currentPageIndex	IntegerProperty	The current page index being displayed.
pageCount	IntegerProperty	The total number of pages available to be displayed.
pageFactory	ObjectProperty<Callback <Integer,Node>>	Callback function that returns the page corresponding to the given index.

Listing 4-14. Instantiating a Pagination control with ten pages

```
Pagination pagination = new Pagination(10, 0);
pagination.setPageFactory(pageIndex -> {
    VBox box = new VBox(5);
    for (int i = 0; i < 10; i++) {
        int linkNumber = pageIndex * 10 + i;
        Hyperlink link = new Hyperlink("Hyperlink #" + linkNumber);
```

```
        link.setOnAction(e -> log("Hyperlink #" + linkNumber + "
        clicked!"));
        box.getChildren().add(link);
    }
    return box;
});
```

ScrollBar

The ScrollBar control is essentially a Slider control with a different style. It consists of a track over which a thumb can be moved, as well as buttons at either end for incrementing and decrementing the value (and thus moving the thumb). ScrollBar typically is not used in the same circumstances as Slider however – instead, it is typically used as part of a more complex UI control. For example, it is used in the ScrollPane control to support vertical and horizontal scrolling and is used in the ListView, TableView, TreeView, and TreeTableView controls discussed later.

Table 4-18 introduces the most important properties of the ScrollBar control.

Table 4-18. *Properties of the ScrollBar class*

Property	Type	Description
blockIncrement	DoubleProperty	How much the thumb moves if the track is clicked.
max	DoubleProperty	The maximum allowed value.
min	DoubleProperty	The minimum allowed value.
orientation	ObjectProperty<Orientation>	Whether the ScrollBar is horizontal or vertical.
unitIncrement	DoubleProperty	The amount by which to adjust the value when the increment/decrement method is called.
value	DoubleProperty	The current value of the ScrollBar.

Separator

The Separator control is perhaps the simplest control in the entire JavaFX UI toolkit. It is a control that lacks any interactivity and is simply designed to draw a line in the relevant section of the user interface. This is commonly used in the ToolBar control to group buttons into subgroups, for example. A similar approach is used in popup menus, but as noted previously, in the case of menus, it is required to use SeparatorMenuItem, rather than the standard Separator control discussed here.

By default, a Separator is oriented vertically such that is draws appropriately when placed in a horizontal ToolBar. This can be controlled by modifying the orientation property.

Spinner

The Spinner control was introduced to JavaFX relatively recently, in JavaFX 8u40. A Spinner can be thought of as a single-line TextField that may or may not be editable, with the addition of increment and decrement arrows to step through some set of values. Table 4-19 introduces the most critical properties of this control.

Because a Spinner can be used to step through various types of value (integer, float, double, or even a List of some type), the Spinner defers to a SpinnerValueFactory to handle the actual process of stepping through the range of values (and precisely how to step). JavaFX ships with a number of built-in SpinnerValueFactory types (for doubles, integers, and Lists), and it is possible to write custom SpinnerValueFactory instances for custom needs. The code example in Listing 4-15 demonstrates the integer value factory, and the double and list value factories function in the same fashion.

Table 4-19. *Properties of the Spinner class*

Property	Type	Description
editable	BooleanProperty	Whether text input is able to be typed by the user.
editor	ReadOnlyObjectProperty<TextField>	The editor control used by the Spinner.
promptText	StringProperty	The prompt text to display when there is no user input.
valueFactory	ObjectProperty<SpinnerValueFactory<T>>	As discussed in the preceding text.
value	ReadOnlyObjectProperty<T>	The value selected by the user.

Listing 4-15. Creating a Spinner with an integer value factory

```
Spinner<Integer> spinner = new Spinner<>();
spinner.setValueFactory(new SpinnerValueFactory.
IntegerSpinnerValueFactory(5, 10));

spinner.valueProperty().addListener((o, oldValue, newValue) -> {
        log("value changed: '" + oldValue + "' -> '" + newValue + "'");
});
```

Tooltip

Tooltips are common UI elements which are typically used for showing additional information about a Node in the scene graph when the Node is hovered over by the mouse. Any Node can show a tooltip. In most cases, a Tooltip is created, and its text property is modified to show plain text to the user. However, a Tooltip is able to show within it an arbitrary scene graph of nodes – this is done by creating the scene graph and setting it inside the tooltip graphic property.

You can use the approach shown in Listing 4-16 to set a tooltip on any node.

Listing 4-16. Adding a tooltip to any Node in the JavaFX scene graph

```
Rectangle rect = new Rectangle(0, 0, 100, 100);
Tooltip t = new Tooltip("A Square");
Tooltip.install(rect, t);
```

This tooltip will then participate with the typical tooltip semantics (i.e., appearing on hover and so on). Note that the Tooltip does not have to be uninstalled: it will be garbage collected when it is not referenced by any Node. It is possible to manually uninstall the tooltip, however, in much the same way.

A single tooltip can be installed on multiple target nodes or multiple controls.

Because most tooltips are shown on UI controls, there is special API for all controls to make installing a Tooltip less verbose. The example in Listing 4-17 shows how to create a tooltip for a Button control.

Listing 4-17. Adding a tooltip to a UI control using convenience API

```
Button button = new Button("Hover Over Me");
button.setTooltip(new Tooltip("Tooltip for Button"));
```

The key properties of the Tooltip class are shown in Table 4-20.

Table 4-20. Properties of the Tooltip class

Property	Type	Description
graphic	ObjectProperty<Node>	An icon or arbitrarily complex scene graph to display within the tooltip popup.
text	StringProperty	The text to display within the tooltip popup.
wrapText	BooleanProperty	Whether to wrap text when it exceeds the tooltip width.

Popup Controls

JavaFX ships with a comprehensive set of controls that "pop up." What this means is that, behind the scenes, they are placed in their own window that is separate from the main stage of the user interface, and as such they may appear outside of the window in situations whether they are taller or wider than the window itself. Developers do not need to concern themselves with the placement, sizing, or any detail related to this, but it is a useful detail to understand.

This section covers all UI controls in JavaFX that make use of this popup functionality. For many of them, they also make use of the same APIs for building menus, so we will firstly cover this common functionality, before talking about each control in turn.

Menu-Based Controls

Menu and MenuItem

Building a menu in JavaFX starts with the Menu and MenuItem classes. Both classes are notable for not actually extending Control, which is because they are designed to represent a menu structure, but the implementation is handled behind the scenes by JavaFX.

MenuItem acts essentially in the same fashion as a Button does. It supports a similar set of properties – text, graphic, and onAction. On top of this, it adds support for specifying keyboard accelerators (e.g., Ctrl+C). These are detailed in Table 4-21.

Because MenuItem simply extends from Object, on its own it is useless and cannot be added to a JavaFX user interface in the standard way. The way in which MenuItem is used is via the Menu class, which acts as a container for MenuItem instances. The Menu class has a getItems() method that works in the standard way of most other JavaFX APIs – developers add MenuItem instances into the getItems() method, and these items will then be displayed in the Menu whenever it is displayed to the user.

This leads to a few important questions:

1. **How does JavaFX support nested menus (i.e., where a menu contains a submenu, which itself may contain more submenus)?** This is handled simply by the fact that the Menu class itself extends from MenuItem. This means that whenever the API allows for a MenuItem, it implicitly supports Menu as well.

2. **How does JavaFX support menu items with checkboxes or radio states?** JavaFX ships with two subclasses – CheckMenuItem and RadioMenuItem – that support this. CheckMenuItem has a selected property that will toggle between true and false every time the user clicks the menu item. RadioMenuItem functions in

a similar fashion to RadioButton – it should be associated with a ToggleGroup, and then JavaFX will enforce that at most one RadioMenuItem will be selected at any one time.

3. **How do I separate menu items into groups?** The common way this is handled in user interfaces is with separators. As mentioned earlier in this chapter, it is not possible to add a Separator directly into a Menu (as it does not extend from MenuItem), and so for this reason JavaFX ships with SeparatorMenuItem, which places a Separator into the Menu at the position the SeparatorMenuItem is placed inside the menu items list.

4. **What about custom menu elements? What if I want to show a Slider or a TextField in a Menu, for example?** JavaFX supports this with the CustomMenuItem class. By using this class, developers can embed any arbitrary Node into the content property.

Table 4-21. *Properties of the MenuItem class*

Property	Type	Description
accelerator	ObjectProperty<KeyCombination>	A keyboard shortcut to access this menu item.
disable	BooleanProperty	Whether the menu item should be user interactive.
graphic	ObjectProperty<Node>	The graphic to show to the left of the menu item text.
onAction	ObjectProperty<EventHandler<ActionEvent>>	The event handler to be called when the menu item is clicked.
text	StringProperty	The text to display in the menu item.
visible	BooleanProperty	Whether the menu item is visible in the menu or not.

MenuBar

So far we have covered the API required to specify a Menu, but not how it may be displayed to the user. By far, the most common way in which menus are added to a JavaFX user interface is through the MenuBar control. This class is traditionally placed at the top of the user interface (e.g., if a BorderLayout is used, it is typically set to be the top node), and it is constructed simply by creating an instance and then adding Menu instances to the list returned by calling getMenus().

On some operating systems (most notably macOS), it is typically quite uncommon to see a menu bar at the top of an application window, as macOS instead has a "system menu bar" that runs across the very top of the screen. This system menu bar is application context specific in that it changes its content whenever the focused application changes. JavaFX supports this, and the MenuBar class has a useSystemMenuBar property that, if set to true, will remove the MenuBar from the application window and instead render the menu bar natively using the system menu bar. This will happen automatically on platforms that have a system menu bar (macOS), but will have no effect on platforms that do not (and in which case, the MenuBar will be positioned in the user interface however it is specified to appear by the application developer).

Listing 4-18 shows how to create a MenuBar with menus and menu items.

Listing 4-18. Creating a MenuBar with two menus (the first of which has a submenu)

```
// Firstly we create our menu instances (and populate with menu items)
final Menu fileMenu = new Menu("File");
final Menu helpMenu = new Menu("Help");

// we are creating a Menu here to add as a submenu to the File menu
Menu newMenu = new Menu("Create New...");
newMenu.getItems().addAll(
        makeMenuItem("Project", console),
        makeMenuItem("JavaFX class", console),
        makeMenuItem("FXML file", console)
);
// add menu items to each menu
fileMenu.getItems().addAll(
```

```
        newMenu,
        new SeparatorMenuItem(),
        makeMenuItem("Exit", console)
);
helpMenu.getItems().addAll(makeMenuItem("Help", console));
// then we create the MenuBar instance and add in the menus
MenuBar menuBar = new MenuBar();
menuBar.getMenus().addAll(fileMenu, helpMenu);
```

MenuButton and SplitMenuButton

Another way menus are commonly shown to users in JavaFX applications is through the MenuButton and SplitMenuButton classes. These classes are quite closely related, but they do function in slightly different fashions, so we will cover them separately in the following.

MenuButton is a button-like control that, whenever clicked, will show a menu consisting of all MenuItem elements added to the items list. Because the MenuButton class extends from ButtonBase (which itself extends from Labeled), there is a significant amount of API overlap with the JavaFX Button control. For example, MenuButton has the same onAction event, as well as text and graphic properties and so on. Note however that for a MenuButton, setting onAction has no effect, as the MenuButton does not fire onAction events, because this is used instead to show a popup. Table 4-22 outlines the properties introduced by MenuItem, and Listing 4-19 demonstrates how to use MenuButton in code.

SplitMenuButton extends the MenuButton class, but unlike MenuButton, the visuals of SplitMenuButton split the button itself into two pieces – an "action" area and the "menu open" area. When a user clicks the "action" area, the SplitMenuButton essentially acts as if it were a Button – executing whatever code is associated with the onAction property. When the user clicks the "menu open" area, the popup menu is shown, and the user may interact with the menu as per usual. Listing 4-20 demonstrates how to use SplitMenuButton in code.

Table 4-22. *Properties of the MenuButton class*

Property	Type	Description
popupSide	ObjectProperty<Side>	The side the context menu should be shown relative to the button.

Listing 4-19. An example of using MenuButton

```
MenuButton menuButton = new MenuButton("Choose a meal...");
menuButton.getItems().addAll(
        makeMenuItem("Burgers", console),
        makeMenuItem("Pizza", console),
        makeMenuItem("Hot Dog", console));
// because the MenuButton does not have an 'action' area,
// onAction does nothing
menuButton.setOnAction(e -> log("MenuButton onAction event"));
```

Listing 4-20. An example of using SplitMenuButton

```
SplitMenuButton splitMenuButton = new SplitMenuButton();
// this is the text in the 'action' area
splitMenuButton.setText("Perform action!");
// these are the menu items to display in the popup menu
splitMenuButton.getItems().addAll(
        makeMenuItem("Burgers", console),
        makeMenuItem("Pizza", console),
        makeMenuItem("Hot Dog", console));
// splitMenuButton does fire an onAction event,
// when the 'action' area is pressed
splitMenuButton.setOnAction(e -> log("SplitMenuButton onAction event"));
```

ContextMenu

ContextMenu is a popup control that contains within it MenuItems. This means that it is never added to a scene graph and instead is called either directly (via the two show() methods) or as a consequence of a user requesting a context menu to show using common mouse or keyboard operations (most commonly via pressing the right button of the mouse).

To make specifying and displaying context menus as easy as possible, the root `Control` class has a `contextMenu` property on it. When certain events happen (e.g., right mouse button press), the UI control is configured to check if a context menu is specified and, if so, to automatically display it. For example, the `Tab` class has one such `contextMenu` property, and whenever a user right-clicks a `Tab` inside of a `TabPane`, they are presented with the context menu as specified by the developer. Listing 4-21 shows a Button that has a ContextMenu set against it, which displays whenever the right mouse button is pressed on it.

Listing 4-21. Specifying a ContextMenu and adding it to a Button instance

```
// create a standard JavaFX Button
Button button = new Button("Right-click Me!");
button.setOnAction(event -> log("Button was clicked"));
// create a ContextMenu
ContextMenu contextMenu = new ContextMenu();
contextMenu.getItems().addAll(
        makeMenuItem("Hello", console),
        makeMenuItem("World!", console),
        new SeparatorMenuItem(),
        makeMenuItem("Goodbye Again!", console)
);
```

In some cases, we want to show a `ContextMenu` on a class that does not extend from `Control`. In these cases, we can simply make use of one of the two `show()` methods on `ContextMenu` to display it when relevant events come up. There are two `show()` methods available:

1. `show(Node anchor, double screenX, double screenY)`: This method will show the context menu at the specified screen coordinates.

2. `show(Node anchor, Side side, double dx, double dy)`: This method will show the context menu at the specified side (top, right, bottom, or left) of the specified anchor node, with the amount of x- and y-axis shifting specified by `dx` and `dy`, respectively (also note that `dx` and `dy` can be negative if desired, but most commonly these values can simply be zero).

By using one of these two show methods in conjunction with appropriate event handlers (in particular onContextMenuRequested and onMousePressed API available on all JavaFX Node subclasses), we can achieve the desired outcome. Listing 4-22 shows how to display a ContextMenu on a JavaFX Rectangle class (which lacks the setContextMenu API from Control subclasses).

Listing 4-22. Adding a ContextMenu to a JavaFX Rectangle by manually showing it when requested

```
Rectangle rectangle = new Rectangle(50, 50, Color.RED);
rectangle.setOnContextMenuRequested(e -> {
    // show the contextMenu to the right of the rectangle with zero
    // offset in x and y directions
    contextMenu.show(rectangle, Side.RIGHT, 0, 0);
});
```

ChoiceBox

ChoiceBox is a JavaFX UI control that displays a popup menu when clicked, but it is not constructed through MenuItem instances. Instead, ChoiceBox is a generic class (e.g., ChoiceBox<T>), where the type of the class is also the type used for the items list. In other words, rather than have users specify menu items, a ChoiceBox is constructed with zero or more objects of type T, and these are what are displayed to the user in the popup menu.

Because the default toString() method of the T class may not be appropriate or overly human readable, ChoiceBox supports the notion of a converter property (which is of type StringConverter<T>). If a converter is specified, the ChoiceBox will take each element from the items list (which is of type T) and pass it through the converter, which should return a more human-readable string to be displayed in the popup menu.

When a user makes a selection in the ChoiceBox, the value property will be updated to reflect this new selection. When the value property changes, the ChoiceBox control also fires an onAction ActionEvent, so developers can choose whether to observe the value property or to add an onAction event handler.

Due to the UI design of ChoiceBox, this control is best suited to relatively small lists of elements. If the number of elements to display is large, it is normally recommended that developers instead use the ComboBox control.

The primary properties of ChoiceBox are outlined in Table 4-23, and their use is demonstrated in Listing 4-23.

Table 4-23. *Properties of the ChoiceBox class*

Property	Type	Description
converter	ObjectProperty<StringConverter<T>>	Allows for a way to convert the visual presentation of the items list.
items	ObjectProperty<ObservableList<T>>	The items to display in the ChoiceBox.
selectionModel	ObjectProperty<SingleSelectionModel<T>>	The selection model for the ChoiceBox.
showing	ReadOnlyBooleanProperty	Indicates if the ChoiceBox popup is visible.
value	ObjectProperty<T>	The current selection in the ChoiceBox.

Listing 4-23. Creating a ChoiceBox with four choices and a listener

```
ChoiceBox<String> choiceBox = new ChoiceBox<>();
choiceBox.getItems().addAll(
    "Choice 1",
    "Choice 2",
    "Choice 3",
    "Choice 4"
);
choiceBox.getSelectionModel()
        .selectedItemProperty()
        .addListener((o, oldValue, newValue) -> log(newValue));
```

ComboBox-Based Controls

Beyond the menu-based controls, there are a lot of other controls that pop up based on user interaction. This section covers a set of controls that all can be classified as controls that are "combo boxes." In JavaFX, the controls in this set all extend from the ComboBoxBase class (whose properties are shown in Table 4-24) and are known as ComboBox, ColorPicker, and DatePicker.

Because all ComboBoxBase subclasses share a common parent, their API is uniform, and there are a number of notable similarities:

- They appear as a button that, when clicked, will pop up some UI that allows the user to make a selection.

- There is a value property that represents the current value selected by the user.

- They typically can be editable or not, by setting the editable property appropriately. When the control is editable, it displays with a TextField and a button on the side – the TextField allows for user input, and the button will show the popup. When the control is not editable, the entire control will appear as a button.

- There are show() and hide() methods to programmatically cause the popup to show itself or, if it is already showing, to hide.

Table 4-24. Properties of the ComboBoxBase class

Property	Type	Description
editable	BooleanProperty	Whether the control shows a text input area to receive user input.
onAction	ObjectProperty<EventHandler <ActionEvent>>	The event handler when the user sets a new value.
promptText	StringProperty	The prompt text to display – whether it displays is dependent on the subclass.
value	ObjectProperty<T>	The latest selection (or input if editable) by the user.

ComboBox

ComboBox is conceptually quite similar to the ChoiceBox control, but is more fully featured and more performant when large lists of elements are needing to be displayed. The properties added in ComboBox are shown in Table 4-25 and demonstrated in code in Listing 4-24.

Table 4-25. *Properties of the ComboBox class*

Property	Type	Description
cellFactory	ObjectProperty<Callback<ListView<T>,ListCell<T>>>	Used to customize rendering of items.
converter	ObjectProperty<StringConverter<T>>	Converts user-typed input (when editable) to an object of type T to set as value.
items	ObjectProperty<ObservableList<T>>	The elements to show in popup.
placeholder	ObjectProperty<Node>	What to show when the ComboBox has no items.
selectionModel	ObjectProperty<SingleSelectionModel<T>>	Selection model of ComboBox.

Listing 4-24. Creating a ComboBox with multiple choices and a listener

```
ComboBox<String> comboBox = new ComboBox<>();
comboBox.getItems().addAll(
        "Apple",
        "Carrot",
        "Orange",
        "Banana",
        "Mango",
        "Strawberry"
);
comboBox.getSelectionModel()
        .selectedItemProperty()
        .addListener((o, oldValue, newValue) -> log(newValue));
```

179

ColorPicker

The ColorPicker control is a specialized form of ComboBox, designed specifically to allow users to select a color value.[7] The ColorPicker control does not add any additional functionality on top of ComboBoxBase, but of course the user interface is vastly different. Using a ColorPicker is very similar to the other controls, as shown in Listing 4-25.

The ColorPicker control provides a color palette with a predefined set of colors. If the user does not want to choose from the predefined set, they can create a custom color by interacting with a custom color dialog. This dialog provides RGB, HSB, and web modes of interaction, to create new colors. It also lets the opacity of the color to be modified.

Once a new color is defined, users can choose whether they want to save it or just use it. If the new color is saved, this color will then appear in the custom colors area on the color palette.

Listing 4-25. Creating a ColorPicker and listening for selection changes

```
final ColorPicker colorPicker = new ColorPicker();
colorPicker.setOnAction(e -> {
    Color c = colorPicker.getValue();

System.out.println("New Color RGB = "+c.getRed()+" "+c.getGreen()+" "+c.
getBlue());
});
```

DatePicker

Much as ColorPicker is a specialization of ComboBoxBase for selecting colors, the DatePicker is a specialization of ComboBoxBase for selecting dates – in this case a java.time.LocalDate value. The properties introduced in DatePicker are shown in Table 4-26, and its use in code is demonstrated in Listing 4-26.

---

[7] More specifically, ColorPicker is a ComboBoxBase<javafx.scene.paint.Color> and therefore does not allow for developers to specify any other generic type for this class.

Table 4-26. *Properties of the DatePicker class*

Property	Type	Description
chronology	ObjectProperty<Chronology>	Which calendar system to use.
converter	ObjectProperty<StringConverter<LocalDate>>	Converts text input into a LocalDate and vice versa.
dayCellFactory	ObjectProperty<Callback<DatePicker,DateCell>>	Cell factory to customize individual day cells in popup.
showWeekNumbers	BooleanProperty	Whether the popup should show week numbers.

Listing 4-26. Creating a DatePicker and listening for selection changes

```
final DatePicker datePicker = new DatePicker();
datePicker.setOnAction(e -> {
    LocalDate date = datePicker.getValue();
    System.err.println("Selected date: " + date);
});
```

JavaFX Dialogs

JavaFX, since the 8u40 release, has shipped with a comprehensive set of dialog APIs to alert, query, and inform users. There exists API for simply popping open an informational alert all the way through creating custom dialogs. At the simplest end of the spectrum, developers should use the Alert class to show pre-built dialogs. Developers who want to prompt a user for text input or to make a choice from a list of options would be better served by using TextInputDialog and ChoiceDialog, respectively. Completely custom dialogs can be created using the Dialog and DialogPane classes.

There are two terms when discussing dialogs that developers should become familiar with. These are "modal" and "blocking" and are often used interchangeably when there is a distinct difference between them. Despite this, the two terms are quite easily defined:

- A **modal** dialog is one that appears atop another window and prevents the user from clicking that window until the dialog is dismissed.

- A **blocking** dialog is one that causes code execution to stop at the very line that caused the dialog to appear. This means that, once the dialog is dismissed, execution continues from that line of code. This can be thought of as a synchronous dialog. Blocking dialogs are simpler to work with, as developers can retrieve a return value from the dialog and continue execution without needing to rely on listeners and callbacks.

In JavaFX, by default all dialogs are modal, but it is possible to be non-modal by using the initModality(Modality) method on Dialog. For blocking, this is up to the developer – they may choose to call showAndWait() for blocking and show() for non-blocking dialogs.

Alert

The Alert class is the simplest option for developers who simply want to display a dialog to the user. There are a number of pre-built options with varying icons and default buttons. Creating an alert is simply a matter of calling the constructor with the desired AlertType specified. AlertType is used to configure which buttons and which graphic are shown by default. Here is a quick summary of the options:

- Confirmation: Best used to confirm that a user is sure before performing some action. Shows with a blue question mark image and "Cancel" and "OK" buttons.

- Error: Best used to inform the user that something has gone wrong. Shows a red "X" image and a single "OK" button.

- Information: Best used to inform the user of some useful information. Shows a blue "I" image (to represent "information") and a single "OK" button.

- None: This will result in no image and no buttons being set. This should rarely be used unless a custom implementation is about to be provided.

- Warning: Best used to warn the user of some fact or pending problem. Shows a yellow exclamation mark image and a single "OK" button.

In most cases, developers should simply choose the appropriate alert type from the options outlined in the preceding text and then provide the text that they wish to display to the user. Once the alert is created, it can be shown as outlined in Listing 4-27.

Listing 4-27. Creating an alert, waiting to see if the user selects the OK button, and, if so, performing an action

```
alert.showAndWait()
    .filter(response -> response == ButtonType.OK)
    .ifPresent(response -> formatSystem());
```

ChoiceDialog

ChoiceDialog is a dialog that shows a list of choices to the user, from which they can pick one item at most. In other words, this dialog will use a control such as a ChoiceBox or ComboBox (it is left as an implementation detail; a developer cannot specify their preference) to enable a user to make a selection. This selection will subsequently be returned to the developer to act on as appropriate, as shown in Listing 4-28.

Listing 4-28. Creating a ChoiceDialog with default choice of "Cat" and three choices. Dialog is modal and blocking, and if the user clicks the "OK" button, output is printed to console

```
ChoiceDialog<String> dialog = new ChoiceDialog<>("Cat", "Dog", "Cat", "Mouse");
dialog.showAndWait()
    .ifPresent(result -> log("Result is " + result));
```

The key property of the ChoiceDialog class is shown in Table 4-27.

Table 4-27. Properties of the ChoiceDialog class

Property	Type	Description
selectedItem	ReadOnlyObjectProperty<T>	The item that was selected by the user in the dialog.

TextInputDialog

TextInputDialog is similar to ChoiceDialog, except rather than allow a user to make a selection from a popup list, it instead enables a user to provide a single line of text input.

The key method for the TextInputDialog class is shown in Table 4-28 along with an example of how to create a TextInputDialog in Listing 4-29.

Table 4-28. *Methods on the TextInputDialog class*

Method	Type	Description
getEditor()	TextField	The TextField the user is shown in the dialog.

Listing 4-29. Creating a TextInputDialog. Dialog is modal and blocking, and if the user clicks the "OK" button, their input is printed to console

```
TextInputDialog dialog = new TextInputDialog ("Please enter your name");
dialog.showAndWait()
    .ifPresent(result -> log("Result is " + result));
```

Dialog and DialogPane

Dialog is the most flexible dialog option in JavaFX, enabling complete configuration of a dialog. This allows for creation of dialogs such as username/password prompts, complex forms, and similar.

When a Dialog is instantiated, developers can specify a single generic type, R, which represents the type of the result property. This is important, because it is what we as developers will receive back when the dialog is dismissed.

This may lead to the obvious question: **What should the R type be**? The answer is that it depends on what exactly is being asked of the user. In the case of a password prompt, it might be an instance of a UsernamePassword class, for example.

Because the Dialog class does not know about the content it is displaying and therefore does not know how to convert the values entered by the user into an instance of the R type, it is necessary for the developer to set the resultConverter property. This is required whenever the R type is not Void or ButtonType. If this is not heeded, developers will find that they get `ClassCastException` thrown in their code, for failure to convert from `ButtonType` via the result converter.

Once a Dialog is instantiated, the next step is to configure it. The most important properties related to creating a custom dialog are shown in Table 4-29.

Table 4-29. *Properties of the Dialog class*

Property	Type	Description
contentText	StringProperty	The main text to display.
dialogPane	ObjectProperty<DialogPane>	The root node in the `Dialog`. Contains most other properties displayed here.
graphic	ObjectProperty<Node>	The graphic to display.
headerText	StringProperty	The text to display in the header area (above the `contentText`).
result	ObjectProperty<R>	The value returned once the dialog is dismissed.
resultConverter	ObjectProperty<Callback<ButtonType, R>>	API to convert the user button click into a result.
title	StringProperty	The dialog title to display to the user.

Internally, Dialog defers all layout handling of the viewable area to an embedded DialogPane instance. In fact, many of the properties simply forward on to this DialogPane.[8] The DialogPane API provides a lot of additional functionality that is not exposed at the Dialog level, and developers can retrieve the currently installed DialogPane by calling getDialogPane() on the Dialog instance.

---

[8] Creating custom DialogPane instances is beyond the scope of this chapter, so please consider referring to the Javadocs.

Advanced Controls

The last set of controls that need to be covered are the "advanced" controls: `ListView`, `TreeView`, `TableView`, and `TreeTableView`. These controls contain the most API and also the most functionality. All four controls share a lot of common concepts, so this section will dive deeply into `ListView` (being the simplest of the four) and then discuss the other three controls at a higher level.

ListView

A `ListView` control is used to show a list of elements to a user. `ListView` is a generic class, so a `ListView<T>` is able to contain items of type T. As with most UI controls, to populate a `ListView` with items is incredibly easy – simply add elements of type T into the `items` list. The order in which elements appear in the items list will correspond to the order in which they are displayed inside the `ListView`.

Because `ListView` (as with all "advanced" controls in this section) is "virtualized," it does not pay a performance penalty as the number of elements in the list increases. This is because, behind the scenes, a `ListView` only creates enough "cells" to contain the elements in the visible area of the `ListView`. For example, if the `ListView` is tall enough to fit 20 rows, the `ListView` may choose to create 22 cells and reuse these as the user scrolls through the list.

The `ListView` control has `selectionModel` and `focusModel` properties, enabling developers to control precisely what is selected and focused on in the user interface. These concepts will be covered in more depth later in the "Selection and Focus Models" section.

Typically, a `ListView` scrolls vertically, but by changing the `orientation` property, it may also be configured to scroll horizontally. This property and other important properties are shown in Table 4-30.

Table 4-30. *Properties of the ListView class*

Property	Type	Description
cellFactory	ObjectProperty<Callback<ListView<T>, ListCell<T>>>	See the "Cells and Cell Factories" section.
editable	BooleanProperty	Whether the ListView supports editing cells.
focusModel	ObjectProperty<FocusModel<T>>	Refer to the "Selection and Focus Models" section.
items	ObjectProperty<ObservableList<T>>	The elements to show within the ListView.
orientation	ObjectProperty<Orientation>	Whether the ListView is vertical or horizontal.
placeholder	ObjectProperty<Node>	Text to display within the ListView if the items list is empty.
selectionModel	ObjectProperty<MultipleSelectionModel<T>>	Refer to the "Selection and Focus Models" section.

Cells and Cell Factories

In the advanced controls in this section (ListView, TreeView, TableView, and TreeTableView), a common aspect to their API is that they all support the concept of a "cell factory." This is similar in concept to other factories we've already covered in this chapter, such as the page factory in the Pagination control.

The purpose of a cell factory is to create cells when requested by the UI control (e.g., ListView), which leads to the question: **What exactly is a cell**? In the JavaFX sense, it is a class that extends from the javafx.scene.control.Cell class. The Cell class is Labeled, meaning it exposes all of the API discussed at the beginning of this chapter, and a cell is used to render a single "row" inside the ListView and other controls. Cells are also used for each individual "cell" inside TableView and TreeTableView.

Every cell is associated with a single data item (represented by the Cell item property). The cell is solely responsible for rendering this item. Depending on the cell type being used, the item may be represented as a string or by using some other UI control such as a CheckBox or Slider.

Cells are "stacked" inside a UI control like ListView, and as noted earlier, cell factories are used to generate these based on the needs of the control. But how then are cells updated when they are reused? There is a critical method called updateItem that is called by the UI control (e.g., ListView) whenever it is about to reuse a cell. When developers provide custom cell factories, it is this method that they must override, as it provides a hook in which a developer may, at the moment a cell is updated to contain new content, also update the presentation of the cell to better represent this new content.

Because by far the most common use case for cells is to show text to a user, this use case is specially optimized for within Cell. This is done by Cell extending from Labeled. This means that subclasses of Cell need only set the text property, rather than create a separate Label and set that within the Cell. However, for situations where something more than just plain text is called for, it is possible to place any Node in the Cell graphic property. Despite the term, a graphic can be any Node and will be fully interactive. For example, a ListCell might be configured with a Button as its graphic. Table 4-31 outlines some of the more critical properties of the Cell class.

Table 4-31. *Properties of the Cell class*

Property	Type	Description
editable	BooleanProperty	Whether the Cell instance can enter an editing state.
editing	ReadOnlyBooleanProperty	Whether the Cell is currently in an editing state.
empty	ReadyOnlyBooleanProperty	Whether the Cell has any item.
item	ObjectProperty<T>	The object the Cell is currently representing.
selected	ReadOnlyBooleanProperty	Whether the Cell has been selected by the user.

There are other use cases too. Supporting editing inside a ListView is easy – when a cell enters its "editing" state, the same updateItem method is called, and inside this code a developer can choose to check the cell's editing state, and if it is true the developer can choose to remove, for example, the text and to replace it with a TextField, allowing for custom input directly from the user.

When working with a UI control, such as ListView, developers do not use Cell directly, but rather a control-specific subclass (in the case of ListView, this would be ListCell). For the TableView and TreeTableView controls, there are in fact two cell types – TableRow/TreeTableRow and TableCell/TreeTableCell – but we will discuss this distinction later in the chapter. Despite this additional complexity, developers can console themselves in the knowledge that by and large they must simply understand the basics of the Cell class, and they will be able to create cell factories for all UI controls in much the same way. Listing 4-30 demonstrates how a developer can create a custom ListCell class.

Listing 4-30. Creating a custom ListCell subclass and overriding updateItem

```
public class ColorRectCell extends ListCell<String> {
    private final Rectangle rect = new Rectangle(100, 20);
    @Override public void updateItem(String item, boolean empty) {
        super.updateItem(item, empty);
        if (empty || item == null) {
            setGraphic(null);
        } else {
            rect.setFill(Color.web(item));
            setGraphic(rect);
        }
    }
}
```

Cell Editing

When a custom cell is to be editable, we enable support for it simply by extending the updateItem method shown in Listing 4-31 to also add checks to see if the cell is being used to represent the current editing index in the control.

For many of the common cases, there already exist a number of pre-built cell factories that support editing shipping with the core JavaFX APIs, contained within the javafx.scene.control.cell package, and discussed in more detail in the next section.

In situations where a pre-built editable cell does not exist, follow the code shown in Listing 4-31 to toggle between editing and non-editing states with ease whenever the user performs the relevant interactions to do this (normally this is double-clicking within the cell, but there are keyboard shortcuts too). Note that to enable editing, not only must the cell support editing but the ListView editable property must be set to true by the developer.

Listing 4-31. Creating a ListCell that supports editing state

```
public class EditableListCell extends ListCell<String> {
    private final TextField textField;
    public EditableListCell() {
        textField = new TextField();
        textField.addEventHandler(KeyEvent.KEY_PRESSED, e -> {
            if (e.getCode() == KeyCode.ENTER) {
                commitEdit(textField.getText());
            } else if (e.getCode() == KeyCode.ESCAPE) {
                cancelEdit();
            }
        });
        setGraphic(textField);
        setContentDisplay(ContentDisplay.TEXT_ONLY);
    }
    @Override public void updateItem(String item, boolean empty) {
        super.updateItem(item, empty);
        setText(item);
        setContentDisplay(isEditing() ?
            ContentDisplay.GRAPHIC_ONLY : ContentDisplay.TEXT_ONLY);
    }
    @Override public void startEdit() {
        super.startEdit();
        setContentDisplay(ContentDisplay.GRAPHIC_ONLY);
        textField.requestFocus();
    }
    @Override public void commitEdit(String s) {
        super.commitEdit(s);
        setContentDisplay(ContentDisplay.TEXT_ONLY);
    }
```

```
@Override public void cancelEdit() {
    super.cancelEdit();
    setContentDisplay(ContentDisplay.TEXT_ONLY);
}
}
```

Pre-built Cell Factories

As mentioned previously, JavaFX ships with a number of pre-built cell factories that make customizing ListView and others a very easy task. If you need to accept text input, there exists a TextFieldListCell class (for ListView). If you want to show progress in a TableColumn, there exists a ProgressBarTableCell (for TableView). Making use of these pre-built cell factories is a no-brainer, as they have been developed and tested in the widest array of configurations and have been developed to avoid common performance concerns. Table 4-32 summarizes all available pre-built cell factories, and Listing 4-32 demonstrates how to use one of these cell factories.

Table 4-32. *Pre-built cell factories*

Type	Supported UI Controls
CheckBox	ListView, TableView, TreeView, TreeTableView
ChoiceBox	ListView, TableView, TreeView, TreeTableView
ComboBox	ListView, TableView, TreeView, TreeTableView
ProgressBar	TableView, TreeTableView
TextField	ListView, TableView, TreeView, TreeTableView

Listing 4-32. Using a pre-built cell factory to customize the editing style of a ListView

```
ListView<String> listView = new ListView<>();
listView.setEditable(true);
listView.setCellFactory(param -> new TextFieldListCell<>());
```

TreeView

The TreeView control is the go-to control inside the JavaFX UI toolkit for displaying tree-like data structures to users, for example, for representing a file system or a corporate hierarchy. The TreeView control displays a hierarchical structure by showing "disclosure" nodes (i.e., arrows) on tree branches, allowing for them to be expanded and collapsed. When a tree branch is expanded, its children are displayed beneath the branch but with a certain amount of indentation to make it clear that the children belong to their parent.

Unlike the JavaFX ListView control, which simply exposes an items list, the TreeView control instead simply has a root property that the developer must specify. The root property is of type TreeItem<T> (where the T corresponds with the type of the TreeView instance itself, as TreeView has one generic type as well). The root property unsurprisingly represents the root element of the TreeView, from which all descendants derive. The primary properties for TreeView are shown in Table 4-33.

Table 4-33. *Properties of the TreeView class*

Property	Type	Description
cellFactory	ObjectProperty<Callback<TreeView<T>,TreeCell<T>>>	Cell factory used for creating all cells.
editable	BooleanProperty	Whether the TreeView is able to enter editing state.
editingItem	ReadOnlyObjectProperty<TreeItem<T>>	The TreeItem currently being edited.
expandedItemCount	ReadOnlyIntegerProperty	The total number of tree nodes able to be visible in the TreeView.
focusModel	ObjectProperty<FocusModel<TreeItem<T>>>	Refer to the "Selection and Focus Models" section.
root	ObjectProperty<TreeItem<T>>	The root tree item in the TreeView.

(continued)

Table 4-33. (*continued*)

Property	Type	Description
selectionModel	ObjectProperty<MultipleSelection Model<TreeItem<T>>>	Refer to the "Selection and Focus Models" section.
showRoot	BooleanProperty	Whether the root is shown or not. If not, all children of the root will be shown as root elements.

TreeItem is a relatively simple class and behaves in a similar manner to MenuItem, discussed earlier, in that it is not a class that extends from Control or even Node. It is purely a model class used to represent the abstract concept of a tree item (either a branch, with children of its own, or a leaf, with no children). The properties of TreeItem are shown in Table 4-34.

Table 4-34. *Properties of the TreeItem class*

Property	Type	Description
expanded	BooleanProperty	Whether this TreeItem is expanded or collapsed.
graphic	ObjectProperty<Node>	The graphic to show beside any text or other representation.
leaf	ReadOnlyBooleanProperty	Whether this TreeItem is a leaf node or has children.
parent	ReadOnlyObjectProperty<T reeItem<T>>	The parent TreeItem of this TreeItem, or null if it is the root.
value	ObjectProperty<T>	The value of the TreeItem – this is what will be rendered in the cell of the TreeView/TreeTableView control.

TableView

TableView, as the name implies, enables developers to display tabular data to users. This control, therefore, can be thought of as a ListView with support for multiple columns of data, rather than the single column in a ListView. With this comes a vast array of additional functionality: columns may be sorted, reordered, resized, and nested, individual columns may have custom cell factories installed, resize policies can be set to control how columns have available space distributed to them, and so much more. The primary properties of TableView are shown in Table 4-35.

TableView has a single generic type, S, which is used to specify the value of the elements allowed in the items list. Each element in this list represents the backing object for one entire row in the TableView. For example, if the TableView was to show Person objects, then we would define a TableView<Person> and add all the relevant people into the items list.

The fact that TableView has an items list is sometimes surprising to developers, as it leads to the question: How are these items transformed into the values required to be displayed in each "cell" of the TableView (e.g., suppose our TableView had columns to display a person's first name, last name, and email address)? The answer is that this is the responsibility of each TableColumn instance created by the developer, and therefore in this case we would expect a developer to create three TableColumn instances, one each for first name, last name, and email address.

Table 4-35. *Properties of the TableView class*

Property	Type	Description
columnResizePolicy	ObjectProperty<Callback <ResizeFeatures, Boolean>>	This handles redistributing column space when columns are resized or the table is resized.
comparator	ReadOnlyObjectProperty<Comp arator<S>>	The current comparator based on the table columns in the sortOrder list.
editable	BooleanProperty	Whether the TableView is able to enter editing state.
editingCell	ReadOnlyObjectProperty<Tabl ePosition<S,?>>	The position of any cell that is currently being edited.
focusModel	ObjectProperty<TableViewFoc usModel<S>>	Refer to the "Selection and Focus Models" section.

(continued)

Table 4-35. (*continued*)

Property	Type	Description
items	ObjectProperty<ObservableList<S>>	The elements to show within the TableView.
placeholder	ObjectProperty<Node>	Text to display within the TableView if the items list is empty.
rowFactory	ObjectProperty<Callback<TableView<S>,TableRow<S>>>	The rowFactory is responsible for creating an entire row of TableCells (for all columns).
selectionModel	ObjectProperty<TableViewSelectionModel<S>>	Refer to the "Selection and Focus Models" section.
sortPolicy	ObjectProperty<Callback<TableView<S>,Boolean>>	Specifies how sorting should be performed.
tableMenuButtonVisible	BooleanProperty	Specifies whether a menu button should show in the top right of TableView.

TableColumn and TreeTableColumn

TableColumn exists in the set of classes in JavaFX UI controls that do not extend from Control (previous examples we've discussed include MenuItem, Menu, and TreeItem). TableColumn extends from TableColumnBase, and as TreeTableView has similar (but not fully identical) API, this therefore necessitated the creation of TreeTableColumn. Despite the need for different classes for TableView and TreeTableView, there is still significant overlap, which is why most API is on TableColumnBase. The key properties for TableColumnBase are shown in Table 4-36.

Table 4-36. *Properties of the TableColumnBase class*

Property	Type	Description
comparator	ObjectProperty<Comparator<T>>	The comparator to use when this column is part of the table sortOrder list.
editable	BooleanProperty	Specifies if this column supports editing.
graphic	ObjectProperty<Node>	Graphic to show in the column header area.
parentColumn	ReadOnlyObjectProperty<TableColumnBase<S,?>>	Refer to the "Nested Columns" section.
resizable	BooleanProperty	Whether the width of the column can be changed by the user.
sortable	BooleanProperty	Whether the column can be sorted by the user.
sortNode	ObjectProperty<Node>	The "sort arrow" to show when the column is part of the sort order list.
text	StringProperty	The text to display in the column header area.
visible	BooleanProperty	Whether the column shows to the user or not.
width	ReadOnlyDoubleProperty	The width of the column.

TableColumn is a generic class with two generic types, S and T, where S is the same type as the TableView generic type and T is the type for the values that will be used in the specific column that the TableColumn represents.

When creating a `TableColumn` instance, the two most important properties to set are the column `text` property (what to show in the column header area) and the column `cellValueFactory` property (which is used to populate individual cells in the column).[9]

TableColumn is obviously designed for use with TableView, but it may surprise some of you that it is not able to be used with TreeTableView (which is covered in more detail soon). This is because TableColumn makes some API assumptions that tie it directly to the TableView API. As such, another class, called TreeTableColumn, is used in conjunction with TreeTableView, to much the same effect. For the most part, the API that we care about is interchangeable, so Table 4-37 introduces these APIs for TableColumn, but rest assured that TreeTableView API exists in much the same form.

***Table 4-37.** Properties of the TableColumn and TreeTableColumn classes*

Property	Type	Description
cellFactory	ObjectProperty<Callback<TableColumn <S,T>,TableCell<S,T>>>	Cell factory for all cells in this table column.
cellValueFactory	ObjectProperty<Callback<CellDataFea tures<S,T>,ObservableValue<T>>>	The cell value factory for all cells in this table column.
sortType	ObjectProperty<SortType>	Specifies, when this column is part of the sort, whether it should be ascending or descending.

---

[9] It's important to note that a cell value factory, responsible for extracting the raw data from a backing row object for a given column, is very different from a cell factory, responsible for displaying the data in a human-presentable form. To avoid confusion, please be discerning when reading this section to note whether a cell value factory or cell factory is being discussed.

Listing 4-33. Code required to create a TableColumn and specify a cell value factory

```
ObservableList<Person> data = ...
TableView<Person> tableView = new TableView<Person>(data);
TableColumn<Person,String> firstNameCol = new TableColumn<Person,String>
("First Name");
firstNameCol.setCellValueFactory(new Callback<CellDataFeatures<Person,
String>, ObservableValue<String>>() {
    public ObservableValue<String> call(CellDataFeatures<Person, String> p) {

// p.getValue() returns the Person instance for a particular TableView row
        return p.getValue().firstNameProperty();
    }
});
tableView.getColumns().add(firstNameCol);
```

The approach in Listing 4-33 assumes that the object returned from `p.getValue()` has a JavaFX `ObservableValue` that can simply be returned. The benefit of this is that the `TableView` will internally create bindings to ensure that, should the returned `ObservableValue` change, the cell contents will be automatically refreshed.

There is a more succinct option available – it makes use of reflection to achieve the same effect, without the need to write the preceding code. This is demonstrated in Listing 4-34 where we use the `PropertyValueFactory` class and pass in the name of the property that we wish to observe (in this case "firstName"). Internally, JavaFX will try to find a property method titled `firstNameProperty()` and, if it finds it, will bind to it. If it does not find it, it will look for `getFirstName()` and display the returned value (without binding, obviously).

Listing 4-34. Example of using PropertyValueFactory

```
TableColumn<Person,String> firstNameCol = new TableColumn<Person,String>
("First Name");
firstNameCol.setCellValueFactory(new PropertyValueFactory("firstName"));
```

In situations where a `TableColumn` must interact with classes created before JavaFX or that generally do not wish to use the JavaFX API for properties, it is possible to wrap the returned value in a `ReadOnlyObjectWrapper` instance. See Listing 4-35 for an example.

Listing 4-35. Wrapping non-property values for use in a JavaFX TableView

```
firstNameCol.setCellValueFactory(new Callback<CellDataFeatures<Person,
String>, ObservableValue<String>>() {
    public ObservableValue<String> call(CellDataFeatures<Person, String> p) {
        return new ReadOnlyObjectWrapper(p.getValue().getFirstName());
    }
});
```

For the `TreeTableView` control, a class similar to the PropertyValueFactory exists, called `TreeItemPropertyValueFactory`. It performs the same function as the `PropertyValueFactory` class, but it is designed to work with the `TreeItem` class that is used as part of the data model of the `TreeTableView` class.

Nested Columns

The JavaFX TableView and TreeTableView controls both have built-in support for column nesting. This means that, for example, you may have a "Name" column that contains two sub-columns, for first name and last name. The "Name" column is for the most part decorative – it isn't involved in providing a cell value factory or cell factory (this is the responsibility of the child columns), but it can be used by the user to reorder the column position and to resize all child columns.

To create nested columns is simple and demonstrated in Listing 4-36.

Listing 4-36. Creating a "Name" column with two nested child columns

```
TableColumn firstNameCol = new TableColumn("First Name");
TableColumn lastNameCol = new TableColumn("Last Name");
TableColumn nameCol = new TableColumn("Name");
nameCol.getColumns().addAll(firstNameCol, lastNameCol);
```

Cell Factories in TableView

We have already covered cell factories in the context of ListView, but cell factories in TableView (and TreeTableView) are slightly more nuanced. This is because, unlike ListView and TreeView, in the TableView and TreeTableView classes, there are two possible places where a cell factory can be placed.

Firstly, a "row factory" can be specified on the TableView and TreeTableView controls. A row factory is responsible for displaying an entire row of information, and therefore a custom row factory must take care to carefully display all columns appropriately. For this reason, row factories are very rarely created by developers.

Instead, developers tend to specify a custom cell factory on a single TableColumn (or TreeTableColumn, for the TreeTableView case). When a cell factory is set on a TableColumn, it functions in much the same way as a cell factory functions when set on a ListView – it is focused solely on representing a single cell (i.e., a column/row intersection) and not an entire row. This works well, as in most cases it is a fact that we wish to display all cells in a given column the same way, and therefore by specifying a custom cell factory on a TableColumn, we can enable this without great difficulty. In fact, the approach to writing a custom cell factory for a TableColumn is essentially exactly the same as for writing one for a ListView.

TreeTableView

Now that we have covered TreeView and TableView, we are left with covering TreeTableView, which from an API point of view takes elements of both TreeView and TableView. Therefore, to simplify the discussion and avoid repetition, this section on TreeTableView will be largely spent detailing from which of the two controls TreeTableView inherits its API.

The high-level summary of TreeTableView is that it uses the same TreeItem API as TreeView, and therefore it is required for developers to set the root node in the TreeTableView. This also means that there is no items list, such as in ListView and TableView. Similarly, the TreeTableView control makes use of the same TableColumn-based approach that the TableView control uses, except instead of using the TableView-specific TableColumn class, developers will need to use the largely equivalent TreeTableColumn class.

In terms of functionality displayed to the end user, the TreeTableView is essentially equivalent to the TableView, with the addition of the ability to expand/collapse branches and indentation of branch children when they are showing. TreeTableView has quite a few properties, which are listed in Table 4-38.

Table 4-38. *Properties of the TreeTableView class*

Property	Type	Description
columnResizePolicy	ObjectProperty<Callback<Resiz eFeatures, Boolean>>	This handles redistributing column space when columns or the table is resized.
comparator	ReadOnlyObjectProperty<Compar ator<TreeItem<S>>>	The current comparator based on the table columns in the sortOrder list.
editable	BooleanProperty	Whether the TreeTableView is able to enter editing state.
editingCell	ReadOnlyObjectProperty<TreeTa blePosition<S,?>>	The position of any cell that is currently being edited.
expandedItemCount	ReadOnlyIntegerProperty	The total number of tree nodes able to be visible in the TreeTableView.
focusModel	ObjectProperty<TreeTTableView FocusModel<S>>	Refer to the "Selection and Focus Models" section.
items	ObjectProperty<ObservableLis t<S>>	The elements to show within the TableView.
placeholder	ObjectProperty<Node>	Text to display within the TreeTableView if the items list is empty.
root	ObjectProperty<TreeItem<S>>	The root tree item in the TreeTableView.

(continued)

Table 4-38. (*continued*)

Property	Type	Description
rowFactory	ObjectProperty<Callback<TreeTableView<S>,TreeTableRow<S>>>	The rowFactory is responsible for creating an entire row of TreeTableCells (for all columns).
selectionModel	ObjectProperty<TreeTableViewSelectionModel<S>>	Refer to the "Selection and Focus Models" section.
sortPolicy	ObjectProperty<Callback<TreeTableView<S>,Boolean>>	Specifies how sorting should be performed.
tableMenuButtonVisible	BooleanProperty	Specifies whether a menu button should show in the top right of TreeTableView.
treeColumn	ObjectProperty<TreeTableColumn<S,?>>	Which column should have the disclosure node drawn within it.

Selection and Focus Models

A number of the UI controls that ship with JavaFX consistently expose selection or focus models. This abstraction makes it simpler for developers to understand all UI controls, as they offer the same API for common scenarios. The SelectionModel API is far more widely used in a number of APIs, so we will cover it first.

SelectionModel

SelectionModel is an abstract class extended with a single generic type, T, that represents the type of the selected item in the related UI control. Because SelectionModel is abstract, most use cases are typically based on one of the two provided subclasses: SingleSelectionModel and MultipleSelectionModel. As their names imply, SingleSelectionModel is used in UI controls where only a single selection can be made at a time (e.g., in TabPane, it is only ever valid to select a single Tab at a time), whereas MultipleSelectionModel supports there being multiple selections existing at the same time (e.g., multiple rows in a ListView may be selected at the same moment).

Beyond the main two properties mentioned in Table 4-39, there are a number of methods for performing selection, clearing selection, and querying whether a given index or item is currently selected.

Table 4-39. *Properties of the SelectionModel class*

Property	Type	Description
selectedIndex	ReadOnlyIntegerProperty	The currently selected cell index in the UI control.
selectedItem	ReadOnlyObjectProperty<T>	The currently selected item in the UI control.

Moving further down the inheritance hierarchy, MultipleSelectionModel introduces additional API for allowing developers to select multiple rows at once and to observe on the selectedIndices and selectedItems lists for when state changes.

The final level of inheritance is table-specific selection models (TableViewSelectionModel and TreeTableViewSelectionModel). These classes add APIs to change selection mode between row and cell selection and, when in cell selection mode, make it possible to select cells based on their row/column intersection points. They also make available a selectedCells list to listen for state changes.

FocusModel

The notion of focus in JavaFX can be a little odd when applied to UI controls, as there is an overloading of the term. In JavaFX, the more correct use of focus is related to what happens when the user "tabs" through a user interface – they are shifting focus between the various UI controls and nodes. Whichever of these elements has focus is then receptive to all other keyboard input.

Some UI controls have overloaded the term focus to also mean what could more precisely be referred to as "internal focus." The ListView, TreeView, TableView, and TreeTableView controls all have focus models to allow for programmatic manipulation and observation of this internal focus. In this regard, the focus is not on a Node, but rather on an element inside the UI control, and we do not concern ourselves with the Node, but the value (of type T) in that row (as well as the index position of that row).

In many regards, a FocusModel can be considered quite similar to a SingleSelectionModel in that there can only ever be one focused element, and this is what makes the API for FocusModel simpler than for the more common MultipleSelectionModel we've already discussed. The two main properties of FocusModel are shown in Table 4-40.

Table 4-40. *Properties of the FocusModel class*

Property	Type	Description
focusedIndex	ReadOnlyIntegerProperty	The currently focused cell index in the UI control.
focusedItem	ReadOnlyObjectProperty<T>	The currently focused item in the UI control.

Summary

This chapter has methodically stepped through all UI controls that ship as part of JavaFX 17. You should now feel that you have sufficient knowledge to more easily create user interfaces consisting of appropriate UI controls.

As noted at the beginning of this chapter, there is a companion application available with the source code samples for this book that demonstrates all UI controls that are available as part of the core JavaFX distribution. You are encouraged to execute this application to become more familiar with how each UI control operates and to also better see how to use the UI control in your own development.

Acknowledgments

The companion application that was developed for this chapter could not have been fully realized without contributions from members of the JavaFX community. I would therefore like to take the opportunity to thank the following people: Abhinay Agarwal, Fouad Almalki, Almas Baimagambetov, Frank Delporte, Cyril Fischer, and Hossein Rimaz. Thanks!

Additionally, this chapter was expertly reviewed by Abhinay Agarwal. Thanks!

CHAPTER 5

Mastering Visual and CSS Design

Written by Eugene Ryzhikov

Cascading Style Sheets or CSS is a stylesheet language that was created to describe the presentation of a document written in XML and its dialects such as HTML, SVG, and MathML. It became a de facto standard in web development for describing all of the presentation aspects of the web pages or web applications. It is one of the core languages of the open Web and is standardized across browsers according to the W3C specification.

So it was only natural that such a mature presentation language was implemented as part of JavaFX to simplify the description of all the presentation aspects of the framework such as fonts, colors, padding, effects, and so on.

In this chapter, we will cover the following topics:

- Introduction to Cascading Style Sheets in JavaFX

- Applying CSS techniques

- Advanced CSS API

- Benefits of using CSS in your JavaFX application

Introduction to Cascading Style Sheets

At the most basic level, CSS has only two building blocks, as shown in Figure 5-1:

Properties: Identifiers, which indicate a feature (font, color, etc.)

Values: Each property has a value, which indicates how the feature, described by the property, has to change.

S. Chin et al., *The Definitive Guide to Modern Java Clients with JavaFX 17*,
https://doi.org/10.1007/978-1-4842-7268-8_5

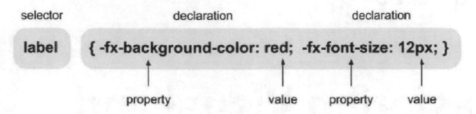

Figure 5-1. Properties and values, the building blocks of CSS

The pair of a property and a value is called a *CSS declaration*. CSS declarations exist within *CSS declaration blocks*, which in turn are paired with **selectors**. The pairs of *selectors* and declaration blocks produce *CSS rulesets* (or simply rules).

The JavaFX dialect of CSS uses the -**fx** prefix for the properties to clearly distinguish them from web ones and avoid any compatibility issues, since many of them share the same names. Here is how such stylesheet may look:

```
/* resources/chapterX/introduction/styles.css */
.root {
    -fx-background-color: white;
    -fx-padding: 20px;
}
.label {
    -fx-background-color: black;
    -fx-text-fill: white;
    -fx-padding: 10px;
}
```

The *.root* selector refers to the root of the scene, and the .label selector refers to an instance of the Label class. This is as simple as it can get – let's use this CSS in the small application:

```
// chapterX/introduction/HelloCSS.java
public void start(Stage primaryStage) {
    Label label = new Label("Stylized label");
    VBox root = new VBox(label);
    Scene scene = new Scene( root, 200, 100 );
    scene.getStylesheets().add(        getClass().getResource("styles.css").
    toExternalForm());
```

```
primaryStage.setTitle("My first CSS application");
primaryStage.setScene(scene);
primaryStage.show();
}
```

The key feature of the preceding code, highlighted in bold, is a part that dynamically loads the stylesheet and applies it to the application scene. Figure 5-2 shows the resulting application next to the one without styling.

As expected, the scene background color and padding are different. Also our label has a different background and text color in addition to its padding.

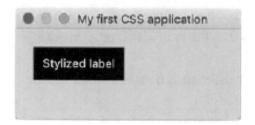
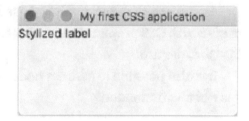

Figure 5-2. *Application with CSS styling (left) and without (right)*

A full description of JavaFX 17 CSS rules can be found in the JavaFX CSS Reference Guide at `https://openjfx.io/javadoc/17/javafx.graphics/javafx/scene/doc-files/cssref.html`. All aspects of JavaFX CSS are documented there.

Styles are applied to the nodes of the scene graph very similarly to the way CSS is applied to elements of the HTML DOM – they are first applied to the parent and then to its children. The code to do this is highly optimized and applies CSS only to the branches of the scene graph that require such changes. The nodes are only styled when they are part of the scene graph, and styles are reapplied on the following conditions:

- Change to the node's pseudo-class state, style class, ID, inline style, or parent.

- Stylesheets are added to or removed from the scene.

Selectors are responsible for matching styles to scene graph nodes and can be based on JavaFX class name, object ID, or just a style class assigned to a specific node. Let's take a look at each use case.

Selectors Based on Class Name

All the top-level JavaFX classes have their selector counterparts, with naming convention being lowercase class name, with words separated by hyphens. Special selector *.root* is reserved to style a root node of the scene. Here is an example of styling a ListView control:

```
.list-view {
    -fx-background-color: lightgrey;
    -fx-pref-width: 250px;
}
```

As you see, the same hyphen-based approach is applied to properties. Here the -fx-pref-width CSS property is automatically interpreted as the prefWidth property of a ListView control.

It is also possible to address nodes by using their short class names as selectors, but it is not recommended.

Selectors Based on Custom Style Classes

Custom style classes can also be used to style scene graph nodes. In this case, the style class has to be assigned to the node manually. Multiple style classes can be assigned to the same node:

```
/* Stylesheet */
.big-bold-text {
    -fx-font-weight: bold;
    -fx-font-size: 20pt;
}
// JavaFX code
label.getStyleClass().add("big-bold-text");
```

Selectors Based on Object ID

Sometimes there is a need to address a specific instance on the node. This is done the same way as the web CSS way by using the # symbol. The ID has to be manually assigned to the node instance that requires special styling and has to be unique in the scene graph:

```
/* Stylesheet */
#big-bold-label {
    -fx-font-weight: bold;
    -fx-font-size: 20pt;
}
// JavaFX code
label.setId("big-bold-label");
```

Applying CSS Styles

Loading CSS Stylesheets

A stylesheet is usually used as a resource in your application, and thus the Java resource API is the best way to load it. The most common way is to add resources to a "stylesheets" property of a scene:

```
// best way of loading stylesheets
  scene.getStylesheets().add(
    getClass().getResource("styles.css").toExternalForm()
  );
  // the following works, but not recommended
  // since it is prone to problems with refactoring
  scene.getStylesheets().add( "package/styles.css");
```

The preceding code loads the stylesheet as a resource from the folder, where the current class is located.

Since the CSS resource is a URL, it is also possible to load remote CSS resources:

```
// remote stylesheet
  scene.getStylesheets().add( "http://website/folder/styles.css" );
```

Note that it is also possible to apply multiple stylesheets to a scene. Those styles will be combined behind the scenes by the JavaFX CSS engine.

In many cases, it is desired to apply global stylesheets to the whole application, that is, all scenes simultaneously. This can be done by calling the Application. setUserAgentStyleSheet API. Passing null will return your application to the default stylesheet. Currently, JavaFX provides two default stylesheets, which are defined as constants:

```
// original stylesheet ( JavaFX 2 and before )
  Application.setUserAgentStylesheet( STYLESHEET_CASPIAN );
  // default stylesheet since JavaFX 8
  Application.setUserAgentStylesheet( STYLESHEET_MODENA );
```

Starting with JavaFX 8u20, it is also possible to set user agent stylesheets for the Scene and SubScene. This allows the Scene and SubScene to have styles distinct from the platform default. When a user agent is set on SubScene, its styles are used instead of the styles from the default platform or any user agent stylesheets set on the Scene.

Applying CSS Styles to JavaFX Nodes

In addition to applying the stylesheets to the whole scene, you can apply them to any node, inherited from javafx.scene.Parent. The API is exactly the same as the one of the Scene class. When you apply CSS to a specific node, it is only applied to the node itself and all the nodes in its children hierarchy.

It is also possible to style the node using its setStyle API. This approach has its own pros and cons, but, before discussing them, let's see how it works:

```
// chapterX/applying/ApplyingStyles.java
public class ApplyingStyles extends Application {
  private Label label = new Label("Stylized label");
  // Simplistic implementation of numeric field
  private TextField widthField = new TextField("250") {
      @Override
      public void replaceText(int start, int end, String text) {
          if (text.matches("[0-9]*")) {
              super.replaceText(start, end, text);
          }
      }
```

```java
    @Override
    public void replaceSelection(String replacement) {
        if (replacement.matches("[0-9]*")) {
            super.replaceSelection(replacement);
        }
    }
};
private void updateLabelStyle() {
    label.setStyle(
            "-fx-background-color: black;" +
            "-fx-text-fill: white;" +
            "-fx-padding: 10;" +
            "-fx-pref-width: " + widthField.getText() + "px;"
    );
}
@Override
public void start(Stage primaryStage) {
    updateLabelStyle();
    widthField.setOnAction( e -> updateLabelStyle());
    VBox root = new VBox(10, label, widthField);
    root.setStyle(
        "-fx-background-color: lightblue;" +
        "-fx-padding: 20px;");
    Scene scene = new Scene( root, 250, 100 );
    primaryStage.setTitle("My first CSS application");
    primaryStage.setScene(scene);
    primaryStage.show();
}
}
```

In the preceding code, styles are applied directly to the root and label controls. In the case of the root, we are applying a static style, that is, the root is always going to be of the light-blue color with the padding of 20 pixels. For the label, we chose to apply a dynamic styling, the preferred width of which comes from the value we enter into widthField. It changes as soon as we press Enter after editing the number. Figure 5-3 shows what the updated UI looks like.

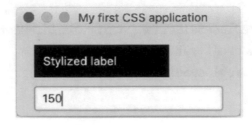

Figure 5-3. *Dynamic style update using setStyle*

This method is only recommended in cases where your styling has to be very dynamic, usually based on your own UI changes, like the preceding example. It is also very useful for quick prototyping.

In all other cases, having external CSS styles is a best choice, since they do not require code changes and thus recompilation and can be edited externally. They also have better performance characteristics.

In many cases, instead of using setStyle, it is possible to call a corresponding API method. This is where you get the ultimate performance since there is not CSS processing involved. Here is how we can replace our preceding dynamic CSS property:

```
// CSS way
  label.setStyle("-fx-pref-width: 500px");
// JavaFX API way
  label.setPrefWidth(500);
```

CSS styles can also be applied in a similar way in FXML. Any component can be styled in one of the following three ways:

- By assigning a style class defined in the external stylesheet

- By setting styles directly using the style property

- By assigning a stylesheet

```
<!-- assign a style class -->
<Label styleClass="fancy-label" />
<!-- assign a style directly -->
<Label style="-fx-pref-width: 500px" />
<!-- assign a stylesheet -->
<Label stylesheets="@styles.css" />
```

You just saw several methods of applying styles to JavaFX nodes. Even though you can apply them interchangeably, JavaFX defines the priority rules for each of them in the following sequence:

1. Apply user agent stylesheets.

2. Apply a value set by a JavaFX API call.

3. Apply styles set by the scene or node stylesheets property.

4. Apply a style from the node's style property.

As you can see, the node's style will override any previous style settings. This is a common source of confusion, but the rules are clear – if you set your style using the setStyle API, all the other methods will be ignored by JavaFX.

Advanced CSS Techniques

Using Descendant Selectors

In a way similar to a web CSS, the JavaFX CSS engine supports selectors to match styles to scene graph nodes. Since the CSS selectors are a widely known subject, we will simply show a few examples of how they are used in JavaFX CSS:

```
/* all labels */
.label,
.text {
   -fx-font-weight: bold;
   -fx-font-size: 20pt;
}
/* all children of #big-bold */
#big-bold .label {
   -fx-font-weight: bold;
   -fx-font-size: 20pt;
}
/* only direct children of #big-bold */
#big-bold > .label {
   -fx-font-weight: bold;
   -fx-font-size: 20pt;
}
```

Using Pseudo-classes

JavaFX CSS also supports pseudo-classes, which allow you to define styles corresponding to a different state of the JavaFX node. JavaFX does not implement a full range of pseudo-classes specified in the CSS standard. Instead, each Node defines a set of supported pseudo-classes, which can be found in the JavaFX CSS Reference Guide.

For example, Button supports the following pseudo-classes:

armed	Applies when the armed variable is true.
cancel	Applies if this Button receives VK_ESC if the event is not otherwise consumed.
default	Applies if this Button receives VK_ENTER if the event is not otherwise consumed.

Here is how we can take advantage of them:

```
/* all buttons will have a font size of 1.1 em */
.button {
    -fx-font-size: 1.1em;
}
/* default buttons will have bigger font size and color*/
.button:default {
    -fx-font-size: 1.2em;
    -fx-font-fill: blue;
}
```

Using Imports

Starting with JavaFX 8u20, the CSS @import rule is partially supported. Currently, only unconditional imports are allowed (media type qualifier is not supported). Also import statements should appear at the top of your stylesheet.

This feature greatly simplifies development of complex styles, allowing separation of concerns.

Styles can be imported from a local or remote stylesheet:

```
@import "styles.css"
@import url ("http://website/folder/styles.css")
```

Font Loading in the Stylesheet

Since JavaFX 8, there is also a partial support for the @font-face rule, which allows custom font loading:

```
@font-face {
    font-family: 'sample';
    font-style: normal;
    font-weight: normal;
    src: local('sample'),    url('http://font.samples/resources/sample.
    ttf';) format('truetype');
}
```

Note that remote font loading using a URL is also supported.

The font-family property defines the name, which can now be used throughout the stylesheet.

Reusing Styles

To allow for higher flexibility, JavaFX CSS supports constants – a nonstandard CSS feature. Currently, only colors can be defined as constants. Besides a lot of predefined named colors, custom constants can be defined, which in the reference guide are called "looked-up colors." With the looked-up colors, you can refer to any other color property that is set on the current node or any of its parents. This power feature allows for generic color theming in your application. The looked-up colors are "live" and react to any style changes since they are not looked up until they are applied.

Here is a simple example of this awesome feature:

```
.root { -my-button-background: #f00 }
.button { -fx-background-color: -my-button-background }
```

There is also another way of reusing styles somewhere else in the stylesheet, which is using the inherit keyword. It simply allows for child elements to reuse the styles defined in their parents:

```
.root {
    -fx-font-fill: green;
.button {
    -fx-font-size: 1.1em;
}
```

215

```
.button:default {
    -fx-font-size: 1.2em;
    -fx-font-fill: inherited;
}
```

In the preceding example, the default button will inherit the color from the root element.

Using Advanced Color Definitions

JavaFX specifies multiple ways to define paint values. Those are of the following:

- Linear gradient

- Radial gradient

- Image pattern with optional repetition

- Solid color

Using Linear Gradients

Linear gradient syntax is defined as follows:

```
linear-gradient( [ [from <point> to <point>] | [ to <side-or-corner>], ]? [
[ repeat | reflect ], ]? <color-stop>[, <color-stop>]+)
where <side-or-corner> = [left | right] || [top | bottom]
```

A linear gradient creates a gradient going through all the stop colors along the line between the "from" point and "to" point. If the points are percentages, they are relative to the size of the area being filled. Percentages and lengths cannot be mixed in a single gradient.

If neither repeat nor reflect is given, then the CycleMethod defaults to "NO_CYCLE."

If neither [from <point> to <point>] nor [to <side-or-corner>] is given, then the gradient direction defaults to "to bottom." Stops are per W3C color-stop syntax and are normalized accordingly. Here are some of the examples:

```
/*
 * gradient from top left to bottom right
 * with yellow at the top left corner and red in the bottom right
 */
```

```
-fx-text-fill: linear-gradient(to bottom right, yellow, red);
/* same as above but using percentages */
-fx-text-fill: linear-gradient(from 0% 0% to 100% 100%, yellow 0%, green
100%);
/*
  * create a 50px high bar at the top with a 3 color gradient
  * white with underneath for the rest of the filled area.
/*
-fx-text-fill: linear-gradient(from 0px 0px to 0px 50px, gray, darkgray
50%, dimgray 99%, white);
```

Using Radial Gradients

Radial gradient syntax is defined as follows:

```
radial-gradient([ focus-angle <angle>, ]? [ focus-distance <percentage>,
]? [ center <point>, ]? radius [ <length> | <percentage> ] [ [ repeat |
reflect ], ]? <color-stop>[, <color-stop>]+)
```

A radial gradient creates a gradient going through all the stop colors radiating outward from the center point to the radius. If the center point is not given, the center defaults to (0,0). Percentage values are relative to the size of the area being filled. Percentages and length sizes cannot be mixed in a single gradient function.

If neither repeat nor reflect is given, then the CycleMethod defaults to "NO_CYCLE."

Stops are per W3C color-stop syntax and are normalized accordingly:

```
-fx-text-fill: radial-gradient(radius 100%, red, darkgray, black);
-fx-text-fill: radial-gradient(focus-angle 45deg, focus-distance 20%,
center 25% 25%, radius 50%, reflect, gray, darkgray 75%, dimgray);
```

Using Image Patterns

This gives the ability to use an image pattern as paint. The following is the syntax for an image pattern:

```
image-pattern(<string>, [<size>, <size>, <size>, <size>[, <boolean>]?]?)
```

Parameters, in order, are defined as follows:

<string>	The URL of the image.
<size>	The *x* origin of the anchor rectangle.
<size>	The *y* origin of the anchor rectangle.
<size>	The width of the anchor rectangle.
<size>	The height of the anchor rectangle.
<boolean>	The proportional flag that indicates whether start and end locations are proportional or absolute.

Here are a few examples of using image patterns:

```
-fx-text-fill: image-pattern("images/wood.png");
-fx-text-fill: image-pattern("images/wood.png", 20%, 20%, 80%, 80%);
-fx-text-fill: image-pattern("images/wood.png", 20%, 20%, 80%, 80%, true);
-fx-text-fill: image-pattern("images/wood.png", 20, 20, 80, 80, false);
```

An image pattern can also be used for producing tiled image-based fills, which are an equivalent of the

```
image-pattern("images/wood.png", 0, 0, imageWith, imageHeight, false);
```

The syntax for tiled or repeating image patterns is

```
repeating-image-pattern(<string>)
```

The only parameter is the URI of the image. Here is an example of a repeating image pattern:

```
repeating-image-pattern("images/wood.png")
```

Using RGB Color Definitions

The RGB color model is used for numerical color applications. It has a number of different supported forms:

```
#<digit><digit><digit>
| #<digit><digit><digit><digit><digit><digit>
| rgb( <integer> , <integer> , <integer> )
| rgb( <integer> %, <integer>% , <integer>% )
| rgba( <integer> , <integer> , <integer> , <number> )
| rgba( <integer>% , <integer>% , <integer> %, <number> )
```

Here are examples of the different RGB formats to set the text fill for a label:

```
.label { -fx-text-fill: #f00           } /* #rgb */
.label { -fx-text-fill: #ff0000        } /* #rrggbb */
.label { -fx-text-fill: rgb(255,0,0)   }
.label { -fx-text-fill: rgb(100%, 0%, 0%) }
.label { -fx-text-fill: rgba(255,0,0,1)   }
```

As you can see, there are three types of RGB formatting:

RGB Hex	The format of an RGB value in the hexadecimal notation is a "#" immediately followed by either three or six hexadecimal characters. The three-digit RGB notation (#rgb) is converted into the six-digit form (#rrggbb) by replicating digits, not by adding zeros. For example, #fb0 expands to #ffbb00. This ensures that white (#ffffff) can be specified with the short notation (#fff) and removes any dependencies on the color depth of the display.
RGB Decimal or Percent	The format of an RGB value in the functional notation is "rgb(" followed by a comma-separated list of three numeric values (either three decimal integer values or three percentage values) followed by ")." The integer value 255 corresponds to 100% and to F or FF in the hexadecimal notation: rgb(255,255,255) = rgb(100%,100%,100%) = #FFF. White space characters are allowed around the numeric values.
RGB + Alpha	This is an extension of the RGB color model to include an "alpha" value that specifies the opacity of a color. This is accomplished via a functional syntax of the form rgba(...) that takes a fourth parameter, which is the alpha value. The alpha value must be a number between 0.0 (representing completely transparent) and 1.0 (completely opaque). As with the rgb() function, the red, green, and blue values may be decimal integers or percentages.

The following examples specify the same color:

```
.label { -fx-text-fill: rgb(255,0,0) } /* integer range 0 - 255*/
.label { -fx-text-fill: rgba(255,0,0,1) /* the same, with explicit opacity
of 1 */
.label { -fx-text-fill: rgb(100%,0%,0%) } /* float range 0.0% - 100.0% */
.label { -fx-text-fill: rgba(100%,0%,0%,1) } /* the same, with explicit
opacity of 1 */
```

Using HSB Color Definitions

Colors can also be specified using the HSB (sometimes called HSV) color model as follows:

```
hsb( <number> , <number>% , <number>% ) |
hsba( <number> , <number>% , <number>% , <number> )
```

The first number is hue, a number in the range 0–360 degrees.

The second number is saturation, a percentage in the range 0–100%.

The third number is brightness, also a percentage in the range 0–100%.

The hsba(...) form takes a fourth parameter at the end, which is an alpha value in the range 0.0–1.0, specifying completely transparent to completely opaque, respectively.

Using Color Functions

The JavaFX CSS engine provides support for some color computation functions. These functions compute new colors from input colors at the same time the color style is applied. This enables a color theme to be specified using a single based color and other variants computed from it. There are two color functions: derive and ladder.

```
derive( <color> , <number>% )
```

The derive function takes a color and computes a brighter or darker version of that color. The second parameter is the brightness offset, representing how much brighter or darker the derived color should be. Positive percentages indicate brighter colors, and negative percentages indicate darker colors. A value of –100% means completely black, 0% means no change in brightness, and 100% means completely white:

```
ladder(<color> , <color-stop> [, <color-stop>]+)
```

The ladder function interpolates between colors. The effect is as if a gradient was created using the stops provided, and then the brightness of the provided <color> is used to index a color value within that gradient. At 0% brightness, the color at the 0.0 end of the gradient is used; at 100% brightness, the color at the 1.0 end of the gradient is used; and at 50% brightness, the color at 0.5, the midway point of the gradient, is used. Note that no gradient is actually rendered. This is merely an interpolation function that results in a single color.

Stops are per W3C color-stop syntax and are normalized accordingly.

For example, you could use the following if you want the text color to be black or white depending upon the brightness of the background:

```
background: white;
-fx-text-fill: ladder(background, white 49%, black 50%);
```

The resulting -fx-text-fill value will be black, because the background (white) has a brightness of 100% and the color at 1.0 on the gradient is black. If we were to change the background color to black or dark gray, the brightness would be less than 50%, giving an -fx-text-fill value of white.

Using Effect Definitions

JavaFX CSS currently supports the DropShadow and InnerShadow effects from the JavaFX platform. See the class documentation in javafx.scene.effect for further details about the semantics of the various effect parameters.

Drop Shadow

DropShadow is a high-level effect that renders a shadow of the given content behind it:

```
dropshadow( <blur-type> , <color> , <number> , <number> , <number> ,
<number> )
```

blur-type	[gaussian | one-pass-box | three-pass-box | two-pass-box].
color	The shadow color.
number	The radius of the shadow blur kernel, in the range [0.0 ... 127.0], typical value 10.

(continued)

number	The spread of the shadow. The spread is the portion of the radius where the contribution of the source material will be 100%. The remaining portion of the radius will have a contribution controlled by the blur kernel. A spread of 0.0 will result in a distribution of the shadow determined entirely by the blur algorithm. A spread of 1.0 will result in a solid growth outward of the source material opacity to the limit of the radius with a very sharp cutoff to transparency at the radius. Values should be in the range [0.0 ... 1.0].
number	The shadow offset in the horizontal direction, in pixels.
number	The shadow offset in the vertical direction, in pixels.

Inner Shadow

Inner shadow is a high-level effect that renders a shadow inside the edges of the given content:

```
innershadow( <blur-type> , <color> , <number> , <number> , <number> ,
<number> )
```

blur-type	[gaussian	one-pass-box	three-pass-box	two-pass-box].
color	The shadow color.
number	The radius of the shadow blur kernel, in the range [0.0 ... 127.0], typical value 10.
number	The choke of the shadow. The choke is the portion of the radius where the contribution of the source material will be 100%. The remaining portion of the radius will have a contribution controlled by the blur kernel. A choke of 0.0 will result in a distribution of the shadow determined entirely by the blur algorithm. A choke of 1.0 will result in a solid growth inward of the shadow from the edges to the limit of the radius with a very sharp cutoff to transparency inside the radius. Values should be in the range [0.0 ... 1.0].
number	The shadow offset in the horizontal direction, in pixels.
number	The shadow offset in the vertical direction, in pixels.

Useful Tips and Tricks

Study the Modena Stylesheet

As was discussed before, Modena is the default user agent stylesheet introduced with JavaFX 8.

It contains a trove of useful definitions and should be studied by anyone who wishes to use CSS styling in JavaFX applications.

Define Themes Based on Modena

Modena stylesheet color definitions are based on few attributes, which you can find in its root section. The most important one is -fx-base, which is the based colors for all the objects:

```
.root {
    /*************************************************************************
     *                                           *
     * The main color palette from which the rest of the colors are
       derived.   *
     *                                           *
     *************************************************************************/
    /* A light grey that is the base color for objects.  Instead of using
     * -fx-base directly, the sections in this file will typically use -fx-
       color.
     */
    -fx-base: #ececec;
    /* A very light grey used for the background of windows.  See also
     * -fx-text-background-color, which should be used as the -fx-text-fill
     * value for text painted on top of backgrounds colored with -fx-
       background.
     */
    -fx-background: derive(-fx-base,26.4%);
    /* Used for the inside of text boxes, password boxes, lists, trees, and
     * tables.  See also -fx-text-inner-color, which should be used as the
     * -fx-text-fill value for text painted on top of backgrounds colored
     * with -fx-control-inner-background.
```

```
      */
    -fx-control-inner-background: derive(-fx-base,80%);
    /* Version of -fx-control-inner-background for alternative rows */
    -fx-control-inner-background-alt: derive(-fx-control-inner-
    background,-2%);
    ....
}
```

This allows us to easily redefine the overall color theme of our stylesheet. For example, create a theme, which closely resembles the famous IntelliJ IDEA "Darcula" theme:

```
.root {
    -fx-base: rgba(60, 63, 65, 255);
}
```

Not only does it set all appropriate object colors but the text color is presented correctly too since the Modena stylesheet uses the ladder method to compute an appropriate contrasting color.

Define Icons Using CSS

Instead of loading and assigning images using Java code, we can do it much simpler using CSS definitions. Let's look at the example of the label, which is given the style class of "image-label":

```
.image-label {
  -fx-graphic: url("icon.jpg");
}
```

Using a URL, we simply assign the appropriate resource the -fx-graphic property. This removes unnecessary styling code from our application while giving a clean separation between styling and the code.

CSS Reusability by Using Color Constants

As we discussed previously, the JavaFX CSS engine supports a nonstandard feature, called color constants. Those constants can only be defined in the root section of your stylesheet, but then can be reused throughout your application. This not only promotes the great reusability but gives your application a nice consistent look.

Using Transparent Colors

In many cases, the design of the application calls for use of specific colors with full control of the background ones. For example, you are styling your custom control, but have no idea where it will be used. You want to style it in such a way that your control's colors blend nicely with any background. Color opacity to the rescue!

Let's see how such technique allows us to blend the colors.

Figure 5-4. *Blending colors using opacity*

In Figure 5-4, you can see how transparent colors are nicely blending with practically any background. In contrast, colors with 100% opacity do not blend and often look out of place.

To appreciate such a design, let's take a look at Trello Boards.

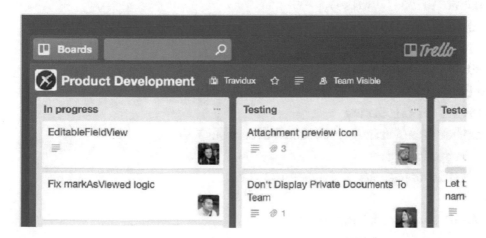

Figure 5-5. *Trello Boards user interface leveraging advanced CSS styling*

In Figure 5-5, you can see how buttons, search fields, and even boards themselves nicely blend with any background chosen by the user.

Advanced CSS API

It is possible to extend standard JavaFX CSS with new custom style classes, properties, and pseudo-classes. Those techniques are especially useful while developing new custom controls and require thorough understanding of the CSS API.

To illustrate the features of the JavaFX CSS API, we will create a simple custom control. This control will represent the weather type, showing associated icon and text. For simplicity, we will extend this control from the standard JavaFX label. In addition, we will also add a custom pseudo style to represent a dangerous type of weather, which will allow us to style the types differently.

First, we define the enums, representing the types of weather we care about. Since we will show our icons using icon font called "Weather Icons Regular," we will pass related font characters into each enum. An additional enum parameter will allow us to define which weather is dangerous:

```
// chapterX/cssapi/WeatherType.java
import javafx.scene.text.Text;

public enum WeatherType {

    SUNNY("\uf00d", false),
    CLOUDY("\uf013", false),
    RAIN("\uf019", false),
    THUNDERSTORM("\uf033", true);
    private final boolean dangerous;
    private final String c;
    WeatherType(String c, boolean dangerous) {
        this.c = c;
        this.dangerous = dangerous;
    }
    public boolean isDangerous() {
        return dangerous;
    }
```

```
Text buildGraphic() {
    Text text = new Text(c);
    text.setStyle("-fx-font-family: 'Weather Icons Regular'; -fx-font-
    size: 25;");
    return text;
    }
}
```

The icons will be represented by the text control. Our icon's characters will be set as text. We will also style it, making sure that it uses an appropriate font family and size. The method buildGraphic will build the text control for a specific enum.

Time to build our custom control!

First, we want to define constants representing our control's style class, weather property, and new pseudo-class:

```
private static final String STYLE_CLASS       = "weather-icon";
private static final String WEATHER_PROP_NAME = "-fx-weather";
private static final String PSEUDO_CLASS_NAME = "dangerous";
```

Next, we will define our styleable property. This is a special type of property, which can be styled from CSS. This property will take the value of our WeatherType and will change the icon and text of our control appropriately:

```
private StyleableObjectProperty<WeatherType> weatherTypeProperty = new Style
ableObjectProperty<>(WeatherType.SUNNY) {
        @Override
        public CssMetaData<? extends Styleable, WeatherType>
        getCssMetaData() {
            return WEATHER_TYPE_METADATA;
        }
        @Override
        public Object getBean() {
            return WeatherIcon.this;
        }
        @Override
        public String getName() {
            return WEATHER_PROP_NAME;
        }
```

```
        @Override
        protected void invalidated() {
            WeatherType weatherType = get();
            dangerous.set( weatherType.isDangerous());
            setGraphic(weatherType.buildGraphic());
            setText(get().toString());
        }
    };
```

Since the value of our property is of enum type, we are using `StyleableObjectP roperty<WeatherType>`. The implementation of the invalidate method defines what happens when our property changes. Here we use the newly instantiated weather type to set the graphic and text of our control. We also set the pseudo-class here, which will be described later.

The property also returns something called `WEATHER_TYPE_METADATA`. In JavaFX, a `CssMetaData` instance provides information about the CSS style and the hooks that allow CSS to set a property value. It encapsulates the CSS property name, the type into which the CSS value is converted, and the default value of the property.

`CssMetaData` is the bridge between a value that can be represented syntactically in a .css file and a `StyleableProperty`. There is a one-to-one correspondence between a CssMetaData and a `StyleableProperty`. Typically, the `CssMetaData` of a Node will include the `CssMetaData` of its ancestors.

To greatly reduce the amount of boilerplate code needed to implement the StyleableProperty and `CssMetaData`, we will use the `StyledPropertyFactory` class. This class defines a lot of methods to create instances of `StyleableProperty` with corresponding `CssMetaData`:

```
private static final StyleablePropertyFactory<WeatherIcon> STYLEABLE_
PROPERTY_FACTORY = new
            StyleablePropertyFactory<>(Region.getClassCssMetaData());
   private static CssMetaData<WeatherIcon, WeatherType> WEATHER_TYPE_
   METADATA =
           STYLEABLE_PROPERTY_FACTORY.createEnumCssMetaData(
                   WeatherType.class, WEATHER_PROP_NAME, x ->
                   x.weatherTypeProperty);
@Override
```

```java
public List<CssMetaData<? extends Styleable, ?>> getControlCss
MetaData() {
    return List.of(WEATHER_TYPE_METADATA);
}
```

We also implement the getControlCssMetaData method, which allows the JavaFX CSS engine to know everything about the control's CSS metadata by returning a list of control styleable properties.

What is left is to implement our pseudo-class. Since we have only two states in our control, dangerous and normal, we can implement our pseudo-class as a Boolean property. Whenever the property changes, we call a special method pseudoClassStateChanged to let the CSS engine know that the state has changed:

```java
private BooleanProperty dangerous = new BooleanPropertyBase(false) {
    public void invalidated() {
        pseudoClassStateChanged(DANGEROUS_PSEUDO_CLASS, get());
    }
    @Override public Object getBean() {
        return WeatherIcon.this;
    }
    @Override public String getName() {
        return PSEUDO_CLASS_NAME;
    }
};
```

There are only few cosmetic changes left now. Let's see the full state of our control:

```java
// chapterX/cssapi/WeatherIcon.java
public class WeatherIcon extends Label {
    private static final String STYLE_CLASS       = "weather-icon";
    private static final String WEATHER_PROP_NAME = "-fx-weather";
    private static final String PSEUDO_CLASS_NAME = "dangerous";

    private static PseudoClass DANGEROUS_PSEUDO_CLASS = PseudoClass.
    getPseudoClass(PSEUDO_CLASS_NAME);

    private static final StyleablePropertyFactory<WeatherIcon> STYLEABLE_
    PROPERTY_FACTORY =
            new StyleablePropertyFactory<>(Region.getClassCssMetaData());
```

```java
    private static CssMetaData<WeatherIcon, WeatherType> WEATHER_TYPE_
    METADATA =
            STYLEABLE_PROPERTY_FACTORY.createEnumCssMetaData(
                    WeatherType.class, WEATHER_PROP_NAME, x ->
                    x.weatherTypeProperty);
    public WeatherIcon() {
        getStyleClass().setAll(STYLE_CLASS);
    }

    public WeatherIcon(WeatherType weatherType ) {
        this();
        setWeather( weatherType);
    }
    private BooleanProperty dangerous = new BooleanPropertyBase(false) {
        public void invalidated() {
            pseudoClassStateChanged(DANGEROUS_PSEUDO_CLASS, get());
        }
        @Override public Object getBean() {
            return WeatherIcon.this;
        }
        @Override public String getName() {
            return PSEUDO_CLASS_NAME;
        }
    };

    private StyleableObjectProperty<WeatherType> weatherTypeProperty = new
    StyleableObjectProperty<>(WeatherType.SUNNY) {

        @Override
        public CssMetaData<? extends Styleable, WeatherType>
        getCssMetaData() {
            return WEATHER_TYPE_METADATA;
        }
        @Override
        public Object getBean() {
            return WeatherIcon.this;
        }
```

```java
    @Override
    public String getName() {
        return WEATHER_PROP_NAME;
    }
    @Override
    protected void invalidated() {
        WeatherType weatherType = get();
        dangerous.set( weatherType.isDangerous());
        setGraphic(weatherType.buildGraphic());
        setText(get().toString());
    }
};
@Override

public List<CssMetaData<? extends Styleable, ?>> getControlCss
MetaData() {
    return List.of(WEATHER_TYPE_METADATA);
}
public WeatherType weatherProperty() {
    return weatherTypeProperty.get();
}
public void setWeather(WeatherType weather) {
    this.weatherTypeProperty.set(weather);
}
public WeatherType getWeather() {
    return weatherTypeProperty.get();
}
}
```

Let's test the control by creating a small application that creates the control in various different states, which set our weather type using CSS as well as Java code.

First, let's define our CSS:

```css
/* resources/chapterX/cssapi/styles.css */
@font-face {
    font-family: 'Weather Icons Regular';
    src: url('weathericons-regular-webfont.ttf');
}
```

```css
.root {
    -fx-background-color: lightblue;
    -fx-padding: 20px;
}
.thunderstorm {
    -fx-weather: THUNDERSTORM;
}
.rain {
    -fx-weather: RAIN;
}
.weather-icon {
    -fx-graphic-text-gap: 30;
    -fx-padding: 10;
}
.weather-icon:dangerous {
    -fx-background-color: rgba(255, 0, 0, 0.25);
}
```

- We load our font first. JavaFX requires the font resource to be in the same location where the CSS file is located.

- Define the root styles.

- Define two custom style classes, .thunderstorm and .rain. They set the weather type accordingly.

- Define styles for both states: normal and dangerous. Dangerous state is shown with a reddish background.

Our test application is almost trivial. We create several WeatherIcon controls setting weather type using CSS style classes or code. We then present them using vertical layout (VBox):

```java
/* chapterX/cssapi/WeatherApp.java */
public class WeatherApp extends Application {
    @Override
    public void start(Stage primaryStage)  {
        WeatherIcon rain = new WeatherIcon();
        rain.getStyleClass().add("rain");
```

```
WeatherIcon thunderstorm = new WeatherIcon();
thunderstorm.getStyleClass().add("thunderstorm");
WeatherIcon clouds = new WeatherIcon( WeatherType.CLOUDY);
VBox root = new VBox(10, rain, thunderstorm, clouds);
root.setAlignment(Pos.CENTER);
Scene scene = new Scene( root);
scene.getStylesheets().add( getClass().getResource("styles.css").
toExternalForm());
primaryStage.setTitle("WeatherType Application");
primaryStage.setScene(scene);
primaryStage.show();
    }
}
```

As you can see in Figure 5-6, the "dangerous" thunderstorm weather is highlighted with red background, while the rest of the weather icons are not.

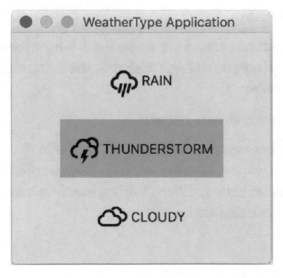

Figure 5-6. *WeatherType application using pseudo-classes for dynamic style updates*

In this example, we chose to change the pseudo-class automatically, as soon as the weather type changed. It is very much possible to expose the pseudo-class property as public, which will give us a way to change it independently from the weather type.

We have shown a very powerful way to extend JavaFX CSS with additional style classes, styleable properties, and pseudo-classes to represent additional component states using advanced JavaFX CSS APIs.

CSS in JavaFX Applications: Summary

Overall, having the ability of styling the UI using CSS stylesheets is a huge leap forward. It brings the following benefits:

- **Division of responsibilities**

  The code and styling are clearly separated and can be updated independently.

- **Greater design consistency**

  CSS stylesheets can easily be reused, giving developers greater design consistency.

- **Lightweight code**

  Since the code is separate from the styling, it is not overloaded with parts that only do styling, which provides for much more lightweight code.

- **Ability to quickly change styling**

  Styling can be changed by simply switching a few definitions in the stylesheet without touching any code. It is also possible to easily provide an entirely different styling based on hardware platform or operating system.

CHAPTER 6

High-Performance Graphics

Written by William Antônio Siqueira

JavaFX is a complete platform for creating rich user interfaces. It has a complete set of controls for use and allows developers to style their applications using CSS. Among all the controls provided by JavaFX, we have the powerful Canvas. Using Canvas, we can create visually impressive graphics applications that make use of JavaFX hardware acceleration graphics. In this chapter, we will explore Canvas capabilities to create dynamic graphics applications using known algorithms and techniques.

Imagine that you were given the task of creating a JavaFX game. You may achieve it using the standard control APIs, but controls are not suitable for it. The same applies if you have to build a simulation or some other kind of application that requires continuous update of the screen. For such cases, we usually use Canvas.

Canvas from the JavaFX API resembles ones from other platforms and programming languages, and since it is Java, we can port it to mobile and embedded devices and make use of JavaFX hardware acceleration. Another great advantage of being part of a Java library is that we could use the infinite number of APIs available to retrieve information that later could be displayed on a canvas, for example, to access a remote service or a database to retrieve data that can be displayed in a unique way using Canvas.

Just like a Button or a Label, javafx.scene.canvas.Canvas is a subclass of Node, which means that it can be added to the JavaFX scene graph and have transformation, event listeners, and effects applied to it. To use Canvas, however, we need another class, GraphicsContext, where all the magic happens. From GraphicsContext, we have access to all the methods to draw on a canvas to build our application. Currently, JavaFX only supports a 2D graphics context, but that's enough to create high-performance graphics.

© Stephen Chin, Johan Vos and James Weaver 2022
S. Chin et al., *The Definitive Guide to Modern Java Clients with JavaFX 17*,
https://doi.org/10.1007/978-1-4842-7268-8_6

Using Canvas

To get started with Canvas, let's draw a few simple geometric forms and a text. In Listing 6-1, you can see a small application that makes use of GraphicsContext to draw simple forms and a text.

Listing 6-1. Hello Canvas application

```java
import javafx.application.Application;
import javafx.scene.Scene;
import javafx.scene.canvas.Canvas;
import javafx.scene.canvas.GraphicsContext;
import javafx.scene.layout.StackPane;
import javafx.scene.paint.Color;
import javafx.scene.text.Font;
import javafx.scene.text.TextAlignment;
import javafx.stage.Stage;
public class HelloCanvas extends Application {
        private static final String MSG = "JavaFX Rocks!";
        private static final int WIDTH = 800;
        private static final int HEIGHT = 600;
        public static void main(String[] args) {
                launch();
        }
        @Override
        public void start(Stage stage) throws Exception {
                Canvas canvas = new Canvas(800, 600);
                GraphicsContext gc = canvas.getGraphicsContext2D();
                gc.setFill(Color.WHITESMOKE);
                gc.fillRect(0, 0, WIDTH, HEIGHT);
                gc.setFill(Color.DARKBLUE);
                gc.fillRoundRect(100, 200, WIDTH - 200, 180, 90, 90);
                gc.setTextAlign(TextAlignment.CENTER);
```

```
gc.setFont(Font.font(60));
gc.setFill(Color.LIGHTBLUE);
 gc.fillText(MSG, WIDTH / 2, HEIGHT / 2);
gc.setStroke(Color.BLUE);
gc.strokeText(MSG, WIDTH / 2, HEIGHT / 2);
stage.setScene(new Scene(new StackPane(canvas), WIDTH,
HEIGHT));
stage.setTitle("Hello Canvas");
stage.show();
    }
}
```

As already mentioned, the javafx.scene.canvas.GraphicsContext class is used to instruct what will be drawn on the canvas, and with it we can fill a geometric form using, for example, fillRect and fillOval. To select the color that will be used to fill the geometric forms, we use the method setFill, which accepts objects of type Paint. Color is a subclass of Paint, and it has built-in colors for our use, so we don't have to select the actual color red, green, and blue values. We can pick some of the available colors. Like setFill, we also have the possibility to stroke geometric forms and text using methods like strokeRect and strokeOval, and to set the stroke color, we can use setStroke. Changing the stroke and the fill is like using a brush with a color palette, where you have to first paint the brush with the desired color before making the actual drawing or painting. The result of this application is shown in Figure 6-1.

Figure 6-1. *A simple Canvas application that draws a rectangle and a text*

When we draw something, we must also provide its x and y position, which is similar to what is done when we have to trace functions in a Cartesian coordinate system. It is important to get familiar with how Canvas sees x and y positions to be able to correctly write forms, and it basically starts considering y from the upper-left corner. For x, it is the same; however, a higher y means that the element you are drawing will be close to the bottom of the application. With the code from Listing 6-2, we can generate the application from Figure 6-2 that shows various x,y coordinates in a canvas. Inside a nested for loop, we stroke rectangles and also paint small ovals with texts to display each x,y point. Notice how we have to change the fill to white before drawing the text and then we select the color red to draw the oval.

Listing 6-2. Drawing x,y coordinates

```
Canvas canvas = new Canvas(WIDTH, HEIGHT);
GraphicsContext gc = canvas.getGraphicsContext2D();
gc.setFont(Font.font(12));
gc.setFill(Color.BLACK);
gc.fillRect(0, 0, WIDTH, HEIGHT);
gc.setStroke(Color.LIGHTGRAY);
for (int i = 0; i < WIDTH; i+=RECT_S) {
        for (int j = 0; j < HEIGHT; j+=RECT_S) {
                gc.strokeRect(i, j, RECT_S, RECT_S);
                gc.setFill(Color.WHITE);
                gc.fillText("x=" + i + ",y=" + j, i + 2, j + 12);
                gc.setFill(Color.RED);
                gc.fillOval(i - 4, j - 4, 8, 8);
        }
}
```

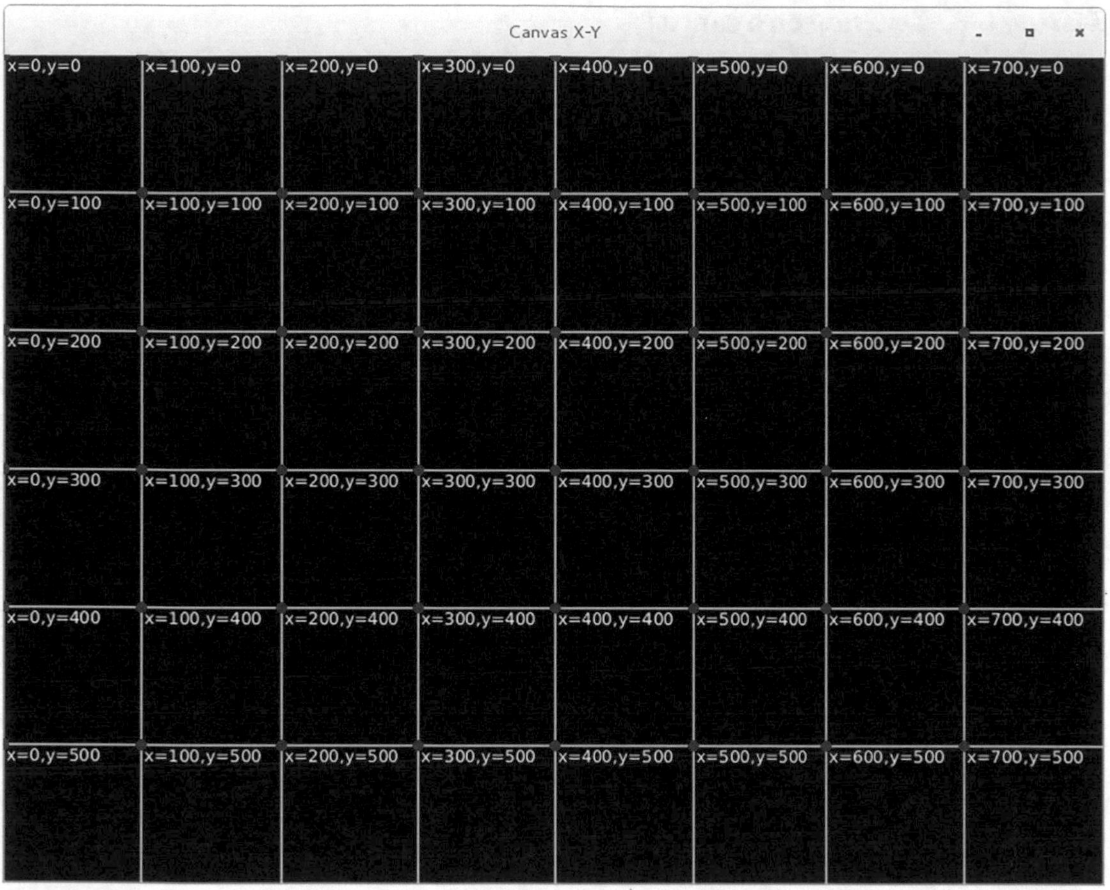

Canvas X-Y							
x=0,y=0	x=100,y=0	x=200,y=0	x=300,y=0	x=400,y=0	x=500,y=0	x=600,y=0	x=700,y=0
x=0,y=100	x=100,y=100	x=200,y=100	x=300,y=100	x=400,y=100	x=500,y=100	x=600,y=100	x=700,y=100
x=0,y=200	x=100,y=200	x=200,y=200	x=300,y=200	x=400,y=200	x=500,y=200	x=600,y=200	x=700,y=200
x=0,y=300	x=100,y=300	x=200,y=300	x=300,y=300	x=400,y=300	x=500,y=300	x=600,y=300	x=700,y=300
x=0,y=400	x=100,y=400	x=200,y=400	x=300,y=400	x=400,y=400	x=500,y=400	x=600,y=400	x=700,y=400
x=0,y=500	x=100,y=500	x=200,y=500	x=300,y=500	x=400,y=500	x=500,y=500	x=600,y=500	x=700,y=500

Figure 6-2. *This application shows how x and y positions work in a JavaFX canvas*

Using event handling and Canvas draw capabilities, we can alter the way that graphics are created. For example, allow the user to freely draw on a canvas as you can see in Listing 6-3, where we register a listener for mouse pressed and we start drawing a path. Then on onMouseDragged, we continuously add lines to the path. If the user stops dragging and presses the mouse button again, a new path is created. When the user clicks the canvas with the secondary mouse button, we draw the background over everything on the canvas, cleaning it. The methods for creating paths allow you to interactively build geometric shapes; in this case, we just used it to make the drawing more precise (we could draw small points instead, creating the path), but there are many other applications for this part of the API. The result is a simple paint application that you can see in Figure 6-3.

Listing 6-3. Drawing on a canvas

```
public void start(Stage stage) throws Exception {
        Canvas canvas = new Canvas(800, 600);
        GraphicsContext ctx = canvas.getGraphicsContext2D();
        ctx.setLineWidth(10);
        canvas.setOnMousePressed(e -> ctx.beginPath());
        canvas.setOnMouseDragged(e -> {
                ctx.lineTo(e.getX(), e.getY());
                ctx.stroke();
        });
        canvas.setOnMouseClicked(e -> {
                if(e.getButton() == MouseButton.SECONDARY) {
                        clear(ctx);
                }
        });
        stage.setTitle("Drawing on Canvas");
        stage.setScene(new Scene(new StackPane(canvas), WIDTH, HEIGHT));
        stage.show();
        clear(ctx);
}
public void clear(GraphicsContext ctx) {
        ctx.setFill(Color.DARKBLUE);
        ctx.fillRect(0, 0, WIDTH, HEIGHT);
        ctx.setStroke(Color.ALICEBLUE);
}
```

Figure 6-3. *A small JavaFX drawing application*

So far, we just explored high-level GraphicsContext methods to create shapes and texts. If we want to build more complex graphics, we may need to handle the pixels directly, one by one. Fortunately, this can be easily achieved using the PixelWriter that can be accessed from GraphicsContext. Using the pixel writer, we can set the color of each individual pixel in the canvas. The number of pixels depends on the canvas size, for example, if it has size 800 × 600, then it has 480000 pixels, which can be accessed individually using x and y points. In other words, we can go through each pixel of a canvas by iterating from x = 0 until x = Canvas.getWidth, and inside this iteration we can have another one from y = 0 until y = canvas.getHeight. Translating it to code, we have what you can see in Listing 6-4, which results in a canvas with random pixels as you can see in Figure 6-4.

Listing 6-4. Writing random colors to each pixel of a canvas

```
Canvas canvas = new Canvas(WIDTH, HEIGHT);
GraphicsContext gc = canvas.getGraphicsContext2D();
for (int i = 0; i < canvas.getWidth(); i++) {
        for (int j = 0; j < canvas.getHeight(); j++) {
                gc.getPixelWriter().setColor(i, j, Color.color(Math.
                random(), Math.random(), Math.random()));
        }
}
```

Figure 6-4. *A canvas with random pixels*

The GraphicsContext class also allows you to draw complex paths, other geometric forms, and images and configure how the content will be displayed. To explore all the Canvas and GraphicsContext possibilities, we recommend you read the Javadocs, where you will find all available methods with information on how to use them.

Giving Life to a Canvas Application

To create the kind of applications we described at the beginning of this chapter, we need to constantly update the canvas to create animations or simulations. There are many different ways to achieve this; however, to keep it simple, we will take inspiration from the Processing programming language and create a method draw that is invoked repeatedly and setup that will be invoked only one time on an abstract class GraphicApp. In this chapter, we will use GraphicApp to explore a few known algorithms because it has some code that would be repeated in all examples. Using this abstract class, we can focus on setup and draw, and we won't have to repeat ourselves in each example. Let's understand what it does by checking its source in Listing 6-5.

Listing 6-5. The GraphicApp abstract class provides a skeleton for creating animated graphics using Canvas

```java
import javafx.animation.KeyFrame;
import javafx.animation.Timeline;
import javafx.application.Application;
import javafx.scene.Node;
import javafx.scene.Scene;
import javafx.scene.canvas.Canvas;
import javafx.scene.canvas.GraphicsContext;
import javafx.scene.layout.BorderPane;
import javafx.scene.paint.Color;
import javafx.scene.paint.Paint;
import javafx.stage.Stage;
import javafx.util.Duration;
public abstract class GraphicApp extends Application {
        protected int width = 800;
        protected int height = 600;
        protected GraphicsContext graphicContext;
        private Paint backgroundColor = Color.BLACK;
        private Timeline timeline = new Timeline();
        private int frames = 30;
        private BorderPane root;
        private Stage stage;
        @Override
        public void start(Stage stage) throws Exception {
                this.stage = stage;
                Canvas canvas = new Canvas(width, height);
                graphicContext = canvas.getGraphicsContext2D();
                canvas.requestFocus();
                root = new BorderPane(canvas);
                stage.setScene(new Scene(root));
                setup();
                canvas.setWidth(width);
                canvas.setHeight(height);
                startDrawing();
```

```
                stage.show();
                internalDraw();
        }
    public abstract void setup();
    public abstract void draw();
    public void title(String title) {
            stage.setTitle(title);
    }
    public void background(Paint color) {
            backgroundColor = color;
    }
    public void frames(int frames) {
            this.frames = frames;
            startDrawing();
    }
    public void setBottom(Node node) {
            root.setBottom(node);
    }
    private void internalDraw() {
            graphicContext.setFill(backgroundColor);
            graphicContext.fillRect(0, 0, width, height);
            draw();
    }
    private void startDrawing() {
            timeline.stop();
            if (frames > 0) {
                    timeline.getKeyFrames().clear();
                    KeyFrame frame = new
                    KeyFrame(Duration.millis(1000 /
                    frames), e -> internalDraw());
                    timeline.getKeyFrames().add(frame);
                    timeline.setCycleCount(Timeline.INDEFINITE);
                    timeline.play();
            }
    }
```

```
public double map(double value, double start1, double stop1, double start2,
double stop2) {
        return start2 + (stop2 - start2) * ((value - start1) / (stop1 -
        start1));
        }
}
```

Notice that the methods draw and setup are abstract. To create applications, we must extend GraphicApp and implement these methods. The method draw call frequency is controlled by a Timeline class as you can see in method startDrawing, where a unique frame duration is controlled by a frame int parameter, which represents the number of frames per second. On the method draw, it is possible to access the parameter grahicsContext, which is of type GraphicsContext, and then start creating your application. Using grahicsContext, you can also access the canvas to register listeners, so you can respond to user input. The method map is a utility to convert values of a range to another range. Finally, you can add custom controls to the bottom using the setBottom method.

Using GraphicApp, we can focus on our visual effects. For example, let's create a bouncing balls application. This application simply draws a few ovals that change direction when they reach the application boundaries. You can see in Listing 6-6 that we focus on our idea, which is a model element that represents a ball using the class Ball, and then generate random values for it; and for each iteration in draw, we update the ball position and draw it on the screen.

Listing 6-6. The bouncing balls example

```
import java.util.ArrayList;
import java.util.List;
import java.util.Random;
import javafx.scene.canvas.GraphicsContext;
import javafx.scene.paint.Color;
public class BouncingBalls extends GraphicApp {
        private static final int TOTAL_BALLS = 20;
        List<Ball> balls = new ArrayList<>();
        public static void main(String[] args) {
                launch(args);
        }
```

```java
    @Override
    public void setup() {
        Random random = new Random();
        for (int i = 0; i < TOTAL_BALLS; i++) {
            Ball ball = new Ball();
            ball.circ = random.nextInt(100) + 10;
            ball.x = random.nextInt(width - ball.circ);
            ball.y = random.nextInt(height - ball.circ);
            ball.xDir = random.nextBoolean() ? 1: -1;
            ball.yDir = random.nextBoolean() ? 1: -1;
            ball.color = Color.color(Math.random(),
            Math.random(), Math.random());
            balls.add(ball);
        }
        background(Color.DARKCYAN);
    }
    @Override
    public void draw() {
        for (Ball ball : balls) {
            ball.update();
            ball.draw(graphicContext);
        }
    }
    public class Ball {
        int x, y, xDir = 1, yDir = 1, circ;
        Color color;
        public void update() {
            if (x + circ > width || x < 0) {
                xDir *= -1;
            }
            if (y + circ > height || y < 0) {
                yDir *= -1;
            }
            x += 5 * xDir;
            y += 5 * yDir;
        }
```

```java
public void draw(GraphicsContext gc) {
        gc.setLineWidth(10);
        gc.setFill(color);
        gc.fillOval(x, y, circ, circ);
        gc.setStroke(Color.BLACK);
        gc.strokeOval(x, y, circ, circ);
    }
  }
}
```

When you run this application, you will see balls on the canvas, moving to all sides, as you can see in Figure 6-5. You can improve it by adding intersection detection, physics, event handling, or any other effect that would make it useful or cool.

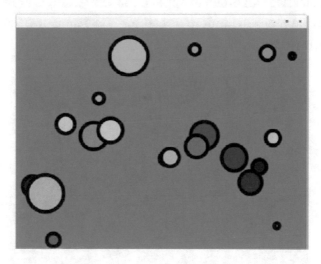

Figure 6-5. *Bouncing balls example*

Having said that, let's explore some known algorithms using our GraphicsApp.

Particle Systems

Particle systems were introduced by William Reeves in the paper "Particle Systems: A Technique for Modeling a Class of Fuzzy Objects" where he defined them as "a collection of many many minute particles that together represent a fuzzy object." You can think of it by having two main components: emitter and particle. An emitter keeps creating particles that will eventually die. The applications for particle systems include the following:

- Games effects: Explosions, collision

- Animations: Fire, cloud, wave hitting a stone

- Simulations: Space, reproduction of living beings

It is possible to create a very simple particle system with a few lines of code, but this type of system can be considerably complex depending on what we want to achieve. For simple and advanced particle systems, we will basically need two classes: Particle and Emitter. The Particle class depends on Emitter, and an emitter can have one or an infinite number of particles.

Using these classes, we can build an application with a single emitter, which generates particles that move to random directions. See Figure 6-6 followed by the code to generate it in Listing 6-7.

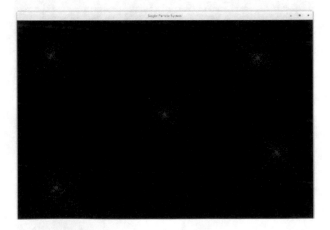

Figure 6-6. *A very simple particle system*

Listing 6-7. Very simple particle system

```
import java.util.ArrayList;
import java.util.List;
import java.util.Random;
import java.util.stream.Collectors;
```

```java
import javafx.scene.canvas.GraphicsContext;
import javafx.scene.paint.Color;
public class ParticleSystem extends GraphicApp {
        private List<Emitter> emitters = new ArrayList<>();
        Random random = new Random();
        public static void main(String[] args) {
                launch();
        }
        @Override
        public void setup() {
                frames(50);
                width = 1200;
                height = 800;
                // you can change it to onMouseDragged
                graphicContext.getCanvas().setOnMouseDragged(e ->
                emitters.
                add(new Emitter(5, e.getSceneX(), e.getSceneY())));
                title("Simple Particle System");
        }
        @Override
        public void draw() {
                for (Emitter emitter : emitters) {
                        emitter.emit(graphicContext);
                }
        }
        public class Emitter {
                List<Particle> particles = new ArrayList<>();
                int n = 1;
                double x, y;
                public Emitter(int n, double x, double y) {
                        this.n = n;
                        this.x = x;
                        this.y = y;
                }
```

```java
        public void emit(GraphicsContext gc) {
                for (int i = 0; i < n; i++) {
                        int duration = random.nextInt(200) + 2;
                        double yDir = random.nextDouble() * 2.0 +
                        -1.0;
                        double xDir = random.nextDouble() * 2.0 +
                        -1.0;
                        Particle p = new Particle(x, y, duration,
                        xDir, yDir);
                        particles.add(p);
                }
                for (Particle particle : particles) {
                        particle.step();
                        particle.show(gc);
                }
                particles = particles.stream().filter(p ->
                p.duration > 0).collect(Collectors.toList());
        }
    }

    public class Particle {
            int duration;
            double x, y, yDir, xDir;
            public Particle(double x, double y, int duration, double
            yDir, double xDir) {
                    this.x = x;
                    this.y = y;
                    this.duration = duration;
                    this.yDir = yDir;
                    this.xDir = xDir;
            }
            public void step() {
                    x += xDir;
                    y += yDir;
                    duration--;
            }
```

```
public void show(GraphicsContext gc) {
        gc.setFill(Color.rgb(255, 20, 20, 0.6));
        gc.fillOval(x, y, 3, 3);
    }
}
}
```

In the code from Listing 6-7, we generate a particle system at the position where the user clicks the canvas. Notice the class Emitter generates particles every time the method emit is called and it also draws the existing particles; these two actions could be separated in two different methods. A particle is a simple oval; and it has a duration, an initial x and y position, and a y and x direction. The emitter emits all particles, and after it is done, all the obsolete particles are removed. The code is flexible and easy to extend, for example, when we remove the mouse clicked event listener in the canvas and change it to use mouse dragged event, we can "write" using particle systems. See Figure 6-7.

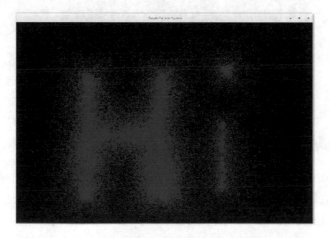

Figure 6-7. *Using mouse dragged with the particle system*

To make the particle system configurable, let's add a control panel at the bottom of our application so users can configure a lot of aspects of the emitters and particles to experiment with the full potential of particle systems. For this purpose, we created an application that allows users to add new emitters when they click the canvas. See our configurable particle system in Figure 6-8.

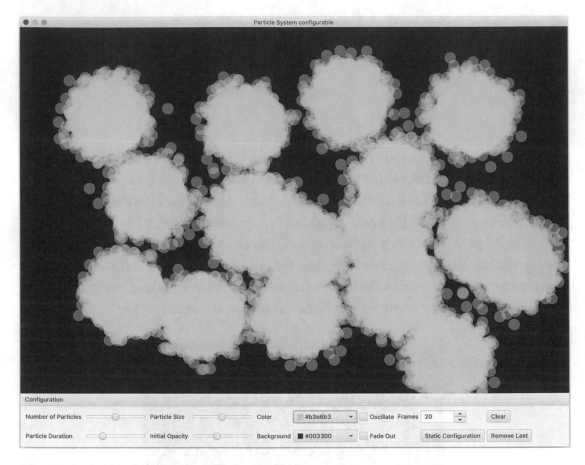

Figure 6-8. *Configurable particle system*

The code for the emitter creation can be found in Listing 6-8. The way it works is simple. When a click happens on the canvas, a new emitter is added to a list; and in the draw method, the emit method of each particle system is called. The configuration in the bottom pane (see Figure 6-8) is passed to each emitter when it is created, and if users select the toggle button Static Configuration, the configuration for that particular emitter won't be updated in real time.

Listing 6-8. Emitter creation and calling draw

```
@Override
public void setup() {
        frames(20);
        width = 1200;
```

```
            height = 800;
            GridPane gpConfRoot = buildConfigurationRoot();
            TitledPane tpConf = new TitledPane("Configuration", gpConfRoot);
            tpConf.setCollapsible(false);
            setBottom(tpConf);
            graphicContext.getCanvas().setOnMouseClicked(e -> {
                    Emitter newEmitter;
                    if (globalConf.cloneConfProperty.get()) {
                            newEmitter = new Emitter(e.getSceneX(),
                                e.getSceneY(), globalConf.clone());
                    } else {
                            newEmitter = new Emitter(e.getSceneX(),
                                e.getSceneY(), globalConf);
                    }
                    emitters.add(newEmitter);
            });
            title("Particle System configurable");
}
@Override
public void draw() {
        for (Emitter emitter : emitters) {
                emitter.emit(graphicContext);
        }
}
```

The configuration object holds diverse information that is used by the emitter to create a particle. The class ParticleSystemConf (see Listing 6-9) uses JavaFX properties so the property values can be bound directly to the controls we added to the bottom pane. These properties control the number of particles produced every time that emit is called, how many frames the particle will live in the application (particle duration), and the size of the oval that represents the particle opacity. You can also select the particle color and if it will move in a straight line or if it will oscillate and if it should have a fade-out effect. Finally, the configuration has also a clone method, which allows us to create a new configuration that won't be bound to the controls as shown in Listing 6-9.

Listing 6-9. The configuration object

```
public class ParticleSystemConf {
        IntegerProperty numberOfParticlesProperty = new
        SimpleIntegerProperty();
        IntegerProperty durationProperty = new SimpleIntegerProperty();
        DoubleProperty sizeProperty = new SimpleDoubleProperty();
        DoubleProperty opacityProperty = new SimpleDoubleProperty();
        BooleanProperty oscilateProperty = new SimpleBooleanProperty();
        BooleanProperty fadeOutProperty = new SimpleBooleanProperty();
        ObjectProperty<Color> colorProperty = new SimpleObjectProperty<>();
        BooleanProperty cloneConfProperty = new SimpleBooleanProperty();

        public ParticleSystemConf clone() {
                ParticleSystemConf newConf = new ParticleSystemConf();
                newConf.numberOfParticlesProperty.
                set(numberOfParticlesProperty.get());
                newConf.durationProperty.set(durationProperty.get());
                newConf.sizeProperty.set(sizeProperty.get());
                newConf.opacityProperty.set(opacityProperty.get());
                newConf.oscilateProperty.set(oscilateProperty.get());
                newConf.fadeOutProperty.set(fadeOutProperty.get());
                newConf.colorProperty.set(colorProperty.get());
                return newConf;
        }
}
```

All the fields of the configuration are later bound to a control that is added to the bottom of the application:

```
cbBackgrounColor.valueProperty().addListener((a, b, c) -> background(c));
globalConf.numberOfParticlesProperty.bind(sldNumberOfParticles.
valueProperty());
globalConf.durationProperty.bind(sldDuration.valueProperty());
globalConf.oscilateProperty.bind(cbOscillate.selectedProperty());
globalConf.sizeProperty.bind(sldPParticleSize.valueProperty());
globalConf.opacityProperty.bind(sldOpacity.valueProperty());
```

```
globalConf.fadeOutProperty.bind(cbFadeOut.selectedProperty());
globalConf.colorProperty.bind(cbColor.valueProperty());
globalConf.cloneConfProperty.bind(tbClone.selectedProperty());
```

Finally, all the configuration is used in Emitter and Particle classes as you can see in Listing 6-10.

Listing 6-10. Particle and Emitter classes using the configuration object

```
public class Emitter {
        List<Particle> particles = new ArrayList<>();
        double x, y;
        private ParticleSystemConf conf;
        public Emitter(double x, double y, ParticleSystemConf conf) {
                this.x = x;
                this.y = y;
                this.conf = conf;
        }
        public void emit(GraphicsContext gc) {
                for (int i = 0; i < conf.numberOfParticlesProperty.get();
                i++) {
                        Particle p = new Particle(x, y, conf);
                        particles.add(p);
                }
                for (Particle particle : particles) {
                        particle.step();
                        particle.show(gc);
                }
            particles = particles.stream().filter(p -> p.duration
>               0).collect(Collectors.toList());
        }
}
public class Particle {
        int duration, initialDuration;
        double x, y, yDir, xDir, size, opacity, currentOpacity;
        Color color = Color.YELLOW;
        boolean oscilate, fadeOut;
```

```java
        public Particle(double x, double y, ParticleSystemConf conf) {
                this.x = x;
                this.y = y;
                this.oscilate = conf.oscilateProperty.get();
                this.size = conf.sizeProperty.get();
                this.initialDuration = conf.durationProperty.get() + 1;
                this.yDir = random.nextGaussian() * 2.0 - 1.0;
                this.xDir = random.nextGaussian() * 2.0 + -1.0;
                this.opacity = conf.opacityProperty.get();
                this.fadeOut = conf.fadeOutProperty.get();
                this.duration = initialDuration;
                this.currentOpacity = opacity;
                this.color = conf.colorProperty.get();
        }
        public void step() {
                x += xDir;
                y += yDir;
                if (oscilate) {
                        x += Math.sin(duration) * 10;
                        y += Math.cos(duration) * 10;
                }
                if (fadeOut) {
                        currentOpacity = map(duration, 0,
                        initialDuration, 0, opacity);
                }
                duration--;
        }
        public void show(GraphicsContext gc) {
                Color cl = Color.color(color.getRed(), color.getGreen(),
                color.getBlue(), currentOpacity);
                gc.setFill(cl);
                gc.fillOval(x, y, size, size);
        }
}
```

Not all the code for the configurable particle system was shared in this chapter; however, you can find it in the GitHub repository associated with this book. When you run this application, you will notice that you can quickly make it slow if you add a lot of emitters with a lot of particles generated by frame and mainly if you have too many frames per second. You can improve the performance following the tips provided at the end of this chapter. There are a few nice features that could be added to this application:

- Particle format selection

- Particle orientation

- Exporting the visualization to a file or in a format that could be reused in other applications

We will leave these tasks as an exercise for you!

Fractals

A rough definition of a fractal is a geometric shape formed of other small geometric shapes that resemble itself. Using fractals, we can create beautiful and intriguing art, but also understand pattern formations in nature. In our case, we will explore Canvas capacity using fractals.

A famous fractal created from a sequence of complex numbers is the Mandelbrot set. To build a Mandelbrot set, you must iterate on function $f(z) = z^2 + c$ filling it with values from its own results starting from 0. This function tends to infinity; however, there are a few intermediate values that may lead to interesting results. For example, if you iterate on an image pixel and map the pixel to the values accepted by the Mandelbrot sent and then, using the pixel writer, set the pixel color as white when the result tends to infinity and as black otherwise, the result will be something like in Figure 6-9. Notice that in this figure the small part resembles the whole. It looks like we have a small Mandelbrot everywhere. The code for it is in Listing 6-11.

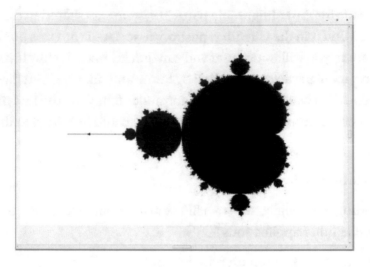

Figure 6-9. *Simplest Mandelbrot set*

Listing 6-11. Simplest Mandelbrot

```
private final int MAX_ITERATIONS = 100;
private double zx, zy, cX, cY, tmp;
int i;
@Override
public void setup() {
        width = 1200;
        height = 800;
        frames(0);
}
@Override
public void draw() {
        long start = System.currentTimeMillis();
        for (int x = 0; x < width; x++) {
                for (int y = 0; y < height; y++) {
                        zx = zy = 0;
                        // the known range of accepted values for cx and cy
                        cX = map(x, 0, width, -2.5, 1.0);
                        cY = map(y, 0, height, -1, 1.0);
                        i = 0;
```

```
        while (zx * zx + zy * zy < 4 && i <
        MAX_ITERATIONS) {
                tmp = zx * zx - zy * zy + cX;
                zy = 2.0 * zx * zy + cY;
                zx = tmp;
                i++;
        }
        // if it is not exploding to infinite
        if (i < MAX_ITERATIONS) {
                graphicContext.getPixelWriter().setColor(
                x, y, Color.WHITE);
        } else {
                graphicContext.getPixelWriter().setColor
                (x, y, Color.BLACK);
        }
    }
}
System.out.println("GEnerating mandelbrot took " + (System.
currentTimeMillis() - start)  + " ms");
}
```

If you search for Mandelbrot in online videos, you will find very interesting special effects such as zooming effects and different colors. This is possible due to coloring algorithms and zoom effects. Let's improve the original Mandelbrot first by allowing a fake zoom. This can be done by manipulating the root pane of the GraphicsApp and wrapping the canvas in a stack pane with a very big size and then wrapping it in a scroll pane, which provides the scrolling functionality. The canvas size can be changed using event listeners: when a user clicks the scroll pane with the left button, it zooms in; when the user clicks using the right button, it zooms out; and clicking with the middle button resets the zoom and centralizes the pane. This is all done in the setup method as in Listing 6-12, where you can see the trick for the zoom: we are actually scaling the canvas; it is not a real zoom. In Figure 6-10, you can see the result without zoom. The zoom effect is shown in Figure 6-11. Notice that it does not adjust the resolution, hence, as we said, a fake zoom.

Listing 6-12. Trick for zoom into the application canvas

```
@Override
public void setup() {
        width = 1200;
        height = 800;
        Canvas canvas = graphicContext.getCanvas();
        BorderPane bp = (BorderPane) canvas.getParent();
        bp.setCenter(null);
        StackPane p = new StackPane(canvas);
        p.setMinSize(20000, 20000);
        ScrollPane sp = new ScrollPane(p);
        sp.setPrefSize(1200, 800);
        sp.setVvalue(0.5);
        sp.setHvalue(0.5);
        bp.setCenter(sp);
        sp.setOnMouseClicked(e -> {
                double zoom = 0.2;
                double scaleX = canvas.getScaleX();
                double scaleY = canvas.getScaleY();
                if (e.getButton() == MouseButton.SECONDARY &&
                  (canvas.getScaleX() > 0.5)) {
                        canvas.setScaleX(scaleX - zoom);
                        canvas.setScaleY(scaleY - zoom);
                } else if (e.getButton() == MouseButton.PRIMARY) {
                        canvas.setScaleX(scaleX + zoom);
                        canvas.setScaleY(scaleY + zoom);
                } else if (e.getButton() == MouseButton.MIDDLE) {
                        sp.setVvalue(0.5);
                        sp.setHvalue(0.5);
                        canvas.setScaleY(1);
                        canvas.setScaleX(1);
                }
        });
        canvas.setOnMousePressed(canvas.getOnMouseClicked());
```

```
        frames(0);
        title("Mandelbrot with color and zoom");
}
```

For coloring, we modify the Mandelbrot color. Instead of white, pick a value relative to the last iteration. Using this value, we can play with the generated color. For example, with the values from Listing 6-13, we have a purplish value for the outer color and greenish values for the borders as you can see in Figure 6-10.

Listing 6-13. Adding colors to the Mandelbrot non-infinite values

```
// if the steps above are not heading towards infinite we draw the pixel
with a specific color
if (i < MAX_ITERATIONS) {
        double newC = ((double) i) / ((double) MAX_ITERATIONS);
        Color c;
        if(newC > 0.4)
        c = Color.color(newC, 0.8, newC);
        else c = Color.color(0.2, newC, 0.2);
        graphicContext.getPixelWriter().setColor(x, y, c);
} else {
        graphicContext.getPixelWriter().setColor(x, y, Color.BLACK);
}
```

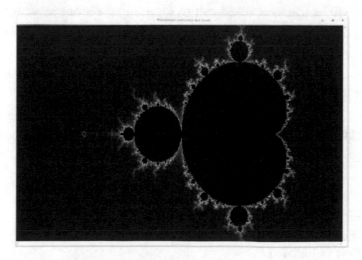

Figure 6-10. *Mandelbrot with colors and zoom*

Figure 6-11. *Zooming in to the Mandelbrot*

That's all for the Mandelbrot. Take some time to modify the code, try to generate more interesting colors, and play with the parameters. As our next visual effect, we will create a panel for real-time experiment and also extend the Mandelbrot to also allow us to test Julia set values, generating other fractal forms.

A Julia set is a collection of fixed values for Mandelbrot imaginary and real values. Using these fixed values, we can create forms that are derived from Mandelbrot. In our code, we just stopped calculating cx and ci variables from Mandelbrot, and instead we let users choose a value for them using a JavaFX slider added to the bottom part of our root pane. The central pane uses the same trick for zoom that we used in Mandelbrot, and this time we will let the user select values for many different parameters of the fractal form, generating unique images. The changes we did in Mandelbrot code to generate Julia sets can be seen in Listing 6-14, where cx and ci are coming from a configuration object, which we will describe soon. Also, the color now is coming from a specific method that will take the user configuration.

Listing 6-14. Code for Julia sets. Now the values come from configuration objects

```
@Override
public void draw() {
        running.set(true);
        totalIterations++;
```

```
        for (int x = 0; x < width; x++) {
                for (int y = 0; y < height; y++) {
                        zx = zy = 0;
                        zx = 1.5 * (x - width / 2) / (0.5 * width);
                        zy = (y - height / 2) / (0.5 * height);
                        i = 0;
                        while (zx * zx + zy * zy < 4 && i <
                        totalIterations) {
                                tmp = zx * zx - zy * zy + conf.cx;
                                zy = 2.0 * zx * zy + conf.ci;
                                zx = tmp;
                                i++;
                        }
                        Color c = conf.infinityColor;
                        if (i < totalIterations) {
                        double newC = ((double) i) / ((double)
                        totalIterations);
                        c = getColor(newC);
                    }
                    graphicContext.getPixelWriter().setColor(x, y, c);
                }
        }
        if (totalIterations > conf.maxIterations) {
                running.set(false);
                frames(0);
        }
}
private Color getColor(double newC) {
        double r = newC, g = newC, b = newC;
        if (newC > conf.threshold) {
                if (!conf.computedLighterR)
                        r = conf.lighterR;
                if (!conf.computedLighterG)
                        g = conf.lighterG;
```

```
                if (!conf.computedLighterB)
                        b = conf.lighterB;
        } else {
                if (!conf.computedDarkerR)
                        r = conf.darkerR;
                if (!conf.computedDarkerG)
                        g = conf.darkerG;
                if (!conf.computedDarkerB)
                        b = conf.darkerB;
        }
        return Color.color(r, g, b);
}
```

The configuration, however, is not using binding for the reason that binding inside the for loop in the draw() method will be much slower than using primitive types. To make the configuration object up to date with the configuration, we make use of listeners, so for each element in the UI, we have a listener that will update the configuration object when the control is changed. This way, the loop that draws the fractal form won't suffer from performance issues due to the use of binding. The configuration and the bottom pane constructions can be found in Listing 6-15. In Figure 6-12, you can see the application in action.

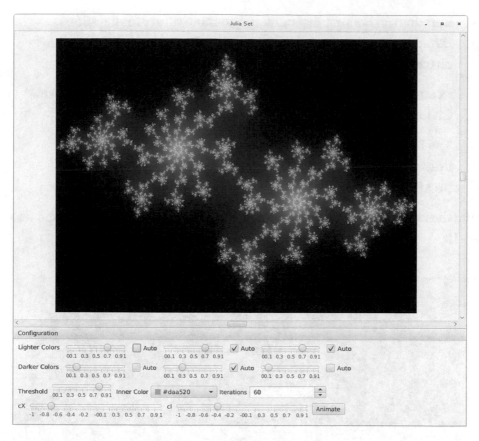

Figure 6-12. *Our Julia set fractals application*

Each control you see in Figure 6-12 is explained in the following:

- Lighter Colors: The colors for values that are above the threshold. You can use a slider for each value (RGB), and if you select Auto, the value for that specific color part is taken from the algorithm we saw in Listing 6-14.

- Darker Colors: Just like lighter colors, but used for the values that are below the threshold.

- Threshold: A threshold for dividing the colors. We can select values for the colors that are above the threshold or below it.

- Inner Color: A Color Picker that allows you to select the default color when the calculated value tends to infinity.

- Iterations: A Spinner that contains possible values for iterations. Iterations are the number of times we make our calculation before checking if it tends to infinity or not.

- cx and cy: These sliders are the range of known values for a Julia set. Changing it will change the fractal form.

- The button Animate will show each step of the fractal evolution by drawing it from iteration 1 until the number you selected in Iterations.

Using these controls, you can create really interesting fractals like the one from Figure 6-13.

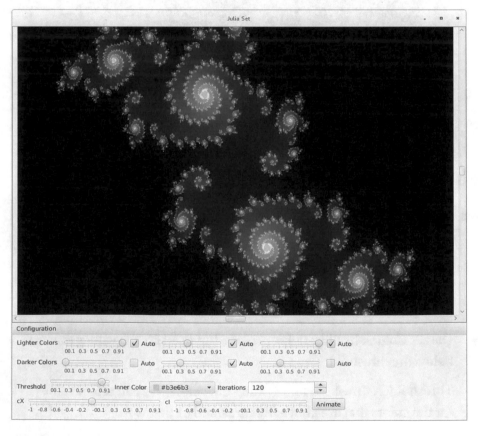

Figure 6-13. *A fractal generated using our application*

Listing 6-15. Code for the Julia set

```java
public static class JuliaSetConf {
        public double threshold = 0.8;
        public double lighterR = 0.7;
        public double lighterG = 0.7;
        public double lighterB = 0.7;
        public double darkerR = 0.3;
        public double darkerG = 0.3;
        public double darkerB = 0.3;
        public double cx = -0.70176;
        public double ci = -0.3842;
        public boolean computedLighterR = true;
        public boolean computedLighterG = true;
        public boolean computedLighterB = true;
        public boolean computedDarkerR = true;
        public boolean computedDarkerG = true;
        public boolean computedDarkerB = true;
        public Color infinityColor = Color.GOLDENROD;
        public int maxIterations = MAX_ITERATIONS / 2;
}
private Node createConfPanel() {
        VBox vbConf = new VBox(5);
        Slider spLigherR = slider(conf.lighterR);
        Slider spLigherG = slider(conf.lighterG);
        Slider spLigherB = slider(conf.lighterB);
        CheckBox chkUseComputedLighterR = checkBox();
        CheckBox chkUseComputedLighterG = checkBox();
        CheckBox chkUseComputedLighterB = checkBox();
        vbConf.getChildren().add(new HBox(10, new Label("Lighter Colors"),
                        spLigherR, chkUseComputedLighterR, spLigherG,
                        chkUseComputedLighterG, spLigherB,
                        chkUseComputedLighterB));
        Slider spDarkerR = slider(conf.darkerR);
        Slider spDarkerG = slider(conf.darkerG);
        Slider spDarkerB = slider(conf.darkerB);
```

```
CheckBox chkUseComputedDarkerR = checkBox();
CheckBox chkUseComputedDarkerG = checkBox();
CheckBox chkUseComputedDarkerB = checkBox();
vbConf.getChildren().add(new HBox(10, new Label("Darker Colors"),
                spDarkerR, chkUseComputedDarkerR, spDarkerG,
                chkUseComputedDarkerG, spDarkerB,
                chkUseComputedDarkerB));
Slider sldThreshold = slider(conf.threshold);
Spinner<Integer> spMaxIterations = new Spinner<>(10,
MAX_ITERATIONS, MAX_ITERATIONS / 2);
spMaxIterations.valueProperty().addListener(c ->
updateConf.run());
ColorPicker clInifinity = new ColorPicker(conf.infinityColor);
clInifinity.valueProperty().addListener(c -> updateConf.run());
HBox hbGeneral = new HBox(5, new Label("Threshold"), sldThreshold,
                new Label("Inner Color"), clInifinity,
                new Label("Iterations"), spMaxIterations);
hbGeneral.setAlignment(Pos.CENTER_LEFT);
vbConf.getChildren().add(hbGeneral);
Slider sldX = slider(-1, 1.0, conf.cx);
sldX.setMinSize(300, 10);
Slider sldI = slider(-1, 1.0, conf.ci);
sldI.setMinSize(300, 10);
Button btnRun = new Button("Animate");
// since we are not using bind we need to get all the properties here
updateConf = () -> {
        conf.lighterR = spLigherR.getValue();
        conf.lighterG = spLigherG.getValue();
        conf.lighterB = spLigherB.getValue();
        conf.darkerR = spDarkerR.getValue();
        conf.darkerG = spDarkerG.getValue();
        conf.darkerB = spDarkerB.getValue();
        conf.threshold = sldThreshold.getValue();
        conf.computedLighterR
=           chkUseComputedLighterR.isSelected();
```

```
                conf.computedLighterG =
                chkUseComputedLighterG.isSelected();
                conf.computedLighterB =
                chkUseComputedLighterB.isSelected();
                conf.computedDarkerR =
                conf.computedDarkerG =
                chkUseComputedDarkerG.isSelected();
                conf.computedDarkerB =
                chkUseComputedDarkerB.isSelected();
                conf.cx = sldX.getValue();
                conf.ci = sldI.getValue();
                conf.infinityColor = clInifinity.getValue();
                conf.maxIterations = spMaxIterations.getValue();
                totalIterations = conf.maxIterations;
                frames(TOTAL_FRAMES);
        };
        btnRun.setOnAction(e -> {
                updateConf.run();
                totalIterations = 1;
        });
        HBox hbSet = new HBox(5, new Label("cX"), sldX, new Label("cI"),
        sldI, btnRun);
        vbConf.getChildren().add(hbSet);
        TitledPane pnConf = new TitledPane("Configuration", vbConf);
        pnConf.setExpanded(true);
        pnConf.setCollapsible(false);
        pnConf.disableProperty().bind(running);
        return pnConf;
}
private CheckBox checkBox() {
        CheckBox checkBox = new CheckBox("Auto");
        checkBox.setSelected(true);
        checkBox.selectedProperty().addListener(c -> updateConf.run());
        return checkBox;
}
```

```
private Slider slider(double d) {
      return slider(0.0, 1.0, d);
}
private Slider slider(double min, double max, double d) {
      Slider slider = new Slider(min, max, d);
      slider.setShowTickLabels(true);
      slider.setShowTickMarks(true);
      slider.setMajorTickUnit(0.1);
      slider.valueProperty().addListener(c -> updateConf.run());
      return slider;
}
```

High Performance

The performance so far has not been discussed. The focus was entirely on creating our algorithms using JavaFX APIs, meaning that we trusted only the JavaFX hardware acceleration feature that was mentioned before. If you run the fractal and particle examples, you will notice that the performance is compromised once we push it to its limits. In the last part of this chapter, we will make a more advanced discussion, discuss why JavaFX itself won't bring the best performance for your application, and propose solutions based on Sean M. Phillips's article published in *Java Magazine* in May–June 2018: "Producer-Consumer Implementations in JavaFX."

JavaFX is single-threaded. All the rendering is done on a single thread, which means that if you hold the thread with a long-running task, it won't show anything until the task is done. When you code something in the start method of a JavaFX application, you are already on the JavaFX main thread. To make clear this behavior, see the application whose code is in Listing 6-16. In this application, we have an animated label; we have also a button. When you click the button, we call Thread.sleep, and the animation simply stops. You can't even click the button. The reason is that the main thread was locked by our Thread.sleep call!

Listing 6-16. Locking the main JavaFX thread

```
import javafx.animation.ScaleTransition;
import javafx.animation.Transition;
import javafx.application.Application;
```

```java
import javafx.scene.Scene;
import javafx.scene.control.Button;
import javafx.scene.control.Label;
import javafx.scene.layout.BorderPane;
import javafx.stage.Stage;
import javafx.util.Duration;
public class LockedThread extends Application {
        public static void main(String[] args) {
                launch();
        }
        @Override
        public void start(Stage stage) throws Exception {
                Label lblHello = new Label("Hello World");
                ScaleTransition st = new
                ScaleTransition(Duration.seconds(1));
                st.setAutoReverse(true);
                st.setCycleCount(Transition.INDEFINITE);
                st.setByX(2);
                st.setByY(2);
                st.setNode(lblHello);
                Button btnLock = new Button("Sleep for 10 seconds");
                BorderPane bp = new BorderPane(lblHello);
                bp.setBottom(btnLock);
                stage.setScene(new Scene(bp, 300, 200));
                stage.show();
                btnLock.setOnAction(e -> {
                        try {
                                Thread.sleep(10000);
                        } catch (InterruptedException e1) {
                                e1.printStackTrace();
                        }
                });
                st.play();
        }
}
```

The lesson is don't do heavy task on the main thread. The solution is to use a separate thread for the actual processing and, once you are done, update the canvas (or the user interface) on the JavaFX thread. With this approach, the load is taken away from the main thread, and the application should run smoothly.

Now that we know this, we will try to call graphic context or make any JavaFX control change on a different thread, and what you will see is an exception of type *java. lang.IllegalStateException* with message *Not on FX application thread*. To assure that something is running on the JavaFX thread, we may use *javafx.application.Platform. runLater* passing a runnable, which will run later on the JavaFX thread: *Platform. runLater(() ➤ gc.fillText("Safe Fill Text", 0, 0))*. In other words, make sure to do JavaFX control updates on the main thread; otherwise, we may face the exception we mentioned previously.

However, Platform.runLater won't solve all the issues we will face with concurrent programming in JavaFX. There are other utilities in the javafx.concurrent package, mainly the javafx.concurrent.Task class, which is very useful for asynchronous tasks. For this chapter, we will explore the high-density data pattern introduced by Sean M. Phillips in *Java Magazine* in May–June 2018: "Producer-Consumer Implementations in JavaFX."

If you check the mentioned article, you will notice that the idea is to have a thread that will do the hard processing and push the result to a queue and then another thread that gets the result once it is available and updates the canvas. The first thread is known as the producer, and it is responsible to do the hard processing without touching the JavaFX thread. The results generated by the producer are added to a **java.util. concurrent.ConcurrentLinkedQueue**, which are received by the second thread, the consumer thread, that will then do the graphical processing on the JavaFX thread.

To show the pattern in a real-world application, let's create an implementation of Conway's Game of Life. In the Wikipedia article of the same name, you will find that Game of Life is a cellular automaton where a cell dies if it has more than three neighbors due to overpopulation, cells with fewer than two neighbors die by underpopulation, dead cells surrounded by exactly three neighbors will be reborn, and cells with two or three neighbors remain alive.

We made our Game of Life implementation in Listing 6-17. The cells are represented by Boolean values, where true means a live cell. We can set the size of each cell and the width and height of the application, which means that the number of cells can be calculated by width divided by the cell's size times the height divided by the cell's size. The application will write a square of size cellSize for each live cell and then calculate the next generation of cells based on the rules we discussed before. To determine if a cell will live or not depends on the number of neighbors, and in method countNeighbours we made a different way to calculate the number of neighbors, which is to check each neighbor position and exclude the cases where the neighbor checking would lead to errors. This approach saved us from an if/else ugly implementation. Since we need to sum the neighbors of each cell, we will have to go through each cell in a for-for loop to find each cell neighbor as you can see in method newGeneration.

Listing 6-17. A Game of Life implementation

```java
import java.util.Arrays;
import javafx.scene.canvas.GraphicsContext;
import javafx.scene.paint.Color;
public class GameOfLife {
        private int columns;
        private int rows;
        private int cellSize;
        public GameOfLife(int columns, int rows, int cellSize) {
                this.columns = columns;
                this.rows = rows;
                this.cellSize = cellSize;
        }
        public boolean[][] newCells() {
                boolean[][] newCells = new boolean[columns][rows];
                for (int i = 0; i < columns; i++) {
                        for (int j = 0; j < rows; j++) {
                                newCells[i][j] = Math.random() > 0.5;
                        }
                }
                return newCells;
        }
        public void drawCells(boolean[][] cells, GraphicsContext
        graphicContext) {
                for (int i = 0; i < columns; i++) {
                        for (int j = 0; j < rows; j++) {
                                if (cells[i][j]) {
                                        graphicContext.setFill(Color.BLACK);
```

```java
                            graphicContext.fillRect(i *
                            cellSize, j * cellSize, cellSize,
                            cellSize);
                }
            }
        }
    }
    public boolean[][] newGeneration(boolean previousGeneration[][]) {
            boolean[][] newGeneration = new boolean[columns][rows];
            for (int i = 0; i < columns; i++) {
                    for (int j = 0; j < rows; j++) {
                            updateCell(previousGeneration,
                            newGeneration, i, j);
                    }
            }
            return newGeneration;
    }
    private void updateCell(boolean[][] previousGeneration, boolean[][]
    newGeneration, int i, int j) {
            int countNeighbours = countNeighbours(previousGeneration,
            i, j);
            if (previousGeneration[i][j] && (countNeighbours < 2 ||
            countNeighbours > 3)) {
                    newGeneration[i][j] = false;
            } else if (!previousGeneration[i][j] && countNeighbours
            == 3) {
                    newGeneration[i][j] = true;
            } else if (previousGeneration[i][j]) {
                    newGeneration[i][j] = true;
            }
    }
    private int countNeighbours(boolean[][] copy, int i, int j) {
            int[][] borders = {
                            {i - 1, j -1}, {i -1, j}, {i -1, j+ 1},
                            {i, j -1}, {i, j + 1},
                            {i +1, j - 1}, {i +1, j}, {i +1, j +1}
```

```
        };
        return (int) Arrays.stream(borders)
                .filter(b -> b[0] > -1 &&
                                b[0] < columns &&
                                b[1] > -1       &&
                                b[1] < rows     &&
                                copy[b[0]][b[1]])
                .count();
    }
}
```

The first and easy way to give life to this game is using a subclass of GraphicApp, which will do all the work in the draw method. Each time draw is called, the current generation will be rendered, and a new generation will replace the current one. As you know, the method draw runs on the JavaFX thread, which means this implementation will use a single thread to do all work. This implementation can be found in Listing 6-18, and the result can be seen in Figure 6-14.

Listing 6-18. Game of Life running on the application main thread

```
import javafx.scene.paint.Color;
public class GameOfLifeFXThread extends GraphicApp {
        final int WIDTH = 2500;
        final int HEIGHT = 2500;
        final int CELL_SIZE = 5;
        boolean currentGeneration[][];
        int columns = WIDTH / CELL_SIZE;
        int rows = HEIGHT / CELL_SIZE;
        private GameOfLife gameOfLife;
        public static void main(String[] args) {
                launch();
        }
        @Override
        public void setup() {
                width = WIDTH;
                height = HEIGHT;
                gameOfLife = new GameOfLife(columns, rows, CELL_SIZE);
```

```
                currentGeneration = gameOfLife.newCells();
                background(Color.DARKGRAY);
                title("Game of Life");
                frames(5);
        }
        @Override
        public void draw() {
                long initial = System.currentTimeMillis();
                gameOfLife.drawCells(currentGeneration, graphicContext);
                System.out.println("Time to render " +
                  (System.currentTimeMillis() - initial));
                initial = System.currentTimeMillis();
                currentGeneration = gameOfLife.newGeneration(currentGenera
                tion);
                System.out.println("Time to calculate new generation: " +
                (System.currentTimeMillis() - initial));
        }
}
```

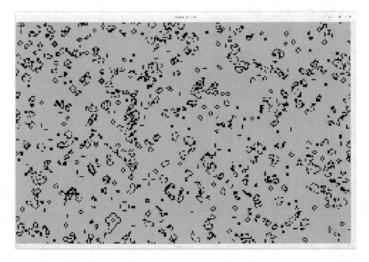

Figure 6-14. *Our Game of Life*

If you run the implementation from Listing 6-18 with size 2500 × 2500 and cell size 5 (2500 × 2500 × 5), you will see in the console that the time to calculate the next generation is approximately 30 times greater than the time used to actually render the cells, meaning that most of the time is used to calculate the new generation while the JavaFX thread is locked. The application becomes very slow and unresponsive when we simply change the size of cell to 2 (remember that the amount of cells is dependent on the cell size) because now the main thread is locked doing the new generation. You can see the output on the console in Figure 6-15, which was collected for 2500 × 2500 × 2.

```
Time to render 7
Time to calculate new generation: 270
Time to render 7
Time to calculate new generation: 201
Time to render 7
Time to calculate new generation: 202
Time to render 7
Time to calculate new generation: 233
Time to render 8
Time to calculate new generation: 228
Time to render 8
Time to calculate new generation: 216
Time to render 7
Time to calculate new generation: 226
Time to render 8
Time to calculate new generation: 206
Time to render 8
Time to calculate new generation: 212
Time to render 7
Time to calculate new generation: 199
Time to render 7
Time to calculate new generation: 201
```

Figure 6-15. *Time to render × the time to calculate a new generation*

Considering that you are running Game of Life on a multiple-core machine, we can make a small change to transform the outer loop (or the columns loop) in the newGeneration method to use a parallel stream instead. This was achieved by adding a new method to the GameOfLife class, which you can see in Listing 6-19. Using 2500 × 2500 with cell size 2, we can have an improvement of about 30% in a four-core machine, making the application much faster. The results can be found in Figure 6-16. Bear in mind that parallel is not a silver bullet solution. You must observe if the load you are making parallel is worth it; otherwise, the time to divide the work between the cores may be greater than the time to do the actual processing, resulting in performance degradation instead of a performance improvement.

Listing 6-19. Method using parallel stream when checking the neighbors for all cells in a column

```java
public boolean[][] newGenerationParallel(boolean previousGeneration[][]) {
        boolean[][] newGeneration = new boolean[columns][rows];
        IntStream.range(0, columns).parallel().forEach(i -> {
                for (int j = 0; j < rows; j++) {
                        updateCell(previousGeneration, newGeneration, i, j);
                }
        });
        return newGeneration;
}
```

```
Time to render 18
Time to calculate new generation: 126
Time to render 19
Time to calculate new generation: 154
Time to render 18
Time to calculate new generation: 126
Time to render 14
Time to calculate new generation: 151
Time to render 12
Time to calculate new generation: 139
Time to render 19
Time to calculate new generation: 143
Time to render 18
Time to calculate new generation: 143
Time to render 17
Time to calculate new generation: 138
Time to render 12
Time to calculate new generation: 124
Time to render 12
Time to calculate new generation: 129
Time to render 26
Time to calculate new generation: 148
Time to render 16
Time to calculate new generation: 142
Time to render 14
Time to calculate new generation: 127
```

Figure 6-16. *Processing time after using a parallel stream when calculating the new generation*

Since we are running everything on the JavaFX thread, we are limited on the improvements that can be done. However, if we use the same idea of the already mentioned high-density pattern, we can have impressive results. The application will rarely become unresponsive because it will take all the processing out of the JavaFX main thread and call Platform.runLater() only to render data. All the processing will be in a producer task, which calculates the new generation, and the result is added to a ConcurrentLinkedQueue. The results are later polled by another task, the consumer task, and then the canvas is updated on the application main thread. We can try to control the number of frames per second by polling the results every X milliseconds, for example, if you want ten frames per second, you can make the consumer thread sleep for 100 milliseconds each time it polls a result from the queue, or you can constantly poll results and update the canvas because the most important result is that the rest of the application will run smoothly without any impact on the end user, which means that the user may see a slow animation, but they still can change controls or do other tasks. The resulting code can be found in Listing 6-20. Further improvements could be done, such as using threads to calculate the new generation. In this case, simply calling parallel on a stream may not help because parallel uses all cores, meaning that it may starve the render thread, because all the cores will be used in the new generation calculation, so a more sophisticated parallel programming will be required.

Listing 6-20. Game of Life with high-density data pattern

```java
import java.util.concurrent.ConcurrentLinkedQueue;
import org.examples.canvas.GraphicApp;
import javafx.application.Platform;
import javafx.concurrent.Task;
import javafx.scene.paint.Color;
public class GameOfLifePublisherConsumer extends GraphicApp {
        final int WIDTH = 2500;
        final int HEIGHT = 2500;
        final int CELL_SIZE = 2;
        boolean currentGeneration[][];
        int columns = WIDTH / CELL_SIZE;
        int rows = HEIGHT / CELL_SIZE;
```

```java
        // this is the desired number of frames
        int numberOfFramesPerSecond = 0;
        private GameOfLife gameOfLife;
        ConcurrentLinkedQueue<boolean[][]> cellsQueue;
        public static void main(String[] args) {
                launch();
        }
        @Override
        public void setup() {
                cellsQueue = new ConcurrentLinkedQueue<>();
                width = WIDTH;
                height = HEIGHT;
                gameOfLife = new GameOfLife(columns, rows, CELL_SIZE);
                currentGeneration = gameOfLife.newCells();
                Task<Void> producerTask = new Task<Void>() {
                        @Override
                        protected Void call() throws Exception {
                                while(true) {
                                        cellsQueue.add(currentGeneration);
                                        currentGeneration =
                                        gameOfLife.newGeneration(current
                                        Generation);
                                }
                        }
                };
                Task<Void> consumerTask = new Task<Void>() {
                        @Override
                        protected Void call() throws Exception {
                                while (true) {
                                        while (!cellsQueue.isEmpty()) {
                                                boolean[][] data =
                                                cellsQueue.poll();
                                                Platform.runLater(() -> {
```

```
                                    // we need to draw
                                    the background
                                    because we are
                                    not using draw
                                    loop anymore
                                    graphicContext.set
                                  Fill(Color.LIGHTGRAY);
                                  graphicContext.
                                  fillRect(0, 0,
                                  width, height);
                                  gameOfLife.
                                  drawCells(data,
                                  graphicContext);
                              });
                              if(numberOfFramesPerSecond
                                  > 0) {
                                  Thread.sleep(1000 /
                                      numberOfFramesPer
                                      Second);
                              }
                        }
                  }
            }
      };
      Thread producerThread = new Thread(producerTask);
      producerThread.setDaemon(true);
      Thread consumerThread = new Thread(consumerTask);
      consumerThread.setDaemon(true);
      producerThread.start();
      consumerThread.start();
      frames(0);
      title("Game of Life Using High-Density Data Pattern");
  }
```

```
        @Override
        public void draw() {
                // we don't use the main loop anymore, but we have to
                draw the background in draw cells
        }
}
```

Conclusion

JavaFX can be used to generate very complex visualizations. As with any framework that allows to create a user interface, it is very easy to create something with a bad performance. However, in this chapter, we explained a number of tips and tricks that allow you to get excellent performance, even with complex scene graphs and a high number of nodes.

With the basic knowledge about the JavaFX Application Thread discussed in this chapter, you can leverage the capabilities JavaFX provides to achieve great performance.

CHAPTER 7

Bridging Swing and JavaFX

Written by Sven Reimers

One of the major advantages of a new UI toolkit is the possibility to protect your investments in existing applications. This chapter will show you how to integrate legacy Swing components into a modern JavaFX UI and how to integrate modern UI elements into an existing Swing application.

Because moving an existing Swing desktop application to a pure JavaFX application is challenging and not always necessary, this chapter describes the technologies available for integration and offers tips and strategies for the migration process.

Note To understand a couple of the concepts, a good understanding of Swing technology is helpful. To grasp some of the examples in full detail, refer to other chapters of this book or some good Swing in-depth material.

Integrating JavaFX into Swing

The typical migration path for a Java desktop application is the usage of a new available control from JavaFX, for example, WebView, which finally allows having a real browser embedded in a standard Swing application.

© Stephen Chin, Johan Vos and James Weaver 2022
S. Chin et al., *The Definitive Guide to Modern Java Clients with JavaFX 17*,
https://doi.org/10.1007/978-1-4842-7268-8_7

JFXPanel: Swing Component with JavaFX Inside

The way to achieve this is to use a special Swing JComponent – the JFXPanel located in the javafx.embed.swing package in the javafx.swing module. It allows you to embed a JavaFX scene graph into a Swing container hierarchy. The interesting method needed from JFXPanel is

- public void setScene(final Scene newScene)

  Attaches a Scene object to display in this JFXPanel. This method can be called either on the event dispatch thread or the JavaFX Application Thread.

Swing coding rules require Swing components to always be created and accessed from the Swing event thread. JFXPanel is different in this respect. It can also be managed from the FX Application Thread. This can be helpful in the case of complex scenes, which may demand JavaFX components to be explicitly created on the FX Application Thread.

Besides the threading aspect, which will be discussed in more detail as we progress further through the integration, the first major thing to recognize here is that the JavaFX embedding does not work on a Node or Control level, rather on a full Scene level. So, if there is a need to embed a Node, for example, a Chart, you cannot just add the Chart instance to the Swing component hierarchy. Instead, you have to create a full Scene and add this using JFXPanel as a Swing component wrapper around your Scene.

With this, a full-fledged small example for an integrated JavaFX Scene can be seen in Listing 7-1.

Note   All following examples are reduced as much as possible so that the integration handling becomes obvious, not the architecture in terms of object-oriented or functional programming. Typically, the only thing needed is a main method into which you can copy and paste the example code. If further special code is needed, this is pointed out in the description for the example.

Listing 7-1. Simple JavaFX in Swing embedding

```
SwingUtilities.invokeLater(() -> {
        var frame = new JFrame("JavaFX 17 integrated in Swing");
        frame.setDefaultCloseOperation(JFrame.EXIT_ON_CLOSE);
        var jfxPanel = new JFXPanel();
        var button = new Button("Hello FX");
        var scene = new Scene(button);
        jfxPanel.setScene(scene);
        jfxPanel.setPreferredSize(new Dimension(100,200));
        var panel = new JPanel(new BorderLayout());
        panel.add(new JLabel("Hello Swing North"), BorderLayout.NORTH);
        panel.add(new JLabel("Hello Swing South"), BorderLayout.SOUTH);
        panel.add(jfxPanel, BorderLayout.CENTER);
        frame.setContentPane(panel);
        frame.pack();
        frame.setLocationRelativeTo(null);
        frame.setVisible(true);
    });
```

This code will produce a Swing JFrame with three visible parts, one Swing JLabel on top of a JavaFX Button on top of another Swing JLabel as shown in Figure 7-1.

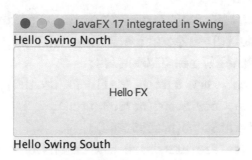

Figure 7-1. *Simple JavaFX integration*

Especially interesting here is the layout of the components. One major aspect is the correct setting of the preferred size of the JFXPanel. If you comment out setting the preferred size, you will see the JFXPanel resizing to the minimum size of the Button after running the example. The initial view you get should be similar to what is shown in Figure 7-2. This is a change in behavior from, for example, JavaFX 11, where the JFXPanel would not have the correct preferred size.

Figure 7-2. *Simple JavaFX integration without setting preferred size*

Having solved this initial integration problem, let's dive deeper into the possibilities this solution offers.

Because JFXPanel is a Swing component, this opens up the opportunity to create multiple component instances and add them to the Swing component hierarchy. For a simple example, the application from Listing 7-1 is changed to use two JavaFX Labels and one Swing JLabel as shown in Listing 7-2.

Listing 7-2. Multiple JavaFX Scenes in Swing

```
SwingUtilities.invokeLater(() -> {
        var frame = new JFrame("JavaFX 17 integrated in Swing (multiple)");
        frame.setDefaultCloseOperation(JFrame.EXIT_ON_CLOSE);
        var northJfxPanel = new JFXPanel();
        var northButton = new Button("Hello FX North");
        var northScene = new Scene(northButton);
        northJfxPanel.setScene(northScene);
        northJfxPanel.setPreferredSize(new Dimension(200,50));
        var southJfxPanel = new JFXPanel();
        var southButton = new Button("Hello FX South");
        var southScene = new Scene(southButton);
        southJfxPanel.setScene(southScene);
        southJfxPanel.setPreferredSize(new Dimension(200,50));
        var panel = new JPanel(new BorderLayout());
        panel.add(northJfxPanel, BorderLayout.NORTH);
```

```
        panel.add(southJfxPanel, BorderLayout.SOUTH);
        panel.add(new JLabel("Hello Swing"), BorderLayout.CENTER);
        frame.setContentPane(panel);
        frame.pack();
        frame.setLocationRelativeTo(null);
        frame.setVisible(true);
});
```

If you run this program, the output shown should be similar to Figure 7-3.

Figure 7-3. *Multiple JavaFX Scenes*

So far, all the examples were extremely simplified in comparison to real-world integration scenarios. A typical scenario is the integration of WebView into an existing Swing application. With some small modifications of Listing 7-1, a WebView is integrated instead of the Button of the original application as shown in Listing 7-3.

Listing 7-3. Adding a WebView to a Swing application

```
SwingUtilities.invokeLater(() -> {
        var frame = new JFrame("JavaFX 17 integrated in Swing");
        frame.setDefaultCloseOperation(JFrame.EXIT_ON_CLOSE);
        var jfxPanel = new JFXPanel();
        var panel = new JPanel(new BorderLayout());
        panel.add(new JLabel("Hello Swing North"), BorderLayout.NORTH);
        panel.add(new JLabel("Hello Swing South"), BorderLayout.SOUTH);
        Platform.runLater(() -> {
            var webView = new WebView();
            var scene = new Scene(webView);
            webView.getEngine().load("https://openjfx.io/");
            jfxPanel.setScene(scene);
```

```
            jfxPanel.setPreferredSize(new Dimension(400,600));
            SwingUtilities.invokeLater(() -> {
                panel.add(jfxPanel, BorderLayout.CENTER);
                frame.pack();
                frame.setLocationRelativeTo(null);
            });
        });
        frame.setContentPane(panel);
        frame.pack();
        frame.setLocationRelativeTo(null);
        frame.setVisible(true);
    });
```

Running this example will show a `WebView` rendering the OpenJFX homepage sitting between two Swing `JLabel`s as shown in Figure 7-4.

Figure 7-4. *WebView embedded in Swing application*

Looking at the code, there is an obvious change in comparison with the original code. The creation of the `Scene` requires a couple of thread changes to get everything done on the correct UI thread. For a better understanding, let us take a peek under the hood to see the details of threading.

Threading

Threading in an application with mixed JavaFX nodes and Swing components is a complex thing to get right.

As already hinted at in the last section, two major threads have to be considered:

- JavaFX Application Thread

- AWT-EventQueue

The first thread is associated with all things JavaFX, for example, adding a new Node to the already rendered (live) scene graph or changing a property of a node belonging to an already rendered scene graph.

The second thread is associated with the Swing UI toolkit (inherited from AWT, hence the name), for example, creation of all Swing components shall occur on this thread. Combining the toolkits will result in a lot of hopping on and off one or the other thread to ensure all things are always triggered and done on the correct thread.

Note   A system property `javafx.embed.singleThread` is available, which switches both UI toolkits to use the same thread if set to `true`. This behavior is experimental and may lead to undesired behavior, so use with caution.

One more special thing should be noted, especially since WebView is probably the most wanted JavaFX control to be integrated with Swing. All other JavaFX controls can be created on any thread besides WebView. Due to some initialization problems, WebView has to be created on the JavaFX Application Thread, quoting from JDK-8087718:

> *In theory, it should be possible to eliminate the restriction by deferring the initialization calls until the first real use of the WebKit code. In practice, such a change is likely to end up being very non-trivial, primarily due to the fact that there is a large number of entry points that may or may not result in the "first real use."*

With this knowledge about the threading, let's look again at the initialization code of the last example.

The first remarkable part of the code sequence is the necessity to execute some code during the setup of the JFXPanel on the JavaFX Application Thread. Once this code is finished, another code fragment is required to run on the AWT-EventQueue. The nesting

289

of the execution blocks guarantees the correct sequence. So a generic sequence of code can roughly look like the pseudo-code in Listing 7-4.

Listing 7-4. Abstract sequence with dedicated thread-sensitive code

```
Platform.runLater(() -> {
    // ensure JavaFX all necessary init is done
    SwingUtilities.invokeLater(() -> {
        // now come back to update Swing component hierarchy accordingly
    });
});
```

> **Note**   There are two utility methods that can be helpful to ensure or detect that code is executed on the correct thread: `javax.swing.SwingUtilities.isEventDispatchThread()` and `javax.application.Platform.isFxApplicationThread()`. Used either in asserts to guarantee the thread or as a simple debugging support, they can help make the usage of threads more transparent.

With a better understanding of how to run which code on the correct thread, the next step of integration is providing interaction between JavaFX Nodes and Swing JComponents.

Interaction Between Swing and JavaFX

The next step in an integration story is interaction between components of both UI toolkits. Looking at the threading models of JavaFX and Swing, this will require some extra ceremony. A change from a JavaFX node/control will be notified on the JavaFX Application Thread, and a Swing component will need to be changed on the AWT-EventQueue. Handling events coming from JavaFX toward Swing will require switching threads, that is, execute code blocks (lambdas) on the correct thread. This pattern will look similar to the following code fragment:

```
NODE.setOnXXX(e ->
        SwingUtilities.invokeLater(() -> JCOMPONENT.setYYY(ZZZZ))).
```

As an example, the text of the south label shall be changed on press and release of the mouse button. Based on the aforementioned code strategy, the necessary code is

```
button.setOnMousePressed(e ->
        SwingUtilities.invokeLater(() -> southLabel.setText("FX Button
        Pressed")));
button.setOnMouseReleased(e ->
        SwingUtilities.invokeLater(() -> southLabel.setText("Hello Swing
        South")));
```

The first statement triggers a change of the southLabel text on pressing the mouse button, and the second statement changes the text back to its original value once the button gets released. The full application can be seen in Listing 7-5.

Listing 7-5. Interactive JavaFX in Swing embedding

```
SwingUtilities.invokeLater(() -> {
    var frame = new JFrame("JavaFX 17 integrated in Swing");
    frame.setDefaultCloseOperation(JFrame.EXIT_ON_CLOSE);
    var jfxPanel = new JFXPanel();
    var button = new Button("Hello FX");
    var scene = new Scene(button);
    jfxPanel.setScene(scene);
    jfxPanel.setPreferredSize(new Dimension(200,100));
    jfxPanel.setBorder(new EmptyBorder(5,5,5,5));
    var panel = new JPanel(new BorderLayout());
    panel.add(new JLabel("Hello Swing North"), BorderLayout.NORTH);
    var southLabel = new JLabel("Hello Swing South");
    panel.add(southLabel, BorderLayout.SOUTH);
    button.setOnMousePressed(e ->
    SwingUtilities.invokeLater(() -> southLabel.setText("FX Button
    Pressed")));
    button.setOnMouseReleased(e ->
    SwingUtilities.invokeLater(() -> southLabel.setText("Hello Swing
    South")));
    panel.add(jfxPanel, BorderLayout.CENTER);
    frame.setContentPane(panel);
```

```
    frame.pack();
    frame.setLocationRelativeTo(null);
    frame.setVisible(true);
});
```

The interaction works the same way in both directions. To show interaction starting from Swing, let's change the last example to contain a Swing JButton in the south area and add some listening to it:

```
southButton.addMouseListener(new MouseAdapter() {
    @Override
    public void mousePressed(MouseEvent e) {
        Platform.runLater(() -> button.setText("Swing Button Pressed"));
    }
    @Override
    public void mouseReleased(MouseEvent e) {
        Platform.runLater(() -> button.setText("Hello FX"));
    }
});
```

As can be seen, interaction will start on the AWT-EventQueue and is then shifted to the JavaFX Application Thread to change the text property of the JavaFX Button. The full example code can be seen in Listing 7-6.

Listing 7-6. Interactive bidirectional JavaFX in Swing

```
SwingUtilities.invokeLater(() -> {
    var frame = new JFrame("JavaFX 17 bidirectional interaction in Swing");
    frame.setDefaultCloseOperation(JFrame.EXIT_ON_CLOSE);
    var jfxPanel = new JFXPanel();
    var button = new Button("Hello FX");
    var scene = new Scene(button);
    jfxPanel.setScene(scene);
    jfxPanel.setPreferredSize(new Dimension(200,100));
    jfxPanel.setBorder(new EmptyBorder(5,5,5,5));
    var panel = new JPanel(new BorderLayout());
    panel.add(new JLabel("Hello Swing North"), BorderLayout.NORTH);
```

```
var southButton = new JButton("Hello Swing South Button");
panel.add(southButton, BorderLayout.SOUTH);
button.setOnMousePressed(e ->
        SwingUtilities.invokeLater(() -> southButton.setText("FX Button
        Pressed")));
button.setOnMouseReleased(e ->
        SwingUtilities.invokeLater(() -> southButton.
        setText("Hello Swing South")));
southButton.addMouseListener(new MouseAdapter() {
    @Override
    public void mousePressed(MouseEvent e) {
        Platform.runLater(() -> button.setText("Swing Button
        Pressed"));
    }
    @Override
    public void mouseReleased(MouseEvent e) {
        Platform.runLater(() -> button.setText("Hello FX"));
    }
});
panel.add(jfxPanel, BorderLayout.CENTER);
frame.setContentPane(panel);
frame.pack();
frame.setLocationRelativeTo(null);
frame.setVisible(true);
});
```

Running this application shows the following states (see Figures 7-5 to 7-7).

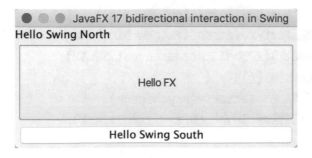

Figure 7-5. *Start state of interaction demo*

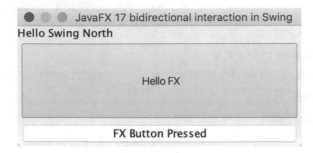

Figure 7-6. *State after JavaFX button clicked*

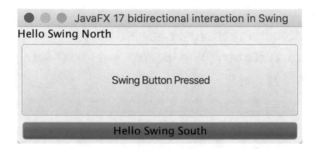

Figure 7-7. *State after Swing button clicked*

The next level of interactivity is to dynamically add a JavaFX scene to the Swing application. This is a feature typically required with more complex application frameworks, because they dynamically change the Swing component hierarchy. Modify the preceding example with multiple JavaFX Scenes so that the second JFXPanel will be added as the result of a Swing button click. The major change is the ActionListener necessary:

```
swingButton.addActionListener(e -> {
    var southJfxPanel = new JFXPanel();
    var southButton = new Button("Hello FX South");
    var southScene = new Scene(southButton);
    southJfxPanel.setPreferredSize(new Dimension(200,50));
    panel.add(southJfxPanel, BorderLayout.SOUTH);
    Platform.runLater(() -> {
        southJfxPanel.setScene(southScene);
        SwingUtilities.invokeLater(frame::pack);
    });
});
```

The creation of the JFXPanel itself can be done on the AWT-EventQueue (as described before), but in this case, the setting of the scene has to be done on the JavaFX Application Thread; and to ensure visibility of the panel, it is necessary to resize the frame again. This has to be done on the AWT-EventQueue, once the scene is set.

Running the example as shown in Listing 7-7 shall display two JFXPanels inside one Swing JFrame as shown in Figure 7-8.

Figure 7-8. *State after Scene has been added*

Listing 7-7. Interactive bidirectional dynamic JavaFX in Swing

```
SwingUtilities.invokeLater(() -> {
    var frame = new JFrame("JavaFX 17 integrated in Swing (multiple,
    dynamic)");
    frame.setDefaultCloseOperation(JFrame.EXIT_ON_CLOSE);
    var northJfxPanel = new JFXPanel();
    var northButton = new Button("Hello FX North");
    var northScene = new Scene(northButton);
    northJfxPanel.setScene(northScene);
    northJfxPanel.setPreferredSize(new Dimension(200,50));
    var panel = new JPanel(new BorderLayout());
    panel.add(northJfxPanel, BorderLayout.NORTH);
    var swingButton = new JButton("Add FX Scene in South");
    swingButton.addActionListener(e -> {
        var southJfxPanel = new JFXPanel();
        var southButton = new Button("Hello FX South");
        var southScene = new Scene(southButton);
        southJfxPanel.setPreferredSize(new Dimension(200,50));
        panel.add(southJfxPanel, BorderLayout.SOUTH);
        Platform.runLater(() -> {
```

```
            southJfxPanel.setScene(southScene);
            SwingUtilities.invokeLater(frame::pack);
        });
    });
    panel.add(swingButton, BorderLayout.CENTER);
    frame.setContentPane(panel);
    frame.pack();
    frame.setLocationRelativeTo(null);
    frame.setVisible(true);
});
```

The next logical step is the interactive removal of a JFXPanel. For demonstration purposes, the last example is enhanced with the additional possibility to remove the north JFXPanel (see Listing 7-8).

Listing 7-8. Adding/removing of JFXPanel in Swing

```
SwingUtilities.invokeLater(() -> {
    var frame = new JFrame("JavaFX 17 integrated in Swing (multiple,
    dynamic)");
    frame.setDefaultCloseOperation(JFrame.EXIT_ON_CLOSE);
    var northJfxPanel = new JFXPanel();
    var northButton = new Button("Hello FX North");
    var northScene = new Scene(northButton);
    northJfxPanel.setScene(northScene);
    northJfxPanel.setPreferredSize(new Dimension(200,50));
    var panel = new JPanel(new BorderLayout());
    panel.add(northJfxPanel, BorderLayout.NORTH);
    var northSwingButton = new JButton("Remove FX Scene in North");
    northSwingButton.addActionListener(e -> {
        panel.remove(northJfxPanel);
        frame.pack();
    });
        var southSwingButton = new JButton("Add FX Scene in South");
        southSwingButton.addActionListener(e -> {
            var southJfxPanel = new JFXPanel();
            var southButton = new Button("Hello FX South");
```

```
        var southScene = new Scene(southButton);
        southJfxPanel.setPreferredSize(new Dimension(200,50));
        panel.add(southJfxPanel, BorderLayout.SOUTH);
        Platform.runLater(() -> {
            southJfxPanel.setScene(southScene);
            SwingUtilities.invokeLater(frame::pack);
        });
    });
    var swingInside = new JPanel(new BorderLayout());
    swingInside.add(northSwingButton, BorderLayout.NORTH);
    swingInside.add(southSwingButton, BorderLayout.SOUTH);
    panel.add(swingInside, BorderLayout.CENTER);
    frame.setContentPane(panel);
    frame.pack();
    frame.setLocationRelativeTo(null);
    frame.setVisible(true);
});
```

Running this example shows two Swing buttons – one for removal of the northern JFXPanel and one for the addition of the southern JFXPanel as seen in Figure 7-9.

Figure 7-9. *Addition/removal of JFXPanels*

The result of the application depends on the sequence of the button clicks. If the button for adding the JFXPanel to the south is clicked first, the panel will show up, and the click of the removal button removes the northern JFXPanel (result is shown in Figure 7-10).

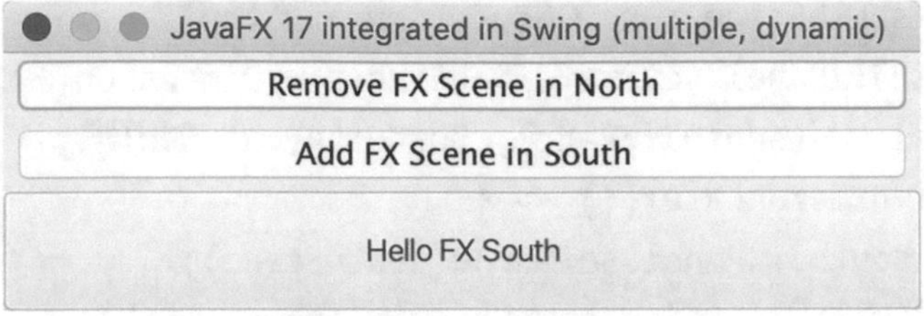

Figure 7-10. *Result of first adding and then removing the JFXPanel*

If the buttons are clicked in the inverse order, the northern panel is removed, but the southern panel cannot be added anymore. This is due to the fact that JavaFX has a feature that automatically initiates a shutdown of the JavaFX runtime as soon as the last JavaFX window is closed. This feature is enabled by default, so that the removal of the only JFXPanel triggers the shutdown, and afterward all calls to the runtime, for example, adding the JFXPanel to the south, do not work anymore. This behavior can be changed by disabling the implicitExit feature:

```
Platform.setImplicitExit(false);
```

Note   If you try to create some generic integration of JavaFX on top of Swing, it is probably always a good idea to disable this feature, to ensure the JavaFX runtime is not accidentally shut down.

Drag and Drop with JavaFX and Swing

More complex Swing applications will typically have some kind of drag-and-drop support, either inside the application or for dragging stuff from outside the application into it. The second use case is not a special case in the integration, because the drop target is either a Swing JComponent or a JavaFX Node. This allows to use the default drop handling for each of the technologies. The first case is more interesting, since drag source and drop target are based on different UI technologies.

An example application is shown in Figure 7-11.

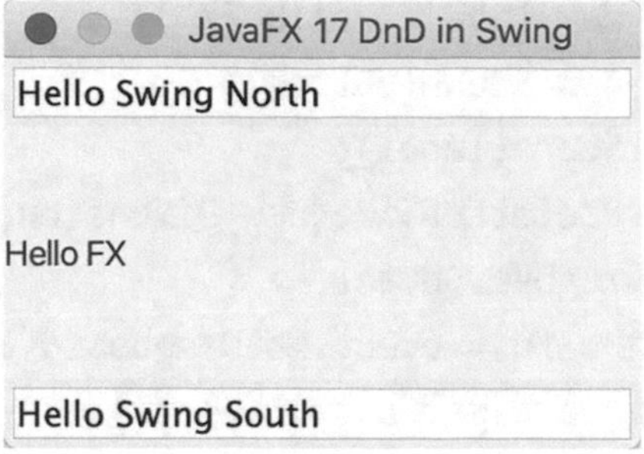

Figure 7-11. *Drag and drop with JavaFX and Swing*

There are two Swing JTextFields and one JavaFX Label. The drag operation allows for dragging selected text from either the north or the south Swing TextField and dropping it onto the JavaFX Label. Although this sounds like a lot of complex threading, it is not. Most of the complex interaction is done on the toolkit level, invisible to the user.

The first thing that is needed is an interaction for the drag start as shown in Listing 7-9.

Listing 7-9. Swing MouseAdapter for drag start

```
private static class MouseDragAdapter extends MouseAdapter {
    @Override
    public void mousePressed(MouseEvent e) {
        var component = (JComponent) e.getSource();
        component.getTransferHandler().
                    exportAsDrag(component, e, TransferHandler.COPY);
    }
  }
```

The shown code fragment defines a MouseListener and just overrides the mousePressed method to ensure that by pressing the mouse button, the content of the component is exported as the drag content. With this, we can now look at the full code in Listing 7-10.

Listing 7-10. Drag from Swing to JavaFX

```
SwingUtilities.invokeLater(() -> {
        var frame = new JFrame("JavaFX 17 DnD in Swing");
        frame.setDefaultCloseOperation(JFrame.EXIT_ON_CLOSE);
        var jfxPanel = new JFXPanel();
```

```
var label = new Label("Hello FX");
var scene = new Scene(button);
jfxPanel.setScene(label);
jfxPanel.setPreferredSize(new Dimension(200, 100));
label.setOnDragOver(event -> {
    var dragboard = event.getDragboard();
    if (dragboard.getContentTypes().
        contains( DataFormat.lookupMimeType("application/
        x-java-serialized-object"))) {
        event.acceptTransferModes(TransferMode.COPY);
    }
    event.consume();
});
label.setOnDragDropped(event -> {
    var dataFormat = DataFormat.
                     lookupMimeType("application/x-java-
                     serialized-object");
    var dragboard = event.getDragboard();
    if (dragboard.hasContent(dataFormat)) {
        String content = (String) dragboard.
        getContent(dataFormat);
        label.setText(content);
    }
    event.setDropCompleted(true);
    event.consume();
});
var panel = new JPanel(new BorderLayout());
var northField = new JTextField("Hello Swing North");
northField.setDragEnabled(true);
northField.addMouseListener(new MouseDragAdapter());
var southField = new JTextField("Hello Swing South");
southField.setDragEnabled(true);
southField.addMouseListener(new MouseDragAdapter());
panel.add(northField, BorderLayout.NORTH);
panel.add(southField, BorderLayout.SOUTH);
```

```
        panel.add(jfxPanel, BorderLayout.CENTER);
        frame.setContentPane(panel);
        frame.pack();
        frame.setLocationRelativeTo(null);
        frame.setVisible(true);
    });
```

There are two distinct pieces ensuring that dropping onto the JavaFX Label works. The first code fragment ensures during detecting the drag is happening over the component that in case of a compatible MimeType in the DragBoard content types, the accept mode for dragging is set. With this done, the only thing missing is the reaction to the real drop. This code fragment ensures the availability of the expected MimeType, retrieves the data from the DragBoard in the correct format, and uses the data to change the displayed text of the Label.

Due to the fact that all those handling methods are called from the UI toolkits, all handling is already on the correct thread, so no thread switching is needed in this example.

Note   Drag and drop from one node in one JFXPanel to another node in another JFXPanel is not different from drag and drop between any two nodes in an ordinary JavaFX scene. Both, source and target of the operation, do know nothing about the embedding in a Swing context. This is an important factor for integrating complex JavaFX nodes/controls into a Swing application.

JavaFX 3D Integrated in Swing

One of the most compelling features of JavaFX is the support for 3D rendering and the mixture of 2D and 3D, which makes the creation of advanced visualization simple. Because JFXPanel just takes any Scene and embeds it into the Swing component hierarchy, this can also be done to 3D-enabled scenes.

Building on top of one of the 3D examples used in this book, Listing 7-11 shows an example of a 3D integration.

Listing 7-11. 3D embedded in Swing

```
SwingUtilities.invokeLater(() -> {
    var frame = new JFrame("JavaFX 17 3D integrated in Swing");
    frame.setDefaultCloseOperation(JFrame.EXIT_ON_CLOSE);
    var jfxPanel = new JFXPanel();
    var camera = createCamera();
    var box = new Box(10, 10, 10);
    var view = new Group(box, camera);
    var scene = new Scene(view, 640, 480);
    scene.setCamera(camera);
    jfxPanel.setScene(scene);
    jfxPanel.setPreferredSize(new Dimension(200,100));
    var panel = new JPanel(new BorderLayout());
    panel.add(new JLabel("Hello Swing North"), BorderLayout.NORTH);
    panel.add(new JLabel("Hello Swing South"), BorderLayout.SOUTH);
    panel.add(jfxPanel, BorderLayout.CENTER);
    frame.setContentPane(panel);
    frame.pack();
    frame.setLocationRelativeTo(null);
    frame.setVisible(true);
    Platform.runLater(() -> animate());
});
private static Camera createCamera() {
    Camera answer = new PerspectiveCamera(true);
    answer.getTransforms().addAll(rotateX, rotateY, rotateZ, translateZ);
    return answer;
}
private static void animate() {
    Timeline timeline = new Timeline(
            new KeyFrame(Duration.seconds(0),
                    new KeyValue(translateZ.zProperty(), -20),
                    new KeyValue(rotateX.angleProperty(), 90),
                    new KeyValue(rotateY.angleProperty(), 90),
                    new KeyValue(rotateZ.angleProperty(), 90)),
            new KeyFrame(Duration.seconds(5),
```

```
                new KeyValue(translateZ.zProperty(), -80),
                new KeyValue(rotateX.angleProperty(), -90),
                new KeyValue(rotateY.angleProperty(), -90),
                new KeyValue(rotateZ.angleProperty(), -90))
    );
    timeline.setCycleCount(Animation.INDEFINITE);
    timeline.setAutoReverse(true);
    timeline.play();
}
```

Running the example shows a Swing application with two Swing labels, one above and one below the 3D animated JavaFX scene as shown in Figure 7-12.

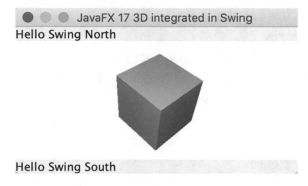

Figure 7-12. *3D rendering integrated in Swing*

Integrating Swing into JavaFX

Having done the integration of new JavaFX controls inside existing Swing applications, this section describes how to use well-known large Swing-based libraries, for example, WorldWind from NASA (`https://worldwind.arc.nasa.gov/java`), inside the JavaFX scene graph.

The way to achieve this is to use a special JavaFX Node – the SwingNode. It allows you to embed a Swing JComponent inside the scene graph. Where JFXPanel is a JComponent wrapping around a JavaFX Scene, SwingNode is a JavaFX Node wrapping a Swing component hierarchy. All things shown and discussed about threading, interaction, and so on are valid for the integration of Swing components in JavaFX applications as well. Because from an interaction standpoint, both elements, the JavaFX Node and the Swing

JComponent, do not know how they are integrated, it does not matter if it is JavaFX inside Swing or Swing inside JavaFX. The main difference is that during the construction of the UI tree, either the Swing or the JavaFX rules apply. A simple example is shown Listing 7-12.

Listing 7-12. Swing embedded in JavaFX

```
@Override
public void start(Stage stage) throws Exception {
    var borderPane = new BorderPane();
    var swingNode = new SwingNode();
    var scene = new Scene(borderPane, 200, 200);
    borderPane.setCenter(swingNode);
    borderPane.setBottom(new Label("JavaFX Bottom"));
    SwingUtilities.invokeLater(() -> {
        var panel = new JPanel();
        panel.setLayout(new BorderLayout());
        panel.add(new JLabel("Swing North"), BorderLayout.CENTER);
        swingNode.setContent(panel);
        borderPane.layout();
    });
    stage.setScene(scene);
    stage.show();
}
```

The result of running this application is shown in Figure 7-13.

Figure 7-13. *Swing embedded in JavaFX*

Migration Strategies

Migrating between UI toolkits is always a tedious and complex process. JavaFX mitigates this by providing quite seamless dual-way integration components – JFXPanel and SwingNode. This allows for arbitrary migration steps from a full Swing-based application to a full JavaFX application.

Typically, the migration path begins with a complex Swing-based application and tries to get rid of as much Swing as possible or tries to integrate better components or controls available from JavaFX. So the first stop is always the JFXPanel-based approach.

Using the strategy "divide et impera," look for components in your existing Swing component hierarchy that can be easily replaced with their JavaFX counterparts.

While you do this, more and more parts of your application will start to be JavaFX, and you can start to regroup already transformed JFXPanels into larger scene graphs. If there is still some Swing component, which cannot be transformed, there is still the possibility to reuse the original Swing component and wrap it inside a SwingNode and use it as a part of the scene graph.

This approach using both JFXPanel and SwingNode allows for at least theoretically transparent and incremental migration, although the details in doing so may be tricky.

Large-Scale Integrations

The enhanced integration possibilities JavaFX offers in terms of building mash-up applications that are originally built on Swing make it easy to create complex combinations of both technologies.

One very prominent example is a project that tries to embed Scene Builder, a JavaFX rapid application development tool, into Apache NetBeans (https://netbeans.apache.org) – a Swing-based IDE. The actual project can be found at https://github.com/svenreimers/nbscenebuilder.

Figure 7-14 shows an example screenshot of the integration.

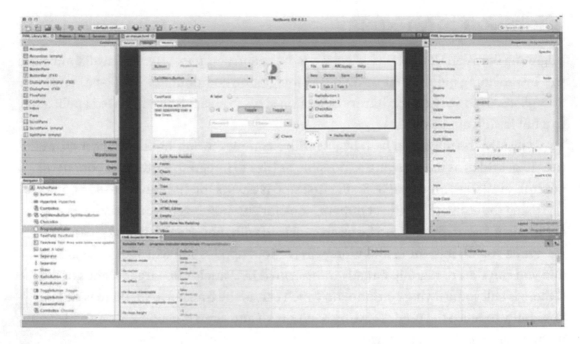

Figure 7-14. *Scene Builder integration in Apache NetBeans*

Conclusion

With two compatibility strategies, allowing for embedding of JavaFX UI parts into existing Swing applications and allowing the reuse of Swing components inside new JavaFX applications, JavaFX is a top choice for building new cross-platform rich client applications. The key points covered in this chapter are as follows:

- JavaFX offers a Swing component called JFXPanel to integrate JavaFX scene graphs into Swing.

- JavaFX offers SwingNode to integrate Swing components into JavaFX.

- Special attention is required while dealing with two UI toolkits providing their own dedicated UI thread.

- Interactions between nodes and components from both UI toolkits are fairly easy to implement.

- Large-scale integrations are certainly possible and can protect your existing investments.

CHAPTER 8

JavaFX 3D

Written by Johan Vos and José Pereda

Modern UI platforms should be capable of dealing with three-dimensional data visualization on a two-dimensional screen. This is often a requirement for applications that are, for example, related to engineering, construction, science, or medical imaging. The JavaFX APIs provide a number of base classes for three-dimensional shapes and a number of ways to manipulate those shapes and their rendering, taking into account environmental circumstances such as light, camera, and material properties.

On top of that, third-party frameworks provide additional shapes and functionality that developers can use to create three-dimensional scenes that are rendered on a two-dimensional screen.

In this chapter, we give an overview of the functionality that is available in the JavaFX APIs, and we briefly cover a third-party extension. We start with the basic concepts, and once we cover those, we will combine some of these concepts into more interactive samples.

Prerequisites

Typically, projecting three-dimensional objects onto a two-dimensional screen, taking into account light, material behavior, and camera viewpoint, is a computationally intensive process. While this can be done using software rendering only, this will often lead to slow rendering, which does not contribute to a great user experience. In its architecture, JavaFX allows to leverage modern rendering solutions and hardware acceleration where possible.

© Stephen Chin, Johan Vos and James Weaver 2022
S. Chin et al., *The Definitive Guide to Modern Java Clients with JavaFX 17*,
https://doi.org/10.1007/978-1-4842-7268-8_8

Therefore, JavaFX will only allow the rendering and manipulation of three-dimensional scenes if the underlying hardware is capable of doing it. The JavaFX platform provides a method

```
javafx.application.Platform.isSupported(ConditionalFeature feature)
```

which returns true only if the specific feature is supported by the running JavaFX platform. Depending on your hardware and operating system, some features will be supported, while other features might not be supported. One particular ConditionalFeature specifies whether 3D is supported:

```
ConditionalFeature.SCENE3D
```

At runtime, the JavaFX platform will select the most optimal rendering pipeline. It will always try to use a hardware-accelerated rendering pipeline. On Windows systems, this is the D3DPipeline, which has support for Direct3D. All implementations have support for ConditionalFeature.SCENE3D and hence are capable of rendering JavaFX 3D scenes.

On Linux, macOS, Android, iOS, and most embedded systems, the ES2Pipeline will be used, which will use OpenGL for the rendering of the JavaFX nodes. OpenGL defines a number of extensions that may or may not be present in a specific implementation. One of those extensions is support for NPOT, which allows storage of textures whose dimensions are not a power of 2. If this extension is available, the JavaFX platform has support for ConditionalFeature.SCENE3D.

In practice, most modern systems provide support for JavaFX 3D. Mobile devices typically have a strong GPU with support for hardware acceleration as well, since those devices are frequently used to render highly dynamic, interactive content (e.g., images, videos). In the case of old or unsupported hardware, JavaFX will gracefully print a message about missing support for 3D, rather than providing the user with a slow and unresponsive interface.

Getting Started with Shapes

The JavaFX platform contains a number of out-of-the-box available three-dimensional shapes. Apart from those predefined shapes, developers can create their own three-dimensional objects. All those shapes are regular JavaFX nodes; hence, they can be combined with those nodes. There are a number of additional features and properties related to three-dimensional objects that are not relevant in two-dimensional worlds, and we will cover those later in the chapter.

As a very simple example, we show how we can combine a simple JavaFX label and a three-dimensional sphere in a single JavaFX scene. The code in Listing 8-1 that can be found at https://github.com/modernclientjava/mcj-samples/tree/master/ch08-3Dgraphics/simplesphere achieves this.

Listing 8-1. SimpleSphere source code

```
package org.modernclientjava.hello3d;
import javafx.application.Application;
import javafx.scene.Group;
import javafx.scene.Scene;
import javafx.scene.control.Label;
import javafx.scene.shape.Sphere;
import javafx.stage.Stage;
public class SimpleSphere extends Application {
    @Override
    public void start(Stage stage) throws Exception {
        Sphere sphere = new Sphere(50);
        Label label = new Label("Hello, JavaFX 3D");
        label.setTranslateY(80);
        Group root = new Group(label, sphere);
        root.setTranslateX(320);
        root.setTranslateY(240);
        Scene scene = new Scene(root, 640, 480);
        stage.setTitle("JavaFX 3D Sphere");
        stage.setScene(scene);
        stage.show();
    }
    public static void main(String[] args) {
        launch();
    }
}
```

The output for this sample is shown in Figure 8-1.

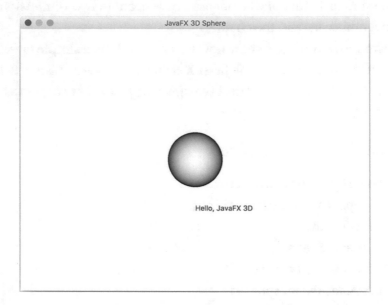

Figure 8-1. *Output from SimpleSphere sample*

While this picture is extremely simple and it doesn't provide lots of real value, the important part is that it is very easy in JavaFX to get started with adding three-dimensional objects to scenes.

We created a sphere with the single-argument constructor

```
Sphere sphere = new Sphere(50);
```

which creates a sphere with a radius of 50 pixels. The center of this sphere is at the center of our coordinate system, which in three dimensions is at (0,0,0).

In order to show how 2D and 3D objects can be combined in a single scene, we create a label as well:

```
Label label = new Label("Hello, JavaFX 3D");
```

We don't want the label to overlap with the sphere; hence, we move it down along the y-axis by 80 pixels:

```
label.setTranslateY(80);
```

We then combine the sphere and the label in a single group as follows:

```
Group root = new Group(label, sphere);
```

We want to center the content of our group to the center of the scene. We will create a scene with a width of 640 pixels and a height of 480 pixels, so we will shift the group to the center by moving it horizontally with 320 and vertically with 240 pixels:

```
root.setTranslateX(320);
root.setTranslateY(240);
Scene scene = new Scene(root, 640, 480);
```

The remaining code will simply assign the scene to the stage, set the title, and show the stage.

Although the developer has to write very little code to get started with JavaFX 3D APIs, there is a lot going on behind the scenes. Shapes have material property, the projection is realized by a camera on the scene, and there is a light source responsible for illuminating the scene. We will discuss material, camera, and light later in the chapter.

The JavaFX APIs allow for a number of primitive 3D shapes to be created out of the box: a sphere, a box, and a cylinder. Developers can easily add their own shapes, by using the MeshView class, which we will describe later.

The following code snippet shows a sphere, a cube, and a box in a single scene:

```
Sphere sphere= new Sphere(50);
sphere.setTranslateX(-100);
Box box = new Box(40,50,60);
Cylinder cylinder = new Cylinder(50, 80);
cylinder.setTranslateX(100);
Group root = new Group(sphere, box, cylinder);
root.setRotationAxis(new Point3D(.2,.5,.7));
root.setRotate(45);
root.setTranslateX(320);
root.setTranslateY(240);
Scene scene = new Scene(root, 640, 480);
```

In order to make it clear that we are dealing with three-dimensional shapes here, we rotated the entire group so that different sides of the shapes are visible. A (non-shown) rotation axis is defined by the center point of the scene with {x,y,z} coordinates of {0,0,0} and the supplied point with pixel coordinates {0.2,0.5,0.7}. Those two points define the line around which the entire group is rotated.

We will talk more about coordinate systems and translations later.

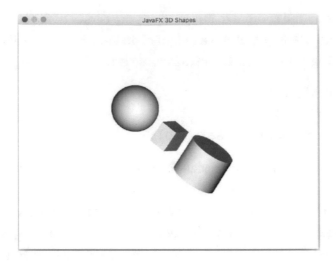

Figure 8-2. *Output of SphereCylinderBox sample*

Running this application that can be found at `https://github.com/` `modernclientjava/mcj-samples/tree/master/ch08-3Dgraphics/spherecylinderbox` results in the screen output in Figure 8-2.

This sample shows the three predefined three-dimensional shapes in JavaFX: Sphere, Box, and Cylinder. Those shapes all are part of the javafx.scene.shape package (which is the same package where also the two-dimensional shapes live), and they extend the javafx.scene.shape.Shape3D class. A fourth class, MeshView, allows developers to create their own shape.

Before we discuss the different shapes, we will explain the coordinate system used by the JavaFX platform. As shown in Figure 8-3, JavaFX uses a right-handed coordinate system. In this system, the x- and y-axes are in the area of the screen, with the z-axis perpendicular on the screen, pointing away from the viewer. The origin of the coordinate system is at the upper-left corner of the screen.

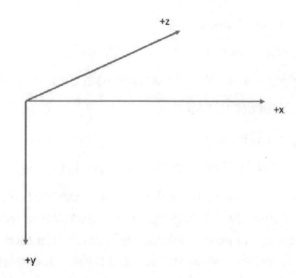

Figure 8-3. *Coordinate system in JavaFX 3D*

By default, JavaFX uses a parallel camera placed at a negative value of z, hence looking into the direction of positive z values. This camera uses an orthographic projection, in which all nodes are vertically projected onto the {x,y} plane. Later, we will discuss another type of camera, the PerspectiveCamera, that uses a different projection.

Since this default camera doesn't render nodes differently if their coordinates along the z-axis change, it is hard to see the shape of a box unless it is rotated. This is what we did in the second sample. We rotated the whole group around an axis starting at (0,0,0) and containing (0.2,0.5,0.7).

The translate and rotate properties, as well as the rotationAxis property, of three-dimensional shapes are inherited from the JavaFX Node class.

Shape3D

The superclass of all JavaFX 3D shapes is `javafx.scene.shape.Shape3D`. This base class provides common functionality shared by all shapes. That functionality is defined by three properties: material, drawMode, and cullFace. Following the JavaFX API conventions, those properties are directly accessible, and their values are reachable via corresponding get and set methods:

- `void setMaterial(Material)`

- `Material getMaterial()`

- `ObjectProperty<Material> materialProperty()`

- `void setDrawMode(DrawMode)`

- `DrawMode getDrawMode()`

- `ObjectProperty<DrawMode> drawModeProperty()`

- `void setCullFace(CullFace)`

- `CullFace getCullFace()`

- `ObjectProperty<CullFace> cullFaceProperty()`

The Material class contains a set of rendering properties that control how the 3D shape reacts to lights. It gives the 3D shape its unique look. We cover the Material class hierarchy in a later section. For now, it is sufficient to know that there is one concrete class in the hierarchy called PhongMaterial and that it has a constructor that takes a single color parameter for its diffuse color.

The DrawMode enum has two declarators: LINE and FILL. A drawMode property of DrawMode.LINE will cause the JavaFX runtime to render the 3D shape as a wireframe. A drawMode property of DrawMode.FILL will cause the JavaFX runtime to render the 3D shape as a solid. By default, FILL is set.

The CullFace enum has three declarators: NONE, BACK, and FRONT. It controls how the JavaFX runtime renders each constituent polygon (also called a face) of the 3D shape. Through a process called face culling, the JavaFX runtime might remove some of the faces in a 3D shape from being rendered, thus improving the performance of the 3D model. A cullFace property of CullFace.NONE will cause the JavaFX runtime to not perform any face culling. A cullFace property of CullFace.BACK will cause the JavaFX runtime to cull all back side faces. A cullFace property of CullFace.FRONT will cause the JavaFX runtime to cull all front side faces. By default, BACK is set.

We discuss faces of 3D shapes in more detail in the section about user-defined 3D shapes.

Sphere

The javafx.scene.shape.Sphere class describes a sphere. There are three constructors for a sphere:

- Sphere()

- Sphere(double radius)

- Sphere(double radius, int division)

In these constructors, the radius describes the radius of the sphere. If this value is not provided, a radius of 1.0 will be used.

The division relates to the number of triangles used to generate the shape of the sphere around its equator. During rendering, a sphere is composed of a number of triangles. The larger this number, the smoother the sphere – but the computational time increases as well. By default, 64 divisions are used, which leads to a mesh with nearly 4000 triangles.

The center of the created sphere is at the origin of the coordinate system, hence at (0,0,0).

Box

The javafx.scene.shape.Box class describes a box. The Box class has two constructors:

- Box()

- Box(double width, double height, double depth)

These constructors are self-explaining. If the width, height, and depth are not specified, they are all set to 2, and 12 triangles will be generated.

Cylinder

The javafx.scene.shape.Cylinder class describes a cylinder. This class has three constructors:

- Cylinder

- Cylinder(double radius, double height)

- Cylinder(double radius, double height, int divisions)

Clearly, the radius parameter corresponds to the radius of the cylinder, while the height parameter corresponds to its height. In case those parameters are not supplied, the default radius is 1, and the default height is 2.

Similar to the division concept in a sphere, the divisions parameter in a cylinder describes the number of triangles used to render the base area of the cylinder. The default value is 64, leading to a mesh of 256 triangles. The Javadoc for Cylinder specifies the minimum number for this parameter:

Note that divisions should be at least 3. Any value less than that will be clamped to 3.

Creating User-Defined 3D Shapes

The previous sections showed how the standard JavaFX 3D shapes can be used easily to create 3D scenes. In reality, typical 3D environments use more complex shapes than a simple sphere, cylinder, or cube.

JavaFX allows developers to completely define their custom shapes, including the geometry and the material. The JavaFX node that allows for this is described by the MeshView class. A MeshView instance has a corresponding Mesh instance, which describes the 3D shape.

The MeshView class has the following constructors:

- MeshView()

- MeshView(Mesh mesh)

The default constructor creates a `MeshView` without a `Mesh`. The one-parameter constructor creates a `MeshView` with the specified `mesh`. The `mesh` is available as a read-write object property. The `Mesh` abstract class and its `TriangleMesh` concrete subclass are where the geometric information of the 3D shape is stored. The geometric information in a `TriangleMesh` includes the following:

- The vertex format that defines the format of the vertices in a mesh: A vertex consists of point and texture coordinates (VertexFormat. POINT_TEXCOORD, by default) or point, normal, and texture coordinates (VertexFormat.POINT_NORMAL_TEXCOORD).

- The three-dimensional coordinates of all the vertices, or points, of the 3D shape.

- The two-dimensional texture coordinates used by the 3D shape.

- The three-dimensional normals used by the 3D shape, if the vertex format is set to POINT_NORMAL_TEXCOORD.

- The faces of the 3D shape, each one a triangle defined by the vertex indices that are from the vertices list and texture indices that are from the texture coordinates list, when POINT_TEXCOORD is used, and also by the normal indices of the normals list when POINT_NORMAL_TEXCOORD is set.

- The face smoothing groups, which cause the JavaFX runtime to
  connect faces in the same smoothing group smoothly across their
  common edges and to leave the edges between faces not in the
  same smoothing group as hard edges. When POINT_NORMAL_
  TEXTCOORD is set, this is not used.

For efficiency reasons, the `TriangleMesh` class stores this information in observable arrays. The following public methods allow you to access these observable arrays and their sizes:

- `ObservableFloatArray getPoints()`

- `ObservableFloatArray getTexCoords()`

- `ObservableFloatArray getNormals()`

- `ObservableFaceArray getFaces()`

- `ObservableIntegerArray getFaceSmoothingGroups()`

- `int getPointElementSize()`

- `int getTexCoordElementSize()`

- `int getNormalElementSize()`

- `int getFaceElementSize()`

The `getPoints()` method returns an `ObservableFloatArray`, which you can use to add three-dimensional vertex coordinates. This observable float array's size must be a multiple of 3, and the elements of the array are interpreted as $x0, y0, z0, x1, y1, z1, \ldots$, where $(x0,y0,z0)$ are the coordinates of the first vertex $p0$, $(x1,y1,z1)$ are the coordinates of the second vertex $p1$, and so on.

The `getTexCoords()` method returns an `ObservableFloatArray`, which you can use to add two-dimensional texture coordinates. This observable float array's size must be a multiple of 2, and the elements of the array are interpreted as $u0, v0, u1, v1, \ldots$, where $(u0,v0)$ is the first texture point, $(u1,v1)$ is the second texture point, and so on. We cover texture coordinates in more detail in the "Material" section. For now, it is sufficient to understand the texture coordinates as points in a two-dimensional image with a top-left point that has coordinates (0,0) and a bottom-right point that has coordinates (1,1).

The getNormals() method returns an ObservableFloatArray, which you can use to add three-dimensional normals. This observable float array's size must be a multiple of 3, and the elements of the array are interpreted as *nx0, ny0, nz0, nx1, ny1, nz1,…* , where (*nx0,ny0,nz0*) is the first normal, (*nx1,ny1,nz1*) is the second normal, and so on. Each normal can be interpreted as the perpendicular direction to the surface of the 3D shape at a given point, pointing outward.

The getFaces() method returns an ObservableFaceArray, which you can use to add faces to the 3D shape. The ObservableFaceArray is a subinterface of the ObservableIntegerArray interface.

When VertexFormat.POINT_TEXTCOORD is used, this array's size must be a multiple of 6, and the elements of the array are interpreted as *p0, t0, p1, t1, p2, t2, p3, t3, p4, t4, p5, t5, …* , where *p0, t0, p1, t1, p2, t2* define the first face, *p3, t3, p4, t4, p5, t5* define the second face, and so on. Of the six integers that define a face, the *p* values are indices into the conceptual points array, which is one-third the length of the actual points array because we consider three float elements from the actual points array as constituting one conceptual point, and the *t* values are indices into the conceptual texture coordinates array, which is one-half the length of the actual texture coordinates array because we consider two float elements from the actual texture coordinates array as constituting one conceptual texture coordinates pair.

If VertexFormat.POINT_NORMAL_TEXTCOORD is used, the array's size must be a multiple of 9, and the elements of the array are interpreted as *p0, n0, t0, p1, n1, t1, p2, n2, t2* for the first face and so on for the rest of the faces.

The getFaceSmoothingGroups() method returns an ObservableIntegerArray, which you can use to define smoothing groups for the faces of the 3D shape. You can leave this array empty, in which case the JavaFX runtime will consider all faces of the 3D shape as belonging to one and the same smoothing group, resulting in a 3D shape with a surface that is smooth everywhere. Such is the case for the underlying TriangleMesh of the Sphere predefined 3D shape. If you fill this array, then you must fill it with the same number of elements as there are conceptual faces, which is one-sixth of the length of the actual faces array because we consider six int elements from the actual faces array as constituting one conceptual face. Each element in the face smoothing group array represents one face of the 3D shape, and two faces belong to the same smoothing group if and only if their representations share a common one bit when each int value is viewed as 32 individual bits. There could be at most 32 face smoothing groups in a TriangleMesh. This limitation can be overcome by using normals and a vertex format of POINT_NORMAL_TEXTCOORD. In this case, it won't be necessary to define face smoothing groups.

The getPointElementSize() method always returns 3. The getTexCoordElementSize() method always returns 2. The getNormalElementSize() method always returns 3. The getFaceElementSize() method returns 6 for vertex format POINT_TEXTCOORD and 9 for vertex format POINT_NORMAL_TEXTCOORD.

Each face in a 3D shape has two sides. In 3D graphics programming, it is important to distinguish these two sides as either the front side or the back side. JavaFX 3D uses the counterclockwise winding order to define the front side. Imagine yourself standing on one side of the triangle, and trace the edges of the triangle according to the order in which each vertex appears in the definition of the face. If it appears that you are tracing the edges in a counterclockwise fashion, then you are standing on the front side of the face. This concept of front side and back side of faces is what CullFace.FRONT and CullFace.BACK enum declarators refer to. By default, Shape3D uses the CullFace.BACK setting, which means the back sides of faces are not rendered.

The following code snippet creates a simple tetrahedron, which is a shape containing four triangular faces:

```
@Override
public void start(Stage stage) throws Exception {
    float length = 100f;
    TriangleMesh mesh = new TriangleMesh();
    mesh.getPoints().addAll(
            0f,0f,0f,
            length,0f,0f,
            0f,length,0f,
            0f,0f,length);
    mesh.getTexCoords().addAll(
            0f,0f,
            0f,1f,
            1f,0f,
            1f,1f);
    mesh.getFaces().addAll(
            0,0,2,1,1,2,
            0,0,3,1,2,2,
            0,0,1,1,3,2,
            1,0,2,1,3,2);
    MeshView meshView = new MeshView(mesh);
```

```
meshView.setRotationAxis(new Point3D(1,1,1));
meshView.setRotate(30);
meshView.setTranslateX(100);
meshView.setTranslateY(100);
Group group = new Group(meshView);
Scene scene = new Scene(group);
stage.setScene(scene);
stage.show();
}
```

In this sample, we create a tetrahedron with an edge size of length. We first define the four points that are used in the tetrahedron. The (x,y,z) coordinates of these points are, respectively, (0,0,0), (length,0,0), (0,length,0), and (0,0,length).

We define four texture coordinates: (0,0), (0,1), (1,0), and (1,1).

Next, the four faces are defined.

Figure 8-4 shows the triangle mesh we have just created. The axes have been added to illustrate the coordinate system.

Let's take for instance the frontal face #0, defined by indices (**0**,*0*,**2**,*1*,**1**,*2*), or (**0,2,1**) for points and (*0,1,2*) for texture coordinates.

Vertex #0 is located at the origin; vertex #1 is located at a length distance of the origin, in the X+ axis; and vertex #2 is located at a length distance of the origin, in the Y+ axis.

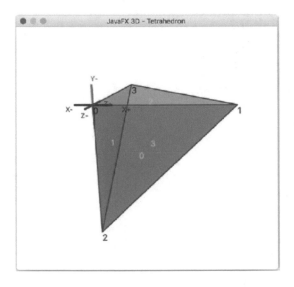

Figure 8-4. *TriangleMesh of a tetrahedron*

Once the mesh is created, we create a MeshView:

```
MeshView meshView = new MeshView(meshView).
```

If we use the above-defined coordinates, the default camera projection in JavaFX will show a single face only. By rotating the mesh, we are able to see more faces. This is done by setting a rotationAxis and a rotateValue. We also move the center of the mesh so that it is inside the visible space:

```
meshView.setRotationAxis(new Point3D(1,1,1));
meshView.setRotate(30);
meshView.setTranslateX(100);
meshView.setTranslateY(100);
```

Finally, we add the meshView to the scene and render the stage.

The result of this program is shown in Figure 8-5.

Figure 8-5. *Tetrahedron rendered in a scene*

Now that we know more about the basic shapes, we can extend the sample we created before. We will add all shapes together and allow the user to modify the draw mode, the culling, the color, and the rotation.

Let's add this custom shape into a more complex scene. The sample in Listing 8-2 can be found at `https://github.com/modernclientjava/mcj-samples/tree/master/ch08-3Dgraphics/shapesandmesh`.

Listing 8-2. ShapesAndMesh source code

```java
public class ShapesAndMesh extends Application {
    private Model model;
    private View view;
    public ShapesAndMesh() {
        model = new Model();
    }
    @Override
    public void start(Stage stage) throws Exception {
        view = new View(model);
        hookupEvents();
        stage.setTitle("Pre-defined 3D Shapes Example");
        stage.setScene(view.scene);
        stage.show();
    }
    private void hookupEvents() {
        view.drawModeComboBox.setOnAction(event -> {
            ComboBox<DrawMode> drawModeComboBox =
                (ComboBox<DrawMode>) event.getSource();
            model.setDrawMode(drawModeComboBox.getValue());
        });
        view.cullFaceComboBox.setOnAction(event -> {
            ComboBox<CullFace> cullFaceComboBox =
                (ComboBox<CullFace>) event.getSource();
            model.setCullFace(cullFaceComboBox.getValue());
        });
    }
    public static void main(String[] args) {
        launch(args);
    }
    private static class Model {
        private DoubleProperty rotate =
            new SimpleDoubleProperty(this, "rotate", 60.0d);
        private ObjectProperty<DrawMode> drawMode =
            new SimpleObjectProperty<>(this, "drawMode", DrawMode.FILL);
```

```
    private ObjectProperty<CullFace> cullFace =
        new SimpleObjectProperty<>(this, "cullFace", CullFace.BACK);
    public final double getRotate() {
        return rotate.doubleValue();
    }
    public final void setRotate(double rotate) {
        this.rotate.set(rotate);
    }
    public final DoubleProperty rotateProperty() {
        return rotate;
    }
    public final DrawMode getDrawMode() {
        return drawMode.getValue();
    }
    public final void setDrawMode(DrawMode drawMode) {
        this.drawMode.set(drawMode);
    }
    public final ObjectProperty<DrawMode>
        drawModeProperty() {
        return drawMode;
    }
    public final CullFace getCullFace() {
        return cullFace.get();
    }
    public final void setCullFace(CullFace cullFace) {
        this.cullFace.set(cullFace);
    }
    public final ObjectProperty<CullFace>
        cullFaceProperty() {
        return cullFace;
    }
}
private static class View {
    public Scene scene;
    public Sphere sphere;
```

```java
    public Cylinder cylinder;
    public Box box;
    public MeshView meshView;
    public ComboBox<DrawMode> drawModeComboBox;
    public ComboBox<CullFace> cullFaceComboBox;
    public Slider rotateSlider;
    public View(Model model) {
        sphere = new Sphere(50);
        cylinder = new Cylinder(50, 100);
        box = new Box(100, 100, 100);
        meshView = createMeshView(100);
        sphere.setTranslateX(100);
        cylinder.setTranslateX(300);
        box.setTranslateX(500);
        meshView.setTranslateX(700);
        sphere.setMaterial(new PhongMaterial(Color.RED));
        cylinder.setMaterial(new PhongMaterial(Color.YELLOW));
        box.setMaterial(new PhongMaterial(Color.BLUE));
        meshView.setMaterial(new PhongMaterial(Color.GREEN));
        setupShape3D(sphere, model);
        setupShape3D(cylinder, model);
        setupShape3D(box, model);
        setupShape3D(meshView, model);
        Group shapesGroup = new Group(sphere, cylinder, box, meshView);
        SubScene subScene = new SubScene(shapesGroup,
            800, 400, true, SceneAntialiasing.BALANCED);
        drawModeComboBox = new ComboBox<>();
        drawModeComboBox.setItems(
            FXCollections.observableArrayList(
                DrawMode.FILL, DrawMode.LINE));
        drawModeComboBox.setValue(DrawMode.FILL);
        cullFaceComboBox = new ComboBox<>();
        cullFaceComboBox.setItems(
            FXCollections.observableArrayList(
                CullFace.BACK, CullFace.FRONT,
                CullFace.NONE));
```

```
        cullFaceComboBox.setValue(CullFace.BACK);
        HBox hbox1 = new HBox(10, new Label("DrawMode:"),
            drawModeComboBox,
            new Label("CullFace:"), cullFaceComboBox);
        hbox1.setPadding(new Insets(10, 10, 10, 10));
        hbox1.setAlignment(Pos.CENTER_LEFT);
        rotateSlider = new Slider(-180.0d, 180.0d, 60.0d);
        rotateSlider.setMinWidth(400.0d);
        rotateSlider.setMajorTickUnit(10.0d);
        rotateSlider.setMinorTickCount(5);
        rotateSlider.setShowTickMarks(true);
        rotateSlider.setShowTickLabels(true);
        rotateSlider.valueProperty().bindBidirectional(
            model.rotateProperty());
        HBox hbox2 = new HBox(10,
            new Label("Rotate Around (1, 1, 1) Axis:"),
            rotateSlider);
        hbox2.setPadding(new Insets(10, 10, 10, 10));
        hbox2.setAlignment(Pos.CENTER_LEFT);
        VBox controlPanel = new VBox(10, hbox1, hbox2);
        controlPanel.setPadding(new Insets(10, 10, 10, 10));
        Group groupSubScene = new Group(subScene);
        BorderPane root = new BorderPane(groupSubScene,
            null, null, controlPanel, null);
        scene = new Scene(root, 800, 600, true,
            SceneAntialiasing.BALANCED);
    }
    private void setupShape3D(Shape3D shape3D,
        Model model) {
        shape3D.setTranslateY(240.0d);
        shape3D.setRotationAxis(
            new Point3D(1.0d, 1.0d, 1.0d));
        shape3D.drawModeProperty().bind(
            model.drawModeProperty());
```

```
            shape3D.cullFaceProperty().bind(
                model.cullFaceProperty());
            shape3D.rotateProperty().bind(
                model.rotateProperty());
        }
        private MeshView createMeshView(float length) {
            TriangleMesh mesh = new TriangleMesh();
            mesh.getPoints().addAll(
                    0f, 0f, 0f,
                    length, 0f, 0f,
                    0f, length, 0f,
                    0f, 0f, length);
            mesh.getTexCoords().addAll(
                    0f, 0f,
                    0f, 1f,
                    1f, 0f,
                    1f, 1f);
            mesh.getFaces().addAll(
                    0, 0, 2, 1, 1, 2,
                    0, 0, 3, 1, 2, 2,
                    0, 0, 1, 1, 3, 2,
                    1, 0, 2, 1, 3, 2);
            MeshView meshView = new MeshView(mesh);
            return meshView;
        }
    }
}
```

When running this sample, the output in Figure 8-6 will be seen.

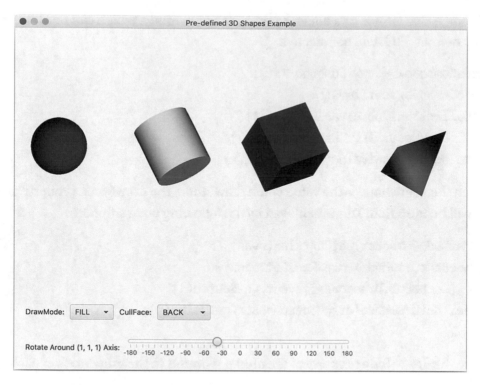

Figure 8-6. *Output from ShapesAndMesh*

In this sample, we combined all the topics we learned so far. And we have included a new one: a SubScene node. We will explain what this node is and what it is intended for.

We create the primitive shapes Box, Cube, and Cylinder, and we create a MeshView like we showed before. For each shape, we call the setupShape3D method that does the following:

```
private void setupShape3D(Shape3D shape3D, Model model) {
    shape3D.setTranslateY(240.0d);
    shape3D.setRotationAxis(new Point3D(1.0d, 1.0d, 1.0d));
    shape3D.drawModeProperty().bind(model.drawModeProperty());
    shape3D.cullFaceProperty().bind(model.cullFaceProperty());
    shape3D.rotateProperty().bind(model.rotateProperty());
}
```

The drawMode of the shape is bound to the value of the drawModeProperty in the model. The same principle holds for the cullFace and the rotate properties.

We add a ComboBox that allows to select the drawMode, which can be LINE or FILL. By default, FILL will be selected:

```
drawModeComboBox = new ComboBox<>();
drawModeComboBox.setItems(
    FXCollections.observableArrayList(
        DrawMode.FILL, DrawMode.LINE));
drawModeComboBox.setValue(DrawMode.FILL);
```

When the user changes the value of the drawMode, the drawMode property on the model will be modified. This is achieved by the following code snippet:

```
view.drawModeComboBox.setOnAction(event -> {
    ComboBox<DrawMode> drawModeComboBox =
        (ComboBox<DrawMode>) event.getSource();
    model.setDrawMode(drawModeComboBox.getValue());
});
```

Since the drawMode property of the model is bound to the drawMode of each shape, due to

```
shape3D.drawModeProperty().bind(model.drawModeProperty());
```

the shape will have a different drawMode when the user selects a different value in the combo box.

The value of the cullFace combo box is transferred to the cullFace property of the shape in exactly the same way.

The value selected by the rotation slider is even more easily transferred.

The rotation slider is created as follows:

```
rotateSlider = new Slider(-180.0d, 180.0d, 60.0d);
rotateSlider.setMinWidth(400.0d);
rotateSlider.setMajorTickUnit(10.0d);
rotateSlider.setMinorTickCount(5);
rotateSlider.setShowTickMarks(true);
rotateSlider.setShowTickLabels(true);
```

Next, the value is immediately bound to the value of the rotateProperty on the model:

```
rotateSlider.valueProperty().bindBidirectional(model.rotateProperty());
```

Since the rotateProperty of each shape is bound to the rotateProperty of the model, whenever the user changes the slide, the rotate value of the shapes is altered.

Given that in this sample we are mixing up a 2D node (the controlPanel) with another one that uses 3D shapes, it is a good practice to restrict the use of 3D features only to the node with 3D shapes.

A SubScene node is a container that can have its own camera and own settings of depth buffering and scene antialiasing. This allows, for instance, applying camera transforms only to the content within this node, and the rest of the scene won't be affected.

A subscene can be embedded into the main scene or into another subscene.

Both a scene and a subscene may request depth buffering support or scene antialiasing support. It is not required that they contain only 2D shapes and without any 3D. But if they do, depth buffering allows depth sorted rendering to avoid depth fighting, related to the visualization of each shape in the z-axis. And antialiasing affects the smoothness of the entire rendered scene or subscene. It can be DISABLED or BALANCED. Both depth buffering and scene antialiasing are conditional features.

In this sample, this is achieved with the use of this constructor:

```
SubScene subScene =
    new SubScene(shapesGroup, 800, 400, true, SceneAntialiasing.BALANCED);
```

Camera

When displaying a three-dimensional world on a two-dimensional screen, somehow a projection from the 3D world onto a 2D world needs to be used. Typically, the projection is managed by the concept of a camera. Even if you don't specify a camera, there is always one assumed to be present. The default camera is a parallel camera that will project the scene graph to a plane located at z=0, and that camera is looking into the positive z direction.

The JavaFX Camera class is an abstract class with two concrete subclasses: ParallelCamera and PerspectiveCamera.

ParallelCamera

The ParallelCamera uses an orthographic projection, ignoring perspective. For a 2D world, that provides very good results, but for three-dimensional objects, this is not realistic. A consequence of an orthographic projection is that the projected dimensions of an object do not depend on the vertical distance between the camera and the object. This is not how, for example, the human visualization works: objects that are closer to our eyes appear to be bigger than objects of the same size but farther away.

A more realistic projection is achieved using a camera that takes into account perspective, as in that case the projection of objects does depend on their relative distance from the camera.

PerspectiveCamera

The `PerspectiveCamera` is the camera implementation in JavaFX that allows for a perspective projection. The PerspectiveCamera class has the following public constructors:

- `PerspectiveCamera()`

- `PerspectiveCamera(boolean fixedEyeAtCameraZero)`

The default constructor creates a `PerspectiveCamera` with the `fixedEyeAtCameraZero` set to false. The one-parameter constructor creates a `PerspectiveCamera` with the specified `fixedEyeAtCameraZero`. Cameras are Nodes and can be placed in a JavaFX scene. A newly created `PerspectiveCamera`, like a newly created `Sphere` or `Cylinder` or `Box`, has its center or eye located in the origin (0,0,0) of the three-dimensional space. The eye looks into the positive z direction. As a Node, the `PerspectiveCamera` itself can be transformed by 3D transformations such as `Rotate`, `Translate`, `Scale`, or even the generic `Affine`. A `fixedEyeAtCameraZero` setting of `true` guarantees that after such transforms, the eye of the `PerspectiveCamera` moves along with it and remains at the camera's zero position. A `fixedEyeAtCameraZero` setting of `false` allows the eye to drift away from the camera's zero position to accommodate what is in the scene. This is useful for rendering 2D scenes and only makes sense when the camera itself is not transformed in any way. Therefore, for use with a 3D model, you should always use the one-parameter constructor, passing in a `fixedEyeAtCameraZero` of `true`.

The PerspectiveCamera class has the following public methods:

- void setFieldOfView(double)

- double getFieldOfView()

- DoubleProperty fieldOfViewProperty()

- void setVerticalFieldOfView(boolean)

- boolean isVerticalFieldOfView()

- BooleanProperty verticalFieldOfViewProperty()

- boolean isFixedEyeAtCameraZero()

These methods define two properties, fieldOfView and verticalFieldOfView, for the PerspectiveCamera class. The fieldOfView is a double property and represents the field of view of the perspective camera in degrees. The default value is 30 degrees. The verticalFieldOfView is a Boolean property that determines if the field of view property applies to the vertical dimension of the projection plane. The isFixedEyeAtCameraZero() method returns the fixedEyeAtCameraZero flag the PerspectiveCamera is constructed with.

The PerspectiveCamera also inherits two double properties from the Camera abstract class: nearClip and farClip. Objects closer to the eye than nearClip and objects farther from the eye than farClip are not rendered in the scene.

In the program in Listing 8-3, available at https://github.com/modernclientjava/mcj-samples/tree/master/ch08-3Dgraphics/perspectivecamera, we create a Box and a PerspectiveCamera. Unlike in previous examples where we transformed the 3D objects themselves like the Box, in this program we keep the Box fixed and transform the PerspectiveCamera with a combination of rotating around the *x*-axis, rotating around the *y*-axis, and a translation along the *z*-axis. We animate the rotation degrees from 90 to –90 and the *z* translation from –20 to –80 in a 5-second Timeline.

Listing 8-3. PerspectiveCamera source code

```
package org.modernclientjava.javafx3d;
import javafx.animation.Animation;
import javafx.animation.KeyFrame;
import javafx.animation.KeyValue;
import javafx.animation.Timeline;
```

```java
import javafx.application.Application;
import javafx.scene.Camera;
import javafx.scene.Group;
import javafx.scene.PerspectiveCamera;
import javafx.scene.Scene;
import javafx.scene.shape.Box;
import javafx.scene.transform.Rotate;
import javafx.scene.transform.Translate;
import javafx.stage.Stage;
import javafx.util.Duration;
public class PerspectiveCameraDemo extends Application {
    private final Rotate rotateX = new Rotate(-20, Rotate.X_AXIS);
    private final Rotate rotateY = new Rotate(-20, Rotate.Y_AXIS);
    private final Rotate rotateZ = new Rotate(-20, Rotate.Z_AXIS);
    private final Translate translateZ = new Translate(0, 0, -100);
    @Override
    public void start(Stage stage) throws Exception {
        Camera camera = createCamera();
        Box box = new Box(10, 10, 10);
        Group view = new Group(box, camera);
        Scene scene = new Scene(view, 640, 480);
        scene.setCamera(camera);
        stage.setTitle("PerspectiveCamera Example");
        stage.setScene(scene);
        stage.show();
        animate();
    }
    private Camera createCamera() {
        Camera camera = new PerspectiveCamera(true);
        camera.getTransforms().addAll(rotateX, rotateY, rotateZ,
        translateZ);
        return camera;
    }
    private void animate() {
        Timeline timeline = new Timeline(
```

```
            new KeyFrame(Duration.seconds(0),
                    new KeyValue(translateZ.zProperty(), -20),
                    new KeyValue(rotateX.angleProperty(), 90),
                    new KeyValue(rotateY.angleProperty(), 90),
                    new KeyValue(rotateZ.angleProperty(), 90)),
            new KeyFrame(Duration.seconds(5),
                    new KeyValue(translateZ.zProperty(), -80),
                    new KeyValue(rotateX.angleProperty(), -90),
                    new KeyValue(rotateY.angleProperty(), -90),
                    new KeyValue(rotateZ.angleProperty(), -90))
        );
        timeline.setCycleCount(Animation.INDEFINITE);
        timeline.play();
    }
    public static void main(String[] args) {
        launch(args);
    }
}
```

Running this sample shows an animation, and Figure 8-7 is a screenshot of this animation.

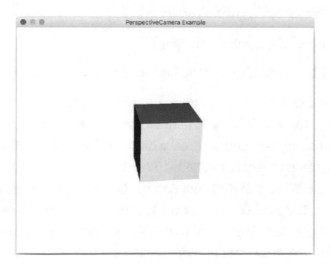

Figure 8-7. *Screenshot of PerspectiveCamera output*

Light

The lighting class hierarchy for the JavaFX 3D graphics API consists of the LightBase abstract class and its concrete subclasses AmbientLight and PointLight. They belong to the javafx.scene package. An AmbientLight is a light source that seems to come from all directions. A PointLight is a light that has a fixed point in space and radiates light equally in all directions away from itself. They are Nodes, so they can be added to a JavaFX scene to provide lighting to the scene. They can also be moved to the desired locations using the Translate transform. If they are added to a container, then they move along with the container when the container is transformed.

Understanding the LightBase Class

The LightBase abstract class has the following public methods:

- void setColor(Color)
- Color getColor()
- ObjectProperty<Color> colorProperty()
- void setLightOn(boolean)
- boolean isLightOn()
- BooleanProperty lightOnProperty()
- ObservableList<Node> getScope()
- ObservableList<Node> getExclusionScope()

These methods define two properties, color and lightOn, for the LightBase class. The color property is of type Color and defines the color of the light. The lightOn property is a Boolean property and controls whether the light is on. The getScope() method returns an ObservableList of Nodes. When this list is empty, the light affects all Nodes in the scene. When this list is not empty, the light only affects the Nodes contained in the list. The getExlusionScope() method, new since JavaFX 13, returns an ObservableList of Nodes. Any Nodes in this list or under a parent in the list are not affected by the light, unless a closer parent exists in the scope list.

Understanding the AmbientLight Class

The AmbientLight class has the following constructors:

- AmbientLight()

- AmbientLight(Color color)

The default constructor creates an AmbientLight with a default color of Color. WHITE. The one-parameter constructor creates an AmbientLight with the specified color. The AmbientLight class has no additional public methods aside from the ones it inherited from the LightBase base class.

Understanding the PointLight Class

The PointLight class has the following constructors:

- PointLight()

- PointLight(Color color)

The default constructor creates a PointLight with a default color of Color.WHITE. The one-parameter constructor creates a PointLight with the specified color. The PointLight class has no additional public methods aside from the ones it inherited from the LightBase class.

Since JavaFX 16, the light's intensity can be set to decrease over distance by attenuating it. The attenuation formula is

```
attn = 1 / (ca + la * dist + qa * dist^2)
```

where ca, la, and qa control the constant, linear, and quadratic behaviors of intensity falloff over the distance dist, respectively. The effective color of the light at a given point in space is color * attn. It is possible, albeit unrealistic, to specify negative values to attenuation coefficients.

Therefore, there are four new properties to set the light attenuation:

- DoubleProperty constantAttenuationProperty()

- DoubleProperty linearAttenuationProperty()

- DoubleProperty quadraticAttenuationProperty()

- DoubleProperty maxRangeProperty()

The program shown in Listing 8-4, available at `https://github.com/modernclientjava/mcj-samples/tree/master/ch08-3Dgraphics/lightdemo`, illustrates the use of lights in a JavaFX 3D scene. Two `PointLights`, one red and one blue, are added to a scene that already has three `Boxes` and a `PerspectiveCamera`. For each light, a control panel is added at the bottom of the window to allow you to see the effect of the lights. For each light, a `CheckBox` allows setting it on or off, and three sliders can alter the coordinates of the light location. For the red light, several `RadioButtons` allow adding each `Box` either to the scope list or to the exclusion list. And for the blue light, several controls allow defining values for the distance and the three constants to attenuate the light.

Listing 8-4. LightDemo source code

```
package org.modernclientjava.javafx3d;

import javafx.application.Application;
import javafx.beans.binding.Bindings;
import javafx.beans.property.DoubleProperty;
import javafx.beans.property.SimpleDoubleProperty;
import javafx.geometry.Insets;
import javafx.geometry.Pos;
import javafx.scene.*;
import javafx.scene.control.*;
import javafx.scene.layout.*;
import javafx.scene.paint.Color;
import javafx.scene.shape.Box;
import javafx.scene.shape.Rectangle;
import javafx.scene.transform.Rotate;
import javafx.scene.transform.Translate;
import javafx.stage.Stage;
import javafx.util.converter.NumberStringConverter;

public class LightDemo extends Application {
    private final Model model;

    public LightDemo() {
        model = new Model();
    }
```

```java
@Override
public void start(Stage stage) {
    View view = new View(model);
    stage.setTitle("Light Example");
    stage.setScene(view.scene);
    stage.show();
}

public static void main(String[] args) {
    launch(args);
}

private static class Model {
    private final DoubleProperty redLightX = new
    SimpleDoubleProperty(this, "redLightX", 20.0d);
    private final DoubleProperty redLightY = new
    SimpleDoubleProperty(this, "redLightY", -15.0d);
    private final DoubleProperty redLightZ = new
    SimpleDoubleProperty(this, "redLightZ", -20.0d);
    private final DoubleProperty blueLightX = new
    SimpleDoubleProperty(this, "blueLightX", 15.0d);
    private final DoubleProperty blueLightY = new
    SimpleDoubleProperty(this, "blueLightY", -15.0d);
    private final DoubleProperty blueLightZ = new
    SimpleDoubleProperty(this, "blueLightZ", -5.0d);

    public DoubleProperty redLightXProperty() {
        return redLightX;
    }

    public DoubleProperty redLightYProperty() {
        return redLightY;
    }

    public DoubleProperty redLightZProperty() {
        return redLightZ;
    }
```

```java
        public DoubleProperty blueLightXProperty() {
            return blueLightX;
        }

        public DoubleProperty blueLightYProperty() {
            return blueLightY;
        }

        public DoubleProperty blueLightZProperty() {
            return blueLightZ;
        }
    }

    private static class View {
        public Scene scene;

        public Box box1;
        public Box box2;
        public Box box3;
        public PerspectiveCamera camera;
        public PointLight redLight;
        public PointLight blueLight;

        private View(Model model) {
            box1 = new Box(10, 10, 10);
            box1.setId("Box1");
            box1.getTransforms().add(new Translate(-15, 0, 0));
            box2 = new Box(10, 10, 10);
            box2.setId("Box2");
            box3 = new Box(10, 10, 10);
            box3.setId("Box3");
            box3.getTransforms().add(new Translate(15, 0, 0));

            camera = new PerspectiveCamera(true);

            Rotate rotateX = new Rotate(-20, Rotate.X_AXIS);
            Rotate rotateY = new Rotate(-20, Rotate.Y_AXIS);
            Rotate rotateZ = new Rotate(-20, Rotate.Z_AXIS);
            Translate translateZ = new Translate(0, 0, -60);
```

```
camera.getTransforms().addAll(rotateX, rotateY, rotateZ,
                              translateZ);

redLight = new PointLight(Color.RED);
redLight.translateXProperty().bind(model.redLightXProperty());
redLight.translateYProperty().bind(model.redLightYProperty());
redLight.translateZProperty().bind(model.redLightZProperty());

blueLight = new PointLight(Color.BLUE);
blueLight.translateXProperty().bind(
    model.blueLightXProperty());
blueLight.translateYProperty().bind(
    model.blueLightYProperty());
blueLight.translateZProperty().bind(
    model.blueLightZProperty());

Group group = new Group(new Group(box1, box2, box3),
        camera, redLight, blueLight);
SubScene subScene = new SubScene(group, 640, 400, true,
                            SceneAntialiasing.BALANCED);
subScene.setCamera(camera);

// Red Light
Tab redTab = new Tab("Red Light");
redTab.setClosable(false);
Rectangle red = new Rectangle(10, 10);
red.fillProperty().bind(
    Bindings.when(redLight.lightOnProperty()).then(Color.RED)
            .otherwise(Color.DARKGREY));
redTab.setGraphic(red);

CheckBox redLightOn = new CheckBox("Light On/Off");
redLightOn.setSelected(true);
redLight.lightOnProperty().bind(redLightOn.selectedProperty());

Slider redLightXSlider = createSlider(20);
Slider redLightYSlider = createSlider(-20);
Slider redLightZSlider = createSlider(-20);
```

```
redLightXSlider.valueProperty().bindBidirectional(
    model.redLightXProperty());
redLightYSlider.valueProperty().bindBidirectional(
    model.redLightYProperty());
redLightZSlider.valueProperty().bindBidirectional(
    model.redLightZProperty());

HBox hbox1 = new HBox(10, new Label("x:"), redLightXSlider,
        new Label("y:"), redLightYSlider,
        new Label("z:"), redLightZSlider);
hbox1.setPadding(new Insets(10, 10, 10, 10));
hbox1.setAlignment(Pos.CENTER);

HBox hbox2 = new HBox(10,
        createScopeToggles(box1),
        createScopeToggles(box2),
        createScopeToggles(box3));
hbox2.setPadding(new Insets(10, 10, 10, 10));
hbox2.setAlignment(Pos.CENTER);

VBox redControlPanel = new VBox(10, redLightOn, hbox1, hbox2);
redControlPanel.setPadding(new Insets(10, 10, 10, 10));
redControlPanel.setAlignment(Pos.CENTER);
redTab.setContent(redControlPanel);

// Blue Light
Tab blueTab = new Tab("Blue Light");
blueTab.setClosable(false);
Rectangle blue = new Rectangle(10, 10);
blue.fillProperty().bind(
    Bindings.when(blueLight.lightOnProperty())
        .then(Color.BLUE)
        .otherwise(Color.DARKGREY));
blueTab.setGraphic(blue);
```

```java
        CheckBox blueLightOn = new CheckBox("Light On/Off");
        blueLightOn.setSelected(true);
        blueLight.lightOnProperty().bind(
            blueLightOn.selectedProperty());

        Slider blueLightXSlider = createSlider(15);
        Slider blueLightYSlider = createSlider(-15);
        Slider blueLightZSlider = createSlider(-15);
        blueLightXSlider.valueProperty().bindBidirectional(
            model.blueLightXProperty());
        blueLightYSlider.valueProperty().bindBidirectional(
            model.blueLightYProperty());
        blueLightZSlider.valueProperty().bindBidirectional(
            model.blueLightZProperty());

        HBox hbox3 = new HBox(10, new Label("x:"), blueLightXSlider,
                new Label("y:"), blueLightYSlider,
                new Label("z:"), blueLightZSlider);
        hbox3.setPadding(new Insets(10, 10, 10, 10));
        hbox3.setAlignment(Pos.CENTER);

        HBox hbox4 = new HBox(50, addLightControls(blueLight));
        hbox4.setPadding(new Insets(10, 10, 10, 10));
        hbox4.setAlignment(Pos.CENTER);

        VBox blueControlPanel = new VBox(10, blueLightOn,
            hbox3, hbox4);
        blueControlPanel.setPadding(new Insets(10, 10, 10, 10));
        blueControlPanel.setAlignment(Pos.CENTER);
        blueTab.setContent(blueControlPanel);

        TabPane tabPane = new TabPane(redTab, blueTab);
        BorderPane borderPane = new BorderPane(
            subScene, null, null, tabPane, null);
        scene = new Scene(borderPane);
    }
```

```java
    private Slider createSlider(double value) {
        Slider slider = new Slider(-40, 40, value);
        slider.setShowTickMarks(true);
        slider.setShowTickLabels(true);
        return slider;
    }

    // since JavaFX 13 -->
    private Pane createScopeToggles(Node node) {
        RadioButton none = new RadioButton("none");
        none.setOnAction(a -> {
            redLight.getScope().remove(node);
            redLight.getExclusionScope().remove(node);
        });

        RadioButton scoped = new RadioButton("scoped");
        scoped.setOnAction(a -> redLight.getScope().add(node));

        RadioButton excluded = new RadioButton("excluded");
        excluded.setOnAction(a ->
            redLight.getExclusionScope().add(node));
        none.setSelected(true);

        ToggleGroup tg = new ToggleGroup();
        tg.getToggles().addAll(none, scoped, excluded);
        var vBox = new VBox(5, none, scoped, excluded);
        return new HBox(10, new Label(node.getId()), vBox);
    }

    // since JavaFX 16 -->
    private HBox addLightControls(PointLight light) {
        VBox range = createSliderControl("range",
            light.maxRangeProperty(), 0, 100, light.getMaxRange());
        VBox c = createSliderControl("constant",
            light.constantAttenuationProperty(), -1, 1,
            light.getConstantAttenuation());
```

```
        VBox lc = createSliderControl("linear",
            light.linearAttenuationProperty(), -1, 1,
            light.getLinearAttenuation());
        VBox qc = createSliderControl("quadratic",
            light.quadraticAttenuationProperty(), -1, 1,
            light.getQuadraticAttenuation());
        return new HBox(10, range, c, lc, qc);
    }

    private VBox createSliderControl(String name,
      DoubleProperty property, double min, double max, double start) {
        Slider slider = new Slider(min, max, start);
        slider.setShowTickMarks(true);
        slider.setShowTickLabels(true);
        property.bindBidirectional(slider.valueProperty());
        TextField tf = new TextField();
        tf.textProperty().bindBidirectional(slider.valueProperty(),
            new NumberStringConverter());
        tf.setMaxWidth(40);
        return new VBox(5, new Label(name), new HBox(slider, tf));
    }
  }
}
```

Running this sample shows the output in Figure 8-8, where you can modify the different controls to see the different effects.

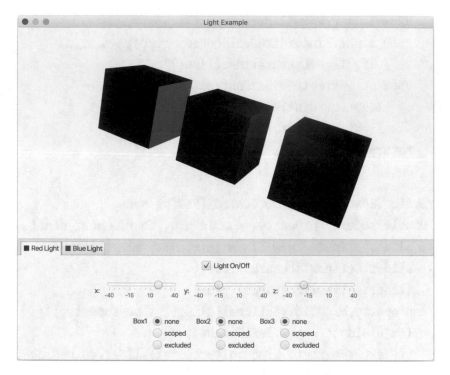

Figure 8-8. *Output of LightDemo*

Material

Now that we have covered the 3D shapes, both predefined and user-defined, the cameras, and the lights, in this section, we deal with the last remaining topic in the JavaFX 3D graphics API. The material API consists of the `Material` abstract class and its concrete subclass `PhongMaterial`. The `Material` class is an abstract base class without any public methods. In all practical situations, it is the `PhongMaterial` class that is used. The Material class describes the physical properties of a 3D surface and how they interact with lights.

Understanding the `PhongMaterial` Class

The `PhongMaterial` class has the following constructors:

- `PhongMaterial()`

- `PhongMaterial(Color diffuseColor)`

- `PhongMaterial(Color diffuseColor, Image diffuseMap, Image specularMap, Image bumpMap, Image selfIlluminationMap)`

The default constructor creates a PhongMaterial with the default diffuseColor of Color.WHITE. The one-parameter constructor creates a PhongMaterial with the specified diffuseColor. The third constructor creates a PhongMaterial with the specified diffuseColor, diffuseMap, specularMap, bumpMap, and selfIlluminationMap. We discuss what these parameters mean after we cover the properties of the PhongMaterial class.

The PhongMaterial class has the following public methods:

- `void setDiffuseColor(Color)`

- `Color getDiffuseColor()`

- `ObjectProperty<Color> diffuseColorProperty()`

- `void setSpecularColor(Color)`

- `Color getSpecularColor()`

- `ObjectProperty<Color> specularColorProperty()`

- `void setSpecularPower(double)`

- `double getSpecularPower()`

- `DoubleProperty specularPowerProperty()`

- `void setDiffuseMap(Image)`

- `Image getDiffuseMap()`

- `ObjectProperty<Image> diffuseMapProperty()`

- `void setSpecularMap(Image)`

- `Image getSpecularMap()`

- `ObjectProperty<Image> specularMapProperty()`

- `void setBumpMap(Image)`

- `Image getBumpMap()`

- `ObjectProperty<Image> bumpMapProperty()`

- `void setSelfIlluminationMap(Image)`

- `Image getSelfIlluminationMap()`

- `ObjectProperty<Image> selfIlluminationMapProperty()`

345

These methods define seven read-write properties for the `PhongMaterial` class. The `diffuseColor` and `specularColor` are object properties of type `Color`. The `specularPower` is a double property. The `diffuseMap`, `specularMap`, `bumpMap`, and `selfIlluminationMap` properties are object properties of type `Image`. Five of the seven properties can be specified in the third constructor. However, once a `PhongMaterial` is constructed, its properties can also be altered.

In several of our earlier examples, we have used the one-parameter `PhongMaterial` constructor, in which we specify the diffuse color of the 3D shapes. The diffuse color is what we normally think of as the color of an object.

The specular color is the color of the highlights reflected off of shiny surfaces, such as a mirror or another well-polished surface.

For more information about the definitions of diffuse color and specular color, you are referred to `https://en.wikipedia.org/wiki/Diffuse_reflection` and `https://en.wikipedia.org/wiki/Specular_highlight`.

The program in Listing 8-5 available at `https://github.com/modernclientjava/mcj-samples/tree/master/ch08-3Dgraphics/specularcolordemo` adds a specular color to the material of a sphere.

Listing 8-5. SpecularColorDemo source code

```
package org.modernclientjava.javafx3d;
import javafx.application.Application;
import javafx.scene.Group;
import javafx.scene.PointLight;
import javafx.scene.Scene;
import javafx.scene.paint.Color;
import javafx.scene.paint.PhongMaterial;
import javafx.scene.shape.Sphere;
import javafx.stage.Stage;
public class SpecularColorDemo extends Application {
    private View view;
    @Override
    public void start(Stage stage) throws Exception {
        view = new View();
        stage.setTitle("Specular Color Example");
```

```java
        stage.setScene(view.scene);
        stage.show();
    }
    public static void main(String[] args) {
        launch(args);
    }
    private static class View {
        public Scene scene;
        public Sphere sphere;
        public PointLight light;
        private View() {
            sphere = new Sphere(100);
            PhongMaterial material =
                new PhongMaterial(Color.BLUE);
            material.setSpecularColor(Color.LIGHTBLUE);
            material.setSpecularPower(10.0d);
            sphere.setMaterial(material);
            sphere.setTranslateZ(300);
            light = new PointLight(Color.WHITE);
            Group group = new Group(sphere, light);
            group.setTranslateY(240);
            group.setTranslateX(320);
            scene = new Scene(group, 640, 480);
        }
    }
}
```

If we run this program, the output is shown in Figure 8-9.

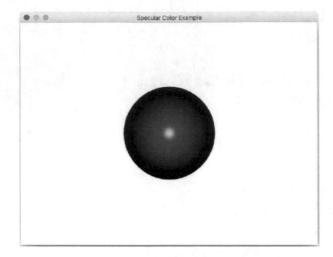

Figure 8-9. *Output of SpecularColorDemo*

In this program, we let a white light shine on a sphere with a diffuse color of blue and a specular color of light blue with a specular power of 10. The default specular power in PhongMaterial is 32.0. Therefore, our sphere shows a less focused spotlight than the default. The higher the value of the specular power, the more focused the white spot would be. A lower value of the specular power will lead to a larger, more blurry white area.

Adding Texture to 3D Shapes

The `diffuseMap` and `specularMap` serve the same purpose as the `diffuseColor` and the `specularColor`, except that the maps provide different color values for different points on the surface of a 3D shape. The `bumpMap` and the `selfIlluminationMap` are similarly mapped to the points on the surface of a 3D shape. The `selfIlluminationMap` provides colors that will shine through even if no light is illuminating the 3D object. The `bumpMap` does not contain color information at all. It contains normal vector information (which just happens to be three numbers, which can be encoded as an RGB color) for each point of the surface, which, when taken into account during the color rendering calculation, will result in a bumped look.

The mapping of the points on the surface to a point on the images is the job of the texture coordinates of the `TriangleMesh`. We built a `MeshView` with a user-defined `TriangleMesh` earlier in this chapter. In fact, the predefined 3D shapes are also based on `TriangleMesh`es internally. Therefore, they are also capable of being texturized. Recall that in a `TriangleMesh`, each face is defined by six indices – *p0, t0, p1, t1, p2, t2*, where *p0, p1, p2* are indices into the points array and *t0, t1, t2* are indices into the `texCoords` array – or nine indices if normals are used, with the same pattern p0, n0, t0,…. Either way, looking up the `texCoords` array with *t0, t1, t2*, we get the (*u0,v0*), (*u1,v1*), and (*u2,v2*) coordinates. The triangular portion of the image determined by these three coordinates is mapped to the face of the 3D shape.

We will now apply an image of a world map as a texture to a sphere and a cube. The image in Figure 8-10 is available as a resource in the code directory at `https://github.com/modernclientjava/mcj-samples/tree/master/ch08-3Dgraphics/earthsphere`.

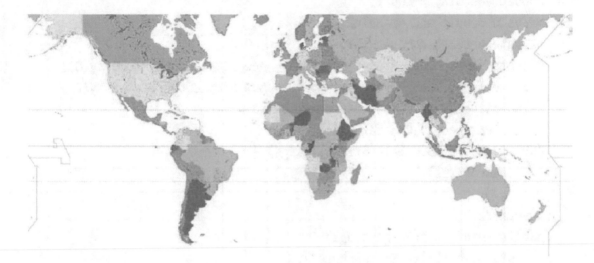

Figure 8-10. *Image of Earth Mercator projection*

Listing 8-6 shows the EarthSphere program, where we use this image as the `diffuseMap` of a sphere to make a globe.

Listing 8-6. EarthSphere source code

```
package org.modernclientjava.javafx3d;
import javafx.application.Application;
import javafx.beans.property.DoubleProperty;
import javafx.beans.property.SimpleDoubleProperty;
import javafx.scene.Group;
import javafx.scene.PerspectiveCamera;
import javafx.scene.PointLight;
```

```
import javafx.scene.Scene;
import javafx.scene.image.Image;
import javafx.scene.input.MouseEvent;
import javafx.scene.paint.Color;
import javafx.scene.paint.PhongMaterial;
import javafx.scene.shape.Sphere;
import javafx.scene.transform.Rotate;
import javafx.stage.Stage;
public class EarthSphere extends Application {
    double anchorX, anchorY;
    private double anchorAngleX = 0;
    private double anchorAngleY = 0;
    private final DoubleProperty angleX = new SimpleDoubleProperty(0);
    private final DoubleProperty angleY = new SimpleDoubleProperty(0);
    PerspectiveCamera scenePerspectiveCamera =
        new PerspectiveCamera(false);
    public static void main(String[] args) {
        launch(args);
    }
    @Override
    public void start(Stage stage) {
        stage.setTitle("EarthSphere");
        Image diffuseMap = new Image(EarthSphere.class
                .getResource("/earth-mercator.jpg")
                .toExternalForm());
        PhongMaterial earthMaterial = new PhongMaterial();
        earthMaterial.setDiffuseMap(diffuseMap);
        final Sphere earth = new Sphere(400);
        earth.setMaterial(earthMaterial);
        final Group parent = new Group(earth);
        parent.setTranslateX(450);
        parent.setTranslateY(450);
        parent.setTranslateZ(100);
        Rotate xRotate;
        Rotate yRotate;
```

```
parent.getTransforms().setAll(
        xRotate = new Rotate(0, Rotate.X_AXIS),
        yRotate = new Rotate(0, Rotate.Y_AXIS)
);
xRotate.angleProperty().bind(angleX);
yRotate.angleProperty().bind(angleY);
final Group root = new Group();
root.getChildren().add(parent);
final Scene scene = new Scene(root, 900, 900, true);
scene.setFill(Color.BLACK);
scene.setOnMousePressed((MouseEvent event) -> {
    anchorX = event.getSceneX();
    anchorY = event.getSceneY();
    anchorAngleX = angleX.get();
    anchorAngleY = angleY.get();
});
scene.setOnMouseDragged((MouseEvent event) -> {
    angleY.set(anchorAngleY + anchorX - event.getSceneX());
});
PointLight pointLight = new PointLight(Color.WHITE);
pointLight.setTranslateX(400);
pointLight.setTranslateY(400);
pointLight.setTranslateZ(-3000);
scene.setCamera(scenePerspectiveCamera);
root.getChildren().addAll(pointLight, scenePerspectiveCamera);
stage.setScene(scene);
stage.show();
    }
}
```

Note that the image is a world map in Mercator projection, which is required by the TriangleMesh that is created internally by the Sphere node. Thanks to the defined texture coordinates, every single point of the sphere surface is mapped into a pixel of the image, based on the interpolation of these points with the texture coordinates of the triangles that they belong to. When the program is run, the EarthSphere window is displayed, as in Figure 8-11.

Figure 8-11. *Output of EarthSphere*

We can apply the same image to the diffuseMap for the material used on a cylinder or a cube.

Interacting with JavaFX 3D Scenes

The 3D shapes in the JavaFX 3D graphics API support the full range of JavaFX mouse and touch events. Your JavaFX 3D program can take full advantage of these events to implement interactive behaviors. In fact, we have implemented mouse interactions in the EarthSphere, EarthCylinder, EarthBox, and MeshCube programs. In the EarthSphere, we set event handlers on the scene:

```
scene.setOnMousePressed((MouseEvent event) -> {
    anchorX = event.getSceneX();
    anchorY = event.getSceneY();
    anchorAngleX = angleX.get();
    anchorAngleY = angleY.get();
});
```

```
scene.setOnMouseDragged((MouseEvent event) -> {
    angleY.set(anchorAngleY + anchorX - event.getSceneX());
});
```

In this code, anchorX and anchorY are double fields of the class, and angleX and angleY are double properties that are bound to the degrees of rotations of the parent node that contains the sphere around the *x*- and *y*-axes. Here, we capture the screen coordinates of the mouse pointer as anchorX and anchorY when the mouse is pressed on the screen. We also query for the degree of rotation about the *x*- and *y*-axes of the parent node that contains the sphere. When the mouse is dragged, we alter the degree of rotation of the parent node that contains the sphere about the *y*-axis by adding the difference between anchorX and the screen *x* coordinate of the new mouse location. Therefore, if you click the screen and drag the mouse to the right, anchorX - event.getScreenX() is a negative number; hence, we decrease the angle of rotation about the *y*-axis. Because in this program, the *y*-axis is pointing down, a decrease of the rotation about the *y*-axis actually makes the sphere to appear to be rotating to the right, matching the direction of the mouse drag.

Understanding the PickResult Class

The JavaFX 3D runtime provides enhanced information about the interplay of the mouse pointer with the 3D scene. This information is provided in terms of an object of class PickResult in the relevant event objects. It is contained in the javafx.scene.input package. The following event objects provide a getPickResult() method that allows you to retrieve this PickResult object:

- ContextMenuEvent
- DragEvent
- GestureEvent
  - RotateEvent
  - ScrollEvent
  - SwipeEvent
  - ZoomEvent

- MouseEvent

    - MouseDragEvent

- TouchPoint

The PickResult class provides the following public constructors:

- PickResult(EventTarget, double, double)

- PickResult(Node, Point3D, double)

- PickResult(Node, Point3D, double, int, Point2D)

- PickResult(Node, Point3D, double, int, Point3D, Point2D)

The first two constructors are used to create PickResults to work with 2D scenes, and the third and four constructors create a PickResult that contains 3D information. The PickResults are usually created by the JavaFX 3D runtime. JavaFX application code usually obtains PickResults by calling the accessor method on the event object.

The PickResult class provides the following public methods:

- Node getIntersectedNode()

- Point3D getIntersectedPoint()

- Point3D getIntersectedNormal()

- double getIntersectedDistance()

- int getIntersectedFace()

- Point2D getIntersectedTexCoord()

When the user presses the mouse on a 3D shape, it touches the 3D shape in a particular point in a particular face. The line segment starting from the eye of the camera in effect for the Scene or SubScene and ending at the point on the 3D shape is called the *pick ray*. The point on the 3D shape is called the *intersected point*. The PickResult provides information about this intersected point. The getIntersectedNode() method returns the 3D shape itself, either a Sphere, a Cylinder, a Box, or a MeshView. The getIntersectedPoint() method returns the 3D coordinates of the intersected point. The coordinates are relative to the 3D shape's local coordinate system. For a Sphere of radius 100, the coordinates (x,y,z) of the returned Point3D will satisfy $x2 + y2 + z2 = 100^2$, regardless of the transforms applied to itself or any of its containing nodes. The getIntersectedNormal() method returns the intersected normal of the picked 3D shape. The getIntersectedDistance() method returns the distance from the eye of the camera to the intersected point. This is the length of the pick ray in the 3D model's world coordinate system. The getIntersectedFace() method returns the face number of the face that contains the intersected point for a MeshView, which has user-defined faces. It returns FACE_UNDEFINED for the predefined 3D shapes Sphere, Cylinder, and Box. The getIntersectedTexCoord() method returns the texture coordinates of the intersected point. Unlike the getIntersectedFace() method, this method will return the texture coordinates for both user-defined and predefined 3D shapes.

The program in Listing 8-7 sets an event handler for the mouse pressed and the mouse dragged event for a sphere and changes the color of the sphere based on the intersected point's coordinates when you press or drag the mouse over the sphere. The code can be also found at https://github.com/modernclientjava/mcj-samples/tree/master/ch08-3Dgraphics/eventdemo.

Listing 8-7. EventDemo source code

```java
package org.modernclientjava.javafx3d;
import javafx.application.Application;
import javafx.beans.property.ObjectProperty;
import javafx.beans.property.SimpleObjectProperty;
import javafx.event.EventHandler;
import javafx.geometry.Point3D;
import javafx.scene.Group;
import javafx.scene.Scene;
import javafx.scene.input.PickResult;
import javafx.scene.paint.Color;
import javafx.scene.paint.Material;
import javafx.scene.paint.PhongMaterial;
import javafx.scene.shape.Sphere;
import javafx.stage.Stage;
import static java.lang.Math.abs;
import static java.lang.Math.min;
public class EventDemo extends Application {
    private Model model;
    private View view;
```

```
public EventDemo() {
    model = new Model();
}
@Override
public void start(Stage primaryStage) throws Exception {
    view = new View(model);
    primaryStage.setTitle("Sphere with MouseEvents");
    primaryStage.setScene(view.scene);
    primaryStage.show();
}
public static void main(String[] args) {
    launch(args);
}
private static class Model {
    private ObjectProperty<Material> material =
        new SimpleObjectProperty<>(
            this, "material", new PhongMaterial());
    public Material getMaterial() {
        return material.get();
    }
    public ObjectProperty<Material> materialProperty() {
        return material;
    }
    public void setMaterial(Material material) {
        this.material.set(material);
    }
}
private static class View {
    public static final int SPHERE_RADIUS = 200;
    public Scene scene;
    public Sphere sphere;
    private View(Model model) {
        sphere = new Sphere(SPHERE_RADIUS);
        sphere.materialProperty().bind(model.materialProperty());
```

```
        EventHandler<javafx.scene.input.MouseEvent> handler = event ->
            {
                PickResult pickResult = event.getPickResult();
                Point3D point = pickResult.getIntersectedPoint();
                model.setMaterial(
                new PhongMaterial(makeColorOutOfPoint3D(point)));
            };
        sphere.setOnMouseClicked(handler);
        sphere.setOnMouseDragged(handler);
        Group group = new Group(sphere);
        group.setTranslateX(320);
        group.setTranslateY(240);
        scene = new Scene(group, 640, 480);
    }
    private Color makeColorOutOfPoint3D(Point3D point) {
        double x = point.getX();
        double y = point.getY();
        double z = point.getZ();
        return Color.color(normalize(x), normalize(y), normalize(z));
    }
    private double normalize(double x) {
        return min(abs(x) / SPHERE_RADIUS, 1);
    }
    }
  }
}
```

When the program is run, a sphere will be rendered, like in Figure 8-12. When you press or drag the mouse, the handler method is called. This method will detect the target Point3D, and using the makeColorOutOfPoint3D method, it will change the color of the sphere.

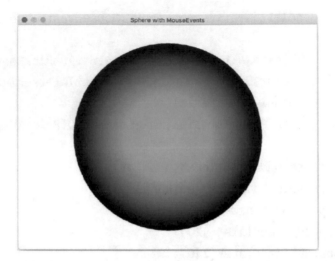

Figure 8-12. *Output of EventDemo*

Third-Party Software: FXyz 3D

FXyz 3D is an open source JavaFX 3D visualization and component library that can be found at `https://github.com/FXyz/FXyz`. Its initial purpose was to enhance the JavaFX built-in 3D features, providing additional primitives, composite objects, controls, and data visualizations. It has been growing over the years. The Deep Space Trajectory Explorer (DSTE) tool used by NASA is one of the well-known use cases of FXyz.

The library contains four subprojects:

- FXyz-Core contains a number of primitives like prisms, pyramids, tetrahedra, segmented spheres, tori, springs, or knots and a number of utility meshes like Polyline3D, SurfacePlot, ScatterPlot, Text3D, SVG3D, or Bezier. All these meshes can be textured with colors, images, patterns, and density maps. There are visualization components like CubeWorld or SkyBox and other many useful tools.

- FXyz-Client is an extended version of the ControlsFX fxsampler, intended for the specific 3D visualization options.

- FXyz importers allow importing complex 3D models from known formats like OBJ or Maya.

- FXyz-Samples provides a number of samples that can be run with the sampler.

The core, client, and importers components are available from Maven Central and can be included in a Maven project as follows:

```
<dependency>
    <groupId>org.fxyz3d</groupId>
    <artifactId>fxyz3d</artifactId>
    <version>0.5.4</version>
</dependency>
or gradle project as follows:
repositories {
    mavenCentral()
}
dependencies {
    implementation 'org.fxyz3d:fxyz3d:0.5.4'
}
```

FXyz 3D Sample

Once the core dependencies have been included, using any of the FXyz primitives in a JavaFX project is straightforward. Listing 8-8 creates a SpringMesh with a density map based on the arc position to generate the texture.

The code is available at https://github.com/modernclientjava/mcj-samples/tree/master/ch08-3Dgraphics/fxyzdemo.

Listing 8-8. FXyzDemo source code

```
package org.modernclientjava.javafx3d;
import javafx.application.Application;
import javafx.scene.paint.Color;
import javafx.scene.shape.CullFace;
import javafx.scene.transform.Rotate;
import javafx.scene.Group;
import javafx.scene.PerspectiveCamera;
import javafx.scene.Scene;
import javafx.scene.SceneAntialiasing;
import javafx.stage.Stage;
import org.fxyz3d.shapes.primitives.SpringMesh;
```

```java
public class FxyzDemo extends Application {
    @Override
    public void start(Stage primaryStage) {
        PerspectiveCamera camera = new PerspectiveCamera(true);
        camera.setNearClip(0.1);
        camera.setFarClip(10000.0);
        camera.setTranslateX(-50);
        camera.setTranslateZ(-30);
        camera.setRotationAxis(Rotate.Y_AXIS);
        camera.setRotate(45);
        SpringMesh spring = new SpringMesh(10, 2, 2, 8 * 2 * Math.PI, 200,
        100, 0, 0);
        spring.setCullFace(CullFace.NONE);
        spring.setTextureModeVertices3D(1530, p -> p.f);
        Scene scene = new Scene(new Group(spring), 600, 400, true,
        SceneAntialiasing.BALANCED);
        scene.setFill(Color.BISQUE);
        scene.setCamera(camera);
        primaryStage.setScene(scene);
        primaryStage.setTitle("FXyz3D Sample");
        primaryStage.show();
    }
}
```

Running this sample shows the output in Figure 8-13.

Figure 8-13.   *Output of FXyzDemo*

Conclusion

The JavaFX core APIs already provide the basis for creating advanced 3D scenes. Those APIs allow for lots of flexibility and configurations, and they use similar concepts as the ones found in other 3D engines.

In the spirit of JavaFX, those APIs mainly provide the foundations for other frameworks to build on top of those APIs and deliver domain-specific functionality – for example, the FXyz framework.

It should also be noted that as a recent addition in JavaFX (starting with JavaFX 13), it is possible to mix content from other (native) applications with JavaFX, using a shared buffer. For an example of this, you can have a look at `https://github.com/miho/NativeFX`.

CHAPTER 9

JavaFX, the Web, and Cloud Infrastructure

Written by Johan Vos, Bruno Borges, and José Pereda

Client applications, as the term itself already hints, are rarely self-contained. In order to function properly, they need to access other components, for example, server applications. JavaFX, being a Java framework, allows application developers to leverage the wide Java ecosystem. Libraries created for interacting with, for example, REST APIs, web components, SOAP endpoints, and encryption APIs can be used in JavaFX applications. As such, there is nothing special about a JavaFX application vs. a non-JavaFX application. However, there are a number of features in JavaFX that enable developers to create an easy, secure, reliable connection to other (backend or server-side) components.

In this chapter, we will discuss two approaches for integrating backend components with JavaFX applications. First, we'll discuss the WebView component. At its core, the JavaFX WebView control has most of the functionalities of a web browser, and it allows for two-way interaction between script elements on the web pages and Java functions in the JavaFX application. It is often used as an easy way to render existing functionality from a web site into a desktop application.

This approach is shown in Figure 9-1.

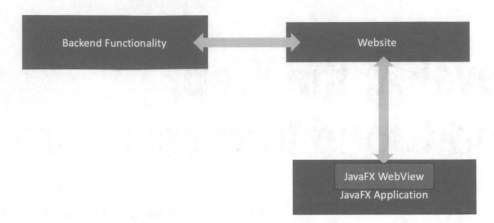

Figure 9-1. *Integrating backend functionality using WebView*

Next, a more flexible and general approach is discussed for connecting JavaFX controls to remote endpoints in cloud or backend infrastructure. In this approach, the JavaFX application communicates directly with the backend APIs, as shown in Figure 9-2.

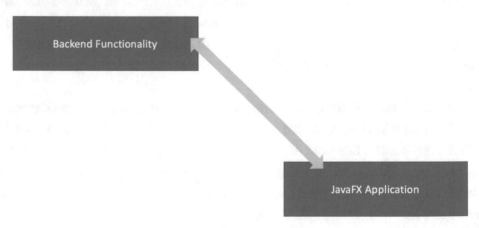

Figure 9-2. *The JavaFX application communicates directly with the backend APIs*

Integrating with the Web

With the WebView component, you can display HTML5 content in your JavaFX application. This works for a local HTML file or a web page. The component is based on WebKit and is quite powerful. The possible applications range from the display of documentation to the integration of complete web applications. What is very practical is that it is easy to interact with the content of the WebView component via a JavaScript bridge. This allows us to modify the page from JavaFX and react to user actions.

Displaying a Web Page

The WebView API itself is very easy to use for simple use cases. The WebView and related classes are part of the javafx.web module. Hence, if we want to use it, we should make sure we add that javafx.web module to our module path. Using a command-line approach, this is done by adding

```
--add-modules javafx.web
```

When using Maven with the javafx-maven-plugin, we can easily add a dependency as follows:

```
<dependency>
    <groupId>org.openjfx</groupId>
    <artifactId>javafx-web</artifactId>
    <version>17.0.1</version>
</dependency>
```

This is also illustrated in the pom.xml file in the webviewdemo sample in the sample repository.

We can start with a code example right away. The core component is the WebView Node. We can add it to the SceneGraph like any other node. We requests its WebEngine and pass a URL to it as follows:

```
public class WebViewDemo extends Application {
    @Override
    public void start(Stage primaryStage) {
        WebView webView = new WebView();
        WebEngine engine = webView.getEngine();
        engine.load("https://openjfx.io");
        Scene scene = new Scene(webView, 300, 250);
        primaryStage.setTitle("JavaFX WebView Demo");
```

```
        primaryStage.setScene(scene);
        primaryStage.show();
    }
}
```

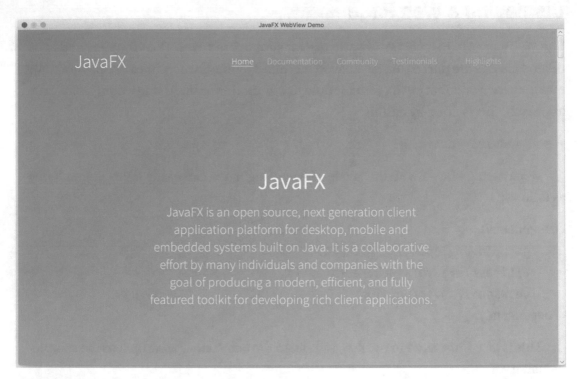

Figure 9-3. *Loading a web site in JavaFX WebView*

The three highlighted lines of code suffice to load the web page as shown in Figure 9-3. With a right-click, you can open a context menu on the page and, depending on the current status, stop or restart the loading of the page. This menu is available by default. For the most common use cases, you won't need it. Let's disable it with the following command:

```
webView.setContextMenuEnabled(false);
```

Adding Navigation and History

To use the WebEngine's load command for navigating between web sites, you can add buttons or menus to your JavaFX application to display a specific page when clicked. In response to a click, just call engine.load("`http://myurl.com`") to instruct the WebEngine to load the page for you. Let's try this in our example with a MenuBar as shown in Figure 9-4. To do this, we first put the WebView into a BorderPane so we can easily insert a MenuBar above it. Change the start method like this:

```java
public void start(Stage primaryStage) {
        WebView webView = new WebView();
        webView.setContextMenuEnabled(false);
        WebEngine engine = webView.getEngine();
        engine.load("https://openjfx.io ");
        BorderPane borderPane= new BorderPane(webView);
        MenuBar menuBar = new MenuBar();
        final Menu navigateMenu = new Menu("Navigate");
        MenuItem home = new MenuItem("Home");
        navigateMenu.getItems().addAll(home);
        home.setOnAction(e -> engine.load("https://github.com/openjdk/jfx"));
        menuBar.getMenus().add(navigateMenu);
        borderPane.setTop(menuBar);
        Scene scene = new Scene(borderPane, 640, 400);
        primaryStage.setTitle("JavaFX WebView Demo");
        primaryStage.setScene(scene);
        primaryStage.show();
    }
```

Figure 9-4. *Adding a MenuBar for navigation*

The WebEngine also makes the navigation history available to us. The WebEngine's getHistory method returns a History object that has a getEntries method. That's an ObservableList we can use to keep track of changes. Let's use that to fill a menu:

```
Menu historyMenu = new Menu("History");
        engine.getHistory().getEntries().addListener((ListChangeListener.
        Change<? extends Entry> c) -> {
            c.next();
            for (Entry e: c.getAddedSubList()) {
                for(MenuItem i: historyMenu.getItems()){
                    if (i.getId().equals(e.getUrl())){
                        historyMenu.getItems().remove(i);
                    }
                }
            }
            for (Entry e: c.getAddedSubList()) {
                final MenuItem menuItem = new MenuItem(e.getUrl());
                menuItem.setId(e.getUrl());
                menuItem.setOnAction(a->engine.load(e.getUrl()));
                historyMenu.getItems().add(menuItem);
            }
        });
        menuBar.getMenus().addAll(navigateMenu, historyMenu);
```

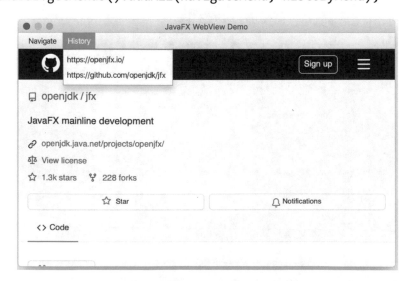

Figure 9-5. *Accessing browsing history*

The result is shown in Figure 9-5. That's not much effort for building a nice basic browser. Now it's time to improve the user experience. Currently, we get no indication of the loading process.

Showing Loading Progress

A progress bar would be very helpful here. We can display it at the bottom of the page while loading new content. Fortunately, the WebEngine is using the javafx concurrency APIs, so we can get a Property to easily track progress. So let's add a ProgressBar to our BorderPane to show the progress:

```
ProgressBar progressBar = new ProgressBar();
progressBar.progressProperty().bind(
        engine.getLoadWorker().progressProperty());
progressBar.visibleProperty().bind(engine.getLoadWorker().
stateProperty().isEqualTo(State.RUNNING));
    borderPane.setBottom(progressBar);
```

We also bind the visibleProperty of our ProgressBar to the stateProperty of the Worker. A very small code sample illustrates perfectly how well properties and bindings are integrated with the rest of the JavaFX APIs. There's no need for listeners, which really helps to improve the readability of our code. The example with a working progress bar is shown in Figure 9-6.

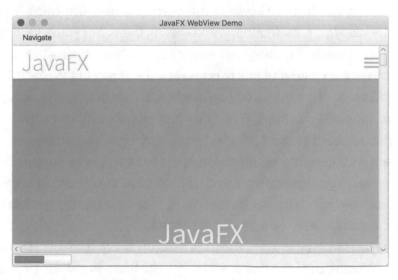

Figure 9-6. *Showing progress while loading a page*

From Web Sites to APIs

In this section, we'll show how existing web sites can easily be rendered in JavaFX applications. By linking JavaScript functionality on the web sites with Java functions in the JavaFX application, it is possible to enhance the web site functionality and make it more interactive or to integrate it with functionality that is not available to web browsers (e.g., connection with devices).

While this is often a quick and simple solution for creating a desktop application based on an existing web site, in most cases it doesn't provide the rich functionality offered by the backend, and it doesn't leverage the rich functionality offered by the JavaFX APIs.

In the second part of this chapter, we will discuss how to access backend functionality and integrate it with JavaFX controls in a more granular way.

Building for the Cloud

Around 2012, the cloud finally went mainstream, but only with very few players that still today dominate the market. And yet, the competition is huge, with services and APIs being announced every quarter. Building applications for the cloud usually means taking advantage of these highly available and scalable infrastructure as a service, as well as highly productive and easy-to-use and easy-to-integrate platforms as a service. Whether it's a virtual machine or a database that is quickly provisioned for you or a face detection API that just needs a subscription key, all these resources have one thing in common: it is not you who is managing, maintaining, and scaling them, but your cloud provider.

Cloud also often means building web-based applications or web-based REST APIs that will run in the cloud and talk to resources also living in the cloud. How these applications and services are built and deployed often falls in the microservices and cloud-native architecture playbook. Scalability patterns of cloud resources apply fairly well to these web applications and microservices. And when everything is on the Internet and applications are accessed through the browser, some automated HTTP-based client, or messaging systems, many challenges that are common to desktop applications such as version update, data caching, service rerouting, and so on simply do not exist or are much easier to be solved in the cloud.

So what happens when the user-facing application is a rich client? How can developers take advantage of the cloud, and why? The focus here is on providing value in their modern client desktop application by not having to develop certain algorithms and business logic within the client itself and instead either moving them to a place where developers can have better control and deliver updates faster or consuming ready-to-use service APIs that would otherwise have consumed a significant time of development to be built in the rich client.

Compared to the scenario where the client is simply displaying a WebView with a web site, this approach is much more powerful. Some parts of the functionality can be implemented in the client, while other parts can be offloaded to the cloud provider.

Architecture of a JavaFX Cloud Application

Most modern enterprise systems have a multitier architecture, in which the web-based frontend and the business logic are separated. Typical web frameworks query the business tier, either using direct (Java) calls or REST APIs. This is shown in the following picture.

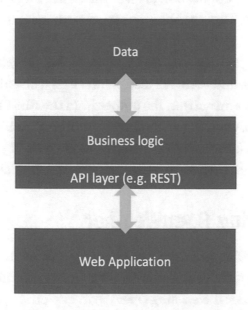

The business logic is not implemented inside the web application, but it is typically implemented in a backend component using some specific enterprise architecture, which provides additional functionality like security, scalability, monitoring, etc. The same concept can be applied to the case of a JavaFX client application, as shown in the following.

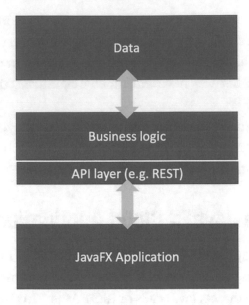

In this case, the JavaFX application invokes the same API layer as a typical web application would invoke. This approach has the advantage that a single API layer is needed to serve different types of clients.

Very often, the API layer exposes a REST interface. Many web frameworks provide access to REST interfaces, and there are also plenty of Java libraries that allow developers to access REST interfaces and convert the output from the REST interface to Java objects.

As an example of this, we will use the OpenWeather API, which is an API layer that is accessed via a REST interface. This API is used by many web-based applications, and we will show three approaches on how to leverage this API in Java client applications.

Use Case: Querying OpenWeather

We will now show a JavaFX application that queries the OpenWeather API (https:// openweathermap.org) to retrieve the weather for a given location. We could have simply used a WebView and render the existing OpenWeather web site, but we want to leverage the power of the JavaFX controls, or we want to integrate seamlessly the weather data within our existing JavaFX UI application.

We will now explain how to write an application that retrieves queries from OpenWeather. In order to do so, the first thing is to sign up in the portal (https://home. openweathermap.org/users/sign_up) and get the default API key or generate a new one (https://home.openweathermap.org/api_keys).

In the following code snippets, you will notice that the API key is sometimes required. The OpenWeather API allows a limited number of calls per hour for a single account. Hence, it is better that you create and use your own API keys rather than using a shared API key. This is why we typically replace the real key with, for example, "XXXXXXXXXXX". Make sure to replace this "XXXXXXXXXXX" with the real API key you obtain from the OpenWeather portal.

For starters, let's create a simple application that will display the weather at a given time and city:

```java
public class WeatherApp extends Application {
    private static final String API_KEY = "XXXXXXXXXXX";
    private static final String CITY = "London";
    private ImageView imageView;
    private Label weatherLabel;
    private Label descriptionLabel;
    private Label tempLabel;
    @Override
    public void start(Stage stage) {
        imageView = new ImageView();
        imageView.setFitHeight(100);
        imageView.setPreserveRatio(true);
        imageView.setEffect(new DropShadow());
        Label label = new Label("The weather in " + CITY);
        weatherLabel = new Label();
        descriptionLabel = new Label();
        descriptionLabel.getStyleClass().add("desc");
        tempLabel = new Label();
        tempLabel.getStyleClass().add("temp");
        VBox root = new VBox(10,
            label, imageView, weatherLabel, descriptionLabel, tempLabel);
        root.setAlignment(Pos.CENTER);
        Scene scene = new Scene(root, 600, 400);
        scene.getStylesheets().add(
            WeatherApp.class.getResource("/styles.css").toExternalForm());
        stage.setScene(scene);
        stage.setTitle("The Weather App");
```

```
        stage.show();
        retrieveWeather();
    }
    private void retrieveWeather() {
        // TODO
    }
}
```

This code is leveraging the layout and controls that we discussed in earlier chapters of this book. The only new part is the "retrieveWeather()" call that is currently not yet implemented. We will implement this in a number of ways in the rest of this chapter.

Apart from code, it is often good to apply some styling information to the application. In this sample, we use the following CSS content:

```
.label {
    -fx-font-size: 1.4em;
    -fx-text-fill: blue;
}
.label.desc {
    -fx-font-size: 1.2em;
    -fx-text-fill: gray;
}
.label.temp {
    -fx-font-size: 1.1em;
    -fx-text-fill: green;
}
```

The query required to get weather data for a given system is defined by the OpenWeather API, and it is described at https://openweathermap.org/current.

Note that the API definitions might change, so the current approach might need minor modifications in case OpenWeather changes its API!

To query OpenWeather for a given city, with our API key, basically we just need to create this query:

```
"https://api.openweathermap.org/data/2.5/weather?appid="
    + API_KEY + "&q=" + CITY
```

When such a query is sent to the OpenWeather API, we will get a response back in the JSON format, similar to the following:

```
{"coord":{"lon":-0.13,"lat":51.51},
 "weather":[{"id":500,"main":"Rain",
 "description":"light rain","icon":"10d"}],"base":"stations",
 "main":{"temp":290.14,"pressure":1012,"humidity":68,
 "temp_min":288.15,"temp_max":292.59},"visibility":10000,
 "wind":{"speed":4.1,"deg":180},"clouds":{"all":40},
 "dt":1563527401,"sys":{"type":1,"id":1414,"message":0.0137,
 "country":"GB","sunrise":1563509115,"sunset":1563566876},
 "timezone":3600,"id":2643743,"name":"London","cod":200}
```

There are multiple ways to process this response. In the Java ecosystem, many libraries exist that deal with JSON input and bind it to a Java object. In order to facilitate the mapping between JSON data and Java objects, we will use model entities to deserialize the JSON string into something like the following:

```
public class Model {
    private long id;
    private long dt;
    private Clouds clouds;
    private Coord coord;
    private Wind wind;
    private String cod;
    private String visibility;
    private long timezone;
    private Sys sys;
    private String name;
    private String base;
    private List<Weather> weather = new ArrayList<>();
    private Main main;
    // Getters & setters
}
public class Clouds {
    private String all;
```

```java
    // Getters & setters
}
public class Coord {
    private float lon;
    private float lat;
    // Getters & setters
}
public class Main {
    private float humidity;
    private float pressure;
    private float temp_max;
    private float temp_min;
    private float temp;
    private float feels_like;
    // Getters & setters
}
public class Sys {
    private String message;
    private String id;
    private long sunset;
    private long sunrise;
    private String type;
    private String country;
    // Getters & setters
}
public class Weather {
    private int id;
    private String icon;
    private String description;
    private String main;
    // Getters & setters
}
public class Wind {
    private float speed;
    private float deg;
```

```
    private float gust;
    // Getters & setters
}
```

As you can see, the model described maps to the output provided by the JSON service. Some frameworks require the names of the object fields to match exactly the names of the JSON fields. Others allow annotations to provide the matching. In some cases, the fields are required, whereas in other cases getters and setters are required.

Case 1: Jackson

A very popular and flexible framework for deserializing JSON into a Java object is the Jackson project that provides a JSON Java parser (`https://github.com/FasterXML/jackson`).

We can simply add the dependency to our project:

```
<dependency>
    <groupId>com.fasterxml.jackson.core</groupId>
    <artifactId>jackson-databind</artifactId>
    <version>2.12.3</version>
</dependency>
 (for Maven)
```

or

```
dependencies {
    implementation "com.fasterxml.jackson.core:jackson-databind:2.12.3"
}
(for Gradle)
```

Now we can complete our `retrieveWeather` call:

```
private void retrieveWeather() {
    try {
            String restUrl =
                "https://api.openweathermap.org/data/2.5/weather?appid="
                + API_KEY + "&q=" + CITY;
            ObjectMapper objectMapper = new ObjectMapper();
            Model model = objectMapper.readValue(
```

```
                new URL(restUrl), Model.class);
            updateModel(model);
        } catch (Throwable e) {
            System.out.println("Error: " + e);
            e.printStackTrace();
        }
    }
    private void updateModel(Model model) throws MalformedURLException,
    URISyntaxException {
        if (model != null) {
            if (!model.getWeather().isEmpty()) {
                Weather w = model.getWeather().get(0);
                imageView.setImage(new Image(new URL("http://
                openweathermap.org/img/wn/" + w.getIcon() + "@2x.png").
                toURI().toString()));
                weatherLabel.setText(w.getMain());
                descriptionLabel.setText(w.getDescription());
            }
            tempLabel.setText(String.format("%.2f °C - %.1f%%",
            model.getMain().getTemp() - 273.15, model.getMain().
            getHumidity()));
        }
    }
```

If you are already using the Jackson API, this code will look very familiar. There is indeed no difference in using the Jackson API from a server-side application vs. from a JavaFX application.

We won't discuss Jackson in detail, but you can understand from the code what is happening.

First, the URL containing the required API request is constructed:

```
String restUrl =
                "https://api.openweathermap.org/data/2.5/weather?appid="
                + API_KEY + "&q=" + CITY;
```

The URL requires the API_KEY and the city of interest to be filled in.

Next, we use the Jackson code to retrieve the information and convert the result into a Java object:

```
ObjectMapper objectMapper = new ObjectMapper();
          Model model = objectMapper.readValue(
               new URL(restUrl), Model.class);
```

The ObjectMapper API, which is part of Jackson, allows to parse the output of a REST method and to create a new instance of a provided class (in this case "Model") and map the fields of that class with the fields in the returned JSON data.

Finally, the "updateModel" call is invoked to make sure the retrieved information is visualized on the Scene. We use the JavaFX APIs that have been discussed earlier in this book for this.

Now we run the application as shown in Figure 9-7.

Figure 9-7. *The application running*

This approach is very easy to implement, especially if you are familiar with Jackson or another JSON parsing library in Java.

While this approach is very convenient, there are some points that are specific to JavaFX and that should be taken into account.

For example, the parsing is done in a synchronous call to do the whole process of querying the given URL, waiting for the result, and retrieving and parsing the response. If anything goes wrong, like a timeout or a network error, there will be only an exception, and possibly the UI will freeze, so we should wrap that call in a JavaFX service.

Also, while the Model class is very generic and a good practice in object-oriented development, it does not leverage the "Observable" concept in JavaFX. Hence, there is boilerplate code needed to update the UI.

The approach we took can be visualized as follows:

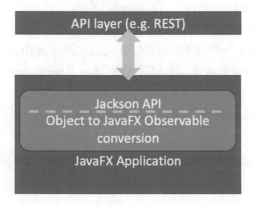

Case 2: Connect

Gluon's Connect library (`https://github.com/gluonhq/connect`) not only deserializes the JSON response like Jackson but also does it in an asynchronous way; and, what's more, it returns a JavaFX observable list or object that can be used directly by the JavaFX UI controls. Using Gluon Connect allows to get rid of the additional step to convert the parsed object into JavaFX Observable instances, as it directly populates or manipulates those instances. Visually, this can be shown as follows:

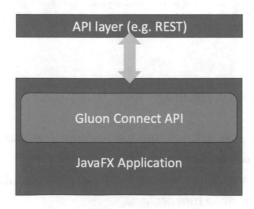

Using Gluon Connect requires adding the following dependencies to our project:

```
<dependency>
    <groupId>com.gluonhq</groupId>
    <artifactId>connect</artifactId>
    <version>2.0.1</version>
</dependency>
<dependency>
    <groupId>org.glassfish</groupId>
    <artifactId>jakarta.json</artifactId>
    <version>1.1.5</version>
    <scope>runtime</scope>
</dependency>
 (for Maven)
```

or

```
dependencies {
    implementation "com.gluonhq:connect:2.0.1"
    runtimeOnly 'org.glassfish:jakarta.json:1.1.5'
}
(for Gradle)
```

And now our updateWeather call can be done as follows:

```
    private void retrieveWeather() {
        GluonObservableObject<Model> weather = getWeather();
        weather.setOnFailed(e -> System.out.println("Error: " + e));
        weather.setOnSucceeded(e -> updateModel(weather.get()));
    }
    private GluonObservableObject<Model> getWeather() {
        RestClient client = RestClient.create()
                .method("GET")
                .host("http://api.openweathermap.org/")
                .connectTimeout(10000)
                .readTimeout(1000)
                .path("data/2.5/weather")
                .header("accept", "application/json")
```

```
            .queryParam("appid", API_KEY)
            .queryParam("q", CITY);
    return DataProvider.retrieveObject(
        client.createObjectDataReader(Model.class));
}
```

Running this application results in the same output as before, but the code is much more concise. The "retrieveWeather" method first creates an instance of a "GluonObservable" object. The creation of this object creates a "RestClient" that defines the REST interface we need to query, and it then uses a "DataProvider" to provide a "GluonObservableObject" that contains the parsed information from the resulting JSON output.

We can set callback methods on this object. For example, when the data is successfully retrieved, we update the model with the provided weather information.

The application we have created is very basic, but you get the point that it can be much more flexible and dynamic than simply rendering a web site in a WebView control. By accessing external APIs, the code in the JavaFX application looks similar to code in a backend that accesses those external APIs, as shown in Figure 9-8.

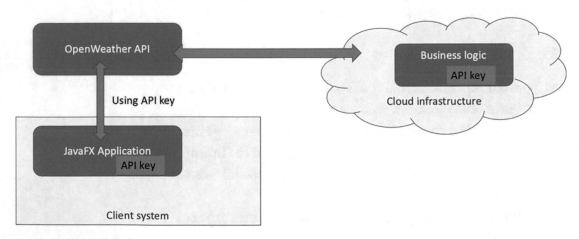

Figure 9-8. *The JavaFX application looks similar to code in a backend that accesses external APIs*

The JavaFX client, or the web client, makes a connection to the API layer, which then probably uses more complex business logic, talks to a data layer, and somehow handles the request.

There is a very important difference between the case where the client code resides in a cloud environment and on a desktop with an end user. In the first case, the cloud environment can in most situations be considered as a trusted environment. However, in the case where the code resides on the end user desktop, this is no longer true. The end user themselves, or other malicious applications on the device, might obtain the API key. As long as the API key is stored on the device, anyone with access to the device might somehow use or abuse this. This is shown in the following picture:

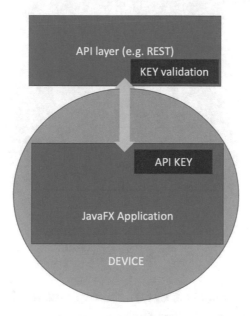

In the case of OpenWeather queries, this is probably not the most fatal issue, but in general, API keys that provide access to critical or sensitive functionality should not be stored on end user systems.

In order to fix this issue, it is beneficial to use a middleware component that acts as a bridge between the trusted cloud infrastructure and the client device (desktop/mobile/embedded) of the user.

The API key is then kept on the middleware component, which is hosted in a secure environment, as shown in the following:

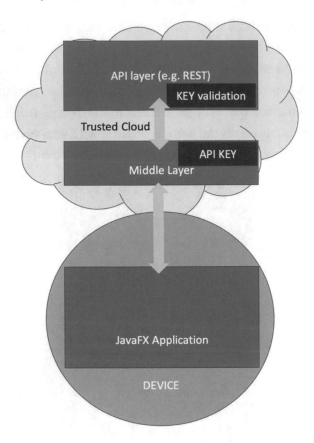

In case the device is now hacked, or the client application is somehow compromised, the hacker has no access to the API key. In the worst case, the hacker can talk to the middle layer, pretending they are the original owner of the device, and then execute calls with the real API key, but they won't have access to this key themselves.

By providing optimal security and authentication between the device and the middle layer, even this scenario can be avoided.

This middleware component can be extended and export general cloud functionality (e.g., access to a serverless container) as well, as shown in Figure 9-9.

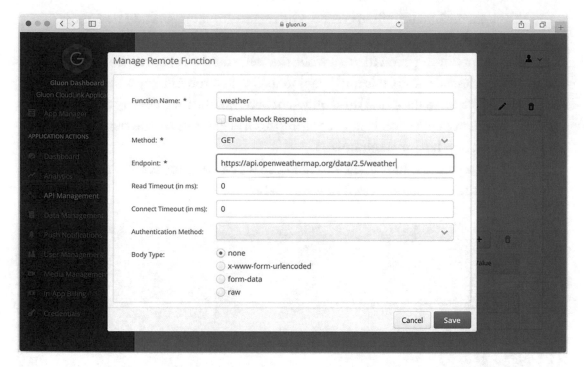

Figure 9-9. *The middleware component can be extended to export general cloud functionality*

In the next paragraph, we will explain how to write the OpenWeather application using Gluon CloudLink (`https://docs.gluonhq.com/cloudlink/`), which is a middleware solution from Gluon that provides specific support for JavaFX applications.

Case 3: Gluon CloudLink

Gluon CloudLink provides much more functionality than simply storing API keys on behalf of devices. We won't go over the functionality in detail, but we will use a handy feature in the following example. Instead of creating the REST request on the JavaFX client, we will compose the request in Gluon CloudLink, using a web-based dashboard.

Before we add the code, we need to access the Gluon Dashboard (`https://gluon.io`), access with our credentials, and go to API Management to add a remote function. A remote function is a component that can be invoked from the Java client (as we will show in the next code snippet), but that is executed on the middleware (hence inside Gluon CloudLink). This has a number of benefits, including flexibility: if the REST API somehow changes (e.g., a parameter is added or renamed), we can redefine the remote function in the Gluon Dashboard console, without having to change the client code. Especially in environments where you can't easily update all client instances immediately, this can make a big difference.

In the client dashboard, when creating the remote function, we add two query parameters for the request: `appid` and `q`. We set the value for the former with our API key, so the client doesn't need to do it, while the value for the latter will be set in the client. As we stressed before, it is important to realize that the API key is stored in the middleware (hosted in the cloud) and only sent between the middleware and the remote service. The client application is not accessing this API key; hence, the risk for the key being obtained by a hacker is minimized.

We can set a pair of values in the test fields, so we can directly test the remote function from the dashboard shown in Figure 9-10.

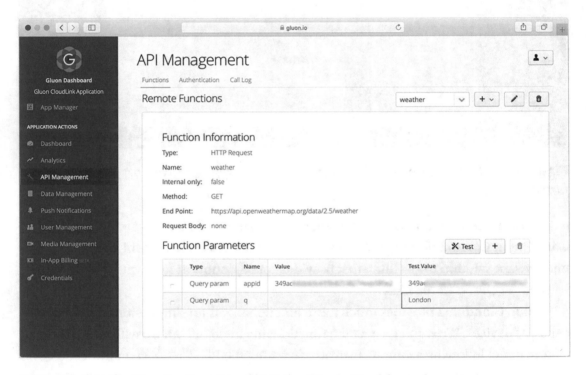

Figure 9-10. *Testing the function from the Gluon Dashboard*

Once the test is successful (we should see a 200 response and a JSON string with the result), we can go back to our project and add the CloudLink dependencies in the pom. xml file. This is done by adding the Gluon repository to the list of repositories:

```
repositories {
    mavenCentral()
    maven {
```

```
    url 'https://nexus.gluonhq.com/nexus/content/repositories/releases/'
  }
}
```

We also have to add a number of dependencies to the pom.xml, as shown in the following:

```
<dependency>
    <groupId>com.gluonhq</groupId>
    <artifactId>charm-cloudlink-client</artifactId>
    <version>6.0.1</version>
 </dependency>
<dependency>
    <groupId>org.glassfish</groupId>
    <artifactId>javax.json</artifactId>
    <version>1.1.4</version>
</dependency>
<dependency>
    <groupId>org.glassfish</groupId>
    <artifactId>jakarta.json</artifactId>
    <version>1.1.5</version>
</dependency>
<dependency>
    <groupId>com.gluonhq.attach</groupId>
    <artifactId>storage</artifactId>
    <version>4.0.11</version>
</dependency>
```

The Gluon CloudLink client code is designed to work on desktop, mobile, and embedded devices. In order to do so, it abstracts some functionality that has different implementations on those different platforms. The open source project Gluon Attach provides this abstraction, as well as implementations for desktop, iOS, and Android platforms. For example, the way data is stored on a platform is different between those targets, and this is used by the Gluon CloudLink client code. Therefore, we added a dependency to the com.gluonhq.attach.storage service. In order to make the application platform independent, we also add the gluonfx-maven-plugin, which makes sure to use the correct native implementation of the attach services:

```
<plugin>
    <groupId>com.gluonhq</groupId>
    <artifactId>gluonfx-maven-plugin</artifactId>
    <version>1.0.2</version>
    <configuration>
        <attachList>
            <list>storage</list>
        </attachList>
        <mainClass>org.modernclientjava.WeatherApp</mainClass>
    </configuration>
 </plugin>
```

Finally, we modify the code to

```
private void retrieveWeather() {
    GluonObservableObject<Model> weather = getWeather();
    weather.setOnFailed(e -> System.out.println("Error: " + e));
    weather.setOnSucceeded(e -> updateModel(weather.get()));
}
private GluonObservableObject<Model> getWeather() {
    RemoteFunctionObject functionObject = RemoteFunctionBuilder
            .create("weather")
            .param("q", CITY)
            .object();
    return functionObject.call(Model.class);
}
```

As you can see, there is only one query parameter in the remote function call from the client.

The only credentials required within the client are those to access the CloudLink middleware. A file named gluoncloudlink_config.json is required at src/main/resources:

```
{
  "gluonCredentials": {
    "applicationKey" : "XXXXXXXX-XXXX-XXXX-XXXX-XXXXXXXXXXXX",
    "applicationSecret": "XXXXXXXX-XXXX-XXXX-XXXX-XXXXXXXXXXXX"
  }
}
```

The content of this file can be retrieved from the Dashboard ➤ Credentials ➤ Client.

Since we want the platform-dependent attach implementations to be handled by the gluonfx plugin, we launch the application using

```
mvn gluonfx:run
```

This will detect the current platform and use the correct implementations.

Conclusion

JavaFX applications are regular Java applications and can use all existing Java functionality. Using the JavaFX WebView control, it is possible to render web pages in a JavaFX application and create interactions between the web page functionality (in JavaScript) and the Java engine running on the client.

For fine-grained, secure, and flexible integrations of client applications with enterprise functionality in the cloud, existing Java frameworks can be used. Developers should be very aware of the specific characteristics of client systems, especially related to security. Therefore, middleware (e.g., Gluon CloudLink) allows developers to shield the security-sensitive information from the client application.

Packaging Apps for the Desktop

Written by José Pereda, Johan Vos, and Gail Anderson

Creating a Java client application is only the first step in the lifecycle of the application. Your application will be used by end users who interact with it. Whether your application is intended for internal, intranet-only usage or for a wide public audience, you want the barrier to use your application to be as low as possible. End users don't like complex procedures before they can start working with an application.

In this chapter, we will explain how to build applications that end users can install and use with the same approach they follow installing other (non-Java) applications. We will explore two important modern tools for creating bundled Java applications that fulfil the expectations of end users: jpackage and GraalVM's Native Image.

Web vs. Desktop Applications

When you create a Java client application, or by extension any client application, the end user will access your application directly. This is very different from creating cloud or web-based applications, where your code is probably running on a cloud or server infrastructure and the end user accesses your code typically via a web browser. In that case, you have to provision your application to a cloud or server, and there are specific tools that help you with this task.

You or your IT department controls the environment in which your application runs. You know the surrounding context, including the operating system, resource constraints, and available software. This situation is shown in Figure 10-1.

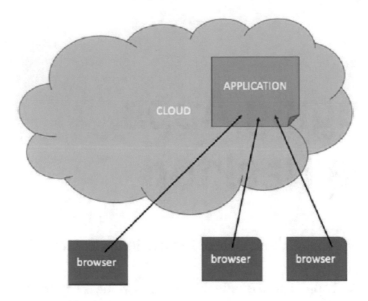

Figure 10-1. *The environment in which an application runs*

In the case of a client application, you need to make sure your application can be installed on all client systems. If you are lucky, your application will be deployed on an intranet that is completely controlled by you or your IT organization. But typically, you do not control the environment in which your application is supposed to run. It is often assumed that your application should work on all operating systems, and you don't know if the end user installed Java or not and, if so, what version or versions. Contrary to deployment in a cloud environment, you cannot install your application yourself on the system of the end user. You rely on this end user to execute the required instructions; hence, you want these instructions to be as simple and familiar as possible. The client deployment scenario is shown in Figure 10-2.

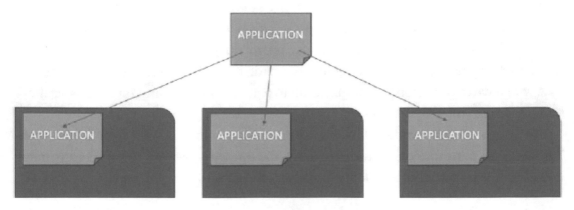

Figure 10-2. *Deployment scenario on desktop*

Evolutions in Application Deployment

In the past, most deployment of Java client applications required a clear separation between your application code, its dependencies, and the Java Virtual Machine (JVM) on which it was required to run. Starting with Java Applets in 1995 and later with Java Web Start, developers of Java client applications could assume there was some Java Virtual Machine already installed on the end user system. If this was not the case, the developer could assume some tool existed to assist the end user in installing a JVM.

Developers, therefore, had to use build tools to bundle program code, dependencies, and resources into an application and then allow end users to install that application on top of the JVM they already installed – see Figure 10-3.

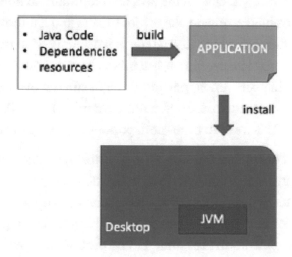

Figure 10-3. *Legacy development process*

The rationale behind this concept was clear: when there are multiple Java applications running on a client, it makes sense to have a single JVM installation to provide the foundation for the different applications. With Java's strong focus on backward compatibility, it was also often fair to assume that your applications would still run with later versions of the JVM. As a consequence, a single JVM on the end user system would be enough to serve the needs of all Java client applications. As a result, this concept requires less disk space (the JVM is shared between applications) and less bandwidth (the JVM code does not need to be transferred with the application; it is assumed to be present).

In recent years, there have been a number of evolutions that make this approach less compelling:

- Typical disk space and bandwidth are increasing. Today's average users are using higher volumes of both storage capacity and streaming capacity. One of the drivers for this is the increase in media streaming and storage. Compared to the requirements of typical streaming services, the transmission and storage of the JVM code is relatively small. Hence, the argument that the JVM code should not be sent with the application or stored with the application because this requires too much bandwidth or storage capacity is less relevant.

- The newer release cadence of the Java Development Kit puts even more responsibilities on end users. Many users find it annoying to see a popup on their PC asking to upgrade to a newer version of Java. Their applications might be using Java, but this should be transparent to end users. While different applications might still run on older JVMs, developers often want to use new features in more recent JVMs for their applications. This leads to even more popups annoying the end user.

- The concept of application stores, or app stores, changed the mobile landscape and is also gaining traction on the desktop. Using app stores, end users simply decide to install an application using a uniform "click and install" concept. Everything that is required to execute the application is assumed to be part of that application. Thus, end users don't manage required components (e.g., JVMs) that are not adding functionality to the user.

The Java ecosystem saw this evolution. The JavaFX libraries previously contained a "javafxpackager" tool that let developers package their JavaFX application, including a Java Virtual Machine and all dependencies, for different platforms (Linux, Windows, macOS).

With the Java Platform Module System, where the JVM itself is broken up into a number of modules, the situation changed. It is now possible to create sub-versions of the JVM that contain only the modules that a specific application needs. Since packaging is relevant to all applications (not just client applications that require a user interface), a new Java packaging tool is part of the JDK in preview since Java 14 and finalized in Java 16. We will discuss this tool, called jpackage, in the next section.

Apart from jpackage, there is another tool that allows you to bundle your application into a self-contained native application, GraalVM's Native Image. With this tool, the application and its dependencies are compiled ahead of time into native applications. We discuss this tool later in this chapter.

The concept of bundling an application with its dependencies and resources, but also with the JVM, is shown in Figure 10-4.

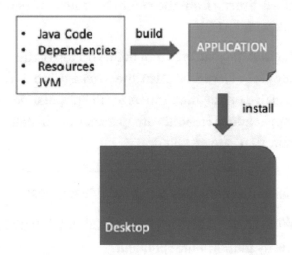

Figure 10-4. *Modern development process*

The jpackage Tool

What Is jpackage?

Starting in preview with JDK 14 and finalized in JDK 16, the jpackage tool is part of the JDK distributions. The specification for jpackage is JEP 392: `https://openjdk.java.net/jeps/392`. (The original specification for jpackage was JEP 343.)

The summary of this JEP is clear:

Create a new tool for packaging self-contained Java applications.

This summary matches what we discussed earlier in this chapter: we want to create self-contained Java applications with the JVM included.

The goals of the JEP, according to the web site, are the following:

Create a packaging tool, based on the JavaFX javapackager tool, that

- Supports native packaging formats to give end users a natural installation experience. These formats include msi and exe on Windows, pkg and dmg on macOS, and deb and rpm on Linux.

- Allows launch-time parameters to be specified at packaging time.

- Can be invoked directly from the command line or programmatically via the ToolProvider API.

From this, it is clear that the jpackage tool builds on top of the JavaFX packaging tool that was previously part of JavaFX 8. Also, the jpackage tool is designed to support existing and common native packaging formats for the popular desktop operating systems. Hence, Java applications created with jpackage are installed similar to how most other native applications are installed.

Java client applications now combine two great advantages:

1. Thanks to the Write Once, Run Anywhere paradigm, the code that a developer has to write is really platform independent.

2. Thanks to the jpackage tool, although the code itself is platform independent, the deployment procedure is completely in line with a specific platform.

Because jpackage is part of the JDK distribution, it is as easy to invoke as the regular java or javac commands. The jpackage executable is located in the same directory as the java and javac executables.

When invoked, jpackage creates a native application based on provided code, dependencies, and resources. It bundles a Java runtime with the native application, and when the application is executed, the packaged Java runtime will execute the Java code, similar to the case where the runtime was installed separately on the system. This is shown in Figure 10-5.

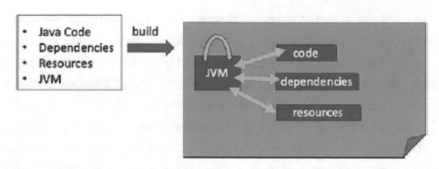

Figure 10-5. *Deployment with jpackage*

Using jpackage

To start using the jpackage tool, you use Java 16 or later; but, as it will be explained later on, you can bundle your application with other versions of the Java runtime.

The jpackage tool supports three application types:

- Non-modular applications that run on the classpath, from one or more jar files

- Modular applications with one or more modular jar files or jmod files

- Modular applications that have been jlinked into a custom runtime image

Note that for the first two cases, jpackage runs jlink to create a Java runtime for the application and bundles that into the final image. In the third case, you provide a custom runtime that is bundled into the image.

The output of jpackage is a self-contained application image. This image can include the following:

- Native application launcher (generated by jpackage)

- Application resources (like jar, icns, ico, png)

- Configuration files (like plist, cfg, properties)

- Helper libraries for the launcher

- The Java runtime image, which includes the files needed to execute Java bytecode

Although jpackage is part of the same directory that also contains the platform-independent java and javac commands, jpackage differs slightly based on the platform you are using. This makes sense, since the output of jpackage is very platform specific. Therefore, jpackage can be considered in the middle of the platformindependent Java bytecode and the platform-dependent native executable.

Since jpackage is capable of building an executable for the current platform, you must run jpackage on all platforms you want to support. Cross-compiling a Java application from one platform into native executables for other platforms is not supported.

Jpackage Usage

The jpackage usage is as follows:

```
jpackage <options>
```

Jpackage Options

Tables 10-1 to 10-7 show the different options you can use with jpackage.

Table 10-1. *jpackage – generic options*

@<filename>	Read options and/or mode from a file. This option can be used multiple times.
--type or -t <type string>	The type of package to create. Valid values are {"app-image", "exe", "msi", "rpm", "deb", "pkg", "dmg"}. If this option is not specified, a platform-dependent default type will be created.
--app-version <version>	Version of the application and/or package.
--copyright <copyright string>	Copyright for the application.
--description <description string>	Description of the application.
--help or -h	Print the usage text with a list and description of each valid option for the current platform to the output stream and exit.

(continued)

Table 10-1. (*continued*)

--name or -n <name>	Name of the application and/or package.
--dest or -d <output path>	Path where the generated output file is placed (absolute path or relative to the current directory). Defaults to the current working directory.
--temp <file path>	Path of a new or empty directory used to create temporary files (absolute path or relative to the current directory). If specified, the temp dir will not be removed upon the task completion and must be removed manually. If not specified, a temporary directory will be created and removed upon the task completion.
--vendor <vendor string>	Vendor of the application.
--verbose	Enables verbose output.
--version	Print the product version to the output stream and exit.

Table 10-2. *jpackage – options for creating the runtime image*

--add-modules <module name>[,<module name>...]	A comma (",")-separated list of modules to add. This module list, along with the main module (if specified), will be passed to jlink as the --add-module argument. If not specified, either just the main module (if --module is specified) or the default set of modules (if --main-jar is specified) are used. This option can be used multiple times.
--module-path or -p <module path>...	Each path is either a directory of modules or the path to a modular jar and is absolute or relative to the current directory. For more than one path, separate the paths with a colon (:) on Linux and macOS or a semicolon (;) on Windows, or use multiple instances of the --module-path option. This option can be used multiple times.
--jlink-options <jlink options>	A space-separated list of options to pass to jlink. If not specified, defaults to "—strip-native-commands –strip-debug –no-man-pages –no-header-files". This option can be used multiple times.
--runtime-image <file paths>	Path of the predefined runtime image that will be copied into the application image (absolute path or relative to the current directory). If --runtime-image is not specified, jpackage will run jlink to create the runtime image using options --strip-debug, --no-header-files, --no-man-pages, and --strip-native-commands.

Table 10-3. *jpackage – options for creating the application image*

--icon <icon file path>	Path of the icon of the application bundle (absolute path or relative to the current directory).
--input or -i <input path>	Path of the input directory that contains the files to be packaged (absolute path or relative to the current directory). All files in the input directory will be packaged into the application image.

Table 10-4. *jpackage – options for creating the application launcher(s)*

--add-launcher <launcher name>=<file path>	Name of the launcher and a path to a properties file that contains a list of key-value pairs (absolute path or relative to the current directory). The keys "module," "add-modules," "main-jar," "main-class," "arguments," "java-options," "app-version," "icon," and "win-console" can be used. These options are added to, or used to overwrite, the original command-line options to build an additional alternative launcher. The main application launcher will be built from the command-line options. Additional alternative launchers may be built using this option, and this option can be used multiple times to build multiple additional launchers.
--arguments <main class arguments>	Command-line arguments to pass to the main class if no command-line arguments are given to the launcher. This option can be used multiple times.
--java-options <java options>	Options to pass to the Java runtime. This option can be used multiple times.
--main-class <class name>	Qualified name of the application main class to execute. This option can only be used if --main-jar is specified.
--main-jar <main jar file>	The main JAR of the application, containing the main class (specified as a path relative to the input path). Either the --module or --main-jar option can be specified but not both.
--module or -m <module name>[/<main class>]	The main module (and optionally main class) of the application. This module must be located on the module path. When this option is specified, the main module will be linked in the Java runtime image. Either the --module or --main-jar option can be specified but not both.

Table 10-5. *jpackage – platform-dependent options for creating the application launcher*

--win-console	Creates a console launcher for the application. Should be specified for the application that requires console interactions. This option is available only when running on Windows.
--mac-package-identifier <ID string>	An identifier that uniquely identifies the application for macOS. Defaults to the main class name. May only use alphanumeric (A–Z, a–z, 0–9), hyphen (-), and period (.) characters. This option is available only when running on macOS.
--mac-package-name <name string>	Name of the application as it appears in the menu bar. This can be different from the application name. This name must be shorter than 16 characters and be suitable for display in the menu bar and the application Info window. Defaults to the application name. This option is available only when running on macOS.
--mac-bundle-signing-prefix <prefix string>	When signing the application bundle, this value is prefixed to all components that need to be signed that don't have an existing bundle identifier. This option is available only when running on macOS.
--mac-sign	Request that the bundle be signed. This option is available only when running on macOS.
--mac-signing-keychain <file path>	Path of the keychain to use (absolute path or relative to the current directory). If not specified, the standard keychains are used. This option is available only when running on macOS.
--mac-signing-key-user-name <team name>	Team name portion in Apple signing identities' names. For example, "Developer ID Application: <team name>".This option is available only when running on macOS.

Table 10-6. *jpackage – options for creating the application package*

--app-image <file path>	Location of the predefined application image that is used to build an installable package (absolute path or relative to the current directory). See create-app-image mode options to create the application image.
--file-associations <file path>	Path to a properties file that contains a list of key-value pairs (absolute path or relative to the current directory). The keys "extension," "mime-type," "icon," and "description" can be used to describe the association. This option can be used multiple times.
--install-dir <file path>	Absolute path of the installation directory of the application on macOS or Linux. Relative sub-path of the installation location of the application such as "Program Files" or "AppData" on Windows.
--license-file <file path>	Path to the license file (absolute path or relative to the current directory).
--resource-dir <path>	Path to override jpackage resources (absolute path or relative to the current directory). Icons, template files, and other resources of jpackage can be overridden by adding replacement resources to this directory.
--runtime-image <file-path>	Path of the predefined runtime image to install (absolute path or relative to the current directory). Option is required when creating a runtime installer.

Table 10-7. *jpackage – platform-dependent options for creating the application package*

--win-dir-chooser	Adds a dialog to enable the user to choose a directory in which the product is installed. This option is available only when running on Windows.
--win-menu	Adds the application to the system menu. This option is available only when running on Windows.
--win-menu-group <menu group name>	Start Menu group in which this application is placed. This option is available only when running on Windows.
--win-per-user-install	Request to perform an install on a per-user basis. This option is available only when running on Windows.
--win-shortcut	Creates a desktop shortcut for the application. This option is available only when running on Windows.
--win-upgrade-uuid <id string>	UUID associated with upgrades for this package. This option is available only when running on Windows.
--linux-package-name <package name>	Name for the Linux package. Defaults to the application name. This option is available only when running on Linux.
--linux-deb-maintainer <email address>	Maintainer for .deb bundle. This option is available only when running on Linux.
--linux-menu-group <menu-group-name>	Menu group in which this application is placed. This option is available only when running on Linux.
--linux-package-deps	Required packages or capabilities for the application. This option is available only when running on Linux.
--linux-rpm-license-type <type string>	Type of the license ("License: <value>" of the RPM <name>.spec). This option is available only when running on Linux.
--linux-app-release <release string>	Release value of the RPM <name>.spec file or Debian revision value of the DEB control file. This option is available only when running on Linux.
--linux-app-category <category string>	Group value of the RPM <name>.spec file or Section value of the DEB control file. This option is available only when running on Linux.
--linux-shortcut	Creates a shortcut for the application. This option is available only when running on Linux.

Requirements

The images created by jpackage are not different from other applications developers create for native platforms. Therefore, the same tools that are used to generate native applications for a specific operating system are used by jpackage as well.

For Windows, in order to generate native packages, developers need to install:

- WiX Toolset, a free third-party tool that generates exe and msi installers

WiX Setup

Download WiX Toolset from `https://wixtoolset.org/releases/`. The current version is 3.11.2. Once downloaded, process with the installer, and when finished, add it to the path, running from the command line

```
setx /M PATH "%PATH%;C:\Program Files (x86)\WiX Toolset v3.11\bin"
```

Samples

We will now present a few samples that show you how to use jpackage. The samples themselves are very simple JavaFX applications, and we will not discuss their functionality in this chapter.

Let's start using jpackage from a terminal window without build tools or plugins. Since you use jpackage slightly differently depending on which platform you are running, we distinguish between using jpackage on Windows, macOS, and Linux.

Non-modular Application: Sample1

As a first sample, we explain how to package a Java application that itself is not a module. The application still uses the JavaFX modules, but there is no specific module-info.java in the application itself.

We describe the instructions on how to package this application into an installer for Windows, Mac, and Linux. The pattern we follow is similar for every platform:

1. Define a number of environment variables.

2. Compile the JavaFX application into Java bytecode.

3. Run and test the application.

4. Create a single jar file, containing the application.

5. Create an installer using jpackage.

Instructions for Windows

These are the required steps to create an installer for a non-modular application, such as this one:

https://github.com/modernclientjava/mcj-samples/tree/master/ch10-packaging/Sample1

Clone the sample and, from a terminal, cd into the application's root.
These first four steps are not different from regular Java compilation and running.

1. Export these environment variables:

    ```
    set JAVA_HOME="C:\Users\<user>\Downloads\jdk-17"
    set PATH_TO_FX="C:\Users\<user>\Downloads\javafx-sdk-17\lib"
    set PATH_TO_FX_MODS="C:\Users\<user>\Downloads\javafx-jmods-17"
    ```

    Note that if you have a different JDK added to the PATH environment variable, this will take precedence.

2. Compile your application and copy the fxml and css resource files to path out\org\modernclients:

    ```
    dir /s /b src\*.java > sources.txt & javac --module-path
    %PATH_TO_FX% --add-modules javafx.controls,javafx.fxml
    -d out @sources.txt & del sources.txt

    copy src\org\modernclients\scene.fxml out\org\
    modernclients\ & copy src\org\modernclients\styles.css
    out\org\modernclients\
    ```

3. Run and test:

    ```
    java --module-path %PATH_TO_FX% --add-modules javafx.
    controls,javafx.fxml
    -cp out org.modernclients.Main
    ```

4. Create a jar:

```
mkdir libs
jar --create --file=libs\sample1.jar --main-class=org.
modernclients.Main -C out .
```

5. Create the installer.

In this step, we use jpackage to create an installer. We showed the different options that can be provided to jpackage in Table 10-1. In the following command, we specify a number of options:

```
%JAVA_HOME%\bin\jpackage --type exe -d installer -i libs --main-jar
sample1.jar -n Sample1 --module-path %PATH_TO_FX_MODS% --add-modules
javafx.controls,javafx.fxml --main-class org.modernclients.Main
```

As a result, jpackage creates Sample1-1.0.exe (26 MB) that can be distributed, and it requires just a double-click to install the application (Figure 10-6).

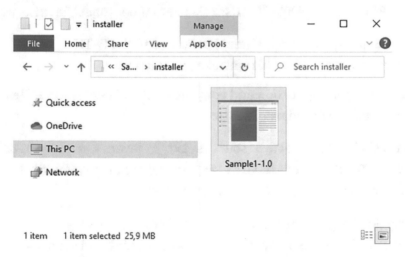

Figure 10-6. *Sample1 Windows installer*

Running the jpackage tool with --verbose shows the following output that helps identify how jpackage builds the installer, where it stores the default resources, and how you can customize these settings:

```
Running candle.exe
Running light.exe
Detected [light.exe] version [3.11.2.4516].
```

Detected [candle.exe] version [3.11.2.4516].

WiX 3.11.2.4516 detected. Enabling advanced cleanup action.

Using default package resource java48.ico [icon] (add Sample1.ico to the resource-dir to customize).

Using default package resource WinLauncher.template [Template for creating executable properties file] (add Sample1.properties to the resource-dir to customize).

MSI ProductCode: 6ad6fbff-52ef-3f2f-959a-a12e4c9b1f68.

MSI UpgradeCode: 4e3a7148-be2c-3a36-bc72-feb6033ea68f.

Using default package resource main.wxs [Main WiX project file] (add main.wxs to the resource-dir to customize).

Using default package resource overrides.wxi [Overrides WiX project file] (add overrides.wxi to the resource-dir to customize).

Preparing MSI config: C:\Users\<user>\AppData\Local\Temp\jdk.jpackage13545744068176887418\images\win-exe.image\Sample1-1.0.msi.

Generating MSI: C:\Users\<user>\AppData\Local\Temp\jdk.jpackage13545744068176887418\images\win-exe.image\Sample1-1.0.msi.

Running candle.exe in C:\Users\<user>\AppData\Local\Temp\jdk.jpackage13545744068176887418\images\win-msi.image\Sample1

Command:

    candle.exe -nologo C:\Users\<user>\AppData\Local\Temp\jdk.jpackage13545744068176887418\config\main.wxs -ext WixUtilExtension -arch x64 [...]

Output:

    main.wxs

Returned: 0

Running candle.exe in C:\Users\<user>\AppData\Local\Temp\jdk.jpackage13545744068176887418\images\win-msi.image\Sample1

Command:

    candle.exe -nologo C:\Users\<user>\AppData\Local\Temp\jdk.jpackage13545744068176887418\config\bundle.wxf -ext WixUtilExtension -arch x64 [...]

Output:

    bundle.wxf

Returned: 0

```
Running light.exe in C:\Users\<user>\AppData\Local\Temp\jdk.
jpackage13545744068176887418\images\win-msi.image\Sample1
Command:
    light.exe -nologo -spdb -ext WixUtilExtension […]
Output:
    C:\Users\<user>\AppData\Local\Temp\jdk.jpackage13545744068176887418\
config\main.wxs(53) : warning LGHT1076 : ICE61: This product should remove
only older versions of itself. No Maximum version was detected for the
current product. (JP_DOWNGRADABLE_FOUND)
Returned: 0
Generating EXE for installer to: C:\Users\<user>\Downloads\mcj-samples\
ch10-packaging\Sample1\installer.
Using default package resource WinInstaller.template [Template for creating
executable properties file] (add WinInstaller.properties to the resource-
dir to customize).
Installer (.exe) saved to: C:\Users\<user>\Downloads\mcj-samples\ch10-
packaging\Sample1\installer
Succeeded in building EXE Installer Package package
```

Modifying the Installer

We can add more options to the jpackage command. For instance, we can add the application to the system menu, create a desktop shortcut, let the user choose the installation directory, and use a custom icon based on the Duke image from

```
https://hg.openjdk.java.net/duke/duke/raw-file/e71b60779736/3D/Duke%20
Waving/openduke.png
```

Running the following jpackage command builds the customized installer that will create the application shown in Figure 10-7:

```
%JAVA_HOME%\bin\jpackage --type exe -d installer -i libs --main-jar
sample1.jar -n Sample1 --module-path %PATH_TO_FX_MODS% --add-modules
javafx.controls,javafx.fxml --main-class org.modernclients.Main --win-menu
--win-shortcut --win-dir-chooser --icon assets\win\openduke.ico
```

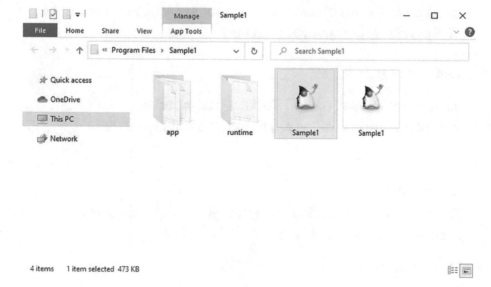

Figure 10-7. *Application with custom icon*

macOS

These are the required steps to create an installer for a non-modular application, similar to Sample1:

https://github.com/modernclientjava/mcj-samples/tree/master/ch10-packaging/Sample1

1. Export these environment variables:

   ```
   export JAVA_HOME=/Users/<user>/Downloads/jdk-17.jdk/
   Contents/Home/
   export PATH_TO_FX=/Users/<user>/Downloads/javafx-sdk-
   17/lib/
   export PATH_TO_FX_MODS=/Users/<user>/Downloads/javafx-
   jmods-17/
   ```

2. Compile your application and copy the fxml and css resource files to path out/org/modernclients:

   ```
   javac --module-path $PATH_TO_FX --add-modules javafx.
   controls,javafx.fxml -d out $(find src -name "*.java")
   ```

```
cp src/org/modernclients/scene.fxml src/org/modernclients/
styles.css out/org/modernclients/
```

3. Run and test:

```
java --module-path $PATH_TO_FX --add-modules javafx.
controls,javafx.fxml -cp out org.modernclients.Main
```

4. Create a jar:

```
mkdir libs
jar --create --file=libs/sample1.jar --main-class=org.
modernclients.Main -C out .
```

5. Create the installer:

```
$JAVA_HOME/bin/jpackage --type dmg -d installer -i
libs --main-jar sample1.jar -n Sample1 --module-path
$PATH_TO_FX_MODS --add-modules javafx.controls,
javafx.fxml --main-class org.modernclients.Main
```

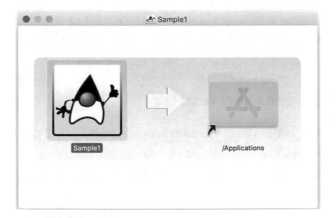

Figure 10-8. *Sample1 macOS installer*

This builds Sample1-1.0.dmg (83 MB), as shown in Figure 10-8, which you can distribute. It requires just a double-click to install the application.

Running the jpackage tool with --verbose shows how jpackage builds the installer and where it stores default resources. Use the --verbose option when you want to determine where jpackage stores the default resources and customize these settings, as shown in the following sample output:

Building DMG package for Sample1
Building PKG package for Sample1
"Adding modules: [javafx.controls, javafx.fxml] to runtime image."
jlink arguments: [--output /var/folders/90/fcwm6f8s0d39jnv8vc0_
rww00000gn/T/jdk.jpackage3310158689456557035/images/
image-8684840536936452979/Sample1.app/Contents/runtime/Contents/
Home --module-path /Users/<user>/Downloads/javafx-jmods-17-ea-13:/
Users/<user>/Downloads/jdk-17.jdk/Contents/Home/jmods --add-modules javafx.
controls,javafx.fxml --strip-native-commands --strip-debug --no-man-pages
--no-header-files]
Using default package resource GenericApp.icns [icon] (add Sample1.icns to
the resource-dir to customize)
Preparing Info.plist: /var/folders/90/fcwm6f8s0d39jnv8vc0_rww00000gn/T/jdk.
jpackage3310158689456557035/images/image-8684840536936452979/Sample1.app/
Contents/Info.plist
Using default package resource Info-lite.plist.template [Application Info.
plist] (add Info.plist to the resource-dir to customize)
Using default package resource Runtime-Info.plist.template [Java Runtime
Info.plist] (add Runtime-Info.plist to the resource-dir to customize)
Using default package resource background_pkg.png [pkg background
image] (add Sample1-background.png to the resource-dir to customize)
Preparing distribution.dist: /var/folders/90/fcwm6f8s0d39jnv8vc0_
rww00000gn/T/jdk.jpackage3310158689456557035/config/distribution.dist
no default package resource [script to run after application image is
populated] (add Sample1-post-image.sh to the resource-dir to customize)
Running [pkgbuild, --root, /var/folders/90/fcwm6f8s0d39jnv8vc0_
rww00000gn/T/jdk.jpackage3310158689456557035/images/
image-9477246125921380963, --install-location, /Applications,
--analyze, -/var/folders/90/fcwm6f8s0d39jnv8vc0_rww00000gn/T/jdk.
jpackage3310158689456557035/config/cpl.plist]
pkgbuild: Inferring bundle components from contents of /var/folders/90/
fcwm6f8s0d39jnv8vc0_rww00000gn/T/jdk.jpackage3310158689456557035/images/
image-9477246125921380963

```
pkgbuild: Writing new component property list to /var/folders/90/
fcwm6f8s0d39jnv8vc0_rww00000gn/T/jdk.jpackage3310158689456557035/config/
cpl.plist
Preparing package scripts
Using default package resource preinstall.template [PKG preinstall
script]  (add preinstall to the resource-dir to customize)
Using default package resource postinstall.template [PKG postinstall
script]  (add postinstall to the resource-dir to customize)
...
```

Modifying the Installer

We can also add a custom icon based on the Duke image available from https://
hg.openjdk.java.net/duke/duke/file/e71b60779736/3D/Duke%20Waving/openduke.
png:

```
$JAVA_HOME/bin/jpackage --type dmg -d installer -i libs --main-jar sample1.
jar -n Sample1 --module-path $PATH_TO_FX_MODS --add-modules javafx.
controls,javafx.fxml --main-class org.modernclients.Main --icon assets/mac/
openduke.icns
```

And we get the result shown in Figure 10-9.

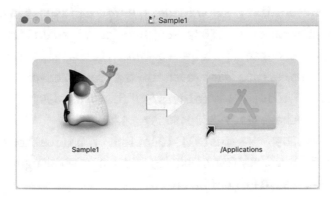

Figure 10-9. *Customized installer*

Linux

These are the required steps to create an installer for a non-modular application, such as Sample1:

https://github.com/modernclientjava/mcj-samples/tree/master/ch10-packaging/Sample1

Here are the instructions to create an installer for a Debian-based distribution:

1. Export these environment variables:

```
export JAVA_HOME=/home/<user>/Downloads/jdk-17/
export PATH_TO_FX=/home/<user>/Downloads/javafx-sdk-17/lib/
export PATH_TO_FX_MODS=/home/<user>/Downloads/javafx-jmods-17/
```

2. Compile your application and copy the fxml and css resource files to path out/org/modernclients:

```
javac --module-path $PATH_TO_FX --add-modules javafx.
controls,javafx.fxml -d out $(find src -name "*.java")

cp src/org/modernclients/scene.fxml src/org/modernclients/
styles.css out/org/modernclients/
```

3. Run and test:

```
java --module-path $PATH_TO_FX --add-modules javafx.
controls,javafx.fxml -cp out org.modernclients.Main
```

4. Create a jar:

```
mkdir libs
jar --create --file=libs/sample1.jar --main-class=org.
modernclients.Main -C out .
```

5. Create the installer:

```
$JAVA_HOME/bin/jpackage --type deb -d installer -i
libs --main-jar sample1.jar -n Sample1 --module-path
$PATH_TO_FX_MODS --add-modules javafx.controls,
javafx.fxml --main-class org.modernclients.Main
```

The result of this command is a file named `sample1-1.0.deb` created in a directory named "installer." Using a file browser to locate this file shows that sample1-1.0.deb is a Debian package (Figure 10-10).

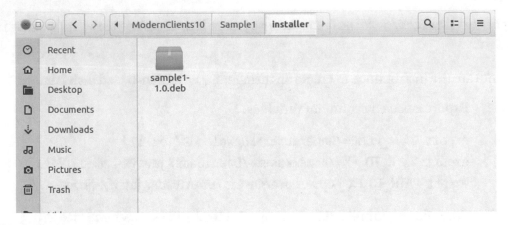

Figure 10-10. *Sample1 Linux installer*

Modular Application: Sample2

Our second application is a modular application. The source code can be found at `https://github.com/modernclientjava/mcj-samples/tree/master/ch10-packaging/Sample2`.

It contains a module-info.java file, and the jpackage tool can process this to deal with the modular dependencies. The module-info file is very simple: it declares dependencies on the javafx.controls and javafx.fxml modules, and it exports the module org.modernclients. Also, module org.modernclients is opened to the javafx.fxml module.

The module-info.java file is shown here:

```
module modernclients {
    requires javafx.controls;
    requires javafx.fxml;
    opens org.modernclients to javafx.fxml;
    exports org.modernclients;
}
```

Windows

These are the required steps to create an installer for a modular application on Windows:

1. Export these environment variables:

    ```
    set JAVA_HOME="C:\Users\<user>\Downloads\jdk-17"
    set PATH_TO_FX="C:\Users\<user>\Downloads\javafx-sdk-17\lib"
    set PATH_TO_FX_MODS="C:\Users\<user>\Downloads\javafx-jmods-17"
    ```

2. Compile your application and copy the fxml and css resource files
    to path out\org\modernclients:

    ```
    dir /s /b src\*.java > sources.txt & javac --module-path
    %PATH_TO_FX% --add-modules javafx.controls,javafx.fxml -d
    mods\modernclients @sources.txt & del sources.txt

    copy src\org\modernclients\scene.fxml mods\modernclients\
    org\modernclients\ & copy src\org\modernclients\styles.css
    mods\modernclients\org\modernclients\
    ```

3. Run and test:

    ```
    java --module-path %PATH_TO_FX%;mods -m modernclients/org.
    modernclients.Main
    ```

4. Create the custom image with jlink:

    ```
    %JAVA_HOME%\bin\jlink --module-path %PATH_TO_FX_MODS%;mods
    --add-modules modernclients --output image
    ```

5. Run and test the image:

    ```
    image\bin\java -m modernclients/org.modernclients.Main
    ```

6. Create the installer:

    ```
    %JAVA_HOME%\bin\jpackage --type exe -d installer -n
    Sample2 -m modernclients/org.modernclients.Main --runtime-
    image image
    ```

As a result, you will get Sample2-1.0.exe (32 MB) that can be distributed, and it requires just a double-click to install the application.

macOS

These are the required steps to create an installer for a modular application on macOS:

1. Export these environment variables:

    ```
    export JAVA_HOME=/Users/<user>/Downloads/jdk-17.jdk/
    Contents/Home/
    export PATH_TO_FX=/Users/<user>/Downloads/javafx-sdk-17/lib/
    export PATH_TO_FX_MODS=/Users/<user>/Downloads/javafx-
    jmods-17/
    ```

2. Compile your application and copy the fxml and css resource files
    to path out/org/modernclients:

    ```
    javac --module-path $PATH_TO_FX -d mods/modernclients
    $(find src -name "*.java")

    cp src/org/modernclients/scene.fxml src/org/modernclients/
    styles.css mods/modernclients/org/modernclients/
    ```

3. Run and test:

    ```
    java --module-path $PATH_TO_FX:mods -m modernclients/org.
    modernclients.Main
    ```

4. Create the custom image with jlink:

    ```
    $JAVA_HOME/bin/jlink --module-path $PATH_TO_FX_MODS:
    mods --add-modules modernclients --output image
    ```

5. Run and test the image:

    ```
    image/bin/java -m modernclients/org.modernclients.Main
    ```

6. Create the installer:

    ```
    $JAVA_HOME/bin/jpackage --type dmg -d installer -n Sample2 -m
    modernclients/org.modernclients.Main --runtime-image image
    ```

As a result, you will get Sample2-1.0.dmg (38.3 MB) that can be distributed, and it requires just a double-click to install the application.

Linux

These are the required steps to create an installer for a modular application on Linux:

1. Export these environment variables:

    ```
    export JAVA_HOME=/home/<user>/Downloads/jdk-17/
    export PATH_TO_FX=/home/<user>/Downloads/javafx-sdk-17/lib/
    export PATH_TO_FX_MODS=/home/<user>/Downloads/javafx-
    jmods-17/
    ```

2. Compile your application and copy the fxml and css resource files
    to path out/org/modernclients:

    ```
    javac --module-path $PATH_TO_FX -d mods/modernclients
    $(find src -name "*.java")

    cp src/org/modernclients/scene.fxml src/org/modernclients/
    styles.css mods/modernclients/org/modernclients/
    ```

3. Run and test:

    ```
    java --module-path $PATH_TO_FX:mods -m modernclients/org.
    modernclients.Main
    ```

4. Create the custom image with jlink:

    ```
    $JAVA_HOME/bin/jlink --module-path $PATH_TO_FX_MODS:
    mods --add-modules modernclients --output image
    ```

5. Run and test the image:

    ```
    image/bin/java -m modernclients/org.modernclients.Main
    ```

6. Create the installer:

    ```
    $JAVA_HOME/bin/jpackage --type deb -d installer -n Sample2 -m
    modernclients/org.modernclients.Main --runtime-image image
    ```

As a result, you will get Sample2-1.0.deb that can be distributed or installed.

Gradle Projects

The previous samples explained how to use the command-line jpackage tool. As with most commands, it often makes sense to use them in existing build tools, for example, with Maven or Gradle.

While you can create a task to add to your build.gradle file with the required options to run the jpackage tool, there is a plugin that does that for you: the org.beryx.jlink plugin, by Serban Iordache (see `https://badass-jlink-plugin.beryx.org/`).

These are the required steps to create an installer for a modular application with Gradle, like this one:

`https://github.com/modernclientjava/mcj-samples/tree/master/ch10-packaging/Sample3`

1. Edit the build.gradle and review the required JDK path. Note that we provide plugin versions that are current as of the publication; you should check for updates to these plugin version numbers.

    ```
    plugins {
        id 'application'
        id 'org.openjfx.javafxplugin' version '0.0.10'
        id 'org.beryx.jlink' version '2.24.1'
    }
    repositories {
        mavenCentral()
    }
    javafx {
       version = 17.0.1
        modules = [ 'javafx.controls', 'javafx.fxml' ]
    }

    application {
        mainModule = "modernclients"
        mainClass = "org.modernclients.Main"
    }
    ```

```
jlink {
    options = ['--strip-debug', '--compress', '2',
    '--no-header-files', '--no-man-pages']
    launcher {
        name = 'sample3'
    }
    jpackage {
        if (javafx.getPlatform().name() == "OSX") {
            installerType = "dmg"
            jpackageHome =
            "/Users/<user>/Downloads/jdk-17.jdk/Contents/Home"
        } else if (javafx.getPlatform().name()
        == "WINDOWS") {
            installerType = "exe"
            jpackageHome = "C:\\Users\\<user>\\Downloads
            \\jdk-17"
            installerOptions = ['--win-menu', '--win-
            shortcut', '--win-dir-chooser']
        } else if (javafx.getPlatform().name() == "LINUX") {
            installerType = "deb"
            jpackageHome = "/home/<user>/Downloads/jdk-17"
        }
    }
}
```

2. Run and test:

```
./gradlew run (Mac OSX or Linux)
gradlew run (Windows)
```

3. Create the custom image:

```
./gradlew jlink (Mac OSX or Linux)
gradlew jlink (Windows)
```

4. Run and test the image:

```
build/image/bin/sample3 (Mac OSX or Linux)
build\image\bin\sample3 (Windows)
```

5. Create the installer:

```
./gradlew jpackage (Mac OSX or Linux)
gradlew jpackage (Windows)
```

As a result, you will get sample3-1.0.dmg (35.8 MB) on macOS, sample3-1.0.exe (34.5 MB) on Windows, or sample3-1.0-1_amd64.deb (33.8 MB) on Linux that can be distributed, and it requires only a double-click to install the application.

Using GraalVM's Native Image

The jpackage tool lets you build native applications for specific operating systems. The Java runtime is bundled with the application, and when the native application is executed, it will internally use the Java runtime to execute the bytecodes. Typically, the Java runtime contains a Just In Time (JIT) compiler that compiles Java bytecode to native code.

Another option for building a native application moves the compilation step to build time. With GraalVM's Native Image, the Java code is compiled Ahead Of Time (AOT). This means the Java bytecode is compiled to native code before it is executed and before it is bundled into an application.

As a result, the resulting binary no longer contains a Java runtime. Figure 10-11 shows this scenario.

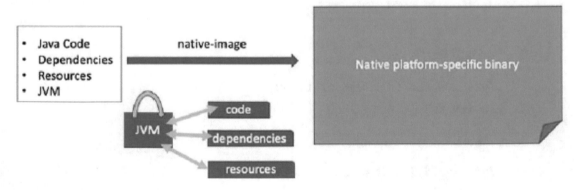

Figure 10-11. *Native Image development process*

Although the GraalVM project ("Run Programs Faster Anywhere") has been active for many years, it only recently became available as a product. GraalVM is still evolving, and parts of it are integrated with the OpenJDK project and vice versa. We recommend that you regularly keep an eye on the `https://graalvm.org` web site and on the GitHub site for the open source code at `https://github.com/oracle/graal`.

While GraalVM provides the AOT compiler that translates Java bytecode into native code for a given platform, there are more actions needed in order to link the program code into an executable. Fortunately, there are open source tools available that help developers achieve this. The GluonFX plugin (from gluonhq.com) lets developers create native images for Linux, macOS, and Windows based on existing Java code.

This same plugin also generates native images for mobile apps, which we discuss in the next chapter.

We will now show you how to build a native executable with the HelloFX sample application using the GluonFX plugin.

Platform Requirements

In order to build a native image, you use JDK 11 or GraalVM JDK 11. We'll briefly describe the requirements for both Maven and Gradle projects on macOS, Linux, and Windows.

You can download JDK 11 or GraalVM JDK 11 for each target system. For example, you can download AdoptOpenJDK from the following URL (choose the appropriate release for the target platform):

`https://adoptopenjdk.net/releases.html`

You can download the Gluon GraalVM release from this URL (choose the appropriate release for the target platform):

`https://github.com/gluonhq/graal/releases/`

Requirements for macOS

To use the plugin to develop and deploy native applications on macOS platforms, you need a Mac with macOS 10.13.2 or higher and Xcode 11 or higher, available from the Mac App Store. Once Xcode is downloaded and installed, open it to accept the license terms.

Once downloaded and installed, set JAVA_HOME to the JDK, for example:

```
export JAVA_HOME=/Users/<user>/Downloads/jdk-11.0.11+9/Contents/Home
```

Requirements for Linux

After downloading a JDK for Linux, export the JAVA_HOME environment variable for the Linux platform JDK, for example:

```
export JAVA_HOME=/home/<user>/Downloads/jdk-11.0.11+9
```

Requirements for Windows

After downloading a JDK for Windows, set the JAVA_HOME environment variable for the Windows platform JDK, for example:

```
set JAVA_HOME=C:\path\to\ jdk-11.0.11+9 2
```

Add JAVA_HOME to the Environment Variables list (Advanced system settings).

In addition to the Java JDK, Microsoft Visual Studio 2019 is also required. The community edition is sufficient, which you can download from

```
https://visualstudio.microsoft.com/downloads/
```

During the installation process, make sure to select at least the following individual components:

- Choose the English Language Pack.

- C++/CLI support for v142 build tools (v 14.25 or later).

- MSVC v142 – VS 2019 C++ x64/x86 build tools (v 14.25 or later).

- Windows Universal CRT SDK.

- Windows 10 SDK (10.0.19041.0 or later).

Note that all build commands must be executed in a Visual Studio 2019 command prompt called x64 Native Tools Command Prompt for VS 2019.

The Code

The code for this example is on GitHub:

https://github.com/gluonhq/gluon-samples/tree/master/HelloFX/src/main/java/hellofx

Listing 10-1 shows the HelloFX main class, and Listing 10-2 shows the styles.css file.

Listing 10-1. HelloFX.java

```java
package hellofx;
import javafx.application.Application;
import javafx.geometry.Pos;
import javafx.scene.Scene;
import javafx.scene.control.Label;
import javafx.scene.image.Image;
import javafx.scene.image.ImageView;
import javafx.scene.layout.VBox;
import javafx.stage.Stage;
public class HelloFX extends Application {
    public void start(Stage stage) {
        String javaVersion = System.getProperty("java.version");
        String javafxVersion = System.getProperty("javafx.version");
        Label label = new Label("Hello, JavaFX " + javafxVersion + ",
            running on Java " + javaVersion + ".");
        ImageView imageView = new ImageView(
            new Image(HelloFX.class.getResourceAsStream("openduke.png")));
        imageView.setFitHeight(200);
        imageView.setPreserveRatio(true);
        VBox root = new VBox(30, imageView, label);
        root.setAlignment(Pos.CENTER);
        Scene scene = new Scene(root, 640, 480);
        scene.getStylesheets().add(
            HelloFX.class.getResource("styles.css").toExternalForm());
        stage.setScene(scene);
        stage.show();
    }
```

```
public static void main(String[] args) {
    launch(args);
  }
}
```

Listing 10-2. File styles.css

```
.label {
    -fx-text-fill: blue;
}
```

Maven Project

If you have a Java or JavaFX project and you are using Maven as a build tool, you can include the plugin to start creating native applications.

The plugin can be found here:

```
https://github.com/gluonhq/gluonfx-maven-plugin
```

Listing 10-3 shows the pom file for a Maven project.

Listing 10-3. pom.xml file

```
<project xmlns="http://maven.apache.org/POM/4.0.0" xmlns:xsi="http://www.
w3.org/2001/XMLSchema-instance" xsi:schemaLocation="http://maven.apache.
org/POM/4.0.0 http://maven.apache.org/xsd/maven-4.0.0.xsd">
    <modelVersion>4.0.0</modelVersion>
    <groupId>hello</groupId>
    <artifactId>hellofx</artifactId>
    <version> 1.0.0-SNAPSHOT</version>
    <packaging>jar</packaging>
    <name>hellofx</name>
    <properties>
        <project.build.sourceEncoding>UTF-8</project.build.sourceEncoding>
        <maven.compiler.source>11</maven.compiler.source>
        <maven.compiler.target>11</maven.compiler.target>
        <javafx.version>17.0.1</javafx.version>
    </properties>
```

```
<dependencies>
    <dependency>
        <groupId>org.openjfx</groupId>
        <artifactId>javafx-controls</artifactId>
        <version>${javafx.version}</version>
    </dependency>
</dependencies>
<build>
    <plugins>
        <plugin>
            <groupId>org.apache.maven.plugins</groupId>
            <artifactId>maven-compiler-plugin</artifactId>
            <version>3.8.1</version>
            <configuration>
                <release>11</release>
            </configuration>
        </plugin>
        <plugin>
            <groupId>org.openjfx</groupId>
            <artifactId>javafx-maven-plugin</artifactId>
            <version> 0.0.8</version>
            <configuration>
                <mainClass>hellofx.HelloFX</mainClass>
            </configuration>
        </plugin>
        <plugin>
            <groupId>com.gluonhq</groupId>
            <artifactId> gluonfx-maven-plugin</artifactId>
            <version>1.0.7</version>
            <configuration>
                <mainClass>hellofx.HelloFX</mainClass>
            </configuration>
        </plugin>
    </plugins>
</build>
<pluginRepositories>
```

```
        <pluginRepository>
            <id>gluon-releases</id>
            <url>
                http://nexus.gluonhq.com/nexus/content/repositories/
                releases
            </url>
        </pluginRepository>
    </pluginRepositories>
</project>
```

Gradle Project

If you have a Java or JavaFX project and you are using Gradle as a build tool, you can include the plugin to start creating native applications.

The plugin can be found here:

https://github.com/gluonhq/gluonfx-gradle-plugin.

Listing 10-4 shows the build.gradle file, and Listing 10-5 shows the settings.gradle file for a Gradle project.

Listing 10-4. File build.gradle

```
plugins {
    id 'application'
    id 'org.openjfx.javafxplugin' version '0.0.10'
    id 'com.gluonhq.gluonfx-gradle-plugin' version '1.0.3'
}
repositories {
    mavenCentral()
}
gluonfx {
}
javafx {
    modules = [ "javafx.controls" ]
}
mainClassName = 'hellofx.HelloFX'
```

Listing 10-5. File settings.gradle

```
pluginManagement {
    repositories {
        gradlePluginPortal()
    }
}
rootProject.name = 'HelloFX'
```

Build the Project

The first step is to build and run the project as a regular Java project (on a regular JVM that you use for your local development, e.g., HotSpot).

With Gradle:

```
./gradlew clean build run (Mac OSX or Linux)
gradlew clean build run (Windows)
```

With Maven:

```
mvn clean javafx:run
```

The result is shown in Figure 10-12.

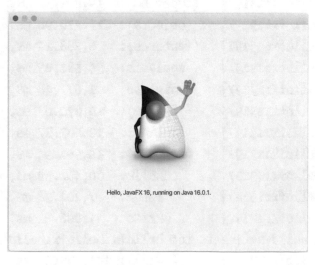

Figure 10-12. *Running HelloFX on OpenJDK 16*

We will now compile, package, and run the native desktop application.

Compile

Run with Gradle:

```
./gradlew nativeCompile (Mac OS or Linux)
gradlew nativeCompile (Windows)
```

Or with Maven:

```
mvn gluonfx:compile
```

You'll need to wait until the task finishes successfully (depending on your machine, it may take 5 minutes or more). You will see the feedback provided during the process, such as in Listing 10-6.

Listing 10-6. Output during the native compilation phase

```
...
[INFO] ==================== COMPILE TASK ====================

[SUB] [hellofx.hellofx:13197]     classlist:    1,810.51 ms,  0.96 GB
[SUB] [hellofx.hellofx:13197]         (cap):    2,187.64 ms,  0.96 GB
[SUB] [hellofx.hellofx:13197]        setup:    4,359.53 ms,  0.96 GB
[SUB] [hellofx.hellofx:13197]      (clinit):      812.63 ms,  4.65 GB
[SUB] [hellofx.hellofx:13197]    (typeflow):  19,802.32 ms,  4.65 GB
[SUB] [hellofx.hellofx:13197]     (objects):  29,770.98 ms,  4.65 GB
[SUB] [hellofx.hellofx:13197]    (features):   2,568.14 ms,  4.65 GB
[SUB] [hellofx.hellofx:13197]     analysis:  54,581.85 ms,  4.65 GB
[SUB] [hellofx.hellofx:13197]     universe:   1,677.48 ms,  4.65 GB
[SUB] [hellofx.hellofx:13197]       (parse):  10,890.07 ms,  5.43 GB
[SUB] [hellofx.hellofx:13197]      (inline):  10,567.77 ms,  6.10 GB
[SUB] [hellofx.hellofx:13197]     (compile):  35,567.94 ms,  6.16 GB
[SUB] [hellofx.hellofx:13197]      compile:  60,462.59 ms,  6.16 GB
[SUB] [hellofx.hellofx:13197]        image:   7,202.38 ms,  6.16 GB
[SUB] [hellofx.hellofx:13197]        write:   1,006.42 ms,  6.16 GB
[SUB] # Printing build artifacts to: hellofx.hellofx.build_artifacts.txt
[SUB] [hellofx.hellofx:13197]      [total]: 131,599.90 ms,  6.16 GB
[INFO] BUILD SUCCESS
[INFO] Total time:  02:22 min
```

As a result, you will see hellofx.hellofx.o (65.0 MB) or hellofx.hellofx.obj under target/gluonfx/{target-architecture}/gvm/tmp/SVM-***/.

If that is not the case, check for any possible failures in the log files under target/gluonfx/{target-architecture}/gvm/log.

Link

Now that the Java code for the application is compiled to native code, we can package the generated code with the required libraries and resources using the nativeLink task.

Run with Gradle:

```
./gradlew nativeLink (Mac OSX or Linux)
gradlew nativeLink (Windows)
```

Or with Maven:

```
mvn gluonfx:link
```

The link step produces the executable in the target subdirectory target/gluonfx/{target-architecture}/HelloFX (65.4 MB) or in target\gluonfx\x86_64-windows\hellofx.exe for Windows. Figure 10-13 shows the executable in a macOS file system.

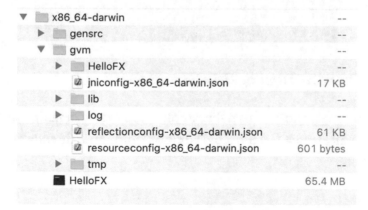

Figure 10-13. *HelloFX executable*

Run

Finally, you can run it with Gradle:

```
./gradlew nativeRun (Mac OS or Linux)
gradlew nativeRun (Windows)
```

Or with Maven:

```
mvn gluonfx:run
```

You should get the output shown in Figure 10-14.

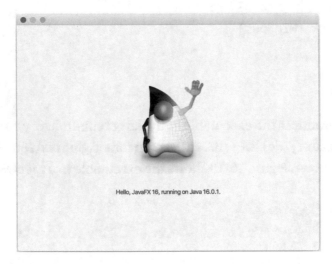

Figure 10-14. *Output of running HelloFX*

Note that you can distribute this native application to any machine with the matching architecture (macOS, Linux, or Windows) and run it directly as any other regular application.

Conclusion

Packaging application code with all the required dependencies, Java runtime, and resources is becoming increasingly popular on desktop, mobile, and embedded devices.

The historical disadvantages, including larger size and longer download times, are less important due to improvements in bandwidth and storage.

The advantages of packaging an application into a self-contained bundle mean less hassle for end users, who can use an installation approach that is familiar and similar to other applications.

JavaFX applications are regular Java applications. Thus, you can use the packaging tools that exist for Java, such as jpackage, jlink, and Graal Native Image, with JavaFX applications as well.

Since these tools are evolving rapidly, we recommend you keep an eye on the samples in the GitHub repository `https://github.com/gluonhq/gluon-samples`, as they will be updated to the latest version once available.

CHAPTER 11

Native Mobile Apps for iOS and Android

Written by José Pereda and Johan Vos

Java started as a programming language for embedded devices. In the early 1990s, a team inside Sun Microsystems worked on a software stack for a set of next-generation hardware products.

The prototype of those hardware products, called the Star7, looked like something between a mobile phone and a tablet. The software for these devices, originally code-named Oak, is what we currently know as Java.

Hardware and software evolutions took very different paths. The Java software made big furor for animating web pages, using Applets, and later became the preferred language for developing enterprise and cloud applications.

The hardware evolution was shaped by complex interactions between phone and device manufacturers, telecom operators, and content providers. The business models were very fragmented, and for a very long time, there was no easy access for developers in general to mobile devices.

With the growing popularity of app stores, it became easier for developers to write applications for mobile platforms. Also, the majority of mobile phones are now either Android based or iOS based. This reduces the fragmentation to two main platforms.

And with Java being originally developed for mobile and embedded systems, it very much makes sense to create Java apps and run them on mobile devices, especially since recent evolutions in the Java area make it easy to deliver high-performant apps to mobile devices.

© Stephen Chin, Johan Vos and James Weaver 2022
S. Chin et al., *The Definitive Guide to Modern Java Clients with JavaFX 17*,
https://doi.org/10.1007/978-1-4842-7268-8_11

Why JavaFX on Mobile

In today's digital infrastructure, web pages are often used to render information from a backend in a simple way.

Desktop and laptop systems are widely used for working with applications that require user interaction, data synchronization, high-performance rendering, and cloud integration. As such, they complement web applications.

An evolution in the IT landscape leads to an increased importance of mobile devices, for example, phones and tablets. As a consequence, IT backends now have to serve three different channels: web-based frontends, desktop applications, and mobile apps. This is shown in Figure 11-1.

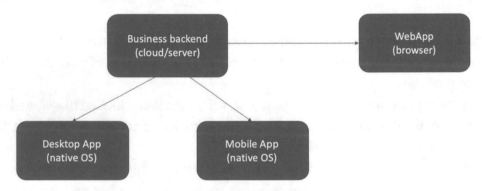

Figure 11-1. *Business backend serving different channels*

JavaFX, thanks to it being Java and hence supporting the Write Once, Run Anywhere paradigm, is very well suited for creating applications that work on desktops and laptops, but also on phones and tablets.

In the previous chapter, we showed how you can convert your JavaFX applications into applications that are native to the client. When we talk about "native," we mean a combination of two things:

1. Code execution is in the native approach of the device. The application that is delivered to the phone directly executes machine code and is not interpreted or translated on the device. This allows for fast execution.

2. There is no intermediate rendering engine (e.g., a browser), and the JavaFX controls are rendered directly using the hardware-accelerated graphics engine available on the client.

In this chapter, we will explain how to deploy your JavaFX applications on mobile devices, thereby leveraging the hardware-accelerated native rendering used on those devices.

Different Approaches for Mobile Apps

There are a number of approaches for creating applications for mobile devices, and they can be divided into a number of categories. Any categorization is artificial, so the one that we use here is only one possibility.

We consider three different approaches, as shown in Figure 11-2:

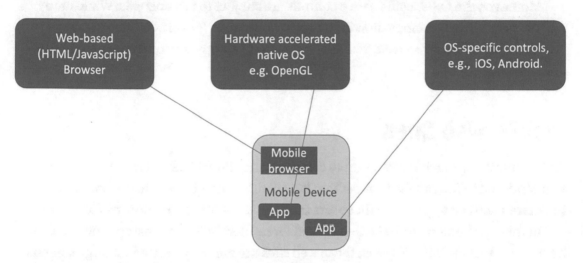

Figure 11-2. *Three possible approaches for mobile apps*

1. Web-based mobile applications

2. Applications using hardware-accelerated native rendering

3. Applications using OS-specific native controls

Each of these options has its advantages, and there are valid use cases for the three options.

OS-Specific Native Controls

Using OS-specific native controls, as is the case in approach 3, allows for a real smooth integration with the native operating system. In this case, the native controls (e.g., buttons, labels, lists, etc.) are used to render the user interface. For the end user, this is convenient, as they recognize the typical UI components they also use in other apps.

This approach requires very specific skills related to the target operating system. Since most mobile apps target both Android and iOS, and since those platforms come with their own approach for native user interfaces, the apps following this approach are typically created by different teams: one for Android and one for iOS.

Moreover, the OS-specific native controls are subject to fast changes. While many end users love the fast innovation in those environments, for software developers, it is often problematic as they have to upgrade their native apps very often or risk that they are outdated.

Mobile Web Sites

The simplest approach is often simply creating a mobile-friendly web site and have that rendered in the mobile browser that is available on mobile devices – optionally integrated with an app icon so that users can start the application more easily.

In theory, the same web site that is used for rendering in the desktop browser can be rendered on mobile. However, those web sites are typically created for large screens and are operated using mouse controls. Clicking a button using a mouse is easier than touching the same button on a touch device. In general, a web experience is much different from a mobile experience. Users who are used to working with native apps on mobile devices often get frustrated with web sites, and this damages the brand.

Device Native Rendering

The JavaFX approach falls into this category. JavaFX has its own set of controls, and developers can easily create their own controls. The rendering of JavaFX is done on top of the hardware-accelerated drivers on the target platform. At this moment, the rendering pipelines for both JavaFX for iOS and JavaFX for Android use OpenGL, using the same code as the rendering on macOS and Linux. OpenGL is a very mature and stable protocol, and changes in the native UI controls of iOS or Android do not impact OpenGL development. In fact, native OpenGL is also used by a number of game developers, who want to achieve maximum performance and flexibility on mobile devices.

Compared to rendering using a web browser, the JavaFX rendering is much more "native" as it doesn't need the intermediate web browser, but directly targets the same native drivers that are also used for rendering native iOS or native Android controls.

At its core, both iOS and most Android devices are systems with an AArch64 processor, running some sort of Linux. Those systems, as well as OpenGL, are widely used in the industry and not controlled by a single mobile device manufacturer. As a consequence, they provide a stable base, avoiding a vendor lock.

The application-specific JavaFX stack is shown in Figure 11-3.

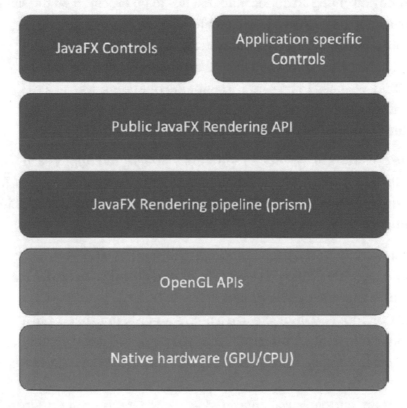

Figure 11-3. *JavaFX stack*

Hello, JavaFX on iOS and Android

While Android and iOS are very different systems, the experience for Java developers will be very similar. Hence, although we only discuss iOS here, the same principles and tools will work for Android as well.

GluonFX Plugins to Reduce Complexity

Deploying applications to mobile devices is slightly more complex than deploying applications on your local development machine (a laptop or a desktop). There are mainly two reasons for this:

- When compiling an application that has to be executed on the same system as the one we use to compile, we can leverage the existing toolchain of our development system, including the compiler and linker. However, when compiling an application for another system, we need to take into account the operating system and the architecture of that system. This is often called cross-compiling, which is considered more complex.

- The operators of the mobile app stores, Google and Apple, each have their own additional requirements for creating mobile apps, for example, related to signing and the structure of the final executable bundles.

One of the reasons for the general success of Java is the large ecosystem. Different companies and individuals provide a set of tools and libraries that make it easier for fellow developers to work on their project.

For JavaFX on mobile, Gluon created a number of plugins that make it much easier for Java developers to deploy Java apps on mobile devices. Those plugins deal with the complexity of cross-compilation and the specific requirements from the respective app stores.

The plugins are currently available for Maven and Gradle projects. Since the popular Java IDEs have first-class support for Maven and Gradle, it is easy to use existing IDEs to create and maintain mobile JavaFX apps.

Using the Maven or Gradle build tool in our project, we can use the GluonFX plugin to run the project on our local (development) system (relying on the JavaFX plugin) and also to create a native image that can be deployed to a target platform.

The Development Flow

While it is, at least in theory, possible to create a mobile app and only test/run it on a mobile device, it is highly recommended to work on desktop first.

A typical deployment cycle contains a number of steps:

- Write some code.

- Compile the code.

- Run the code.

- Test if the output and behavior are as expected.

These steps often have to be repeated, resulting in a number of deployment cycles for a given project.

It should be clear that the deployment cycle on mobile devices takes more time than the deployment cycle on desktop devices. Especially compiling the code takes more time for mobile devices. Therefore, it is better to use your desktop or laptop development system for deployment. The tools that we will describe in the following enable you to use the exact same code on mobile and desktop devices, and the behavior is similar too.

Of course, the mobile experience is still different, and that can only be really tested on mobile devices. For example, gestures like rotate, pinch, and zoom have to be fine-tuned on specific mobile devices, in order to be as intuitive as possible.

A typical development flow for mobile apps is shown in Figure 11-4.

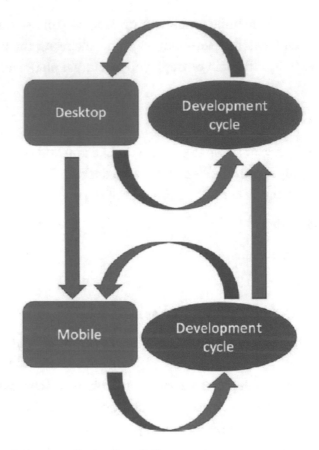

Figure 11-4. *Development flow of mobile apps*

In the referred figure, most of the development is done on desktop. The application is improved, both the business logic part and the UI part. In this stage, issues like NullPointerExceptions, wrong values, or incorrect UI elements are fixed.

At a given moment, the application works as expected on desktop. The business logic fits the requirements, and the UI follows the design. At this point, the application is deployed on a mobile device and tested. As a result of these tests, a new cycle is performed on desktop or on mobile. For example, if tests on the mobile device lead to a hidden issue to surface, it is recommended to go back to the desktop cycle and add a test that fails. This issue can be worked on at the desktop.

On the other hand, if an issue is detected that is specific to mobile (e.g., zooming goes too fast), this issue can directly be fixed in a development cycle on the mobile device.

The Code

We will run you through a very simple HelloFX application that is executed on desktop and an iPhone or an Android device. This sample can be found here (Gradle and Maven):

```
https://github.com/modernclientjava/mcj-samples/tree/master/ch11-Mobile/
Gradle/HelloFX
https://github.com/modernclientjava/mcj-samples/tree/master/ch11-Mobile/
Maven/HelloFX
```

Listing 11-1 shows the HelloFX main class, and Listing 11-2 shows the styles.css file.

Listing 11-1. HelloFX.java file

```java
package hellofx;
import javafx.application.Application;
import javafx.geometry.Pos;
import javafx.scene.Scene;
import javafx.scene.control.Label;
import javafx.scene.image.Image;
import javafx.scene.image.ImageView;
import javafx.scene.layout.VBox;
import javafx.stage.Stage;
public class HelloFX extends Application {
    public void start(Stage stage) {
        String javaVersion = System.getProperty("java.version");
        String javafxVersion = System.getProperty("javafx.version");
        Label label = new Label("Hello, JavaFX " + javafxVersion +
            ", running on Java " + javaVersion + ".");
        ImageView imageView = new ImageView(
            new Image(HelloFX.class.getResourceAsStream("openduke.png")));
        imageView.setFitHeight(200);
        imageView.setPreserveRatio(true);
        VBox root = new VBox(30, imageView, label);
        root.setAlignment(Pos.CENTER);
        Scene scene = new Scene(root, 640, 480);
        scene.getStylesheets().add(
```

```
            HelloFX.class.getResource("styles.css").toExternalForm());
        stage.setScene(scene);
        stage.show();
    }
    public static void main(String[] args) {
        launch(args);
    }
}
```

Listing 11-2. File styles.css

```css
.label {
    -fx-text-fill: blue;
}
```

Listing 11-3 shows the build.gradle file, and Listing 11-4 shows the settings.gradle file for a Gradle project.

Listing 11-3. File build.gradle

```
plugins {
    id 'application'
    id 'org.openjfx.javafxplugin' version '0.0.10'
    id 'com.gluonhq.gluonfx-gradle-plugin' version '1.0.3'
}

repositories {
    mavenCentral()
}

dependencies {
}

gluonfx {
    target = 'host'
    if (project.hasProperty('target')) {
        target = project.getProperty('target')
    }
}
```

```
javafx {
    version = "17.0.1"
    modules = [ "javafx.controls" ]
}

mainClassName = 'hellofx.HelloFX'
```

Listing 11-4. File settings.gradle

```
pluginManagement {
    repositories {
        gradlePluginPortal()
    }
}
rootProject.name = 'HelloFX'
```

The `build.gradle` file shows that we use two special plugins, apart from the regular application one:

```
id 'org.openjfx.javafxplugin' version '0.0.10'
id 'com.gluonhq.gluonfx-gradle-plugin' version '1.0.3'
```

`javafxplugin` is the general plugin for developing JavaFX applications and dealing with the JavaFX modules and dependencies. This is the plugin you typically use for developing JavaFX applications.

The `gluonfx-gradle-plugin` is Gluon's plugin that is capable of cross-compiling code for iOS and Android devices.

In order to use those plugins, we have to tell Gradle where to search for plugins, which are hosted in the general Gradle plugin portal. This explains the `settings.gradle` file shown in Listing 11-4.

Similar to the build file for Gradle, you can use a pom file to declare how to build the application using Maven.

Listing 11-5 shows the equivalent pom file for a Maven project.

Listing 11-5. File pom.xml

```xml
<?xml version="1.0" encoding="UTF-8"?>
<project xmlns="http://maven.apache.org/POM/4.0.0" xmlns:xsi="http://www.
w3.org/2001/XMLSchema-instance" xsi:schemaLocation="http://maven.apache.
org/POM/4.0.0 http://maven.apache.org/xsd/maven-4.0.0.xsd">
    <modelVersion>4.0.0</modelVersion>

    <groupId>hello</groupId>
    <artifactId>hellofx</artifactId>
    <version>1.0-SNAPSHOT</version>
    <packaging>jar</packaging>

    <name>hellofx</name>

    <properties>
        <project.build.sourceEncoding>UTF-8</project.build.sourceEncoding>
        <maven.compiler.release>11</maven.compiler.release>
        <javafx.version>17.0.1</javafx.version>
        <mainClassName>hellofx.HelloFX</mainClassName>
    </properties>

    <dependencies>
        <dependency>
            <groupId>org.openjfx</groupId>
            <artifactId>javafx-controls</artifactId>
            <version>${javafx.version}</version>
        </dependency>
    </dependencies>

    <build>
        <plugins>
            <plugin>
                <groupId>org.apache.maven.plugins</groupId>
                <artifactId>maven-compiler-plugin</artifactId>
                <version>3.8.1</version>
            </plugin>
```

```xml
        <plugin>
            <groupId>org.openjfx</groupId>
            <artifactId>javafx-maven-plugin</artifactId>
            <version>0.0.8</version>
            <configuration>
                <mainClass>${mainClassName}</mainClass>
            </configuration>
        </plugin>

        <plugin>
            <groupId>com.gluonhq</groupId>
            <artifactId>gluonfx-maven-plugin</artifactId>
            <version>1.0.7</version>
            <configuration>
                <target>${gluonfx.target}</target>
                <mainClass>${mainClassName}</mainClass>
            </configuration>
        </plugin>

    </plugins>
</build>

<profiles>
    <profile>
        <id>ios</id>
        <properties>
            <gluonfx.target>ios</gluonfx.target>
        </properties>
    </profile>
    <profile>
        <id>android</id>
        <properties>
            <gluonfx.target>android</gluonfx.target>
        </properties>
```

```
        </profile>
    </profiles>
```

```
</project>
```

iOS

Requirements

To use the plugin to develop and deploy native applications on iOS platforms, you need a Mac with macOS 10.15.6 or superior and Xcode 11 or superior, available from the Mac App Store. Once Xcode is downloaded and installed, open it to accept the license terms.

Alternatively, without a Mac, GitHub Actions can be used to build and deploy remotely (see `https://docs.gluonhq.com/#platforms_ios_github_actions`).

JavaFX applications can run on a JVM without any additional requirement, so any JDK 11+ should be enough. However, to create native images and deploy to mobile, you will need GraalVM. The latest version of the Gluon built version can be found at `https://github.com/gluonhq/graal/releases/latest`. Select the Darwin version for macOS.

Once downloaded and installed, you need to set `GRAALVM_HOME` pointing to it, like

```
export GRAALVM_HOME=
    /path/to/graalvm-svm-darwin-gluon-21.2.0-dev/Contents/Home
export JAVA_HOME=$GRAALVM_HOME
```

Finally, if you want to test and distribute your app via the App Store, you'll need to enroll in the Apple Developer Program. However, if you only want to test on your own iOS device, you can use *free provisioning*.

Follow the instructions in this link to get a valid provisioning profile and a valid signing identity: `https://docs.gluonhq.com/client/#_ios_deployment`.

Build the Project

The first step is to build and run the project as a regular Java project (on a regular JVM that you use for your local development).

With Gradle:

```
./gradlew clean run
```

With Maven:

```
mvn clean gluonfx:run
```

The result is shown in Figure 11-5.

Hello, JavaFX 17–ea, running on Java 11.0.2.

Figure 11-5. *Running HelloFX on OpenJDK 11.0.2*

These instructions will compile the application and its dependencies and run the resulting classes using the default Java Virtual Machine of your system. This is very similar to any other regular Java development. There is no cross-compilation involved here.

As we said before, it is important to verify the app works without errors on your development system, with a regular VM. The AOT compilation that will be performed when we deploy to mobile devices takes a long time, so it should be called only when the project is ready to go to this stage.

Compile

The typical Gradle run task will check if the application is compiled; otherwise, it will compile the required classes again.

For running apps on mobile devices, the compile task has to be called manually, as it can take a long time. This is to allow developers to modify things that are not related to the Java files (but, e.g., to application icons) without having to go through the long compilation phase each time.

Compilation can be done both with Gradle and Maven.

Run with Gradle:

```
./gradlew -Ptarget=ios nativeCompile
```

Run with Maven:

```
mvn -Pios gluonfx:compile
```

Then wait for a while (depending on your machine, it could easily be 5 minutes or more) until the task finishes successfully. If you check the terminal, you could see the feedback provided during the process, like in Listing 11-6.

Listing 11-6. Output during the native compilation phase for iOS

```
==================== COMPILE TASK ====================
We will now compile your code for arm64-apple-ios. This may take some time.
[SUB] [hellofx.hellofx:19668]      classlist:   2,087.16 ms,  0.96 GB
[SUB] [hellofx.hellofx:19668]         (cap):     206.66 ms,  0.96 GB
[SUB] [hellofx.hellofx:19668]          setup:   2,126.59 ms,  0.96 GB
[SUB] [hellofx.hellofx:19668]       (clinit):     850.75 ms,  5.56 GB
[SUB] [hellofx.hellofx:19668]     (typeflow):  36,924.18 ms,  5.56 GB
[SUB] [hellofx.hellofx:19668]      (objects):  29,823.15 ms,  5.56 GB
[SUB] [hellofx.hellofx:19668]     (features):   2,873.60 ms,  5.56 GB
[SUB] [hellofx.hellofx:19668]       analysis:  72,256.12 ms,  5.56 GB
[SUB] [hellofx.hellofx:19668]       universe:   2,483.79 ms,  5.66 GB
[SUB] [hellofx.hellofx:19668]        (parse):   3,013.34 ms,  5.66 GB
[SUB] [hellofx.hellofx:19668]       (inline):  12,337.56 ms,  7.09 GB
[SUB] [hellofx.hellofx:19668]      (compile):  41,955.76 ms,  6.97 GB
[SUB] [hellofx.hellofx:19668]      (bitcode):   4,023.85 ms,  6.97 GB
[SUB] [hellofx.hellofx:19668]      (prelink):   8,245.57 ms,  6.97 GB
[SUB] [hellofx.hellofx:19668]         (llvm): 118,298.09 ms,  6.97 GB
[SUB] [hellofx.hellofx:19668]     (postlink):  12,859.86 ms,  6.97 GB
[SUB] [hellofx.hellofx:19668]        compile: 201,311.01 ms,  6.97 GB
[SUB] [hellofx.hellofx:19668]          image:  11,973.28 ms,  7.05 GB
[SUB] [hellofx.hellofx:19668]          write:   2,908.47 ms,  7.05 GB
[SUB] [hellofx.hellofx:19668]        [total]: 295,742.00 ms,  7.05 GB
```

As a result, hellofx.hellofx.o, with 54.6 MB, can be found under `target/gluonfx/arm64-ios/gvm/tmp/SVM-16***/hellofx.hellofx.o`.

If that is not the case, check for any possible failure in the log files under `target/gluonfx/arm64-ios/gvm/log`.

The next steps will go faster, but they will require a valid signing identity and a valid provisioning profile in order for you to sign the app before it can be deployed to the device.

Link and Package

Now that the Java code for the application is compiled to native code, we can package the generated code with the required libraries and resources, sign the application, and perform more iOS-specific tasks.

The plugins combine this packaging in the `nativeLink` task.

Run with Gradle:

```
./gradlew -Ptarget=ios nativeLink
```

Run with Maven:

```
mvn -Pios gluonfx:link
```

It produces target/gluonfx/arm64-ios/hellofx.app (136.3 MB).

Now, if you want to build an IPA file that can be submitted to the App Store (see `https://docs.gluonhq.com/#platforms_ios_distribution`), you can run

```
./gradlew -Ptarget=ios nativePackage
```

Or run with Maven:

```
mvn -Pios gluonfx:package
```

Run

Congratulations! Your mobile app is ready now! You can deploy this app to your phone as explained in the following.

Plug in your iOS device, and run with Gradle:

```
./gradlew -Ptarget=ios nativeRun
```

Or run with Maven:

```
mvn -Pios gluonfx:nativerun
```

Note that you will need to unlock your device. Once installed, it will launch (Figure 11-6).

Figure 11-6. *HelloFX app on iOS*

Android

Requirements

To use the plugin to develop and deploy native applications on Android, you need a Linux machine. Alternatively, you can use WSL2 (`https://docs.microsoft.com/en-us/windows/wsl/install-win10`) from a Windows PC, or you can do it remotely using GitHub Actions (see `https://docs.gluonhq.com/#platforms_android_github_actions`).

JavaFX applications can run on a JVM without any additional requirement, so any JDK 11+ should be enough. However, to create native images and deploy to mobile, you will need GraalVM. The latest version of the Gluon built version can be found at `https://github.com/gluonhq/graal/releases/latest`. Select the Linux version.

Once downloaded and installed, you need to set `GRAALVM_HOME` pointing to it, like

```
export GRAALVM_HOME=
    /path/to/graalvm-svm-linux-gluon-21.2.0-dev/
export JAVA_HOME=$GRAALVM_HOME
```

Android SDK and NDK are required to build applications for the Android platform. Both will be downloaded automatically by the GluonFX plugin and configured with the required packages.

Compile

Compilation can be done both with Gradle and Maven.

Run with Gradle:

```
./gradlew -Ptarget=android nativeCompile
```

Run with Maven:

```
mvn -Pandroid gluonfx:compile
```

Then wait for a while (depending on your machine, it could easily be 3 minutes or more) until the task finishes successfully. If you check the terminal, you could see the feedback provided during the process, like in Listing 11-7.

Listing 11-7. Output during the native compilation phase for Android

```
==================== COMPILE TASK ====================
We will now compile your code for aarch64-linux-android. This may take some time.
[SUB] Warning: Ignoring server-mode native-image argument --no-server.
[SUB] [hellofx.hellofx:4176]     classlist:   1,692.66 ms,   0.96 GB
[SUB] [hellofx.hellofx:4176]         (cap):     222.33 ms,   0.96 GB
[SUB] [hellofx.hellofx:4176]        setup:   2,350.95 ms,   0.96 GB
[SUB] [hellofx.hellofx:4176]      (clinit):   1,055.23 ms,   5.45 GB
[SUB] [hellofx.hellofx:4176]    (typeflow):  26,771.58 ms,   5.45 GB
[SUB] [hellofx.hellofx:4176]     (objects):  30,115.69 ms,   5.45 GB
[SUB] [hellofx.hellofx:4176]    (features):   2,812.99 ms,   5.45 GB
[SUB] [hellofx.hellofx:4176]      analysis:  62,782.08 ms,   5.45 GB
[SUB] [hellofx.hellofx:4176]      universe:   2,307.81 ms,   5.45 GB
[SUB] [hellofx.hellofx:4176]       (parse):   2,497.79 ms,   5.45 GB
[SUB] [hellofx.hellofx:4176]      (inline):   3,905.41 ms,   5.66 GB
[SUB] [hellofx.hellofx:4176]     (compile):  46,861.15 ms,   6.27 GB
[SUB] [hellofx.hellofx:4176]       compile:  56,083.83 ms,   6.27 GB
[SUB] [hellofx.hellofx:4176]         image:   9,097.73 ms,   5.37 GB
[SUB] [hellofx.hellofx:4176]         write:     558.92 ms,   5.37 GB
[SUB] [hellofx.hellofx:4176]       [total]: 135,607.09 ms,   5.37 GB
```

As a result, hellofx.hellofx.o, with 84.7 MB, can be found under target/gluonfx/
aarch64-android/gvm/tmp/SVM-16***/hellofx.hellofx.o.

If that is not the case, check for any possible failure in the log files under target/
gluonfx/aarch64-android/gvm/log.

Link and Package

Now that the Java code for the application is compiled to native code, we can link and
package the generated code with the required libraries and resources.

The plugins combine this packaging in the nativeLink and nativePackage task.

Run with Gradle:

```
./gradlew -Ptarget=android nativeLink nativePackage
```

Run with Maven:

```
mvn -Pandroid gluonfx:link gluonfx:package
```

It produces target/gluonfx/aarch64-android/gvm/hellofx.apk (28.1 MB). This
file can be submitted to Google Play, provided it is signed for release (see https://docs.
gluonhq.com/#platforms_android_distribution).

Run

You can now deploy this apk to your Android phone as explained in the following.

Plug in your Android device, and run with Gradle:

```
./gradlew -Ptarget=android nativeInstall nativeRun
```

Or run with Maven:

```
mvn -Pandroid gluonfx:install gluonfx:nativerun
```

Once installed, it will launch (Figure 11-7).

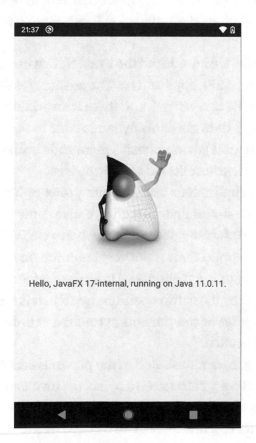

Figure 11-7. *HelloFX app on Android*

How Does It Work?

As a Java developer in general, and a JavaFX developer in particular, you can focus on the Java APIs and implement the required code that makes your application work. The Java platform itself will make sure that your Java application is translated to Java bytecode, which is not dependent on the operating system (e.g., Windows, macOS, Linux variants, iOS) or processors (e.g., ARM 64, Intel x86-64, ARMv6hf).

The typical Java approach is that the next step, executing the Java bytecode on a native system, is achieved using a Java Virtual Machine (JVM) running on the target system. In this case, the JVM interprets the bytecode and executes it, using target-specific native instructions. Most JVMs also contain a Just In Time (JIT) compiler that converts frequently used Java methods on the fly into native code. In general, native code runs much faster than interpreted code; hence, the performance of a Java application typically improves after it is running for a while. Compiling the Java bytecode to native code takes some time, and in the meantime the application is running, so peak performance is not immediately achieved.

In the previous chapter, we introduced the Graal Native Image tool for creating native packages based on JavaFX applications. The advantages discussed in the previous chapter apply for the mobile case as well, and there is an additional reason for using this approach on mobile. Apple does not allow dynamic code to be generated at runtime on iOS devices. Hence, the typical Java approach, where code is first interpreted and later (while running) optimized, is not allowed on iOS devices.

Running mobile Java applications using an interpreter only at runtime is possible, but the interpreter is much slower than executing native code.

On top of that, the (old) server-side approach where one JVM installation can handle a large number of applications is not very common on mobile. Mobile apps are self-contained applications that bundle all their dependencies – apart from a small set of APIs that are offered by the native operating system. It is absolutely not done to download additional libraries or components at runtime in order to satisfy dependencies needed by a specific application.

The Gluon Client plugin, demonstrated in the previous section, contains the required tools to convert Java applications to bytecode; invokes the Graal Native Image tool to convert the bytecode into native code, including the required VM functionality; and links the result into an executable that can be deployed to mobile devices.

Schematically, this is shown in Figure 11-8.

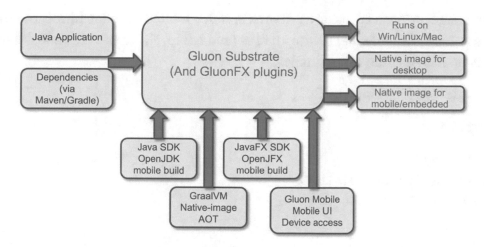

Figure 11-8. *Native application workflow*

The resulting native image obtained by the Gluon Client tools is conceptually not different from a native image created using the OS-specific tools (e.g., Xcode for creating iOS apps and Android Studio for creating Android apps). The developer still needs to upload this image to the app stores, thereby documenting the application, providing screenshots, and so on.

Using the Plugin Options

By default, the plugin will use the best configuration to deploy your application to mobile devices. Different components in the plugin and in GraalVM analyze your code and its dependencies to decide on things like including native libraries, using reflection and JNI, and so on. It is expected that those analysis tools will improve over time.

Since it is currently not possible to cover all edge cases with the analysis tools, the plugin allows developers to set configuration-specific settings (e.g., additional classes to be used for reflection, including native symbols, etc.)

bundlesList

A list of additional fully qualified bundle resources that will be added to the default bundles list that already includes

```
com/sun/javafx/scene/control/skin/resources/controls
com.sun.javafx.tk.quantum.QuantumMessagesBundle
```

For instance, if you are using a resource bundle for internalization purposes, like src/resources/hellofx/hello.properties (and hello_EN.properties and others), you will need to include, using Gradle,

```
bundlesList = ["hellofx.hello"]
```

or using Maven

```
<bundlesList>
    <list>hellofx.hello</list>
</bundlesList>
```

resourcesList

A list of additional resource patterns or extensions that will be added to the default resources list that already includes

```
png, jpg, jpeg, gif, bmp, ttf, raw
xml, fxml, css, gls, json, dat,
license, frag, vert, obj
```

For instance, if you are using a properties file (not included as a resource bundle), like src/resources/hellofx/logging.properties, you will need to include, using Gradle,

```
resourcesList = ["properties"]
```

or using Maven

```
<resourcesList>
    <list>properties</list>
</resourcesList>
```

reflectionList

A list of additional fully qualified classes that will be added to the default reflection list that already includes most of the JavaFX classes.

The current list is added to the file under

```
{build/target}/gluonfx/gvm/reflectionconfig-$target.json
```

jniList

A list of additional fully qualified classes that will be added to the default JNI list that already includes most of the JavaFX classes.

The current list is added to the file under

```
{build/target}/gluonfx/gvm/jniconfig-$target.json
```

runAgent Task/Goal

Alternatively to the reflection and JNI lists, the runAgent task runs the project on desktop, in combination with the `javafx-maven-plugin`, with GraalVM's JVM (HotSpot) and with the `native-image-agent` to record the behavior of the Java application. It generates the configuration files for reflection, JNI, resource, proxy, and serialization that will be used by the native image generation.

If needed, this goal should be executed before the others and requires user intervention to discover all reachable classes, by running with Gradle:

```
./gradlew runAgent
```

Or run with Maven:

```
mvn gluonfx:runagent
```

Creating Real Mobile-Looking Apps

While a JavaFX application created for desktop works on mobile devices, in many cases, you can achieve an improved user experience by tuning your application for mobile usage. Doing so, you end up with code that is specific to mobile vs. specific to desktop, and you may ask what is then the advantage compared to doing mobile development in native languages. There are some very good reasons for this though:

- Most of your application code can still be shared. All business logic, but also a large part of the UI code, can be shared between mobile and desktop.

- With the appropriate frameworks (e.g., Glisten), many existing JavaFX controls get styled for mobile usage. In that case, the exact same JavaFX code is used.

- For the UI components that are completely different between mobile and desktop, at the very least the code is all written in Java and can be written by the same developers, compiled by the same tools, and integrated in the same CI infrastructure.

A good architecture for client applications makes a clean separation between business logic and UI components. In JavaFX, the UI part of an application can be separated even more. The data is often maintained in instances of `ObservableObject` or `ObservableList`, which do not directly relate to the rendering details of the UI components – hence, they can be considered part of the general components.

There are a number of approaches to make the UI components of your JavaFX application more mobile specific, and we will briefly discuss the following:

- Use different stylesheets for mobile vs. desktop.

- Use specific controls for mobile.

The Glisten framework [see `https://docs.gluonhq.com/#_glisten_apis`] from Gluon, which is part of Gluon Mobile, combines both approaches.

Different Stylesheets

One of the reasons why JavaFX user interfaces are flexible and easy to change is because of the support for CSS, which is discussed in Chapter 5, "Mastering Visual and CSS Design." Stylesheets define the look and feel of different components of the user interface in a declarative way, using a CSS file. They are decoupled from the implementation logic, and this allows for a number of combinations.

Looking at the code for the HelloFX app we discussed earlier in this chapter, adding a stylesheet in a JavaFX application is easily done, for example, in the `start` method of the application:

```
Scene scene = new Scene(root, 640, 480);
scene.getStylesheets().add(
    HelloFX.class.getResource("styles.css").toExternalForm());
```

In this code snippet, we add the stylesheet called `styles.css` to the scene graph. The stylesheet we used here is very simple, and it describes the style of the text in a `Label` control:

```
.label {
    -fx-text-fill: blue;
}
```

We can create a second stylesheet, where we set the `-fx-text-fill` property to a different color, for example, red.

We can copy the `styles.css` file to `styles2.css` and edit it as follows:

```
.label {
    -fx-text-fill: red;
}
```

We modify our application now so that we load this stylesheet instead of the original one:

```
Scene scene = new Scene(root, 640, 480);
scene.getStylesheets().add(
    HelloFX.class.getResource("styles2.css").toExternalForm());
```

If we now run the application, we will see that the text color has changed indeed, as shown in Figure 11-9.

This shows how easy the user interface of an application can be reconfigured by supplying a different stylesheet, but we now changed the stylesheet for all deployments. What we really want is to load a different stylesheet based on the target platform.

An easy solution to this is to check for the system property "`os.name`" and based on that load a different stylesheet, as shown in this snippet:

```
Scene scene = new Scene(root, 640, 480);
If (System.getProperty("os.name").equals("ios")) {
    scene.getStylesheets().add(
        HelloFX.class.getResource("styles.css").toExternalForm());
} else {
    scene.getStylesheets().add(
        HelloFX.class.getResource("styles2.css").toExternalForm());
}
```

This snippet will cause the "`styles.css`" stylesheet to be applied in the case where we are running on iOS systems (both device or simulator), and it will use the "`styles2.css`" stylesheet in all other cases.

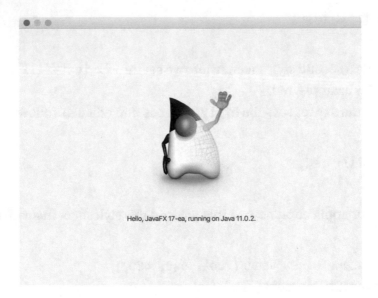

Figure 11-9. *HelloFX application with CSS*

With Gluon Mobile, you can go further. One of the components that are bundled with Gluon Mobile is the open source framework Gluon Attach, which is developed at `https://github.com/gluonhq/attach`.

Gluon Attach contains a number of services that expose a Java API and that are implemented on the different platforms using specific APIs. Example services implemented by Gluon Attach are position, storage, in-app billing, pictures, Bluetooth Low Energy, and so on.

Using Attach, it is possible to detect the platform (e.g., iOS or Android) and the dimensions (e.g., phone or tablet). This allows to load a specific stylesheet for, for example, iPad systems and another specific stylesheet for Android phones.

The following code snippet shows how you can detect this, and it will use a different stylesheet in each case:

```
Scene scene = new Scene(root, 640, 480);
if (Platform.isIOS()) {
    scene.getStylesheets().add(
        HelloFX.class.getResource("styles.css").toExternalForm());
} else if (Platform.isAndroid()) {
```

```
        scene.getStylesheets().add(
            HelloFX.class.getResource("styles2.css").toExternalForm());
    }
```

In this case, we make use of `com.gluonhq.attach.util.Platform`, to get the current platform where the application is running on.

In order to be able to import this class, we need dependencies in the build.gradle file, shown in Listing 11-8.

Listing 11-8. Adding Attach to a Gradle project

```
repositories {
    mavenCentral()
    maven {
        url 'https://nexus.gluonhq.com/nexus/content/repositories/releases'
    }
}
dependencies {
    implementation "com.gluonhq:charm-glisten:6.0.6"
    implementation "com.gluonhq.attach:util:4.0.11"
}
```

We need similar dependencies in the pom file, shown in Listing 11-9.

Listing 11-9. Adding Attach to a Maven project

```
<dependencies>
    <dependency>
        <groupId>com.gluonhq</groupId>
        <artifactId>charm-glisten</artifactId>
        <version>6.0.6</version>
    </dependency>
    <dependency>
        <groupId>com.gluonhq.attach</groupId>
        <artifactId>util</artifactId>
        <version>4.0.11</version>
    </dependency>
</dependencies>
```

```
<repositories>
  <repository>
      <id>Gluon</id>
      <url>
          https://nexus.gluonhq.com/nexus/content/repositories/releases
      </url>
  </repository>
</repositories>
```

Mobile-Specific Controls

While there is a lot we can do with stylesheets, some controls are really only relevant on mobile devices.

Creating a control for a mobile device is not different from creating a control for a desktop application, and it has already been discussed in Chapter 7, "Bridging Swing and JavaFX."

Gluon Mobile contains a number of mobile-specific controls that are often encountered in typical mobile applications. A list of those controls is available at

```
https://docs.gluonhq.com/charm/javadoc/6.0.6/com.gluonhq.charm.glisten/com/
gluonhq/charm/glisten/control/package-summary.html
```

As an example, we will show an application that uses a `FloatingActionButton` control. The project can be found here (Gradle and Maven):

```
https://github.com/modernclientjava/mcj-samples/tree/master/ch11-Mobile/
Gradle/HelloGluon
https://github.com/modernclientjava/mcj-samples/tree/master/ch11-Mobile/
Maven/HelloGluon
```

The Code

Listing 11-10 shows the `build.gradle` file, and Listing 11-11 shows the `settings.gradle` file for a Gradle project.

Listing 11-10. File build.gradle

```
plugins {
    id 'application'
    id 'org.openjfx.javafxplugin' version '0.0.10'
    id 'com.gluonhq.gluonfx-gradle-plugin' version '1.0.3'
}

repositories {
    mavenCentral()
    maven {
        url 'https://nexus.gluonhq.com/nexus/content/repositories/
releases/'
    }
}

dependencies {
    implementation "com.gluonhq:charm-glisten:6.0.6"
}

gluonfx {
    target = 'host'
    if (project.hasProperty('target')) {
        target = project.getProperty('target')
    }

    attachConfig {
        version = "4.0.11"
        services 'display', 'lifecycle', 'statusbar', 'storage'
    }

}

javafx {
    version = "17-ea+16"
    modules = [ "javafx.controls" ]
}

mainClassName = "$moduleName/com.gluonhq.hello.HelloGluon"
```

Listing 11-11. File settings.gradle

```
pluginManagement {
    repositories {

gradlePluginPortal()
    }
}
rootProject.name = 'HelloGluon'
```

If you have a Maven project, Listing 11-12 shows the equivalent pom file.

Listing 11-12. pom.xml file

```
<?xml version="1.0" encoding="UTF-8"?>
<project xmlns="http://maven.apache.org/POM/4.0.0" xmlns:xsi="http://www.
w3.org/2001/XMLSchema-instance" xsi:schemaLocation="http://maven.apache.
org/POM/4.0.0 http://maven.apache.org/xsd/maven-4.0.0.xsd">
    <modelVersion>4.0.0</modelVersion>

    <groupId>com.gluonhq.hello</groupId>
    <artifactId>hellogluon</artifactId>
    <version>1.0-SNAPSHOT</version>
    <packaging>jar</packaging>

    <name>hellogluon</name>

    <properties>
        <project.build.sourceEncoding>UTF-8</project.build.sourceEncoding>
        <maven.compiler.release>11</maven.compiler.release>
        <javafx.version>17.0.1</javafx.version>
        <attach.version>4.0.11</attach.version>
        <mainClassName>com.gluonhq.hello.HelloGluon</mainClassName>
    </properties>

    <dependencies>
        <dependency>
            <groupId>org.openjfx</groupId>
            <artifactId>javafx-controls</artifactId>
```

```xml
        <version>${javafx.version}</version>
    </dependency>
    <dependency>
        <groupId>com.gluonhq</groupId>
        <artifactId>charm-glisten</artifactId>
        <version>6.0.6</version>
    </dependency>
    <dependency>
        <groupId>com.gluonhq.attach</groupId>
        <artifactId>display</artifactId>
        <version>${attach.version}</version>
    </dependency>
    <dependency>
        <groupId>com.gluonhq.attach</groupId>
        <artifactId>lifecycle</artifactId>
        <version>${attach.version}</version>
    </dependency>
    <dependency>
        <groupId>com.gluonhq.attach</groupId>
        <artifactId>statusbar</artifactId>
        <version>${attach.version}</version>
    </dependency>
    <dependency>
        <groupId>com.gluonhq.attach</groupId>
        <artifactId>storage</artifactId>
        <version>${attach.version}</version>
    </dependency>
    <dependency>
        <groupId>com.gluonhq.attach</groupId>
        <artifactId>util</artifactId>
        <version>${attach.version}</version>
    </dependency>
</dependencies>

<repositories>
    <repository>
```

```xml
            <id>Gluon</id>
            <url>https://nexus.gluonhq.com/nexus/content/repositories/
            releases</url>
        </repository>
    </repositories>

    <build>
        <plugins>
            <plugin>
                <groupId>org.apache.maven.plugins</groupId>
                <artifactId>maven-compiler-plugin</artifactId>
                <version>3.8.1</version>
            </plugin>

            <plugin>
                <groupId>org.openjfx</groupId>
                <artifactId>javafx-maven-plugin</artifactId>
                <version>0.0.6</version>
                <configuration>
                    <mainClass>${mainClassName}</mainClass>
                </configuration>
            </plugin>

            <plugin>
                <groupId>com.gluonhq</groupId>
                <artifactId>gluonfx-maven-plugin</artifactId>
                <version>1.0.7</version>
                <configuration>
                    <target>${gluonfx.target}</target>
                    <attachList>
                        <list>display</list>
                        <list>lifecycle</list>
                        <list>statusbar</list>
                        <list>storage</list>
                    </attachList>
                    <mainClass>${mainClassName}</mainClass>
                </configuration>
```

```
            </plugin>
        </plugins>

    </build>

    <profiles>
        <profile>
            <id>ios</id>
            <properties>
                <gluonfx.target>ios</gluonfx.target>
            </properties>
        </profile>
        <profile>
            <id>android</id>
            <properties>
                <gluonfx.target>android</gluonfx.target>
            </properties>
        </profile>
    </profiles>
</project>
```

Listing 11-13 shows the HelloGluon main class, and Listing 11-14 shows the styles.
css file.

Listing 11-13. HelloFX.java file

```java
package hellofx;

import com.gluonhq.attach.display.DisplayService;
import com.gluonhq.attach.util.Platform;
import com.gluonhq.charm.glisten.application.MobileApplication;
import com.gluonhq.charm.glisten.control.AppBar;
import com.gluonhq.charm.glisten.control.FloatingActionButton;
import com.gluonhq.charm.glisten.mvc.View;
import com.gluonhq.charm.glisten.visual.MaterialDesignIcon;
import com.gluonhq.charm.glisten.visual.Swatch;
import javafx.geometry.Dimension2D;
import javafx.geometry.Pos;
```

```java
import javafx.scene.Scene;
import javafx.scene.control.Label;
import javafx.scene.image.Image;
import javafx.scene.image.ImageView;
import javafx.scene.layout.VBox;

public class HelloGluon extends MobileApplication {
    @Override
    public void init() {
        addViewFactory(HOME_VIEW, () -> {
            FloatingActionButton fab =
                new FloatingActionButton(MaterialDesignIcon.SEARCH.text,
                    e -> System.out.println("Search"));
            ImageView imageView = new ImageView(new Image(
                HelloGluon.class.getResourceAsStream("openduke.png")));
            imageView.setFitHeight(200);
            imageView.setPreserveRatio(true);
            Label label = new Label("Hello, Gluon Mobile!");
            VBox root = new VBox(20, imageView, label);
            root.setAlignment(Pos.CENTER);
            View view = new View(root) {
                @Override
                protected void updateAppBar(AppBar appBar) {
                    appBar.setTitleText("Gluon Mobile");
                }
            };
            fab.showOn(view);
            return view;
        });
    }
    @Override
    public void postInit(Scene scene) {
        Swatch.LIGHT_GREEN.assignTo(scene);
        scene.getStylesheets().add(
            HelloGluon.class.getResource("styles.css").toExternalForm());
```

```java
        if (Platform.isDesktop()) {
            Dimension2D dimension2D = DisplayService.create()
                    .map(display -> display.getDefaultDimensions())
                    .orElse(new Dimension2D(640, 480));
            scene.getWindow().setWidth(dimension2D.getWidth());
            scene.getWindow().setHeight(dimension2D.getHeight());
        }
    }
    public static void main(String[] args) {
        launch();
    }
}
```

Listing 11-14. File styles.css

```css
.label {
    -fx-font-size: 2em;
    -fx-text-fill: -primary-swatch-700;
}
```

Build the Project

The first step is to build and run the project as a regular Java project (on a regular JVM that you use for your local development, e.g., HotSpot).

With Gradle:

```
./gradlew clean build run
```

With Maven:

```
mvn clean gluonfx:run
```

The result is shown in Figure 11-10.

Hello, Gluon Mobile!

Figure 11-10. *Running HelloGluon on desktop*

Once the project is ready, we will now compile, package, and run the application on iOS (the same applies to Android).

Compile and Link

Run with Gradle:

```
./gradlew -Ptarget=ios nativeBuild
```

Or run with Maven:

```
mvn -Pios gluonfx:build
```

Run

Run with Gradle:

```
./gradlew -Ptarget=ios nativeRun
```

Or run with Maven:

```
mvn -Pios gluonfx:nativerun
```

The result is shown in Figure 11-11.

Hello, Gluon Mobile!

Figure 11-11. *HelloGluon app on iOS*

Summary

JavaFX applications are very well suited for being deployed on mobile devices. The combination of the JavaFX platform and the Graal Native Image component, integrated in the Gluon Mobile client packages, makes it possible for all Java developers to use their Java skills and create apps that can be uploaded to the popular mobile app stores.

There are a number of tools available that help developers to deploy Java and JavaFX apps to mobile devices in a very familiar way.

In order to make applications really mobile-friendly and adapt to the mobile device context, a number of frameworks can be used (e.g., Gluon Attach and Glisten).

CHAPTER 12

JavaFX 17 on Raspberry Pi

Written by José Pereda

In this chapter, you will learn about how to get started with a Raspberry Pi device and about the required steps to run Java and JavaFX 17 applications, discussing the ways to do local or remote development and how to do remote deployment.

You will be presented different samples, starting from the very basic Java and JavaFX applications, and finally you will be shown a more complex project that tries to create a homemade in-car navigation system, with the help of a GPS device.

Intro to Raspberry Pi

Raspberry Pi and Arduino are the cornerstones of the Maker movement that has been going on for more than 10 years. But these are also the foundation of the Internet of Things (IoT) that has been taking off for years not only for hobbyists but in many industrial sectors. And they even reach more relevance in the STEAM (Science, Technology, Engineering, Art, and Mathematics) initiative, which targets directly the education of our children.

In fact, the Raspberry Pi was born as a small, inexpensive computer intended to be used by kids to learn programming in the school at early stages. As the Raspberry Pi Foundation states (`www.raspberrypi.org`)

> *Our mission is to put the power of computing and digital making into the hands of people all over the world.*

As proof of that, the usual distributions for Raspberry Pi come with Scratch, Python, or Java preinstalled. By the beginning of 2021, more than 40 million units have been sold, where most of these correspond to the Raspberry Pi 3 Model B, released in 2016, and their most recent model, Raspberry Pi 4 Model B, released in 2019.

Whether you are a hobbyist, you work on professional IoT projects, or you have children who want to learn computing, there are many reasons why you should consider doing a very small investment in a Raspberry Pi.

This chapter will give you a brief introduction on getting started with it and programming and running Java and JavaFX applications on this embedded device.

Getting Started with a Raspberry Pi

You can follow www.raspberrypi.org/documentation/ on how to get started.

Initial Kit

There, you will find what components are required, depending on your budget. The following are the minimum requirements to get started and complete the samples of this chapter.

Raspberry Pi

Buy a Raspberry Pi 4 Model B[1] if you haven't done it yet. You will have to choose either 1, 2, 4, or 8 GB of RAM (depending on your needs and your budget).

Its main specifications are as follows:

- SoC: Broadcom BCM2711, Cortex-A72 (ARMv8), 64-bit SoC at 1.5 GHz

- GPU: Broadcom VideoCore VI at 500 MHz

- RAM: 1, 2, 4, or 8 GB LPDDR2 SDRAM

- Wi-Fi and Bluetooth: 2.4 GHz and 5 GHz IEEE 802.11.b/g/n/ac wireless LAN, Bluetooth 5.0

- Networking: Gigabit Ethernet over USB 2.0

- Graphics: H.264 MPEG-4 decode (1080P30); H.264 encode (1080P30); OpenGL ES 3.1/3.2 graphics

- General-Purpose Input/Output (GPIO): Extended 40-pin GPIO header

---

[1] By the time of this writing, the 4 B was the latest model available.

- Ports: 2 USB 2.0 ports, 2 USB 3.0 ports, and 2 HDMI via micro-HDMI; CSI camera port for connecting a Pi camera; DSI display port for connecting a Pi touchscreen display; 4-pole stereo output and composite video port

- PoE: Power-over-Ethernet (PoE) support

Power Adaptor

You may buy it with a complete starting kit or select just the required accessories, including at least a 5 V USB-C power adaptor supplying at least 2 A and an SD card.

SD Card

Follow www.raspberrypi.org/documentation/setup/.

- Choose an SD card of 8 or 16 GB. I'll choose a SanDisk Ultra microS-DHC 16 GB Class 10.

    There are SD cards with NOOBS preinstalled, but the images can be easily downloaded and installed as well using the Raspberry Pi Imager application that can be found at www.raspberrypi.org/software/.

- Keyboard and mouse are optional. Both will require USB connection.

Monitor

You can use any monitor or TV display with HDMI connection, but there is a dedicated Raspberry Pi touch display monitor, as explained in this link:

www.raspberrypi.org/documentation/hardware/display/README.md

- It is a 7" LCD display that connects to the Raspberry Pi through the DSI connector:

www.raspberrypi.org/products/raspberry-pi-touch-display/

- Resolution: The full color display outputs up to 800 × 480 (not that good compared to an HDMI connection) and features a capacitive touch sensing capable of detecting ten fingers.

– It requires external power supply (using another micro-USB power supply is more convenient than connecting through the same Pi board).

– A good case to mount both Raspberry Pi and display is convenient.

– It requires to rotate the display 180° (see later in this chapter).

Install SD

Follow `www.raspberrypi.org/documentation/installation/installing-images/README.md`.

I'll choose the Raspberry Pi OS[2] with desktop software image from `www.raspberrypi.org/software/operating-systems/`. You can choose Lite (without desktop and preinstalled software) or any other distribution of course.

In summary:

– Download and install Raspberry Pi Imager for your OS. After opening it, you see the image shown in Figure 12-1

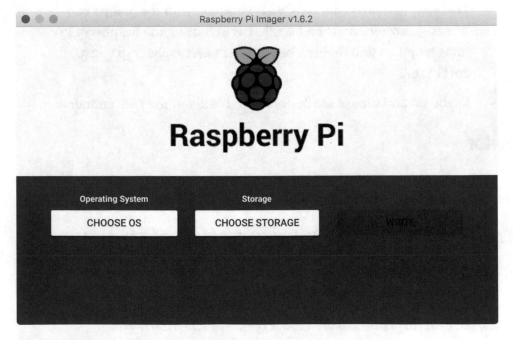

Figure 12-1. *Running Raspberry Pi Imager on Mac*

---

[2] By the time of this writing, Raspberry Pi OS was the latest distribution available.

- Select the image, by default, Raspberry Pi OS (32 bits) with desktop.

  Alternatively, for 64 bits you can download the image from `https://downloads.raspberrypi.org/raspios_arm64/images/`. Download the zip file and unzip it, to extract the .iso file. Then select the `Use custom` option at the end of the menu.

- Once you have plugged the SD card, click Choose Storage to write the file into it. You might need an SD card reader. A USB SD card reader is simple and very convenient. Wait until it finishes, and extract the SD card.

Raspberry Pi Configuration

See `www.raspberrypi.org/documentation/configuration/`. The first time booting, if you have desktop installed, it will start X11, and a configuration dialog will show up. Follow the instructions to configure your language, keyboard settings, and Wi-Fi. Apply the changes and reboot.

Once it has restarted and X11 starts, from the top menu, select Preferences ➤ Raspberry Pi Configuration.

Alternatively, if you are running from the command line, or via SSH, you can get the terminal-based tool shown in Figure 12-2 by running:

```
$ sudo raspi-config
```

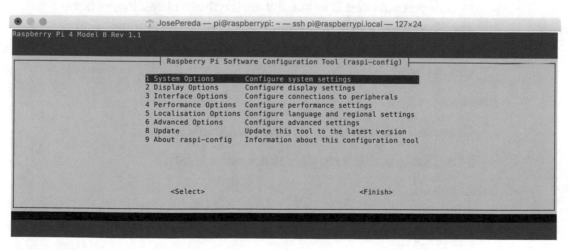

Figure 12-2. *Running raspi-config*

raspi-config

See `www.raspberrypi.org/documentation/configuration/raspi-config.md`.

- Configure system settings:

    - Change user password: The default user on Raspbian is `pi` with the password `raspberry`. You can change that here. For convenience, I'll set the same password: `pi`, which comes handy. But it is quite the opposite of a secure password, of course.

    - Hostname: It is the visible name for this Pi on a network. Change the default `raspberrypi`, if required, for instance, if you have more than one device.

    - Wireless LAN: In case you didn't set it before during the first X11 session, enter SSID and passphrase. It allows connecting to a wireless network using the Raspberry Pi 4's built-in wireless connectivity and will let you work remotely on it from your usual development machine, using SSH.

    - Boot/Auto login: Use this option to change your boot preference to Console or Desktop. We'll choose console/command line, but desktop can be used too. You can also choose auto-login for convenience.

- Localization options:

    - In case you didn't set it before during the first X11 session, choose from keyboard layout, time zone, locale, and Wi-Fi country code. All options on these menus default to British or GB until you change them.

- Interface options:

    - Camera: If you have one, you have to enable it here.

    - SSH: Enable it; this is required to access remotely.

- Performance options:

    - GPU memory: Set at least 256–512 MB for GPU if you are going to run JavaFX.

- Update: Recommended, but it might take a while (only with the Pi connected to the network).

- When finished, reboot.

Note that you can find directly the applied settings in the /boot/config.txt file. After logging in again, you can check the Wi-Fi settings:

```
$ sudo nano /etc/wpa_supplicant/wpa_supplicant.conf
```

You can add as many SSIDs as you need. You can use

```
$ sudo iwlist wlan0 scan
```

to find the available networks at any given location.

Run ifconfig to find if your Pi is connected to the network. As you can see in Figure 12-3, wlan0 is connected, at a given local IP address, and data packages are being received and transmitted (RX, TX).

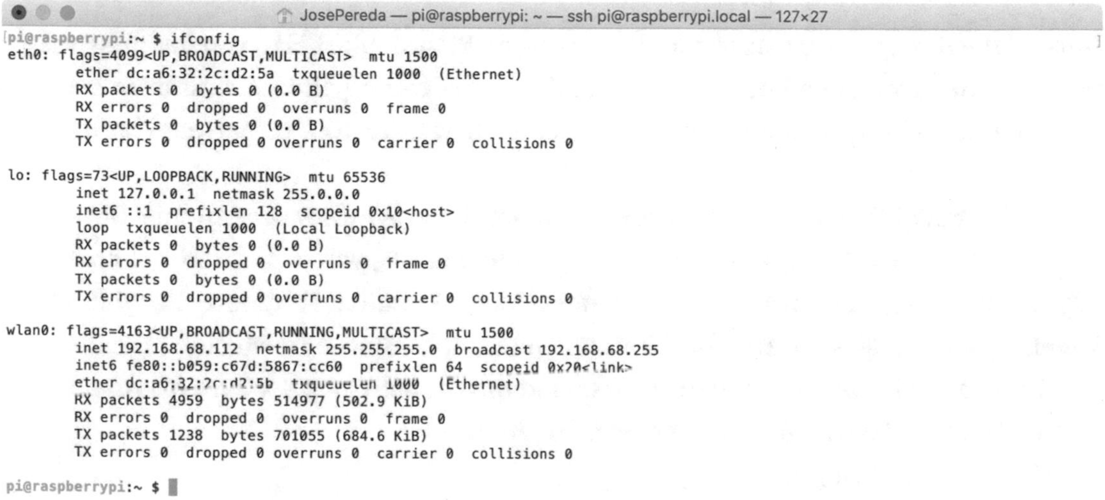

```
●  ●  ●                    JosePereda — pi@raspberrypi: ~ — ssh pi@raspberrypi.local — 127×27
[pi@raspberrypi:~ $ ifconfig
eth0: flags=4099<UP,BROADCAST,MULTICAST>  mtu 1500
        ether dc:a6:32:2c:d2:5a  txqueuelen 1000  (Ethernet)
        RX packets 0  bytes 0 (0.0 B)
        RX errors 0  dropped 0  overruns 0  frame 0
        TX packets 0  bytes 0 (0.0 B)
        TX errors 0  dropped 0 overruns 0  carrier 0  collisions 0

lo: flags=73<UP,LOOPBACK,RUNNING>  mtu 65536
        inet 127.0.0.1  netmask 255.0.0.0
        inet6 ::1  prefixlen 128  scopeid 0x10<host>
        loop  txqueuelen 1000  (Local Loopback)
        RX packets 0  bytes 0 (0.0 B)
        RX errors 0  dropped 0  overruns 0  frame 0
        TX packets 0  bytes 0 (0.0 B)
        TX errors 0  dropped 0 overruns 0  carrier 0  collisions 0

wlan0: flags=4163<UP,BROADCAST,RUNNING,MULTICAST>  mtu 1500
        inet 192.168.68.112  netmask 255.255.255.0  broadcast 192.168.68.255
        inet6 fe80::b059:c67d:5867:cc60  prefixlen 64  scopeid 0x20<link>
        ether dc:a6:32:2c:d2:5b  txqueuelen 1000  (Ethernet)
        RX packets 4959  bytes 514977 (502.9 KiB)
        RX errors 0  dropped 0  overruns 0  frame 0
        TX packets 1238  bytes 701055 (684.6 KiB)
        TX errors 0  dropped 0 overruns 0  carrier 0  collisions 0

pi@raspberrypi:~ $ █
```

Figure 12-3. *Running ifconfig*

By default, DHCP is used. If you need a static IP address, check the link www.raspberrypi.org/documentation/configuration/tcpip/README.md and run

```
$ sudo nano /etc/dhcpcd.conf
```

to configure your eth0 or wlan0 static IP addresses.

In case you have the 7" Raspberry Pi display, you will need to rotate it 180°. Edit the config.txt file:

```
$ sudo nano /boot/config.txt
```

Add the following at the end of the file:

```
lcd_rotate=2
```

Then, save (Ctrl+O), and exit (Ctrl+X).

Finally, note that you should never power off your Raspberry Pi by unplugging it from the power source while it is on, before shutting it down, to prevent the risk of damaging the file system. For a proper way to shut it down, run

```
$ sudo shutdown -h now
```

Then wait a bit, and disconnect power.

Remote Connection via SSH

Most of the time, we will connect to the Raspberry Pi through SSH to run headlessly (i.e., without a dedicated monitor and keyboard on the Pi), having direct access from our developing machine (including copy/paste and file transfer options between both of them).

SSH is built into Linux distributions and macOS. For Windows and mobile devices, third-party SSH clients are available. On Linux and macOS, you can use SSH to connect to your Raspberry Pi from a Linux computer, a Mac, or another Raspberry Pi, without installing additional software. On Windows, the most commonly used client is called PuTTY and can be downloaded from greenend.org.uk. See `www.raspberrypi.org/documentation/remote-access/ssh/windows10.md`.

Usually you will log in via

```
$ ssh pi@<IP>
```

where you need to supply the IP of the device. You can use `hostname -I` to find this IP if you are already connected to it, but if that's not the case, you can try to find the device's IP in the local network using `nmap` or a mobile app, like Fing.

Usually the Raspberry Pi uses DHCP, which means it doesn't have a fixed address, and after rebooting it can probably change. That is not convenient for an SSH connection. We can try to set a fixed IP, or we can also try to use its hostname to connect to it, providing it is broadcasted to the network. This works with Raspberry Pi OS as it uses the multicast DNS protocol.

```
●  ●  ●                🏠 JosePereda — pi@raspberrypi: ~ — ssh pi@raspberrypi.local — 111×23
[JosePereda@MacBook-Pro-de-Jose ~ % ssh pi@raspberrypi.local                                   ]
Linux raspberrypi 5.10.17-v8+ #1403 SMP PREEMPT Mon Feb 22 11:37:54 GMT 2021 aarch64

The programs included with the Debian GNU/Linux system are free software;
the exact distribution terms for each program are described in the
individual files in /usr/share/doc/*/copyright.

Debian GNU/Linux comes with ABSOLUTELY NO WARRANTY, to the extent
permitted by applicable law.
Last login: Tue Jul  6 12:35:18 2021 from fe80::cd1:b2b8:3fdf:68b1%wlan0
pi@raspberrypi:~ $ ▮
```

Figure 12-4. *Starting an SSH session*

Since macOS and Linux use Bonjour, both support mDNS. On Windows, you can install Bonjour from here, `https://support.apple.com/kb/DL999`, for instance.

Then you can log in via `hostname.local`, in this case

```
$ ssh pi@raspberrypi.local
```

After you enter the password, you will have access to the Raspberry Pi (Figure 12-4). The first time you will see a security/authenticity warning. Type yes to continue.

Finally, it is convenient to add the SSH public key of your developing machine to the device, so when running SSH or SCP commands you won't get prompted for the password all the time:

```
$ ssh-copy-id pi@<IP>
```

You can have a look at `www.raspberrypi.org/documentation/remote-access/ssh/passwordless.md` for more details.

Java 11

Raspberry Pi OS comes with Java for ARM installed. If you run `java -version`, it will print

```
$ java -version
openjdk version "11.0.11" 2021-04-20
OpenJDK Runtime Environment (build 11.0.11+9-post-Debian-1deb10u1)
OpenJDK 64-Bit Server VM (build 11.0.11+9-post-Debian-1deb10u1, mixed mode)
```

However, if you run on a distribution without Java installed (like Raspberry Pi OS Lite), you can easily install it with

```
$ sudo apt update
$ sudo apt install default-jdk
```

Testing Java 11

Let's test Java 11 and the Launch Single-File Source-Code Programs feature:

```
$ cd /home/pi/
$ mkdir ModernClients
$ cd ModernClients
$ nano Test.java
```

Add a main method as shown in Listing 12-1 or copy the file from Sample0: https://github.com/modernclientjava/mcj-samples/tree/master/ch12-RaspberryPi/Sample0.

Listing 12-1. Sample0

```java
public class Test {
    public static void main(String... args) {
        System.out.println("Hello Java " +
            System.getProperty("java.version") + " for ARM!");
    }
}
```

Save, exit (Ctrl+O, Ctrl+X), and run:

```
$ java Test.java
```

It should print the result of Figure 12-5.

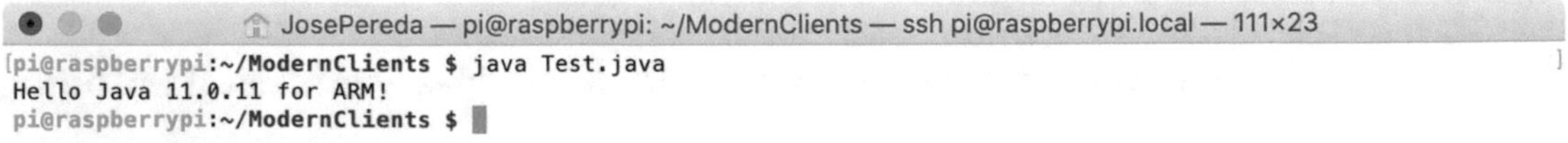

```
● ● ●              🏠 JosePereda — pi@raspberrypi: ~/ModernClients — ssh pi@raspberrypi.local — 111×23
[pi@raspberrypi:~/ModernClients $ java Test.java
Hello Java 11.0.11 for ARM!
pi@raspberrypi:~/ModernClients $ █
```

Figure 12-5. *Running Java 11 on the Raspberry Pi*

Congratulations on running your first Java 11 application on your brand-new Raspberry Pi! Now that Java has been installed successfully, you can move to the next step: installing JavaFX.

Installing JavaFX 17

JavaFX 17 builds for ARM 32 or AArch64 can be downloaded from `https://gluonhq.com/products/javafx`. These are 100% the same JavaFX sources that are used on desktop platforms (Windows, macOS, Linux), but with specific drivers for ARM and 32/64 bits. Note the regular JavaFX distribution for Linux won't work, as it is built for x86-64.

32 Bits

From an SSH session, download the SDK, move it to `/opt`, and unzip it:

```
$ wget https://gluonhq.com/download/javafx-17-ea-sdk-linux-arm32/ -O
openjfx-17-ea+14_linux-arm32_bin-sdk.zip
$ sudo mv openjfx-17-ea+14_linux-arm32_bin-sdk.zip /opt
$ cd /opt
$ sudo unzip openjfx-17-ea+14_linux-arm32_bin-sdk.zip
$ sudo rm openjfx-17-ea+14_linux-arm32_bin-sdk.zip
```

If you look at the list of files under the lib folder, you will find the jars for the different JavaFX modules, as well as the native libraries for ARM.

Note While you will find the media and web JavaFX modules, these are not supported yet on ARM. Neither is Swing.

---

64 Bits

From an SSH session, download the SDK, move it to /opt, and unzip it:

```
$ wget https://gluonhq.com/download/javafx-17-ea-sdk-linux-aarch64-monocle/
-O openjfx-17-ea+14_monocle-linux-aarch64_bin-sdk.zip
$ sudo mv openjfx-17-ea+14_monocle-linux-aarch64_bin-sdk.zip /opt
$ cd /opt
$ sudo unzip openjfx-17-ea+14_monocle-linux-aarch64_bin-sdk.zip
$ sudo rm openjfx-17-ea+14_monocle-linux-aarch64_bin-sdk.zip
```

If you look at the list of files under the lib folder, you will find the jars for the different JavaFX modules, as well as the native libraries for ARM.

Note   JavaFX SDK 64 bits has support for media and web JavaFX modules on ARM. Swing is not supported.

Direct Rendering Manager (DRM)

The DRM is a kernel module that gives direct hardware access to the Direct Rendering Infrastructure clients.

Raspberry Pi has support for the open source VC4/V3D DRM driver. The GPU bundled with Raspberry Pi 4 is a Broadcom VideoCore VI capable of OpenGL ES 3.2 and uses the V3D driver, while the Broadcom VideoCore IV present in Raspberry Pi 3 could only do OpenGL ES 2.0 and uses the VC4 one.

If it is not enabled yet, to get access to hardware acceleration, you can enable the optional overlay editing the `config.txt` file

```
$ sudo nano /boot/config.txt
```

At the end of the file you should have

```
# Enable DRM VC4 V3D drive
dtoverlay=vc4-fkms-v3d
```

Then, save if you made any modification (Ctrl+O), and exit (Ctrl+X). Reboot if needed.

You should check that the device `/dev/dri/card0` (or `/dev/dri/card1`) exists.

Running JavaFX Applications

In order to support hardware-accelerated rendering, JavaFX relies on a number of low-level drivers and libraries that are not always installed by default on all embedded systems. That is the case of the Raspberry Pi OS Lite distribution, for instance, and you can install additional required libraries with

```
$ sudo apt install libegl-mesa0 libegl1 libgbm1 libgles2 libpango-1.0.0
libpangoft2-1.0-0
```

JavaFX support for DRM is a commercial extension from Gluon. You can enable it by setting the environment variable ENABLE_GLUON_COMMERCIAL_EXTENSIONS, either if your application is noncommercial or if you obtained a valid license from Gluon (visit https://gluonhq.com/contact-embedded/).

To enable it on your current session, run

```
$ export ENABLE_GLUON_COMMERCIAL_EXTENSIONS=true
```

Or add it to your .bash file (and for convenience, let's also export PATH_TO_FX):

```
$ nano /home/pi/.bashrc
export ENABLE_GLUON_COMMERCIAL_EXTENSIONS=true
export PATH_TO_FX=/opt/javafx-sdk-17/lib
```

Save and exit.

To enable it also for any remote session, it is convenient to add it to the environment file too:

```
$ nano /etc/environment
ENABLE_GLUON_COMMERCIAL_EXTENSIONS=true
```

Save and exit.

Sample1

Let's try now running the HelloFX sample from the link https://github.com/modernclientjava/mcj-samples/tree/master/ch12-RaspberryPi/Sample1, which is based on the https://openjfx.io/openjfx-docs/ samples.

Listing 12-2 contains the code for a HelloFX Java class that extends from the application JavaFX class.

Listing 12-2. Sample1

```
package org.modernclients.raspberrypi;
import javafx.application.Application;
import javafx.scene.Scene;
import javafx.scene.control.Label;
import javafx.scene.layout.StackPane;
import javafx.stage.Stage;
```

```java
public class HelloFX extends Application {
    @Override
    public void start(Stage stage) {
        String javaVersion = System.getProperty("java.version");
        String javafxVersion = System.getProperty("javafx.version");
        Label label = new Label("Hello, JavaFX " + javafxVersion +
            ", running on Java " + javaVersion + ".");
        Scene scene = new Scene(new StackPane(label), 800, 480);
        stage.setScene(scene);
        stage.setTitle("Hello JavaFX");
        stage.show();
    }
    public static void main(String[] args) {
        launch(args);
    }
}
```

To run it now, from an SSH session, let's first clone the repository with the samples:

```
$ cd /home/pi/Downloads
$ wget https://github.com/modernclientjava/mcj-samples/archive/master.zip
$ unzip master.zip
$ mv mcj-samples-master /home/pi/ModernClients
```

And now enter Sample1:

```
$ cd /home/pi/ModernClients/ch12-RaspberryPi/Sample1
$ javac --module-path $PATH_TO_FX --add-modules=javafx.controls \
    src/org/modernclients/raspberrypi/HelloFX.java -d dist
$ sudo -E java --module-path $PATH_TO_FX --add-modules=javafx.controls \
    -Dmonocle.platform=EGL -Dembedded=monocle -Dglass.platform=Monocle \
    -Dmonocle.egl.lib=$PATH_TO_FX/libgluon_drm-1.1.6.so \
    -cp dist/. org.modernclients.raspberrypi.HelloFX
```

The application will run, but it will be displayed only in a connected monitor. You can quit the application with Ctrl+C from the SSH terminal. Alternatively, you can also try to kill the Java processes:

```
$ sudo killall -9 java
```

If everything works as expected, you will get the result in Figure 12-6, and the output of the process will show something like

```
[GluonDRM] use GPU at /dev/dri/card0 and display id -1
```

But in case the process fails and you get a warning about the device not having DRM capabilities, you can try again adding to the preceding command line this option:

```
-Degl.displayid=/dev/dri/card1
```

Figure 12-6. *Running JavaFX 11 on the Raspberry Pi*

JavaFX mouse events require write permissions to access the hardware, and that's why we need to use sudo; otherwise, the application will start, but an exception will be printed to the console:

```
Udev: Failed to write to /sys/class/input/mice/uevent
```

Check that you have permission to access input devices:

```
java.io.FileNotFoundException: /sys/class/input/mice/uevent (Permission
denied)
    at java.base/java.io.FileOutputStream.open0(Native Method)
...
    at javafx.graphics/com.sun.glass.ui.monocle.SysFS.write(SysFS.java:121)
...
```

Now that we have the sample running, we can try to run it as well from an X11 session, provided we installed Raspberry Pi OS with desktop software.

From the Raspberry Pi now, we run startx; then we open a terminal and type

```
$ cd /home/pi/ModernClients/ch12-RaspberryPi/Sample1
$ sudo java --module-path $PATH_TO_FX --add-modules=javafx.controls \
    -cp dist/. org.modernclients.raspberrypi.HelloFX
```

Since we have removed the Monocle options, now we have a regular windowed application (Figure 12-7). And we can use the mouse to close it and stop the Java process.

Figure 12-7. *Running JavaFX on X11*

Sample2

Let's now try to simplify the command-line process, by using a build tool like Gradle or Maven and taking advantage of the fact that the JavaFX artifacts for ARM 32/AArch64 are available on Maven Central.

In any case, you still need to retrieve the Gluon DRM library. You can download the whole SDK that includes it under /opt/javafx-sdk-17/lib/libgluon_drm-1.1.6.so, or you can download it from the following:

- 32 bits:

```
$ sudo wget http://download2.gluonhq.com/drm/lib-1.1.6/arm32/libgluon_drm.
so -O /opt/javafx-sdk-17/lib/libgluon_drm-1.1.6.so
```

- 64 bits:

```
$ sudo wget http://download2.gluonhq.com/drm/lib-1.1.6/aarch64/libgluon_
drm.so -O /opt/javafx-sdk-17/lib/libgluon_drm-1.1.6.so
```

Gradle

Let's run Sample2:

```
$ cd /home/pi/ModernClients/ch12-RaspberryPi/Sample2/
```

The build.gradle file shown at Listing 12-3 includes the task run that adds the necessary JVM arguments to run the process.

Listing 12-3. Sample2 build.gradle file

```
plugins {
  id 'application'
}

repositories {
    mavenCentral()
}

def osArch = System.properties['os.arch']
def version = "17-ea+14"
def platform = osArch == "arm" ? "linux-arm32-monocle" :
                "linux-aarch64-monocle"
```

```
mainClassName = "org.modernclients.raspberrypi.HelloFX"

dependencies {
    implementation "org.openjfx:javafx-base:$version:$platform"
    implementation "org.openjfx:javafx-graphics:$version:$platform"
    implementation "org.openjfx:javafx-controls:$version:$platform"
}

compileJava {
    doFirst {
        options.compilerArgs = [
                '--module-path', classpath
                    .filter(j -> j.toString().contains(osArch)).asPath,
                '--add-modules', 'javafx.controls'
        ]
    }
}

run {
    doFirst{
        environment "ENABLE_GLUON_COMMERCIAL_EXTENSIONS", "true"
        jvmArgs = [
                '-Dmonocle.platform=EGL', '-Dembedded=monocle',
                '-Dglass.platform=Monocle',
                "-Dmonocle.egl.lib=
                    /opt/javafx-sdk-17/lib/libgluon_drm-1.1.6.so",
                '--module-path', classpath
                    .filter(j -> j.toString().contains(osArch)).asPath,
                '--add-modules', 'javafx.controls'
        ]
    }
}
```

You can directly run

```
$ ./gradlew run
```

The first time it will download Gradle 7.0.1, and it will create a Gradle daemon, so it can take a while before the process starts.

Press Ctrl+C to quit the app. Note that sometimes the app doesn't close, because there are still some Gradle daemon threads running. You can stop them by finding the ID of the Java process(es)

```
$ ps -aux
$ sudo kill <pid of Java process>
```

or directly with

```
$ sudo killall -9 java
```

Note also that you can give sudo access to the Gradle process by editing the file

```
$ nano gradlew
```

and adding at the very end

```
exec sudo "$JAVACMD"...
```

Save and exit (Ctrl+O, Ctrl+X).

Maven

Another alternative is the use of Maven tools and the javafx-maven-plugin. You can easily install Maven on your Pi with

```
$ sudo apt-get install maven
```

Listing 12-4 shows the pom.xml file that is required to run the sample.

Listing 12-4. Sample2 pom.xml file

```
<project xmlns="http://maven.apache.org/POM/4.0.0" xmlns:xsi="http://www.
w3.org/2001/XMLSchema-instance"
        xsi:schemaLocation="http://maven.apache.org/POM/4.0.0 http://
        maven.apache.org/maven-v4_0_0.xsd">
    <modelVersion>4.0.0</modelVersion>
    <groupId>org.modernclients.raspberrypi</groupId>
    <artifactId>hellofx</artifactId>
    <version>1.0-SNAPSHOT</version>
```

```xml
<properties>
    <project.build.sourceEncoding>UTF-8</project.build.sourceEncoding>
    <maven.compiler.release>11</maven.compiler.release>
    <javafx.version>17-ea+14</javafx.version>
    <main.class>org.modernclients.raspberrypi.HelloFX</main.class>
    <runtime.jvm.options/>
</properties>

<dependencies>
    <dependency>
        <groupId>org.openjfx</groupId>
        <artifactId>javafx-controls</artifactId>
        <version>${javafx.version}</version>
    </dependency>
</dependencies>

<profiles>
    <profile>
        <id>default</id>
        <activation>
            <activeByDefault>true</activeByDefault>
        </activation>
    </profile>
    <profile>
        <id>pi</id>
        <properties>
            <runtime.jvm.options>-Dmonocle.platform=EGL,
                -Dembedded=monocle,-Dglass.platform=Monocle,
    -Dmonocle.egl.lib=/opt/javafx-sdk-17/lib/libgluon_drm-1.1.6.so
            </runtime.jvm.options>
        </properties>
    </profile>
</profiles>

<build>
    <plugins>
        <plugin>
```

```
            <groupId>org.apache.maven.plugins</groupId>
            <artifactId>maven-compiler-plugin</artifactId>
            <version>3.8.1</version>
        </plugin>
        <plugin>
            <groupId>org.openjfx</groupId>
            <artifactId>javafx-maven-plugin</artifactId>
            <version>0.0.8</version>
            <configuration>
                <mainClass>${main.class}</mainClass>
                <options>${runtime.jvm.options}</options>
            </configuration>
        </plugin>
    </plugins>
  </build>

</project>
```

On desktop you can run it with

```
mvn javafx:run
```

while on your Raspberry Pi you can run with

```
mvn -Ppi -Djavafx.monocle=true javafx:run
```

Note that all the JavaFX dependencies are downloaded from Maven Central now, and we have to use -Djavafx.monocle=true to select those that include Monocle.

Running JavaFX Applications Remotely

While these projects are compiled and built locally on the Raspberry Pi, it is quite slower compared to building on your machine, and the lack of IDE or the inconveniences of development over SSH invite to look for a different approach: develop on your regular machine and then deploy and run on the Pi.

On the other hand, development on our machine is way faster, but then we still have the deployment issue: we'll need to copy the related files of our application to the Raspberry Pi, before we can run on it.

There are a few options to copy the required files, like the classic FTP or even SCP (a command for sending files over SSH). This means you can copy files between computers, either from your Raspberry Pi to your desktop or laptop or the other way around.

For instance, let's say we have Sample3: modernclientjava/mcj-samples/tree/ master/ch12-RaspberryPi/Sample3. We compile it and build it with Maven on our machine, and then we copy the resulting classes to the Raspberry Pi:

```
$ cd mcj-samples-master/ch12-RaspberryPi/Sample3
$ mvn clean compile
$ cd ..
$ scp -r Sample3 pi@raspberrypi.local:/home/pi/ModernClients/ch12-
RaspberryPi/Sample3
(add password)
```

Now, we can run from the SSH terminal:

```
$ cd /home/pi/ModernClients/ch12-RaspberryPi/Sample3/target
$ sudo -E java --module-path $PATH_TO_FX:classes -Dmonocle.platform=EGL \
    -Dembedded=monocle -Dmonocle.egl.lib=
        /opt/javafx-sdk-17/lib/libgluon_drm-1.1.6.so \
  -Dglass.platform=Monocle \
  -m hellofx/org.modernclients.raspberrypi.MainApp
```

While this works, it is a tedious error-prone manual process, and it would be better if we could have this step integrated within our IDE, or we could have a plugin for our build tool.

Let's examine some options.

Java Remote Platform

NetBeans created a while ago the concept of a remote platform. You can define the settings of a JVM on another machine and use an Ant task to deploy and run over SSH on that machine.

This comes very handy of course in the case of the Raspberry Pi.

To install Apache NetBeans 12.4, you can go to the link https://netbeans.apache. org/download/nb124/nb124.html and choose the installer for your platform.

Once installed, go to Tools ➤ Java Platforms. Click Add Platform… and select Remote Java Standard Edition.

Provide some details about the platform: name of the remote platform, (e.g. Pi 17); host (it can be raspberrypi.local); user, pi; password; and remote JRE path, /usr/lib/jvm/java-11-openjdk-arm64. See Figure 12-8.

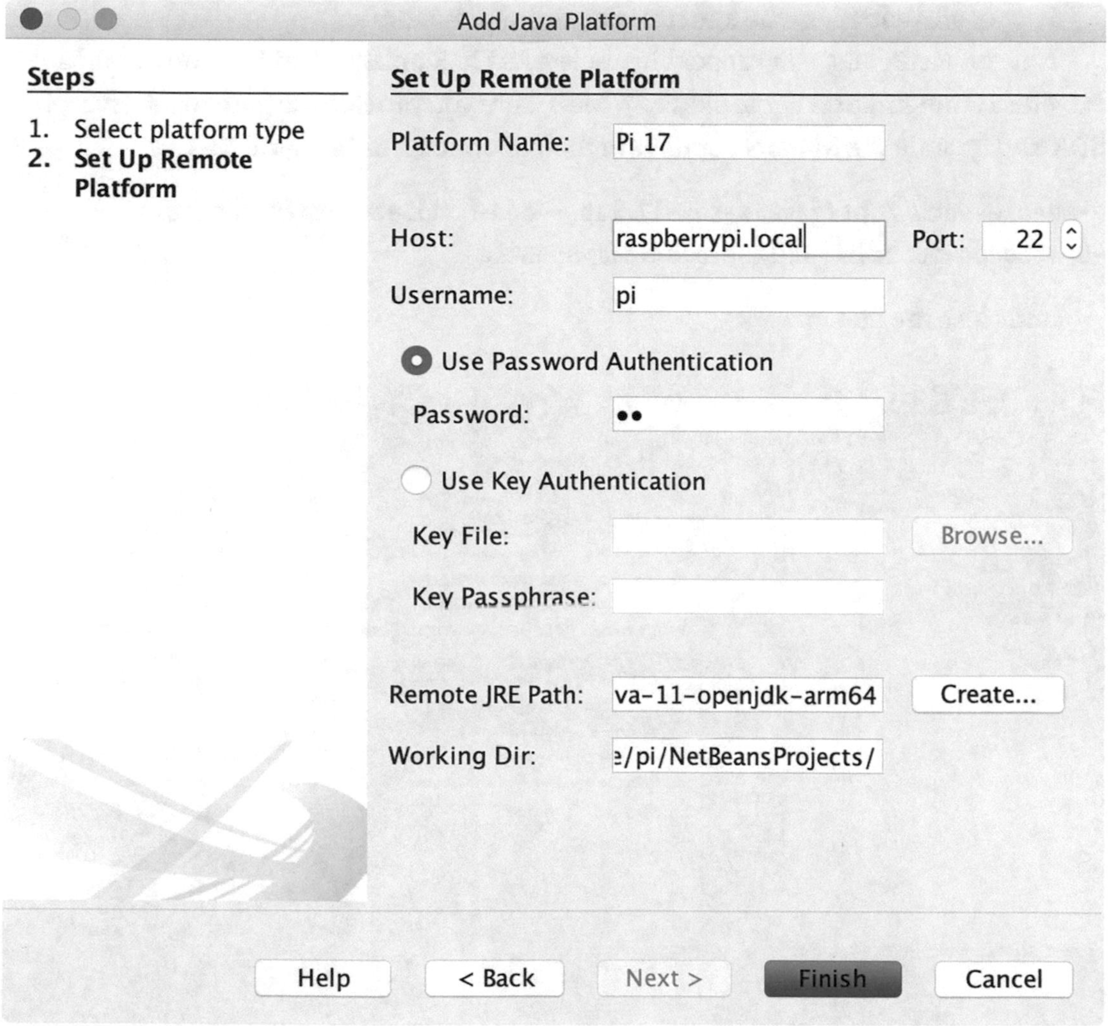

Figure 12-8. *Remote platform configuration*

When the remote platform has been created, make sure you add sudo to the exec prefix, as in Figure 12-9.

Finally, with the Raspberry Pi available, click Test Platform and see that the test is successful. Otherwise, make sure all the fields are correctly set.

Let's try the remote platform with an example. Follow the instructions here, `https://openjfx.io/openjfx-docs/#IDE-NetBeans`, to create a new Java application without build tools, or download Sample4 from the link `https://github.com/modernclientjava/mcj-samples/tree/master/ch12-RaspberryPi/Sample4`.

First of all, make sure the app runs fine on your machine.

Now on NetBeans, edit `Properties`, select Run ➤ `Runtime Platform`, and pick `Pi 17`. Provide a configuration name like `Pi17`. Make sure you provide the path to the JavaFX SDK and include the Monocle options in the VM options, as in Figure 12-10

```
--module-path /opt/javafx-sdk-17/lib --add-modules=javafx.controls
-Dembedded=monocle -Dglass.platform=Monocle
```

and close the dialog.

Figure 12-9. *Adding exec prefix to the remote platform*

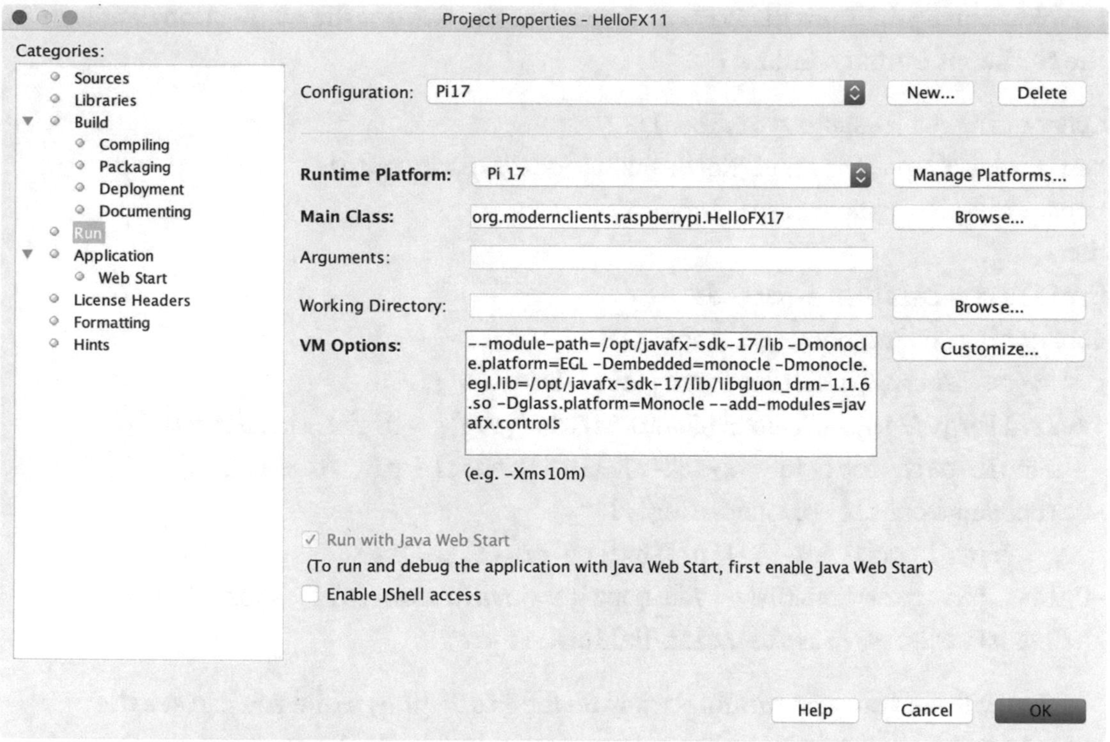

Figure 12-10. *Set project properties to run with a remote platform*

When running the same application on desktop or on the Raspberry Pi, it can be convenient to adapt its window size based on the platforms it is run on, as shown in Listing 12-5.

Listing 12-5. Configure window size based on platform

```
String platform = System.getProperty("glass.platform");
Rectangle2D bounds;
if ("Monocle".equals(platform)) {
    bounds = Screen.getPrimary().getBounds();
} else {
    bounds = new Rectangle2D(0, 0, 600, 400);
}
Scene scene = new Scene(
    new StackPane(label), bounds.getWidth(), bounds.getHeight());
```

497

Now run again, from the Pi17 configuration. You will see the connection details in the NetBeans output window:

```
Connecting to raspberrypi.local:22
cmd : mkdir -p '/home/pi/NetBeansProjects//Sample4/dist'
Connecting to raspberrypi.local:22
done.
profile-rp-calibrate-passwd:
Connecting to raspberrypi.local:22
cmd : cd '/home/pi/NetBeansProjects//Sample4';
'/usr/lib/jvm/java-11-openjdk-arm64/bin/java'  -Dfile.encoding=UTF-8
 --module-path=/opt/javafx-sdk-17/lib -Dmonocle.platform=EGL
-Dembedded=monocle -Dmonocle.egl.lib=
       /opt/javafx-sdk-17/lib/libgluon_drm-1.1.6.so
-Dglass.platform=Monocle --add-modules=javafx.controls  -jar /home/pi/
NetBeansProjects//Sample4/dist/HelloFX11.jar
```

You will see your app running nicely on the Pi's display, while you can see the output from the process in the NetBeans output window. And you can even debug the application.

However, this approach has a few problems: it only works on NetBeans, and it is not valid for Maven or Gradle projects.

Gradle SSH Plugin

Another option is the SSH Gradle plugin from `https://gradle-ssh-plugin.github.io`. It will work on Gradle projects from the terminal or any IDE with Gradle support.

Let's run now this sample, `https://github.com/modernclientjava/mcj-samples/tree/master/ch12-RaspberryPi/Sample5`, from IntelliJ (or any IDE of your choosing).

Edit the `build.gradle` file, and verify the required configuration: working dir, Java home, JavaFX path, and your remote configuration (host, user, and password), as in Listing 12-6.

Listing 12-6. Gradle build file for Sample5

```
plugins {
    id 'application'
    id 'org.openjfx.javafxplugin' version '0.0.10'
```

```
    id 'org.hidetake.ssh' version '2.10.1'
}
repositories {
    mavenCentral()
}
javafx {
    modules = [ 'javafx.controls', 'javafx.fxml' ]
}
mainClassName = "$moduleName/org.modernclients.raspberrypi.MainApp"
def workingDir = '/home/pi/ModernClients/ch12-RaspberryPi/'
def javaHome = '/usr'
def javafxHome = '/opt/javafx-sdk-17/lib'
task libs(type: Copy) {
    dependsOn 'jar'
    into "${buildDir}/libs/"
    from configurations.compileClasspath
}
remotes {
    pi17 {
        host = 'raspberrypi.local'
        user = 'pi'
        password = 'pi'
    }
}
task runRemoteEmbedded {
    dependsOn 'libs'
    ssh.settings {
        knownHosts = allowAnyHosts
    }
    doLast {
        ssh.run {
            session(remotes.pi17) {
                execute "mkdir -p ${workingDir}/${project.name}/dist"

                fileTree("${buildDir}/libs")
```

```
                    .filter { it.isFile() && ! it.name.
                    startsWith('javafx')}
                    .files
                    .each { put from:it,
               into: "${workingDir}/${project.name}/dist/${it.name}"}
            executeSudo "-E ${javaHome}/bin/java -Dfile.encoding=UTF-8
            " +
                    "--module-path=${javafxHome}/lib:
                    ${workingDir}/${project.name}/dist " +
                    "-Dmonocle.platform=EGL -Dembedded=monocle
                     -Dglass.platform=Monocle " +
                    "-Dmonocle.egl.lib=
                       ${javafxHome}/libgluon_drm-1.1.6.so " +
                       "-classpath '${workingDir}/${project.name}/
                       dist/*' " +
                    "-m ${project.mainClassName}"
            }
        }
    }
}
```

Note   For convenience, the task sets `allowAnyHosts`, and host key checking is turned off. It will print a warning message that the process is vulnerable to man-in-the-middle attacks and it is not recommended for production.

With this plugin, pressing Ctrl+C from the terminal just kills the Gradle process, but not the application. To solve this issue, make sure you add an "exit" button to the UI.

Run the `runRemoteEmbedded` task from your IDE Gradle's window, like in Figure 12-11, or run from a terminal:

```
$ ./gradlew runRemoteEmbedded
```

The app will be built, deployed to the Pi, and executed on it, and you will get the output from the process in your terminal, like in Figure 12-11.

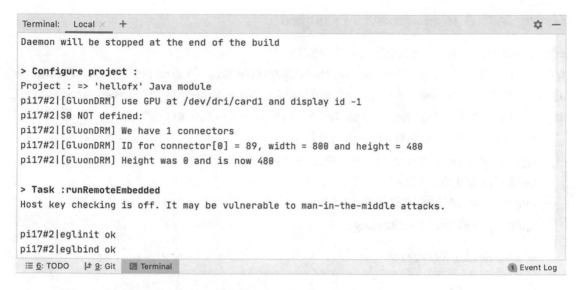

```
Terminal:    Local ×    +                                                          ⚙  —
Daemon will be stopped at the end of the build

> Configure project :
Project : => 'hellofx' Java module
pi17#2|[GluonDRM] use GPU at /dev/dri/card1 and display id -1
pi17#2|S0 NOT defined:
pi17#2|[GluonDRM] We have 1 connectors
pi17#2|[GluonDRM] ID for connector[0] = 89, width = 800 and height = 480
pi17#2|[GluonDRM] Height was 0 and is now 480

> Task :runRemoteEmbedded
Host key checking is off. It may be vulnerable to man-in-the-middle attacks.

pi17#2|eglinit ok
pi17#2|eglbind ok
 ≡ 6: TODO    ⌐ 9: Git    ▣ Terminal                                    ① Event Log
```

Figure 12-11. *Executing the runRemoteEmbedded task*

Creating JavaFX Native Images

You can create a native image of your JavaFX application and run it on the Raspberry Pi, with the only requirement that the AArch64 (64 bits) architecture is currently the only one supported.

Given the device's hardware limitation and the high CPU/memory requirements of the native image process, the recommended way to create the native image is cross-compiling from a desktop Linux machine (x86-64).

This machine should have GraalVM for Linux downloaded and installed from https://github.com/gluonhq/graal/releases/latest, including

```
$ export GRAALVM_HOME=/path/to/graalvm-svm-linux-gluon-21.2.0-dev
```

Then, for cross-compiling, you also need

```
$ sudo apt-get install g++-aarch64-linux-gnu
```

Listing 12-7 shows the pom file for Sample6 where the pi profile has been defined. It includes some properties that might change based on your setup.

Listing 12-7. Maven pom file for Sample6

```xml
<?xml version="1.0" encoding="UTF-8"?>
<project xmlns="http://maven.apache.org/POM/4.0.0" xmlns:xsi="http://www.
w3.org/2001/XMLSchema-instance" xsi:schemaLocation="http://maven.apache.
org/POM/4.0.0 http://maven.apache.org/xsd/maven-4.0.0.xsd">
    <modelVersion>4.0.0</modelVersion>
    <groupId>org.modernclients.raspberrypi</groupId>
    <artifactId>hellofx</artifactId>
    <version>1.0-SNAPSHOT</version>
    <packaging>jar</packaging>

    <name>HelloFX</name>

    <properties>
        <project.build.sourceEncoding>UTF-8</project.build.sourceEncoding>
        <maven.compiler.release>11</maven.compiler.release>
        <javafx.version>17-ea+14</javafx.version>
        <javafx.maven.plugin.version>0.0.6</javafx.maven.plugin.version>
        <gluonfx.maven.plugin.version>1.0.3</gluonfx.maven.plugin.version>
        <runtime.jvm.options/>
        <runtime.options/>
        <remote.host.name/>
        <remote.dir/>
        <main.class>org.modernclients.raspberrypi.HelloFX</main.class>
    </properties>

    <dependencies>
        <dependency>
            <groupId>org.openjfx</groupId>
            <artifactId>javafx-controls</artifactId>
            <version>${javafx.version}</version>
        </dependency>
    </dependencies>

    <build>
        <plugins>
            <plugin>
```

```xml
            <groupId>org.apache.maven.plugins</groupId>
            <artifactId>maven-compiler-plugin</artifactId>
            <version>3.8.1</version>
        </plugin>

        <plugin>
            <groupId>org.openjfx</groupId>
            <artifactId>javafx-maven-plugin</artifactId>
            <version>${javafx.maven.plugin.version}</version>
            <configuration>
                <mainClass>${main.class}</mainClass>
                <options>${runtime.jvm.options}</options>
            </configuration>
        </plugin>

        <plugin>
            <groupId>com.gluonhq</groupId>
            <artifactId>gluonfx-maven-plugin</artifactId>
            <version>${gluonfx.maven.plugin.version}</version>
            <configuration>
                <target>${gluonfx.target}</target>
                <mainClass>${main.class}</mainClass>
                <runtimeArgs>${runtime.options}</runtimeArgs>
                <remoteHostName>${remote.host.name}</remoteHostName>
                <remoteDir>${remote.dir}</remoteDir>
            </configuration>
        </plugin>
    </plugins>
</build>

<profiles>
    <profile>
        <id>pi</id>
        <properties>
            <gluonfx.target>linux-aarch64</gluonfx.target>
            <remote.host.name>pi@raspberrypi.local</remote.host.name>
            <remote.dir>/home/pi/ModernClients/
```

```
                        ch12-RaspberryPi/Sample6</remote.dir>
                <runtime.options>-Duse.fullscreen=true,
                    -Dmonocle.platform=EGL,-Dembedded=monocle,
                    -Dglass.platform=Monocle</runtime.options>
                <runtime.jvm.options>-Dmonocle.egl.lib=
                    /opt/javafx-sdk-17/lib/libgluon_drm-1.1.6.so,
                    ${runtime.options}</runtime.jvm.options>
            </properties>
        </profile>
    </profiles>

</project>
```

Get Sample6 on your Linux machine:

```
$ wget https://github.com/modernclientjava/
mcj-samples/archive/refs/heads/master.zip -O ~/Downloads/ModernClients.zip
$ unzip ~/Downloads/ModernClients.zip
$ cd ~/Downloads/mcj-samples-master/ch12-RaspberryPi/Sample6
```

The native image can be built now using

```
$ mvn -Ppi gluonfx:build
```

This will run the compilation phase and link the compiled objects into an executable. After some minutes, once the process is finished, you can deploy the binary to your Pi, providing you have correctly defined remoteHostName and remoteDir in the pom:

```
$ mvn -Ppi gluonfx:install
```

Finally, you can run from your machine, via SSH, using

```
$ mvn -Ppi gluonfx:nativerun
```

Press Ctrl+C to finalize the application.

Alternatively, you can also run the native image directly on your Pi from the command line with

```
$ cd /home/pi/ModernClients/ch12-RaspberryPi/Sample6
$ sudo -E ./HelloFX -Dmonocle.platform=EGL \
-Dembedded=monocle -Dglass.platform=Monocle
```

Working with Dependencies

So far, we have seen very simple use cases that were helpful to getting us started and setting everything properly.

Time now to have a look at a more complex example.

The DIY In-Car Navigation System

The following project is a Proof of Concept of a Do It Yourself homemade in-car navigation system. For that, we are going to install a GPS to the Raspberry Pi. A JavaFX application will display a map, and the GPS readings will be used to center the map in our current location.

Bill of Materials

Raspberry Pi 4 Model B

7″ display 800 × 480; cage is optional but recommended.

5 V power adaptors for Raspberry Pi and display. Power bank is optional but recommended for field testing.

GPS: Universal Asynchronous Receiver-Transmitter (UART) Serial GPS Neo-7M (micro-USB is optional) (Figure 12-12), for instance, this one: `http://wiki.keyestudio.com/index.php/KS0319_keyestudio_GPS_Module`.

Four female-female jumper wires for GPIO connection.

Micro-USB: USB adaptor (in case the GPS breakout mounts micro-USB) is optional.

Antenna for the GPS is optional (but when used, the capacitor C2 has to be removed).

Figure 12-12. *UART Serial GPS Neo-7M. Image from* `http://wiki.keyestudio.`
`com/File:KSO319.png`

Setup for GPIO

We are going to use the General-Purpose Input/Output (GPIO) pins to get serial readings
from the GPS.

The Raspberry Pi serial port consists of two signals, a *transmit* signal (TxD) and a
receive signal (RxD), that are available at pins 8 and 10 on the 4 Model B (equivalent to
WiringPi numbers #15 and #16 from Figure 12-13, in that order).

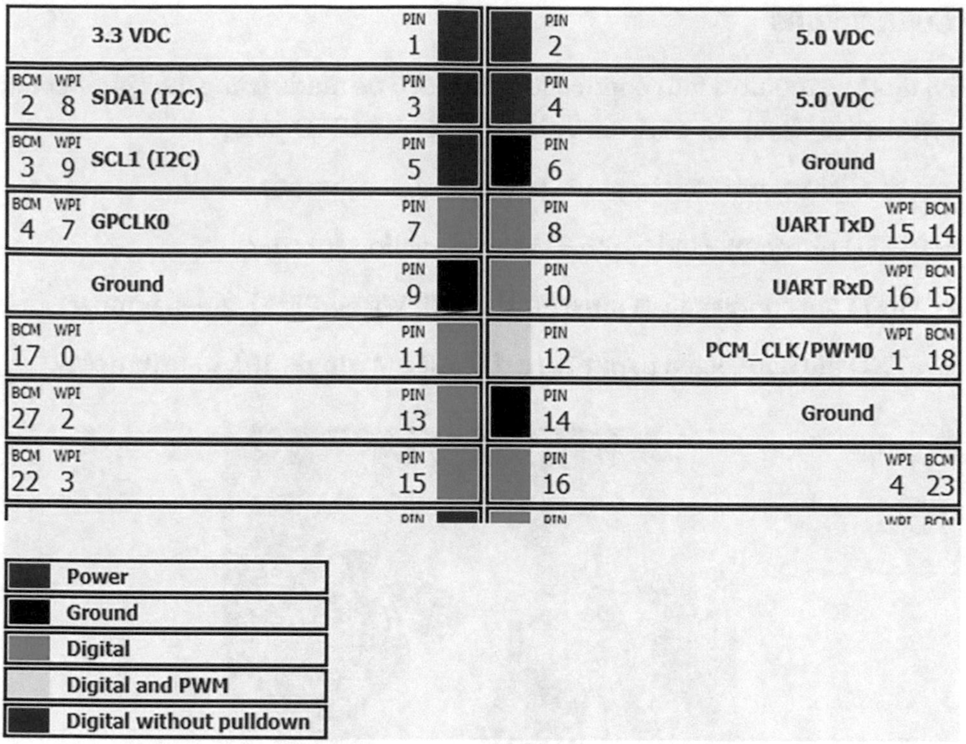

			PIN 1	■	■	PIN 2		5.0 VDC		
		3.3 VDC								

BCM 2	WPI 8	SDA1 (I2C)	PIN 3	■	■	PIN 4	5.0 VDC		

BCM 3	WPI 9	SCL1 (I2C)	PIN 5	■	■	PIN 6	Ground		

BCM 4	WPI 7	GPCLK0	PIN 7	■	■	PIN 8	UART TxD	WPI 15	BCM 14

	Ground		PIN 9	■	■	PIN 10	UART RxD	WPI 16	BCM 15

BCM 17	WPI 0		PIN 11	■	■	PIN 12	PCM_CLK/PWM0	WPI 1	BCM 18

BCM 27	WPI 2		PIN 13	■	■	PIN 14	Ground		

BCM 22	WPI 3		PIN 15	■	■	PIN 16		WPI 4	BCM 23
			PIN	■	■	PIN		WPI	BCM

■	Power
■	Ground
■	Digital
■	Digital and PWM
■	Digital without pulldown

Figure 12-13. *Raspberry Pi 4 Model B GPIO pinout. Image from* `https://pi4j.com/assets/documentation/headerpins_in_header.png`

By default, the serial port on the Raspberry Pi is configured as a console port for communicating with the Linux OS shell. In order to access the serial port from a software program, we have to configure it. Open an SSH session, and run

```
$ sudo raspi-config
```

Select Interface Options and now select Serial Port.

Now you have to select No to disable the login shell access to serial and then select Yes to enable the hardware serial port (or UART for Universal Asynchronous Receiver-Transmitter). Accept and reboot your Raspberry Pi.

GPIO Connections

The GPS module requires four connections that can be made using four jumper female-female wires; see Figure 12-14, from right to left of the GPIO pins:

- VCC pin connected to pin 2 (power 5 V), red jumper

- GND pin connected to pin 6 (ground), yellow jumper

- RXD pin connected to pin 8 (TxD UART, WiringPi 15), green jumper

- TXD pin connected to pin 10 (RxD UART, WiringPi 16), blue jumper

Figure 12-14. *GPS and Raspberry Pi 4 Model B GPIO connection*

Note that a breakout board and pin ribbon cable can be used instead, extending the GPIO pins to a breadboard, where the connection to the GPS can be done more easily.

Required GPS Software

We need to install the following software from a terminal

```
$ sudo apt-get install gpsd gpsd-clients
```

where gpsd is the interface daemon for GPS receivers. When finished, if the GPS is already attached, you can start reading it from the lowest-numbered serial port with

```
$ gpsd /dev/ttyS0
```

or in case you have connected the USB instead with

```
gpsd /dev/ttyUSB0
```

The best option to launch the gpsd is with this service:

```
$ sudo service gpsd start
```

Once the service has started, you can verify its status with

```
$ sudo systemctl status gpsd.socket
```

that will display something like that shown in Figure 12-15.

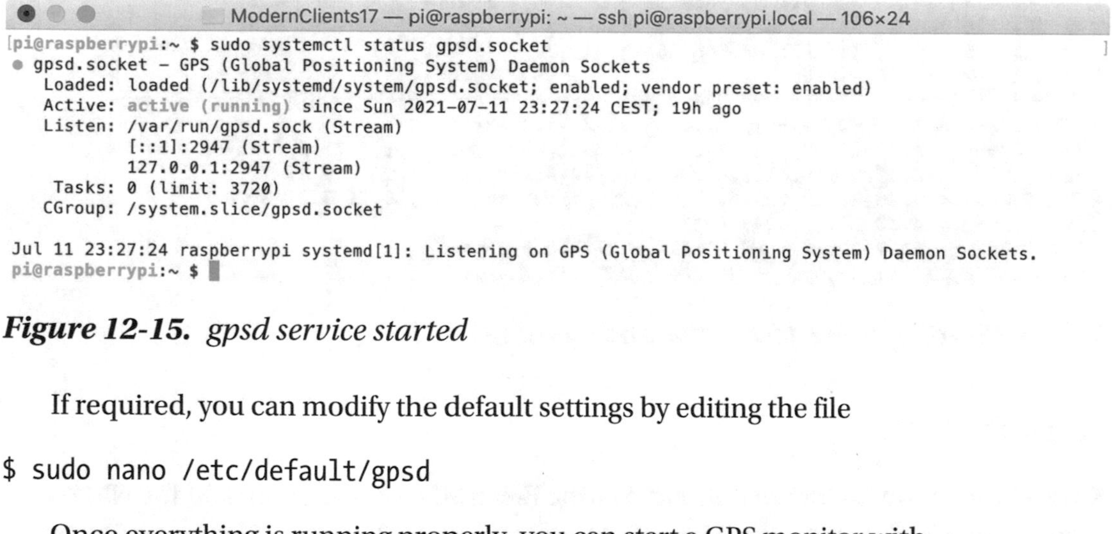

```
● ● ●                ModernClients17 — pi@raspberrypi: ~ — ssh pi@raspberrypi.local — 106×24
[pi@raspberrypi:~ $ sudo systemctl status gpsd.socket                                                  ]
● gpsd.socket – GPS (Global Positioning System) Daemon Sockets
   Loaded: loaded (/lib/systemd/system/gpsd.socket; enabled; vendor preset: enabled)
   Active: active (running) since Sun 2021-07-11 23:27:24 CEST; 19h ago
   Listen: /var/run/gpsd.sock (Stream)
           [::1]:2947 (Stream)
           127.0.0.1:2947 (Stream)
    Tasks: 0 (limit: 3720)
   CGroup: /system.slice/gpsd.socket

Jul 11 23:27:24 raspberrypi systemd[1]: Listening on GPS (Global Positioning System) Daemon Sockets.
pi@raspberrypi:~ $ ▮
```

Figure 12-15. *gpsd service started*

If required, you can modify the default settings by editing the file

```
$ sudo nano /etc/default/gpsd
```

Once everything is running properly, you can start a GPS monitor with

```
$ cgps /dev/ttyS0
```

or with

```
$ gpsmon /dev/ttyS0
```

If you are indoors, it is probable that the GPS won't be able to connect to any satellite and you won't receive any value. But you will still get some readings.

If you take your Raspberry Pi outdoors, as long as the Wi-Fi connection holds, you can still be connected through SSH to your machine and visualize these readings and get something like that shown in Figure 12-16.

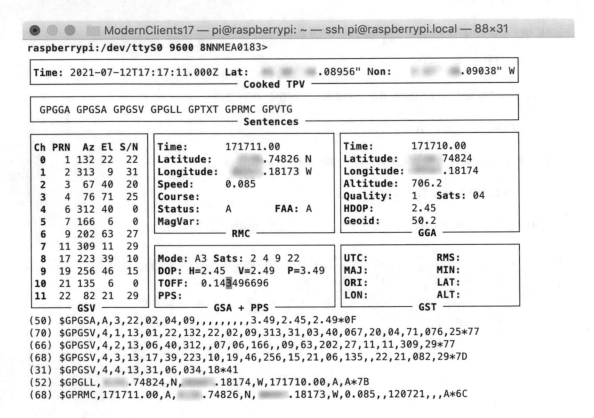

Figure 12-16. gpsd service active and running

NMEA Readings

NMEA is an acronym for the National Marine Electronics Association, and the NMEA 0183 is a standard data format supported by all GPS manufacturers that uses an ASCII serial communication protocol. There are different message types or *sentences*, and all of them start with a header $GP and a code for the sentence like GLL that stands for geographic position, latitude, longitude, ending with * and a checksum. A possible message will look like

```
$GPGLL,5139.69658,N,00947.18207,W,200557.00,A,A*72
```

To find out about all the possible sentences and how to parse them, you can see this link: http://aprs.gids.nl/nmea/.

Listing 12-8 shows the model class we are going to use in our application to keep track of a few of the variables coming from the GPS, like latitude, longitude, altitude, or number of satellites, and Listing 12-9 shows a possible parser of the most significant NMEA messages like GPRMC or GPGGA.

Listing 12-8. GPSPosition class

```
package org.modernclients.raspberrypi.gps.model;
import javafx.beans.property.*;
public class GPSPosition {
    // time
    private final FloatProperty time = new SimpleFloatProperty(this, "time");
    public final FloatProperty timeProperty() { return time; }
    // getter & setter
    // latitude
    private final FloatProperty latitude = new SimpleFloatProperty(this,
        "latitude");
    public final FloatProperty latitudeProperty() { return latitude; }
    // getter & setter
    // longitude
    private final FloatProperty longitude = new SimpleFloatProperty(this,
        "longitude");
    public final FloatProperty longitudeProperty() { return longitude; }
    // getter & setter
    // direction
    private final FloatProperty direction = new SimpleFloatProperty(this,
        "direction");
    public final FloatProperty directionProperty() { return direction; }
    // getter & setter
    // altitude
    private final FloatProperty altitude = new SimpleFloatProperty(this,
        "altitude");
    public final FloatProperty altitudeProperty() { return altitude; }
    // getter & setter
```

```
// velocity
private final FloatProperty velocity = new SimpleFloatProperty(this,
    "velocity");
public final FloatProperty velocityProperty() { return velocity; }
// getter & setter
// satellites
private final IntegerProperty satellites = new
SimpleIntegerProperty(this,
    "satellites");
public final IntegerProperty satellitesProperty() { return satellites; }
// getter & setter
// quality
private final IntegerProperty quality = new SimpleIntegerProperty(this,
    "quality");
public final IntegerProperty qualityProperty() { return quality; }
// getter & setter
// fixed
private final BooleanProperty fixed = new SimpleBooleanProperty(this,
    "fixed");
public final BooleanProperty fixedProperty() { return fixed; }
// getter & setter
public void updatefix() {
    fixed.set(quality.get() > 0);
}
@Override
public String toString() {
    return "GPSPosition{" +
            "time=" + time.get() +
            ", latitude=" + latitude.get() +
            ", longitude=" + longitude.get() +
            ", direction=" + direction.get() +
            ", altitude=" + altitude.get() +
            ", velocity=" + velocity.get() +
            ", quality=" + quality.get() +
            ", satellites =" + satellites.get() +
```

```
                ", fixed=" + fixed.get() +
                '}';
    }
}
```

Listing 12-9. NMEAParser class

```
package org.modernclients.raspberrypi.gps.service;
import javafx.beans.property.FloatProperty;
import javafx.beans.property.Property;
import org.modernclients.raspberrypi.gps.model.GPSPosition;
import java.util.HashMap;
import java.util.Map;
import java.util.concurrent.atomic.AtomicInteger;
import java.util.function.BiFunction;
import java.util.function.Function;
import java.util.function.UnaryOperator;
import java.util.logging.Logger;
public class NMEAParser {
    private static final Logger logger =
        Logger.getLogger(NMEAParser.class.getName());
    interface SentenceParser {
        boolean parse(String [] tokens, GPSPosition position);
    }
    private static final Map<String, SentenceParser> sentenceParsers =
        new HashMap<>();
    private final GPSPosition position;
    public NMEAParser(GPSPosition position) {
        this.position = position;
        sentenceParsers.put("GPGGA", new GPGGA());
        sentenceParsers.put("GPGGL", new GPGGL());
        sentenceParsers.put("GPRMC", new GPRMC());
        sentenceParsers.put("GPRMZ", new GPRMZ());
        sentenceParsers.put("GPVTG", new GPVTG());
    }
```

```java
    public GPSPosition parse(final String line) {
        if (line.startsWith("$") && checksum(line)) {
            String[] tokens = line.substring(1).split(",");
            String type = tokens[0];
            if (sentenceParsers.containsKey(type)) {
                sentenceParsers.get(type).parse(tokens, position);
            }
            position.updatefix();
        }
        return position;
    }
    // parsers
    class GPGGA implements SentenceParser {
        @Override
        public boolean parse(String [] tokens, GPSPosition position) {
            parseCoordinate(tokens[2], tokens[3], "S",
                position.latitudeProperty());
            parseCoordinate(tokens[4], tokens[5], "W",
                position.longitudeProperty());
            doParse(tokens[1], Float::parseFloat, position.timeProperty());
            doParse(tokens[6], Integer::parseInt, position.
            qualityProperty());
            doParse(tokens[7], Integer::parseInt, position.
            satellitesProperty());
            return doParse(tokens[9], Float::parseFloat,
                position.altitudeProperty());
        }
    }
    class GPGGL implements SentenceParser {
        @Override
        public boolean parse(String [] tokens, GPSPosition position) {
            parseCoordinate(tokens[1], tokens[2], "S",
                position.latitudeProperty());
            parseCoordinate(tokens[3], tokens[4], "W",
                position.longitudeProperty());
```

```java
            return doParse(tokens[5], Float::parseFloat, position.
            timeProperty());
        }
    }
    class GPRMC implements SentenceParser {
        @Override
        public boolean parse(String [] tokens, GPSPosition position) {
            doParse(tokens[1], Float::parseFloat, position.timeProperty());
            parseCoordinate(tokens[3], tokens[4], "S",
                position.latitudeProperty());
            parseCoordinate(tokens[5], tokens[6], "W",
                position.longitudeProperty());
            doParse(tokens[7], Float::parseFloat, position.
            velocityProperty());
            return doParse(tokens[8], Float::parseFloat,
                position.directionProperty());
        }
    }
    class GPVTG implements SentenceParser {
        @Override
        public boolean parse(String [] tokens, GPSPosition position) {
            return doParse(tokens[3], Float::parseFloat,
                position.directionProperty());
        }
    }
    class GPRMZ implements SentenceParser {
        @Override
        public boolean parse(String [] tokens, GPSPosition position) {
            return doParse(tokens[1], Float::parseFloat,
                position.altitudeProperty());
        }
    }
    private boolean parseCoordinate(String token, String direction, String
        defaultDirection, FloatProperty property) {
        if (token == null || token.isEmpty() || direction == null ||
```

```
                direction.isEmpty()) {
            return false;
        }
        int minutesPosition = token.indexOf('.') - 2;
        if (minutesPosition < 0) {
            return false;
        }
        float minutes = Float.parseFloat(token.substring(minutesPosition));
        float decimalDegrees = Float.parseFloat(token.
        substring(minutesPosition))
            / 60.0f;
        float degree = Float.parseFloat(token) - minutes;
        float wholeDegrees = (int) degree / 100;
        float coordinateDegrees = wholeDegrees + decimalDegrees;
        if (direction.startsWith(defaultDirection)) {
            coordinateDegrees = -coordinateDegrees;
        }
        property.setValue(coordinateDegrees);
        return true;
    }
    private <T> boolean doParse(String token, Function<String, T> operator,
        Property<T> property) {
        if (token == null || token.isEmpty()) {
            return false;
        }
        try {
            property.setValue(operator.apply(token));
            return true;
        } catch (NumberFormatException nfe) { }
        return false;
    }
    private static boolean checksum(String line) {
        if (line == null || ! line.contains("$") || ! line.contains("*")) {
            return false;
        }
```

```java
        String sentence = line.substring(1, line.lastIndexOf("*"));
        String lineChecksum = "0x" + line.substring(line.lastIndexOf("*") + 1);
        int c = 0;
        for (char s : sentence.toCharArray()) {
            c ^= s;
        }
        String hex = String.format("0x%02X", c);
        boolean result = hex.equals(lineChecksum);
        if (! result) {
            logger.warning("There was an error in the checksum of " + line);
        }
        return result;
    }
}
```

GPIO and Java

Pi4J

Pi4J is a Java library that can be used to access the GPIO pins of the Raspberry Pi. As you can read at http://pi4j.com/

> *This project is intended to provide a friendly object-oriented I/O API and implementation libraries for Java Programmers to access the full I/O capabilities of the Raspberry Pi platform. This project abstracts the low-level native integration and interrupt monitoring to enable Java programmers to focus on implementing their application business logic.*

We are going to use its latest stable version available, 1.4, so we'll simply need to include the dependency in our build:

```gradle
dependencies {
    implementation 'com.pi4j:pi4j-core:1.4'
}
```

With Pi4J, creating a Serial object is as easy as

```java
Serial serial = SerialFactory.createInstance();
```

Then we can add a listener to it so we can react to any incoming serial events, and we can configure the serial based on the usual settings.

Note that the library only works on the Raspberry Pi, but it can be used and compiled on your machine.

WiringPi

Before using Pi4J, there is a native dependency that has to be available on the Raspberry Pi: WiringPi.

While Raspberry Pi 3 models had it built-in, on a Model 4 B you need to perform the following steps to install the latest (unofficial) version:

```
sudo apt-get remove wiringpi -y
sudo apt-get --yes install git-core gcc make
cd ~/Downloads
git clone https://github.com/WiringPi/WiringPi --branch master
    --single-branch wiringpi
sudo ~/buildings/wiringpi/build
```

GPS Service

Listing 12-10 shows the service class that opens the serial port and starts listening to the serial events, extracting one by one all the sentences received from the gpsd process.

Listing 12-10. GPSService class

```
package org.modernclients.raspberrypi.gps.service;
import com.pi4j.io.gpio.GpioController;
import com.pi4j.io.gpio.GpioFactory;
import com.pi4j.io.serial.*;
import javafx.application.Platform;
import javafx.beans.property.SimpleStringProperty;
import javafx.beans.property.StringProperty;
import org.modernclients.raspberrypi.gps.model.GPSPosition;
import javax.annotation.PostConstruct;
import javax.inject.Inject;
```

```java
import java.io.IOException;
import java.nio.charset.Charset;
import java.util.logging.Logger;
public class GPSService {
    private static final Logger logger =
        Logger.getLogger(GPSService.class.getName());
    @Inject
    private GPSPosition gpsPosition;
    private Serial serial;
    private GpioController gpio;
    private NMEAParser nmea;
    private StringBuilder gpsOutput;
    private final StringProperty line = new SimpleStringProperty();
    @PostConstruct
    private void postConstruct() {
        if (!"monocle".equals(System.getProperty("embedded"))) {
            return;
        }
        nmea = new NMEAParser(gpsPosition);
        gpsOutput = new StringBuilder();
        gpio = GpioFactory.getInstance();
        serial = SerialFactory.createInstance();
        serial.addListener(event -> {
            try {
                String s = event.getString(Charset.defaultCharset())
                        .replaceAll("\n", "")
                        .replaceAll("\r", "");
                gpsOutput.append(s);
                processReading();
            } catch (IOException e) {
                logger.warning("Error processing event " + event);
                e.printStackTrace();
            }
        });
```

```
        SerialConfig config = new SerialConfig();
        try {
            String defaultPort = SerialPort.getDefaultPort();
            logger.info("Connecting to default port = " + defaultPort);
            config.device(defaultPort)
                    .baud(Baud._9600)
                    .dataBits(DataBits._8)
                    .parity(Parity.NONE)
                    .stopBits(StopBits._1)
                    .flowControl(FlowControl.NONE);
            serial.open(config);
            logger.info("Connected: " + serial.isOpen());
        } catch (IOException | InterruptedException e) {
            e.printStackTrace();
        }
    }
    private void processReading() {
        if (gpsOutput == null || gpsOutput.toString().isEmpty()) {
            return;
        }
        String reading = gpsOutput.toString().trim();
        if (!reading.contains("$")) {
            return;
        }
        String[] split = reading.split("\\$");
        for (int i = 0; i < split.length - 1; i++) {
            String line = "$" + split[i];
            gpsOutput.delete(0 , line.length());
            if (line.length() > 1) {
                logger.fine("GPS: " + line);
                Platform.runLater(() -> {
                    nmea.parse(line);
                    this.line.set(line);
                });
            }
```

```
            if (i == split.length - 2) {
                gpsOutput.insert(0, "$");
            }
        }
    }
    public final StringProperty lineProperty() {
        return line;
    }
    public void stop() {
        logger.info("Stopping Serial and GPIO");
        if (serial != null) {
            try {
                serial.close();
            } catch (IOException e) {
                e.printStackTrace();
            }
        }
        if (gpio != null) {
            gpio.shutdown();
        }
    }
}
```

While reading from a serial port, we have to be aware that we have a continuous flow of bytes, so we have to take care of converting them properly to string and taking out each sentence. That's what the processReading method does, with the help of a single StringBuilder.

Also, notice that this thread runs in the background, so whenever there is a new sentence, we'll use Platform::runLater to use it with the JavaFX properties, on the JavaFX Application Thread.

For every sentence, we'll call the NMEA parser and update the GPSPosition object with the new values.

The UI

Let's define now the JavaFX interface: we are going to display a map that will be centered into the latitude and longitude coordinates retrieved from the GPS reading.

Gluon Maps

Gluon Maps (`https://gluonhq.com/labs/maps/`) is an open source JavaFX 11+ library that provides a map viewer component, rendering tile-based maps from OpenStreetMap. The project is available here: `https://github.com/gluonhq/maps`.

We can add a `MapView` container to the center of our view and use a `MapLayer` to render our position. On mobile devices with a built-in GPS sensor, we could use the Gluon Attach position service, but on the Raspberry Pi (or any desktop machine with a connected GPS sensor), we can use the `GPSService` listed in the preceding text.

To add the map, we need the following dependencies:

```
repositories {
    mavenCentral()
    maven {
        url 'https://nexus.gluonhq.com/nexus/content/repositories/releases/'
    }
}
dependencies {
    implementation 'com.gluonhq:maps:2.0.0-ea+4'
    implementation 'com.gluonhq.attach:storage:4.0.11:desktop'
    implementation 'com.gluonhq.attach:util:4.0.11'
}
```

For convenience, we will define a `PoiLayer` that can place JavaFX nodes on top of the base map that will be our Points of Interest, based on latitude and longitude (Listing 12-11).

Listing 12-11. PoiLayer class

```
package org.modernclients.raspberrypi.gps.view;
import com.gluonhq.maps.MapLayer;
import com.gluonhq.maps.MapPoint;
import javafx.collections.FXCollections;
import javafx.collections.ObservableList;
import javafx.geometry.Point2D;
import javafx.scene.Node;
import javafx.util.Pair;
```

```java
public class PoiLayer extends MapLayer {
    private final ObservableList<Pair<MapPoint, Node>> points;
    public PoiLayer() {
        points = FXCollections.observableArrayList();
    }
    public void addPoint(MapPoint p, Node icon) {
        points.add(new Pair(p, icon));
        this.getChildren().add(icon);
        this.markDirty();
    }
    @Override
    protected void layoutLayer() {
        for (Pair<MapPoint, Node> candidate : points) {
            MapPoint point = candidate.getKey();
            Node icon = candidate.getValue();
            Point2D mapPoint = getMapPoint(point.getLatitude(),
                point.getLongitude());
            icon.setVisible(true);
            icon.setTranslateX(mapPoint.getX());
            icon.setTranslateY(mapPoint.getY());
        }
    }
}
```

Afterburner

Afterburner is a convenient minimalistic MVP framework based on Convention over Configuration and Dependency Injection from Adam Bien that can be found at this link: https://github.com/AdamBien/afterburner.fx. To use it we need

```
repositories {
    mavenCentral()
}
dependencies {
    implementation 'com.airhacks:afterburner.fx:1.7.0'
    implementation 'javax.annotation:javax.annotation-api:1.3.2'
}
```

Scene Builder

Finally, we'll use Scene Builder 16.0 from https://gluonhq.com/products/scene-builder/ to design the UI with FXML on our machine.

It is convenient to import Gluon Maps into the Scene Builder custom controls library (Figure 12-17).

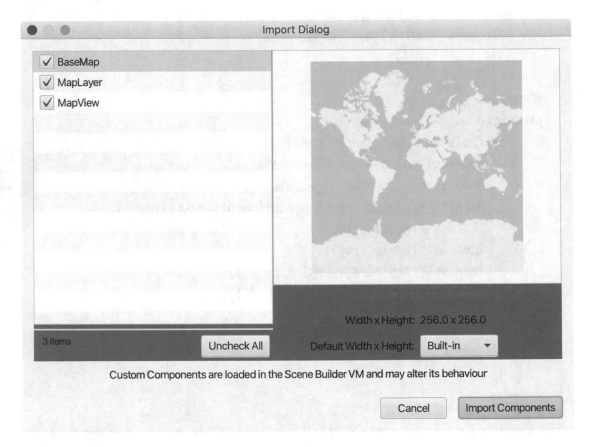

Figure 12-17. *Importing Gluon Maps into Scene Builder*

Then we can create a new FXML file, with a top BorderPane container, and drag and drop the required components: a toolbar on top, the MapView on the center, a VBox with labels on the right to display the current GPSPosition values, and a ListView to display the NMEA sentences at the bottom (Figure 12-18).

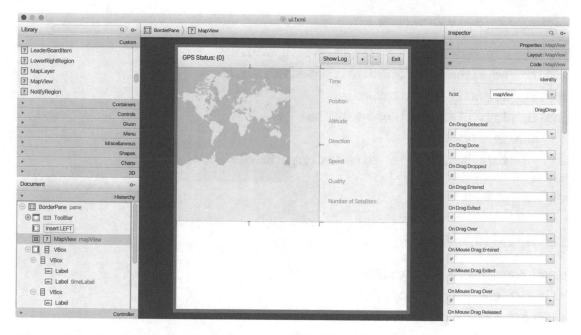

Figure 12-18. *Designing the UI in Scene Builder*

Note that with Afterburner, we will create the following files:
Java classes:

- `org.modernclients.raspberrypi.gps.view.UIView` (Listing 12-12)
  that extends from FXMLView, a convenient container that takes care
  of loading the FXML, CSS, or properties files by convention

- `org.modernclients.raspberrypi.gps.view.UIPresenter`
  (Listing 12-16)

Resource files:

- org.modernclients.raspberrypi.gps.view.ui.fxml (Listing 12-13)

- org.modernclients.raspberrypi.gps.view.ui.css (Listing 12-14)

- org.modernclients.raspberrypi.gps.view.ui.properties (Listing 12-15)

Listing 12-12. UIView class

```
package org.modernclients.raspberrypi.gps.view;
import com.airhacks.afterburner.views.FXMLView;
import java.util.ResourceBundle;
public class UIView extends FXMLView {
    public UIView() {
        this.bundle = ResourceBundle.getBundle(bundleName);
    }
}
```

Listing 12-13. ui.fxml file

```
<?xml version="1.0" encoding="UTF-8"?>
<?import com.gluonhq.maps.MapView?>
<?import javafx.geometry.Insets?>
<?import javafx.scene.control.Button?>
<?import javafx.scene.control.Label?>
<?import javafx.scene.control.ListView?>
<?import javafx.scene.control.Separator?>
<?import javafx.scene.control.ToggleButton?>
<?import javafx.scene.control.ToolBar?>
<?import javafx.scene.layout.BorderPane?>
<?import javafx.scene.layout.Pane?>
<?import javafx.scene.layout.VBox?>
<BorderPane fx:id="pane" xmlns="http://javafx.com/javafx/11.0.1"
xmlns:fx="http://javafx.com/fxml/1" fx:controller="org.modernclients.
raspberrypi.gps.view.UIPresenter">
    <bottom>
        <ListView fx:id="listView" maxHeight="200.0" BorderPane.
        alignment="CENTER" />
    </bottom>
    <right>
        <VBox prefHeight="250.0" prefWidth="200.0" styleClass="box"
            BorderPane.alignment="CENTER">
            <children>
                <VBox>
```

```
    <children>
       <Label styleClass="gps" text="%label.time" />
       <Label fx:id="timeLabel" styleClass="gps-data" />
    </children>
</VBox>
<VBox>
    <children>
       <Label styleClass="gps" text="%label.position" />
       <Label fx:id="positionLabel" styleClass="gps-data" />
    </children>
</VBox>
<VBox>
    <children>
       <Label styleClass="gps" text="%label.altitude" />
       <Label fx:id="altitudeLabel" styleClass="gps-data" />
    </children>
</VBox>
<VBox>
    <children>
       <Label styleClass="gps" text="%label.direction" />
       <Label fx:id="directionLabel" styleClass="gps-data" />
    </children>
</VBox>
<VBox layoutX="10.0" layoutY="112.0">
    <children>
       <Label styleClass="gps" text="%label.speed" />
       <Label fx:id="speedLabel" styleClass="gps-data" />
    </children>
</VBox>
<VBox layoutX="10.0" layoutY="146.0">
    <children>
       <Label styleClass="gps" text="%label.quality" />
       <Label fx:id="qualityLabel" styleClass="gps-data" />
    </children>
</VBox>
```

```
            <VBox layoutX="10.0" layoutY="146.0">
                <children>
                    <Label styleClass="gps" text="%label.satellites" />
                    <Label fx:id="satellitesLabel" styleClass="gps-data" />
                </children>
            </VBox>
        </children>
    </VBox>
</right>
<top>
    <ToolBar BorderPane.alignment="CENTER">
        <items>
            <Label fx:id="statusLabel" styleClass="gps-data" text="%label.
            gps" />
            <Pane maxWidth="1.7976931348623157E308" prefWidth="200.0" />
            <Separator orientation="VERTICAL" />
            <ToggleButton fx:id="showLog"
                mnemonicParsing="false" text="%button.show.log" />
            <Separator layoutX="324.0" layoutY="10.0"
            orientation="VERTICAL" />
            <Button mnemonicParsing="false"
                onAction="#onZoomIn" text="%button.zoom.in" />
            <Button layoutX="10.0" layoutY="10.0" mnemonicParsing="false"
                onAction="#onZoomOut" text="%button.zoom.out" />
            <Separator layoutX="440.0" layoutY="10.0"
            orientation="VERTICAL" />
            <Button layoutX="20.0" layoutY="20.0"
                mnemonicParsing="false" onAction="#onExit"
                text="%button.exit" />
        </items>
        <padding>
            <Insets bottom="10.0" left="10.0" right="10.0" top="10.0" />
        </padding>
    </ToolBar>
</top>
<center>
```

```
        <MapView fx:id="mapView" BorderPane.alignment="CENTER" />
    </center>
</BorderPane>
```

Listing 12-14. ui.css file

```css
.box {
    -fx-padding: 20;
    -fx-spacing: 10;
    -fx-border-color: darkgray;
    -fx-border-width: 0 0 0 1;
}
.label.gps-data {
    -fx-text-fill: blue;
    -fx-font-size: 1.1em;
}
.label.gps {
    -fx-text-fill: darkgray;
    -fx-font-size: 1.0em;
}
```

Listing 12-15. ui.properties file

```
button.show.log=Show Log
button.zoom.in=+
button.zoom.out=-
button.exit=Exit
label.time=Time
label.position=Position
label.altitude=Altitude
label.direction=Direction
label.speed=Speed
label.quality=Quality
label.satellites=Number of Satellites
label.gps=GPS Status: {0}
label.gps.fixed=fixed
label.gps.not-fixed=not fixed
```

Once we have all these files, it is time to add now the presenter (Listing 12-16).

Listing 12-16. UIPresenter class

```
package org.modernclients.raspberrypi.gps.view;
import com.gluonhq.maps.MapPoint;
import com.gluonhq.maps.MapView;
import javafx.application.Platform;
import javafx.beans.binding.Bindings;
import javafx.fxml.FXML;
import javafx.scene.control.Label;
import javafx.scene.control.ListView;
import javafx.scene.control.ToggleButton;
import javafx.scene.layout.BorderPane;
import javafx.scene.paint.Color;
import javafx.scene.shape.Circle;
import org.modernclients.raspberrypi.gps.model.GPSPosition;
import org.modernclients.raspberrypi.gps.service.GPSService;
import javax.inject.Inject;
import java.text.MessageFormat;
import java.util.ResourceBundle;
import java.util.logging.Logger;

public class UIPresenter {
private static final Logger logger =
    Logger.getLogger(UIPresenter.class.getName());
    @FXML private BorderPane pane;
    @FXML private Label statusLabel;
    @FXML private MapView mapView;
    @FXML private ListView<String> listView;
    @FXML private Label timeLabel;
    @FXML private Label positionLabel;
    @FXML private Label altitudeLabel;
    @FXML private Label directionLabel;
    @FXML private Label speedLabel;
    @FXML private Label qualityLabel;
```

```java
@FXML private Label satellitesLabel;
@FXML private ToggleButton showLog;
@FXML private ResourceBundle resources;
@Inject private GPSService service;
@Inject private GPSPosition gpsPosition;
private MapPoint mapPoint;
public void initialize() {
    logger.info("Platform: " + System.getProperty("embedded"));
    mapView = new MapView();
    mapPoint = new MapPoint(50.0d, 4.0d);
    mapView.setCenter(mapPoint);
    mapView.setZoom(15);
    PoiLayer poiLayer = new PoiLayer();
    poiLayer.addPoint(mapPoint, new Circle(7, Color.RED));
    mapView.addLayer(poiLayer);
    pane.setCenter(mapView);
    service.lineProperty().addListener((obs, ov, nv) -> {
        logger.fine(nv);
        listView.getItems().add(nv);
        listView.scrollTo(listView.getItems().size() - 1);
        if (listView.getItems().size() > 100) {
            listView.getItems().remove(0);
        }
    });
    gpsPosition.timeProperty().addListener((obs, ov, nv) -> {
        statusLabel.setText(
            MessageFormat.format(resources.getString("label.gps"),
                gpsPosition.isFixed() ?
                    resources.getString("label.gps.fixed") :
                    resources.getString("label.gps.not-fixed")));
        mapPoint.update(gpsPosition.getLatitude(),
            gpsPosition.getLongitude());
        mapView.setCenter(mapPoint);
    });
```

```
    timeLabel.textProperty().bind(Bindings.createStringBinding(() -> {
        float time = gpsPosition.getTime();
        int hour = (int) (time / 10000f);
        int min = (int) ((time - hour * 10000) / 100f);
        int sec = (int) (time - hour * 10000 - min * 100);
        return String.format("%02d:%02d:%02d UTC", hour, min, sec);
    }, gpsPosition.timeProperty()));
    positionLabel.textProperty().bind(Bindings.format("%.6f, %.6f",
        gpsPosition.latitudeProperty(),
        gpsPosition.longitudeProperty()));
    altitudeLabel.textProperty().bind(Bindings.format("%.1f m",
        gpsPosition.altitudeProperty()));
    speedLabel.textProperty().bind(Bindings.format("%.2f m/s",
        gpsPosition.velocityProperty()));
    directionLabel.textProperty().bind(Bindings.format("%.2f °",
        gpsPosition.directionProperty()));
    qualityLabel.textProperty().bind(Bindings.format("%d",
        gpsPosition.qualityProperty()));
    satellitesLabel.textProperty().bind(Bindings.format("%d",
        gpsPosition.satellitesProperty()));
    statusLabel.setText(MessageFormat.format(resources.
    getString("label.gps"),
        resources.getString("label.gps.not-fixed")));
    listView.managedProperty().bind(listView.visibleProperty());
    listView.visibleProperty().bind(showLog.selectedProperty());
    showLog.setSelected(false);
}
public void stop() {
    service.stop();
}
@FXML private void onExit(){
    Platform.exit();
}
@FXML private void onZoomIn() {
    if (mapView.getZoom() < 19) {
```

```
            mapView.setZoom(mapView.getZoom() + 1);
        }
    }
    @FXML private void onZoomOut() {
        if (mapView.getZoom() > 1) {
            mapView.setZoom(mapView.getZoom() - 1);
        }
    }
}
```

The GPSPosition and the GPSService objects are injected into the presenter, and the text properties of the different labels are bound to the JavaFX properties. Note that it is important to stop the service when the application is closed. This will close the serial port and release the GPIO controller.

The Application Class

Our main class will create a view for the scene and launch the application (Listing 12-17). It is important to set the scene dimensions based on the Raspberry Pi screen.

Listing 12-17. MainApp class

```
package org.modernclients.raspberrypi.gps;
import com.airhacks.afterburner.injection.Injector;
import javafx.application.Application;
import javafx.geometry.Rectangle2D;
import javafx.scene.Scene;
import javafx.stage.Screen;
import javafx.stage.Stage;
import org.modernclients.raspberrypi.gps.view.UIPresenter;
import org.modernclients.raspberrypi.gps.view.UIView;
public class MainApp extends Application {
    private UIPresenter controller;
    @Override
    public void start(Stage stage) throws Exception {
        Rectangle2D bounds = Screen.getPrimary().getBounds();
        UIView ui = new UIView();
```

```
        controller = (UIPresenter) ui.getPresenter();
        Scene scene = new Scene(ui.getView(),
            bounds.getWidth(), bounds.getHeight());
        stage.setTitle("Embedded Maps");
        stage.setScene(scene);
        stage.show();
    }
    @Override
    public void stop() throws Exception {
        controller.stop();
        Injector.forgetAll();
    }
    public static void main(String[] args) {
        launch(args);
    }
}
```

Finally, Listing 12-18 shows the module-info descriptor to generate the module `org.modernclients.raspberrypi.gps`, and Listing 12-19 shows the `build.gradle` file.

Listing 12-18. module-info.java descriptor

```
module org.modernclients.raspberrypi.gps {
    requires javafx.controls;
    requires javafx.fxml;
    requires pi4j.core;
    requires com.gluonhq.maps;
    requires afterburner.fx;
    requires java.annotation;
    requires java.logging;
    opens org.modernclients.raspberrypi.gps.model to afterburner.fx;
    opens org.modernclients.raspberrypi.gps.service to afterburner.fx;
    opens org.modernclients.raspberrypi.gps.view to afterburner.fx, javafx.fxml;
    exports org.modernclients.raspberrypi.gps;
}
```

Listing 12-19. build.gradle file

```
plugins {
    id 'application'
    id 'org.openjfx.javafxplugin' version '0.0.10'
    id 'org.hidetake.ssh' version '2.10.1'
}
repositories {
    mavenCentral()
    maven {
        url 'http://nexus.gluonhq.com/nexus/content/repositories/releases/'
    }
}
dependencies {
    implementation 'com.pi4j:pi4j-core:1.4'
    implementation 'com.gluonhq:maps:2.0.0-ea+4'
    implementation 'com.gluonhq.attach:storage:4.0.11:desktop'
    implementation 'com.gluonhq.attach:util:4.0.11'
    implementation 'com.airhacks:afterburner.fx:1.7.0'
    implementation 'javax.annotation:javax.annotation-api:1.3.2'
}
javafx {
    modules = [ 'javafx.controls', 'javafx.fxml' ]
}
mainClassName = "$moduleName/org.modernclients.raspberrypi.gps.MainApp"
jar {
    manifest {
        attributes 'Main-Class': 'org.modernclients.raspberrypi.gps.MainApp'
    }
}
def workingDir = '/home/pi/ModernClients/ch12-RaspberryPi/Sample7'
def javaHome = '/usr'
def javafxHome = '/opt/javafx-sdk-17/lib'
```

```
task libs(type: Copy) {
    dependsOn 'jar'
    into "${buildDir}/libs/"
    from configurations.runtimeClasspath
}
remotes {
    pi17 {
        host = 'raspberrypi.local'
        user = 'pi'
        password = 'pi'
    }
}
task runRemoteEmbedded {
    dependsOn 'libs'
    ssh.settings {
        knownHosts = allowAnyHosts
    }
    doLast {
        ssh.run {
            session(remotes.pi17) {
                execute "mkdir -p ${workingDir}/${project.name}/dist"

                fileTree("${buildDir}/libs")
                        .filter { it.isFile() && ! it.name.
                        startsWith('javafx')}
                        .files
                        .each { put from:it,
                    into: "${workingDir}/${project.name}/dist/${it.name}"}
                executeSudo "-E ${javaHome}/bin/java -Dfile.encoding=UTF-8 " +
                        "--module-path=${javafxHome}/lib:
                        ${workingDir}/${project.name}/dist " +
                        "-Dmonocle.platform=EGL -Dembedded=monocle
                         -Dglass.platform=Monocle " +
                        "-Dmonocle.egl.lib=
                            ${javafxHome}/libgluon_drm-1.1.6.so " +
```

```
                    "-classpath '${workingDir}/${project.name}/
                    dist/*' " + "-m ${project.mainClassName}"
            }
        }
    }
}
```

The complete project can be found here:

https://github.com/modernclientjava/mcj-samples/tree/master/ch12-
RaspberryPi/Sample7

Deploy and Test

Download the project, build it, and run it, to verify it works on your machine. Even if you don't have GPS, it should display the UI with a map at a fixed location.

Then power up your Raspberry Pi, verify the display and the GPS are connected and located outdoors, and launch the gpsd service from an SSH terminal:

```
$ sudo service gpsd start
```

Now run from your machine

```
$ ./gradlew runRemoteEmbedded
```

And check that the app is deployed to the Raspberry Pi. If everything is working, you should be reading GPS sentences every second and getting updated latitude and longitude coordinates, and a map will be centered at your current location (Figure 12-19).

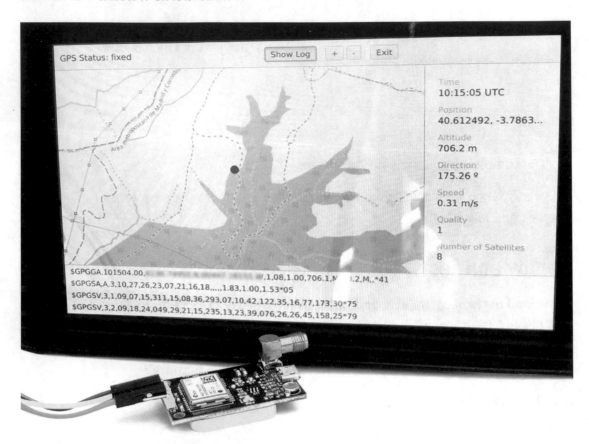

Figure 12-19. *DIY in-car navigation system running*

You can run it directly as well from the SSH terminal (or from the Raspberry Pi with a keyboard):

```
$ cd /home/pi/ModernClients/ch12-RaspberryPi/embeddedGPS/dist
$ sudo -E java -p /opt/javafx-sdk-17/lib:. -Dmonocle.platform=EGL
  -Dembedded=monocle -Dglass.platform=Monocle
  -Dmonocle.egl.lib/opt/javafx-sdk-17/lib/libgluon_drm-1.1.6.so
  -cp . -m org.modernclients.raspberrypi.gps/org.modernclients.raspberrypi.
  gps.MainApp
```

Next Challenge

If you were able to make it work, now the next challenge for you is to get your Raspberry Pi and display powered from a power bank, so you can run the app while moving, either walking or with a vehicle. It will be convenient to use tethering, creating a hotspot with your mobile device so the required maps can be downloaded from OpenStreetMap. You can add the SSID of your device to the `wpa_supplicant.conf` file as discussed at the beginning of this chapter.

Conclusions

In this chapter, you learned about how to configure a Raspberry Pi 4 Model B to work with Java 11+ and JavaFX 17. With the help of basic samples, you saw how to run applications locally and how it was more convenient to use SSH and remote deployment while doing the development on your regular desktop machine.

Once the basics for running JavaFX applications were covered, you had the chance to learn about a more complex project involving a GPS sensor connected via GPIO pins, parsing NMEA readings, and using Gluon Scene Builder with the Afterburner framework to create the UI, which included Gluon Maps, to track your location.

While the Raspberry Pi is an embedded device and it can't be really compared with your regular machine, the actual Pi 4 Model B is a very capable device to run UI applications in places where a desktop machine wouldn't fit.

CHAPTER 13

Machine Learning and JavaFX

Written by William Antônio Siqueira

Machine learning has become a hot topic again recently mostly due to the high amount of data being generated and stored and also the improvement in processing capabilities. Machine learning algorithms are much more than a research topic; they are being used by companies as a competitive advantage. In this chapter, we will discuss the most famous machine learning algorithms focusing on artificial neural networks and show how JavaFX can be used along with a solid machine learning library, DeepLearning4J (DL4J). We will focus on visual neural network models that can interact directly with JavaFX.

What Is Machine Learning

When you develop a system, you have to program exactly what it is supposed to do. You develop an algorithm that step by step describes how a specific flow must be executed.

Machine learning techniques are different, since they don't require explicit programming steps. These techniques return results without being explicitly programmed. Instead of programming it, you "teach" the machine how to use data.

In the machine learning world, we have two different types of algorithms for different tasks, with different performances and precisions. We divide these algorithms in two main categories:

- Supervised learning

- Unsupervised learning

Both categories require data as input.

Supervised Learning

In supervised learning, we have algorithms that make use of labeled data, which means that you will provide sample instances of a problem for the algorithm so it can learn how to classify new unlabeled instances of the same problem. For example, let's say you have certain images of dogs and cats, and you use these images on some of the algorithms. After teaching the algorithm, you can input new images into it, and it should tell you if the new image contains a cat or a dog.

To teach the algorithm, you need to input information, a lot of information, and adjust the algorithm parameters until it can reasonably predict new data. This process is called training. Imagine you want to identify your family in photos and you have thousands of photos of your family members. Once these photos are correctly labeled, you can use them to feed an algorithm, and once the algorithm has a good precision, it can be used to predict new pictures, hopefully identifying members of your family!

Unsupervised Learning

When you have data that you don't have further information about, but still you want to retrieve some knowledge from, you can use unsupervised learning; and depending on the chosen algorithm, it can group certain instances of your data. A known example for unsupervised learning is the recommendation system, where you use user data on certain systems to suggest to them other products or movies.

To use machine learning techniques, one can choose between multiple algorithms available. For supervised learning, we have regression, decision trees, and more. For unsupervised learning, you will find clustering, anomaly detection, and others. For supervised and unsupervised learning, we have neural networks, which we will explore in this chapter.

Artificial Neural Networks

Artificial neural networks are famous and highly discussed and researched due to the high amount of data available for training and high-performance CPUs and GPUs. Neural network basic elements are artificial neurons, which are based on "neurological neurons" and composed of input numbers (x) that are multiplied by their weight (w) and summed by a bias, and the result is inserted in an activation function. Then we have the result (y). These neurons are organized in layers that can have n neurons. Layers are connected in different architectures, and finally we have an artificial neural network as shown in Figure 13-1. Nowadays, artificial neural networks are composed of thousands of neurons, sometimes with hundreds of layers. These large artificial neural networks are part of deep learning methods, and we will see some of the famous deep neural network architectures in this chapter.

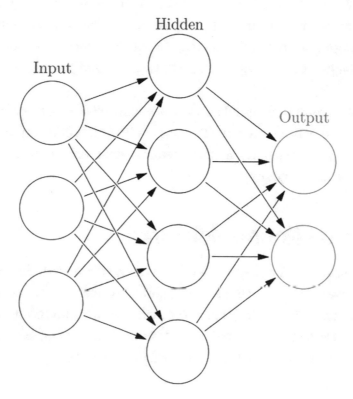

Figure 13-1. *An example of a neural network*

The training process is the key for a neural network to be useful. Before training, the neural network starts with random weights. Training consists of inputting data in the neural network, measuring how far it is from the actual information, and then adjusting the weights until the results are close to the actual values (also called ground truth). For example, if you have a neural network that can predict if a given image is a cat or a dog, you input a cat, and it returns that the cat has 80% of being a dog, you calculate an error (how far is the result from the ground truth data) and then use the process called backpropagation to adjust the neural network weights and repeat it with thousand images of cats and dogs until you have a good result. During training, you should be concerned about overfitting, but this is out of this book's scope.

There are quite a few very known neural network architectures available for use, most of which were proposed by big companies or artificial intelligence researchers. You may create your own neural network, get a lot of data, and train it, so you can use it in your application; however, in this chapter, we will use pretrained neural networks. Yes, good souls out there got some of the very known neural network architectures, trained them using some known dataset (e.g., ImageNet), and, once they were trained, made them available for use in applications; these are called pretrained neural network models.

The power of a pretrained neural network is that it will have all weights already adjusted for a certain dataset, meaning that it is ready for use and you can adjust the weights again with your own data, making it ready to deal with new classes reusing knowledge from other images or data.

Convolutional Neural Networks

It is out of the scope of this book to go deep in all neural network architectures and techniques; however, since we will use mostly convolutional neural networks (CNNs), whose architecture is useful to detect patterns in images without having to write specific patterns, let's discuss it. To understand how CNNs work, take as an example Figure 13-2, a bee drawn by my wife, in an application we will discuss later.

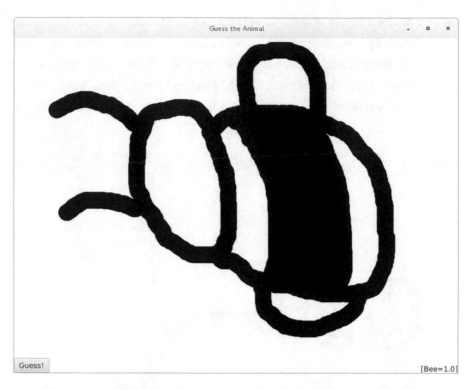

Figure 13-2. *An example of an image to be analyzed by a CNN*

Looking at this bee, we can identify some patterns: a wing is a curve, the body also has a few curves and a filled part, the head is an oval form, and so on. You probably don't know how, but your brain identifies these patterns and concludes that this is a bee drawing. A CNN contains a convolutional layer used with pooling and normalization layers that can identify these patterns, and you don't have to hard-code it. This is all learned during the training process.

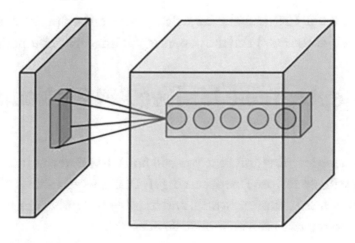

The output of CNN layers is then passed on to a fully connected architecture, which will end in neurons representing each class of images (bee, frogs, dogs, etc.). When you actually predict an image, each class will have a percent chance of being of a certain class. See the following example where the CNN behind the application knows that we tried to input a mouse image (~78% of a mouse), but it also says that there's a small chance that it is a lion (~13%) as shown in Figure 13-3!

Figure 13-3. *The results of an image prediction performed by a CNN*

To learn more about CNNs, check the article from Stanford (`http://cs231n.github.io/convolutional-networks/`) and the papers of the ImageNet competition winners.

Eclipse DeepLearning4J: Java API for Neural Networks

If you search for deep learning and Java, you will find a few libraries out there. For our purpose, we will use Eclipse DeepLearning4J (DL4J), which allows easy data vectorization, creation of neural networks, and training and offers pretrained models for immediate use and can run even on mobile devices.

546

The core library used by DL4J is ND4J. We can perform vectors of n-size operations with ND4J; hence, it is used in all neural network operations in DL4J. For example, every data you want to load for training or predictions is converted to an ND4J INDArray object, so it can feed a neural network during the training process. For more information about ND4J, see Chapter 14, "Scientific Applications Using JavaFX."

On top of ND4J, we have the DataVec library. Deal with neural networks is deal with data, and data on a neural network is represented by number vectors of n size. You can't simply input the binaries of an image or a text string into a neural network. You must convert it; and DataVec has all the tools to go through images, text, CSV files, and more into a neural network. Later, we will make use of DataSetIterators, and it will make clear how it is useful.

DeepLearning4J setup using Maven is simple; you have to add the nd4j-native-platform and deeplearning4j-core dependencies. For this chapter, we will also need deeplearning4j-zoo to make use of available neural network models. For this chapter, we use deeplearning4j 1.0.0-beta7:

```
<dependency>
  <groupId>org.nd4j</groupId>
  <artifactId>nd4j-native-platform</artifactId>
  <version>${dl4j.version}</version>
</dependency>
<dependency>
  <groupId>org.deeplearning4j</groupId>
  <artifactId>deeplearning4j-core</artifactId>
  <version>${dl4j.version}</version>
</dependency>
<dependency>
  <groupId>org.deeplearning4j</groupId>
  <artifactId>deeplearning4j-zoo</artifactId>
  <version>${dl4j.version}</version>
</dependency>
```

We won't be creating neural networks, but to have a taste of how neural networks are created with DeepLearning4J, it looks like you may check DeepLearning4J examples (https://github.com/eclipse/deeplearning4j-examples), like the version of LeNet (the first CNN architecture) that is available and will be used in the first JavaFX application from this chapter:

```
MultiLayerConfiguration conf = new NeuralNetConfiguration.Builder().
seed(seed)
                .activation(Activation.IDENTITY)
                .weightInit(WeightInit.XAVIER)
                .optimizationAlgo(OptimizationAlgorithm.STOCHASTIC_
                GRADIEN T_DESCENT)
                .updater(updater)
                .cacheMode(cacheMode)
                .trainingWorkspaceMode(workspaceMode)
                .inferenceWorkspaceMode(workspaceMode)
                .cudnnAlgoMode(cudnnAlgoMode)
                .convolutionMode(ConvolutionMode.Same)
                .list()
                // block 1
                .layer(0, new ConvolutionLayer.Builder(new int[] {5,
                5}, new int[] {1, 1}).name("cnn1")
                                .nIn(inputShape[0]).nOut(20).
                                activation(Activation.RELU).build())
                .layer(1, new SubsamplingLayer.Builder(SubsamplingLayer.
                PoolingType.MAX, new int[] {2, 2},
                                new int[] {2, }).name("maxpool1").build())
                // block 2
                .layer(2, new ConvolutionLayer.Builder(new int[] {5, 5},
                new int[] {1, 1}).name("cnn2").nOut(50)
                                .activation(Activation.RELU).build())
                .layer(3, new SubsamplingLayer.Builder(SubsamplingLayer.
                PoolingType.MAX, new int[] {2, 2},
                                new int[] {2, 2}).name("maxpool2").build())
                // fully connected
```

```
.layer(4, new DenseLayer.Builder().name("ffn1").
activation(Activation.RELU).nOut(500).build())
// output
.layer(5, new OutputLayer.Builder(LossFunctions.
LossFunction.MCXENT).name("output")
                .nOut(numClasses).activation(Activation.
                SOFTMAX) // radial basis function required
                .build())
.setInputType(InputType.convolutionalFlat(inputShape[2],
inputShape[1], inputShape[0]))
.build();
```

Training Neural Networks from a JavaFX Application

If you don't have a pretrained model, you can train your own. It will require data, a lot of it, and knowledge of neural network parameters and architecture. To interact and visualize the progress of a neural network training process, we will use a JavaFX application.

To demonstrate how a neural network can be trained from JavaFX, we create a small application with the following features:

- See the progress of training and testing. This can take months, days, or a few hours. In our case, we will do a quick training, which will take a few hours. You follow the progress in the JavaFX application.

- Be able to adjust some hyperparameters: number of epochs, iterations, and batch size. Also select paths for train and test input image files along with the image information.

- Export the model after training and import a model configuration to be trained.

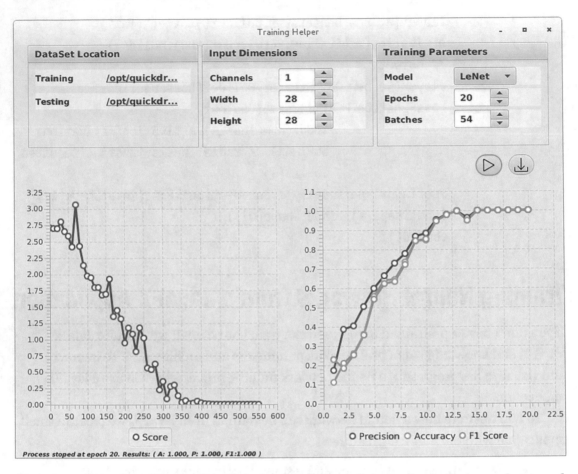

Figure 13-4. *A JavaFX application that visualizes the progress of a neural network training process*

The application shown in Figure 13-4 is built using the controls already discussed in this book. Charts are also used to show the progress of the neural network "learning," and when the process is finished, you can save the now trained neural network to your disk. The exported model can be used for real prediction of new instances of the data.

To explore the full code, you can check the class TrainingHelperApp (accessible at github.com/Apress/definitive-guide-modern-java-clients-javafx17). Here we will focus on how JavaFX accesses DL4J APIs. The DL4J base model used for training is wrapped in the NeuralNetModel interface, and it is possible to implement this interface to provide custom models using Java Service Provider Interface. By default, we have a built-in DL4J model based on LeNet, the first convolutional neural network created by Yann LeCun. The neural network type is org.deeplearning4j.nn.multilayer. MultiLayerNetwork. DL4J also provides ComputationalGraphs. For this example, let's keep MultiLayerNetwork:

```
import org.deeplearning4j.nn.multilayer.MultiLayerNetwork;
public interface NeuralNetModel {
    public String getId();
    public MultiLayerNetwork getModel(int[] inputShape, int numClasses);
}
```

A combo box is filled with the available implementations of NeuralNetModel, and the actual model is accessed using the method getModel. Before running the training process, users must select the training and testing directories. The directories should have a structure where images are under a folder that is corresponding to its class, for example, cat images must be in a folder named cat. When the button Run is clicked, all the entered information is retrieved and then passed on to method prepareForTraining:

```
private void prepareForTraining(String modelId, int[] inputShape,
int epochs, int batchSize, File trainingDir, File testingDir) {
    status("Preparing for training...");
    runningProperty.set(true);
    try {
        DataSetIterator trainingIterator = DL4JHelper.
        createIterator(trainingDir, inputShape[1], inputShape[2],
        inputShape[0], batchSize, SEED);
        DataSetIterator testingIterator = DL4JHelper.
        createIterator(testingDir, inputShape[1], inputShape[2],
        inputShape[0], batchSize, SEED);
        var currentModel = getNeuralNetById(modelId).
        getModel(inputShape, trainingIterator.getLabels().size());
        lastModel.set(currentModel);
        currentModel.setListeners(new AsyncScoreIterationListener(this:
        :updateScore));
        clearSeries();
        launchTrainingThread(epochs, trainingIterator, testingIterator);
    } catch (IOException e) {
```

```
            e.printStackTrace();
        }
    }
```

In prepareForTraining, the directories selected by users are used to create a
DataSetIterator. DL4J provides us an API of iterators that makes easy to load external files
to feed into a neural network. In our case, we create an iterator based on image files, and
the labels are generated based on the parent path for a given image file. It is responsible
to handle all hard work for us; otherwise, we would have to load the image in an
INDArray in order to feed into the neural network. The created iterators also provide the
information about how many labels (or classes) we have in our dataset and we use plus
the entered input shape and the neural network model ID to retrieve the actual model.
After this, we register a listener that is called every time the score is updated, we use a
method reference to update the score to register it, and finally we launch the training
process calling launchTrainingThread passing the number of epochs and the iterators
we created:

```java
private void launchTrainingThread(int epochs, DataSetIterator
trainingIterator, DataSetIterator testingIterator) {
    var currentModel = lastModel.get();
    new Thread(() -> {
            var result  = "";
            int epochNum = 0;
            for (int i = 0; i < epochs; i++) {
                epochNum = (i +1);
                currentModel.fit(trainingIterator);
                status("Evaluating...");
                Evaluation eval = currentModel.
                evaluate(testingIterator);
                double progress = (double) i / (double) epochs;
                var accuracy =  eval.accuracy();
                var precision = eval.precision();
                var f1 = eval.f1();
                updateSeries(accuracySeries, epochNum, accuracy);
                updateSeries(precisionSeries, epochNum, precision);
                updateSeries(f1Series, epochNum, f1);
```

```
                testingIterator.reset();
                trainingIterator.reset();
                result = "( A: " + evalutionFormat.format(accuracy)   +
                        ", P: " + evalutionFormat.format(precision) +
                        ", F1:" + evalutionFormat.format(f1) + " )";
                if (stopRequested) {
                    status("Stop Requested on epoch "  + epochNum +
                        Results: " + result);
                    stopRequested = false;
                    break;
                } else {
                    status("Epoch " + epochNum  + "/" + epochs + " "
                        result);
                    setProgress(progress);
                }
            }
            status("Process stoped at epoch " + epochNum  + ".
            Results: " + result);
            Platform.runLater(() -> runningProperty.set(false));
        }).start();
    }
```

In this method, we start getting the model that the user has selected; then we start a thread that contains the procedure to perform the training. The reason to make this in a different thread is to avoid locking the JavaFX thread; this way we can stop the process if we think that we reached good results already. The training process basically fits the iterator in the model and evaluates the model. The model evaluation returns the commonly used metrics to see how good the model is: accuracy, precision, and f1 score. Each metric has a corresponding chart XYSeries, which is updated during the training process. Everything happens epoch times, hence in a for loop from 0 to number of epochs; however, if the user clicks the Run button while the application is running, then the flag stopRequested becomes true, and the process is stopped and allows the user to export the model.

You may have noticed that we don't interact directly with JavaFX controls on this method; instead, we have to call status, updateSeries, and setProcess. These methods update JavaFX-related classes in the JavaFX thread. See the following:

```
private void setProgress(final double progress) {
    Platform.runLater(() ->  progressProperty.set(progress));
}
private void updateScore(Integer i, Double d) {
    updateSeries(scoreSeries, i, d);
}
private void updateSeries(XYChart.Series<Number, Number>
series, Integer i, Double d) {
    Platform.runLater(() -> series.getData().add(new XYChart.
    Data<>(i, d)));
}
private void status(String txt) {
    Platform.runLater(() ->  txtProgress.set(txt));
}
```

When the training process is finished or stopped, it is possible to export the model, now trained, which means that it will have the weights adjusted and ready to predict new data. This is simply done on method exportModel:

```
private void exportModel(ActionEvent event) {
    var source = (Button) event.getSource();
    var modelOutputFile = fileChooser.showSaveDialog(source.getScene().
    getWindow());
    if (modelOutputFile != null) {
        try {
            ModelSerializer.writeModel(lastModel.get(),
            modelOutputFile, true);
            status("Model saved to " + modelOutputFile.
            getAbsolutePath());
        } catch (IOException e1) {
            e1.printStackTrace();
        }
    }
}
```

Read an Image from JavaFX to a Neural Network

It is possible that you face a situation where you have to get content from inside a JavaFX application to input into a neural network to consume its output. For example, in a game, you want to pass the actual screen to a neural network to adjust the game parameters; or if you are running a simulation, you can input the state of the simulation into a neural network to have real-time predictions. In these cases, we need to know how to get snapshots from JavaFX to input into a neural network.

You may have heard of Quick, Draw!, an online tool from Google that guesses what you are drawing. Google put this open for everyone to play with the tool and also stored all drawings, which surpassed one billion drawings. The good news is that they made the data available for everyone to use (`https://quickdraw.withgoogle.com/data`).

The data is available in a few different binary formats, and it has hundreds of classes, thousands of images per classes. To simplify the training process, we took only the animal classes (dog, cat, etc.) and converted them to a human-readable format, PNG, which can also be accessed from DL4J dataset iterator classes. We also made the images black-and-white and resized them to 28 × 28, the same size used by images of a famous dataset of handwritten digits, MNIST. With this we can use an MNIST neural network architecture from DL4J examples, MnistClassifier (`http://projects.rajivshah.com/blog/2017/07/14/QuickDraw`). We will use a simple LeNet neural network trained using these images to predict what doodle is entered; however, the application we will show can be adapted to other neural network models.

The application can be found in a single class GuessTheAnimal. Running this application results in a screenshot similar to Figure 13-5. The first step is declare constants that contain the input image size, the model location, and the classes we used when we trained the model. In our case, we selected a few animal classes. We used a model with 68% of accuracy and 15 classes. You can use the application from our last section to train your own model and build one with better accuracy:

```
private static final String MODEL_PATH = "/quickdraw-model-15-68.zip";
private static final String CLASSES[] = { "Bee", "Bird", "Cat",
"Dog", "Duck", "Elephant", "Fish", "Frog", "Horse", "Lion", "Mouse",
"Pig", "Rabbit", "Snake", "Spider" };
private static final int INPUT_WIDTH = 28;
private static final int INPUT_HEIGHT = 28;
private static final Double THRESHOLD = 0.1d;
```

Figure 13-5. *A drawing to be analyzed by a LeNet neural network*

The application consists of two parts: load the model and build the UI. To load
the model, we use the ModelSerializer class. Notice you can use any model exported
from the application we discussed before. Just make sure to adjust the constants
accordingly. Loading the model is simple. We just need a call to ModelSerializer.
restoreMultiLayerNetwork and pass the file or input stream containing the model. See
the method initModelAndLoader. In this method, we also create the NativeImageLoader
that is the class that will actually do the conversion of the content to an INDArray,
making it useful with a neural network:

```
private void initModelAndLoader() throws IOException {
    model = ModelSerializer
            .restoreMultiLayerNetwork(GuessTheAnimal.class.
            getResource AsStream(MODEL_PATH));
    model.init();
    loader = new NativeImageLoader(INPUT_WIDTH, INPUT_HEIGHT, 1, true);
}
```

The UI is built in method buildUI(), and it consists of three controls: a canvas used to receive the user's drawings, a button to trigger the prediction process, and a label that contains the output. When the user drags the mouse on the canvas, the application draws small circles, giving the idea of a pencil writing on a sheet. A right-click cleans the canvas and the result label:

```
private StackPane buildUI() {
    var canvas = new Canvas(APP_WIDTH, APP_HEIGHT);
    var btnGuess = new Button("Guess!");
    var lblOutput = new Label("");
    var root = new StackPane(canvas, btnGuess, lblOutput);
    lblOutput.setTextFill(Color.RED);
    txtOutput = lblOutput.textProperty();
    ctx = canvas.getGraphicsContext2D();
    ctx.setLineWidth(30);
    canvas.setOnMouseDragged(e -> {
        ctx.setFill(Color.BLACK);
        ctx.fillOval(e.getX() - 15, e.getY() - 15, 30, 30);
    });
    canvas.setOnMouseClicked(e -> {
        if (e.getButton() == MouseButton.SECONDARY) {
            clearCanvas();
        }
    });
```

```
    btnGuess.setOnAction(evt -> {
        var predictions = predictCanvasContent();
        var pairs = sortAndMap(predictions);
        txtOutput.set(pairs.toString());
    });
    StackPane.setAlignment(btnGuess, Pos.BOTTOM_LEFT);
    StackPane.setAlignment(lblOutput, Pos.BOTTOM_RIGHT);
    return root;
}
```

The most important part of this code is where we get the canvas content and convert it to an INDArray so it can be entered in the neural network model. This is done in methods predictCanvasContent and getScaledImage. On getScaledImage, we get a screenshot of the canvas to a WritableImage, convert it to a java.awt.Image using SwingFXUtils, and finally write it to a BufferedImage that also scales the image to the same size of the image used in the neural network model. We also save the last predicted image to an external file; it can be useful for debugging. In predictCanvasContent, we convert the scaledImage to an INDArray that is then input in the neural network model. The model itself returns an INDArray that has 1 × 15 positions; hence, after the prediction, we convert it to a map and filter the result that had results below the threshold we defined as a constant (by default 0.1):

```
private Map<String, Double> predictCanvasContent() {
    try {
        var img = getScaledImage();
        INDArray image = loader.asRowVector(img);
        INDArray output = model.output(image);
        double[] doubleVector = output.toDoubleVector();
        var results = new HashMap<String, Double>();
        for (int i = 0; i < doubleVector.length; i++) {
            results.put(CLASSES[i], doubleVector[i]);
        }
        return results.entrySet().stream().filter(e -> e.getValue() >
        THRESHOLD)
        .collect(Collectors.toMap(Map.Entry::getKey, Map.Entry::getValue));
    } catch (Exception e) {
```

```java
        throw new RuntimeException(e);
    }
}
private BufferedImage getScaledImage() {
    var canvas = ctx.getCanvas();
    WritableImage writableImage = new WritableImage((int) canvas.
    getWidth(), (int) canvas.getHeight());
    canvas.snapshot(null, writableImage);
    Image tmp = SwingFXUtils.fromFXImage(writableImage, null).
    getScaledInstance(INPUT_WIDTH, INPUT_HEIGHT, Image.SCALE_SMOOTH);
    BufferedImage scaledImg = new BufferedImage(INPUT_WIDTH, INPUT_HEIGHT,
    BufferedImage.TYPE_BYTE_GRAY);
    Graphics graphics = scaledImg.getGraphics();
    graphics.drawImage(tmp, 0, 0, null);
    graphics.dispose();
    try {
        File outputfile = new File("last_predicted_image.jpg");
        ImageIO.write(scaledImg, "jpg", outputfile);
    } catch (IOException e) {
        e.printStackTrace();
    }
    return scaledImg;
}
```

Detecting Objects in a Video

For the next application, we will explore a neural network model architecture called
YOLO (You Only Look Once). A summary of how YOLO works can be found in its paper:[1]

> *We reframe object detection as a single regression problem, straight from
> image pixels to bounding box coordinates and class probabilities. Using
> our system, you only look once (YOLO) at an image to predict what objects
> are present and where they are.*

---

[1] You Only Look Once: Unified, Real-Time Object Detection, by Joseph Redmon, Santosh Divvala,
Ross Girshick, and Ali Farhadi (https://arxiv.org/pdf/1506.02640.pdf).

The paper also brings the following image that simplifies how it works.

The original paper is from 2016. Later, more papers were introduced. The latest one is for YOLO3, which is more precise and faster. Training a YOLO neural network would require bigger images than usual; the input size for the first YOLO version is 448 × 448, which means that it would take a long time in a personal computer. Luckily, DL4J provides TinyYOLO and YOLO2, ready for our use. In this section, we explore a JavaFX application used to detect objects in a running video.

The application starts declaring a few constants important for the application. Let's go through each constant:

```
private static final double APP_WIDTH = 800;
private static final double APP_HEIGHT = 600;
private static final String TARGET_VIDEO = "/path/to/video";
private static final double THRESHOLD = 0.65d;
private static final String[] LABELS = { "person", "bicycle", "car",
"motorbike", "aeroplane", "bus", "train", "truck", "boat", "traffic
light", "fire hydrant", "stop sign", "parking meter", "bench", "bird",
"cat", "dog", "horse", "sheep", "cow", "elephant", "bear", "zebra",
"giraffe", "backpack", "umbrella", "handbag", "tie", "suitcase",
"frisbee", "skis", "snowboard", "sports ball", "kite", "baseball
bat", "baseball glove", "skateboard", "surfboard", "tennis racket",
"bottle", "wine glass", "cup", "fork", "knife", "spoon", "bowl",
"banana", "apple", "sandwich", "orange", "broccoli", "carrot", "hot
dog", "pizza", "donut", "cake", "chair", "sofa", "pottedplant", "bed",
"diningtable", "toilet", "tvmonitor", "laptop", "mouse", "remote",
"keyboard", "cell phone", "microwave", "oven", "toaster", "sink",
"refrigerator", "book", "clock", "vase", "scissors", "teddy bear",
"hair drier", "toothbrush" };
private final int INPUT_WIDTH = 608;
private final int INPUT_HEIGHT = 608;
private final int INPUT_CHANNELS = 3;
private final int GRID_W = INPUT_WIDTH / 32;
private final int GRID_H = INPUT_HEIGHT / 32;
private final double FRAMES_PER_SECOND = 20d;
```

- APP_WIDTH and APP_HEIGHT: The actual image size.

- TARGET_VIDEO: The URL to a supported video file. If it is in the classpath, you can use the path to it directly; however, JavaFX also supports URL protocol, so local files can be loaded using protocol file:/{path to file}.

- THRESHOLD: The cut value. Objects detected with value less than THRESHOLD will not be in the neural network output.

- LABELS: The labels used to train the neural network model. By default it has the classes used to train the DL4J default model, but it is possible to change it to a custom YOLO model.

- INPUT_WIDTH, INPUT_HEIGHT, INPUT_CHANNELS: The input image information used by the YOLO neural network. It is also using the values for the YOLO2 DL4J model.

- GRID_W and GRID_H: The original image is divided in a grid, and the output-detected object positions are related to this grid; hence, when calculating the output box, it is required to use the grid size. It can be calculated using org.deeplearning4j.zoo.model.helper. DarknetHelper getGridWidth and getGridHeight methods.

- FRAMES_PER_SECOND: The number of frames scanned by second. If higher, the processing will be longer, but the detected object highlight will look more precise.

The application UI is composed of a media view for the video playback, a pane that will hold the rectangles that will highlight the detected objects, and a label to show the progress of the running task execution. Everything is stacked on StackPane, and the Label is oriented to be on the bottom. This is all done in the start method, but before building the UI, we generate colors for each rectangle that will highlight the detected object and initialize the YOLO2 model. Notice that the first time this code is executed, it will download the pretrained model; hence, it may take a while:

```
for (int i = 0; i < LABELS.length; i++) {
    colors.put(LABELS[i], Color.hsb((i + 1) * 20, 0.5, 1.0));
}
```

```
var yoloModel = (ComputationGraph)  YOLO2.builder().build().
initPretrained();
String videoPath = DetectObjectsInVideoImproved.class.getResource(TARGET_
VIDEO).toString();
imageLoader = new NativeImageLoader(INPUT_WIDTH, INPUT_HEIGHT, INPUT_
CHANNELS,
        new ColorConversionTransform(COLOR_BGR2RGB));
var media = new Media(videoPath);
var mp = new MediaPlayer(media);
var view = new MediaView(mp);
Label lblProgress = new Label();
lblProgress.setTextFill(Color.LIGHTGRAY);
view.setFitWidth(APP_WIDTH);
view.setFitHeight(APP_HEIGHT);
view.setPreserveRatio(false);
pane = new Pane();
pane.setMinWidth(APP_WIDTH);
pane.setMinHeight(APP_HEIGHT);
var root = new StackPane(view, pane, lblProgress);
StackPane.setAlignment(lblProgress, Pos.BOTTOM_CENTER);
stage.setScene(new Scene(root, APP_WIDTH, APP_HEIGHT));
stage.show();
stage.setTitle("Detect Objects");
```

The application also allows users to pause the video by clicking it, and since we have a pane on top of the media view, we register the mouse listener on the pane and not on the media view:

```
pane.setOnMouseClicked(e -> {
    if (mp.getStatus() == Status.PLAYING) {
        mp.pause();
    } else if (mp.getStatus() == Status.PAUSED) {
        mp.play();
    } else if (mp.getStatus() == Status.STOPPED) {
        mp.seek(mp.getStartTime());
        mp.play();
```

```
        }
    });
    mp.setOnEndOfMedia(() -> {
        mp.stop();
        pane.getChildren().forEach(c -> c.setVisible(false));
    });
```

The prediction is not done in real time. The reason is that a single prediction takes almost 500 ms in a machine without GPU processing. When having GPU, part of the prediction process will be done by the multiple GPU cores, making it much faster. The YOLO paper talks about 155 frames per second; however, this result will hardly be achieved taking a snapshot of a JavaFX node, but in this application, snapshot is used because you can preprocess the media view node and only then run YOLO (e.g., zoom or apply effects), uniting the power of JavaFX with YOLO. Also, you may not want to run YOLO on a video. Any JavaFX node can be subject of a YOLO prediction, so it is open for more possibilities.

The trick in our case is not make the prediction in real time, but collect frames when the application is running and schedule a prediction task, create the JavaFX nodes that will contain the detected object highlight, and then display it on top of the video. Notice that once the group is created, we give it an ID so we can hide or show it according to the current frame that is being displayed for the user. We track each task to avoid redundant execution, and a group with the detected object is added to the pane only after the task is finished (see target.setOnSucceeded). In other words, the video needs to play at least one time so all frames are collected and scheduled to be processed. The scheduled tasks are tracked in trackTasks, and once a task for a given frame ID is done, we show the group that contains the detected object highlight and hide the others. Everything is done in a listener attached to the current time of the media player playback, so it is invoked only when the video is playing; otherwise, it won't collect frames for processing:

```
    var finishedTasks = new AtomicInteger();
    var previousFrame = new AtomicLong(-1);
    mp.currentTimeProperty().addListener((obs, o, n) -> {
        if(n.toMillis() < 50d) return;
        Long millis = Math.round(n.toMillis() / (1000d / FRAMES_PER_
        SECOND));
        final var nodeId = millis.toString();
```

```
        if(millis  == previousFrame.get()) {
            return;
        }
        previousFrame.set(millis);
        trackTasks.computeIfAbsent(nodeId, v -> {
            var scaledImage = getScaledImage(view);
            PredictFrameTask target = new PredictFrameTask(yoloModel,
            scaledImage);
            target.setOnSucceeded(e -> {
                var detectedObjectGroup = getNodesForTask(nodeId,
                target);
                Platform.runLater(() -> pane.getChildren().
                add(detectedObjectGroup));
                updateProgress(lblProgress, trackTasks.size(),
                finishedTasks.incrementAndGet());
            });
            Thread thread = new Thread(target);
            thread.setDaemon(true);
            thread.start();
            return true;
        });
        updateProgress(lblProgress, trackTasks.size(),
        finishedTasks.get());
        pane.getChildren().forEach(node -> node.setVisible(false));
        Optional.ofNullable(pane.lookup("#" + nodeId)).ifPresent
        (node -> node.setVisible(true));
    });
}
```

Now that you understand how we collect frames and process them, let's think about the actual frame processing. Before scheduling the task, there's a call to getScaledImage, whose result will be passed to the task. This method gets a snapshot of the media view just like we did before, but this time we are not getting a black-and-white image, but a colored one. YOLO input images use three channels, one for each color (red, green, and blue):

```
private BufferedImage getScaledImage(Node targetNode) {
    writableImage = new WritableImage((int) targetNode.
    getBoundsInLocal().getWidth(), (int) targetNode.getBoundsInLocal().
    getHeight());
    targetNode.snapshot(null, writableImage);
    Image tmp = SwingFXUtils.fromFXImage(writableImage, null).
    getScaledInstance(INPUT_WIDTH, INPUT_HEIGHT, Image.SCALE_SMOOTH);
    BufferedImage scaledImg = new BufferedImage(INPUT_WIDTH, INPUT_
    HEIGHT, BufferedImage.TYPE_INT_RGB);
    Graphics graphics = scaledImg.getGraphics();
    graphics.drawImage(tmp, 0, 0, null);
    graphics.dispose();
    return scaledImg;
}
```

On the setOnSucceeded listener, we will then process the detected objects returned by the task. Each object has the initial points for each detected rectangle and also other information, but only points xs are required to build a rectangle to highlight the detected object. However, the coordinates are needed to be transformed before creating our rectangle. First, we need to figure it out if a scale is needed because the app size may be bigger than the image input and all coordinates are relative to the input, then calculate the actual coordinates on the original image because all the coordinates are relative to the grid, and finally calculate the rectangle width and height. Along with the rectangle, we also add a label to show the class that was predicted, and it is added to a group, so we can handle both label and rectangle uniquely. This is done for each detected object:

```
private Group getNodesForTask(final String nodeId,
PredictFrameTask    target) {
    try {
        var predictedObjects = target.get();
        var detectedObjectGroup = getPredictionNodes(predictedObjects);
        detectedObjectGroup.setId(nodeId);
        detectedObjectGroup.setVisible(false);
        return detectedObjectGroup;
    } catch (Exception e) {
```

```java
            throw new RuntimeException(e);
        }
    }
    private Group getPredictionNodes(List<DetectedObject> objs) {
        Group grpObject = new Group();
        objs.stream().map(this::createNodesForDetectedObject)
                    .flatMap(l -> l.stream())
                    .forEach(grpObject.getChildren()::add);
        return grpObject;
    }
    private List<Node> createNodesForDetectedObject(DetectedObject obj) {
        double[] xy1 = obj.getTopLeftXY();
        double[] xy2 = obj.getBottomRightXY();
        var w  = INPUT_WIDTH;
        var h  = INPUT_HEIGHT;
        var wScale  = (APP_WIDTH / w);
        var hScale  = (APP_HEIGHT / h);
        var x1 = (w * xy1[0] / GRID_W) * wScale;
        var y1 = (h * xy1[1] / GRID_H) * hScale;
        var x2 = (w * xy2[0] / GRID_W) * wScale;
        var y2 = (h * xy2[1] / GRID_H) * hScale;
        var rectW = x2 - x1;
        var rectH = y2 - y1;
        var label = LABELS[obj.getPredictedClass()];
        Rectangle rect = new Rectangle(x1, y1, rectW, rectH);
        rect.setFill(Color.TRANSPARENT);
        Color color = colors.get(label);
        rect.setStroke(color);
        rect.setStrokeWidth(2);
        Label lbl = new Label(label);
        lbl.setTranslateX(x1 + 2);
        lbl.setTranslateY(y1 + 2);
        lbl.setTextFill(color);
```

```
lbl.setFont(Font.font(Font.getDefault().getFamily(), FontWeight.
EXTRA_BOLD, FontPosture.ITALIC, 10));
return List.of(rect, lbl);
}
```

Finally we have the task, which implements javafx.concurrent.Task and gives it a type of List<DetectedObject>. The JavaFX concurrent task allows us to run some heavy action and later retrieve the result, not holding the main JavaFX thread. The prediction is almost the same thing as done in our Quick, Draw! example. The main difference is that to extract the object, now we use a utility method that is in the org.deeplearning4j. nn.layers.objdetect.Yolo2OutputLayer class to get the predicted objects from the result INDArray:

```
public class PredictFrameTask extends Task<List<DetectedObject>> {
    ComputationGraph yoloModel;
    BufferedImage scaledImage;
    public PredictFrameTask(ComputationGraph yoloModel,
    BufferedImage scaledImage) {
        this.yoloModel = yoloModel;
        this.scaledImage = scaledImage;
    }
    @Override
    protected List<DetectedObject> call() throws Exception {
        return predictObjects();
    }
    private List<DetectedObject> predictObjects() {
        org.deeplearning4j.nn.layers.objdetect.Yolo2OutputLayer yout =
                (org.deeplearning4j.nn.layers.objdetect.Yolo2Output
                Layer)yoloModel.getOutputLayer(0);
        try {
            var imgMatrix = imageLoader.asMatrix(scaledImage);
            var scaler = new ImagePreProcessingScaler(0, 1);
            scaler.transform(imgMatrix);
            INDArray output = yoloModel.outputSingle(imgMatrix);
            return yout.getPredictedObjects(output, THRESHOLD);
```

```
        } catch (IOException e) {
            throw new RuntimeException(e);
        }
    }
```

This is a very simple starting point to build your own application. Think about the possibilities to build your own YOLO-powered application, like finding invaders in a property, counting the number of cars on a street, looking for objects in a big image, and so on!

CHAPTER 14

Scientific Applications Using JavaFX

Written by Johan Vos

Many of the spectacular advances that are being achieved recently are in the field of data science, or at least related to it. Different forms of machine learning, big data calculations, and quantum computing are rapidly getting an increased impact on society in general.

The technical foundations of these advances are based on different scientific research areas. As is often the case, technical foundations are implementation agnostic. Different languages, platforms, and binaries can be used to implement the technical foundations.

In this chapter, we will explain why Java in general, and client Java (including JavaFX) in particular, is a great choice for developers who want to create scientific applications, using the language they master.

We will first demonstrate a few real samples and then explain a more general way that allows you to create scientific applications in Java, including doing the research work related to the scientific application.

JavaFX for Space Exploration

A great scientific application using JavaFX technologies is the Deep Space Trajectory Explorer, or DSTE. This is a product created by a.i. solutions and used by NASA. The product is described on the web site of a.i. solutions at `https://ai-solutions.com/dste`.

© Stephen Chin, Johan Vos and James Weaver 2022
S. Chin et al., *The Definitive Guide to Modern Java Clients with JavaFX 17*,
https://doi.org/10.1007/978-1-4842-7268-8_14

According to the web site, the Deep Space Trajectory Explorer is an interactive software package that combines cutting-edge multibody trajectory design techniques with innovative visualizations to dramatically reduce time spent on trajectory design.

With DSTE, users can design trajectories of objects in space, which typically requires heavy calculations. Often, those calculations are done without any visualization or interactivity until the calculation is done. The DSTE product makes the design process more "agile" and interactive.

One of the key benefits of DSTE is that it allows the usage of interactive visualization in the design process for missions. Doing so, it becomes easier and more intuitive to select orbits that satisfy specific mission constraints.

The requirement to combine high-performant computing and complex visualization is a great use case for Java and JavaFX. Java itself is very scalable, and there are plenty of powerful Java APIs and frameworks that help developers and operators to scale Java code in multicore environments. The JavaFX platform allows for visualization including 3D models and Canvas rendering and thereby uses hardware-accelerated rendering, leveraging the availability of the GPU. Since JavaFX is pure Java, this rendering can easily be integrated with the pieces of code that are responsible for the high-performant computations.

The Deep Space Trajectory Explorer leverages the performance offered by the JavaFX platform in a number of ways. It contains different views, both in 2D and 3D. Many views allow for click-and-drag functionality. Canvas components are used to render millions of linked data points onscreen, without freezing the layout. Filters allow to select and deselect a number of options, and the resulting changes are real time rendered in the views.

Figure 14-1[1] shows a screenshot generated by the DSTE product that shows some of the views offered by the tool.

---

[1]https://ai-solutions.com/wp-content/uploads/2017/12/DTSE_DataSheet.pdf

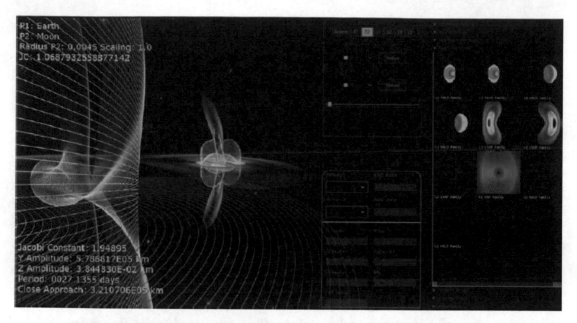

Figure 14-1. *Screenshot generated by DSTE*

The Deep Space Trajectory Explorer is not an application that is easily created. It requires deep knowledge about the physics behind orbits, about high-performance computing, and about UI development. JavaFX is a crucial component in the total solution, proving the power of the platform.

JavaFX for Quantum Computing

Quantum computing is rapidly gaining interest, both in scientific environments and in IT departments.

One of the promises of quantum computing is that some problems that are extremely hard or practically impossible to solve using classic computers can easily be tackled with quantum computers. Especially in areas where algorithms show exponential time behavior, quantum computers can make a big difference.

Quantum computers use some core concepts that are fundamentally present in nature, but not in classical computers.

In a classic computer, the most granular unit is a bit. A bit is either 0 or 1. In a quantum computer, the most granular unit is a qubit. A qubit can hold the value 0 or 1, but it can also be in a so-called superposition state, in which it holds a linear combination of 0 and 1. When measured though, a qubit always returns either 0 or 1. Therefore, the algorithms for quantum computing must take advantage of the superposition states without measuring the qubits during the processing.

In classic computing, bits are manipulated by gates. For example, the NOT gate will flip the value of a bit. When the bit was 0 before it entered the gate, the result after the gate will be 1 and vice versa.

Similarly, in quantum computing, qubits are manipulated by quantum gates.

While there are some very early experimental chips for quantum computers available, quantum computing is by no means ready yet for mainstream development. The practical requirements to create a quantum computer with sufficient qubits that stay available for a reasonable amount of time are huge. Therefore, only a few prototypes exist with a limited amount of qubits.

However, because of the huge potential impact of quantum computing, many developers are already working on algorithms that might benefit from quantum computing. Typically, local or cloud-based simulators are used to develop these algorithms, and some companies are now starting to offer real quantum computers as a cloud service.

These algorithms are often developed in a programming language and visualized using circuit visualization.

One of those quantum simulators, Strange, is using a companion tool called StrangeFX, which is built using JavaFX to render the circuits. StrangeFX is available on GitHub at `https://github.com/redfx-quantum/strangefx`.

StrangeFX allows developers to drag quantum gates onto qubit wires. While they do this, the local simulator evaluates the circuit and shows the results in real time. The draganddrop capabilities of JavaFX provide a very intuitive way for developing quantum circuits, and the integration with the quantum simulation algorithms is straightforward since both components are written in Java.

Figure 14-2 shows a simple screenshot of StrangeFX, showing three qubits and a number of gates in a toolbar that can be dragged to the qubit wires.

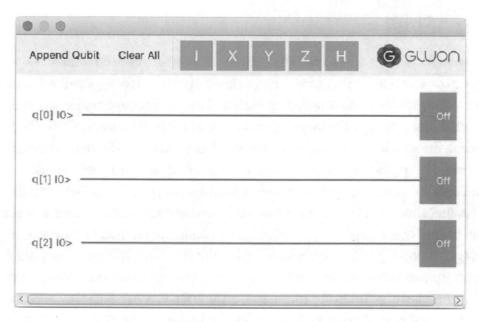

Figure 14-2. *StrangeFX allows developers to drag quantum gates onto qubit wires*

A more complex example includes a simulation of Grover's search shown in Figure 14-3, a famous quantum algorithm.

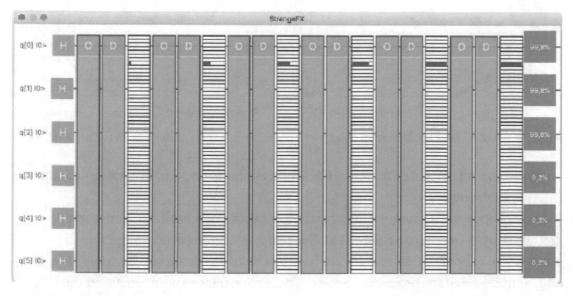

Figure 14-3. *A simulation of Grover's sarch*

Using JShell

In the not so far past, we saw a fault line between activities in two different areas: developers on one hand, using programming languages to create applications, and people working on infrastructure and operations. Developers were mainly working on business solutions for a particular problem in an isolated environment. Once the problem was solved, the solution was handed over to the IT department, who had to bring it into production. The gap between those worlds caused lots of issues related to scalability, documentation, versioning, accountability, dependencies, and so on. Too often the "it works for me" situation blocked the transition from developers who created a business solution toward operational people bringing the solution to high-scale production.

This gap is now typically being tackled by the so-called "DevOps" approach, where some overlapping parts of development and operations are brought together in one approach or team. A number of software improvements, including containerization, allowed for development and operations to work more closely with each other as shown in Figure 14-4.

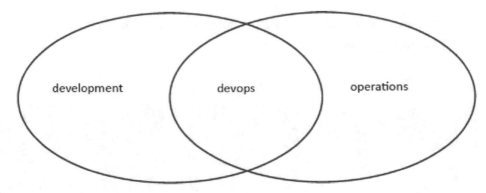

Figure 14-4. *The DevOps approach*

Overlapping parts of development and operations are tackled in a cross-domain DevOps environment.

Today, the growing interest in data science shows a new fault line between two groups: people working on research and developers working on development in production. Very often, the research is done by scientists who have extremely difficult and complex scientific problems to solve. Those researchers should focus on the core problem and not on the syntax or specific behavior of specific programming languages. Therefore, great scientific platforms or languages like Matlab and Python are often used by scientists to tackle those core problems.

Once the core problem is solved, though, it often needs to be integrated in a product and brought into production. This often creates new issues. Scientific platforms are focused on helping researchers finding the best solution to a scientific problem, not on finding the best way to integrate with databases, web services, and high-availability and security services.

The latter are areas where Java excels in. However, when scientists would have to use the same environment as Java enterprise developers, their productivity would most likely drop.

When doing pure research, the iteration cycles are very different from developing business applications and running integration tests. During research, scientists want to measure the impact of changing a single variable, or they want to add a new layer to an existing deep learning model. They should be able to inspect the parameters and intermediate values of their algorithms. This is different from debugging business applications. It requires faster and deeper interactions with the algorithm itself, without the need of recompiling applications or running unit tests.

In the following, we will show how modern Java allows for this rapid scientific development, thanks to JShell. The JShell tool is included in the Java SE distributions starting from Java 9. It is a so-called REPL, which is an acronym for "read-eval-print-loop," and it provides developers with a simple and interactive environment for creating and inspecting applications and algorithms. JShell is built on top of Java, and you can leverage all Java APIs with JShell, including the JavaFX APIs.

Therefore, JShell is a great tool allowing the transition between scientific research and development for production as illustrated in Figure 14-5.

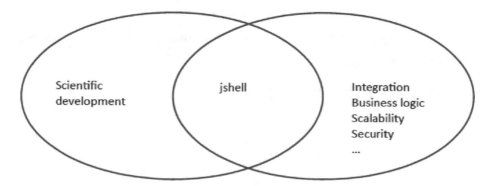

Figure 14-5. *JShell allows for a transition between the scientific development and the integration in business environments*

We will first show the basic functionalities of JShell. Next, we will show how you can easily work with linear algebra in JShell, using the ND4J library. Finally, we will demonstrate how using JavaFX with JShell allows for real easy and fast visualization during prototyping.

Using JShell

Starting JShell is very easy. JShell is a tool located in the same directory as the javac and java wrapper. Hence, if you managed to add java and javac to your path, simply invoking

```
jshell
```

should start the tool. Once JShell is started, you enter the JShell environment in which you can enter commands or statements.

After starting JShell, you see the following:

```
⏺ ◯ ◯                ⌂ johan — java ‹ jshell — 80×24
[~ $ jshell                                                                    ]
|  Welcome to JShell -- Version 17-internal
|  For an introduction type: /help intro

jshell>
```

Note that the version number says "17-internal." The reason for this is that this screenshot (and the next screenshots as well) is created with a custom-built version of OpenJDK 17 before the binary release was available.

JShell allows you to create Java statements. For example, the following statement can be written after the JShell prompt:

```
System.out.println("Hello, JShell");
```

It will result immediately in the following response:

```
● ○ ●                    ⌂ johan — java ‹ jshell — 80×24
[~ $ jshell                                                                   ]
|   Welcome to JShell -- Version 17-internal
|   For an introduction type: /help intro

[jshell> System.out.println("Hello, JShell");                                 ]
 Hello, JShell

 jshell> █
```

While this looks very similar to how a regular Java application is created, it is important to notice that we didn't have to create a package or a class or a main method. The following statement is equivalent to creating a class HelloWorld containing the following definition:

```
public class HelloWorld {
    public static void main(String[] args) {
        System.out.println("Hello, Jshell");
    }
}
```

Next, we would have to compile the class

```
javac HelloWorld.java
```

and run it using

```
java HelloWorld
```

Note   As of Java 11, it is possible to skip the compilation step and directly run the class using `java HelloWorld.java`.

While the end result is the same ("Hello, JShell" is being printed), the steps are very different. Creating a class and a method with modifiers is very important when working on complex or modular software, and it should not be seen as overhead in this case. However, when we simply want to know what would be printed in the preceding snippet, the approach using JShell is giving us much faster answers.

Using JShell for printing "Hello, JShell" is not very ambitious, but we showed that you can use the same Java syntax in Java applications and in JShell. Hence, the familiarity with Java is one of the key advantages of JShell.

Scientific applications often require mathematical operations. We will now show an example that has more mathematical functionality.

The following snippet will print the value of the sine of a parameter that takes the value of 0, 30, 60, and 90 degrees:

```
jshell> IntStream.range(0, 4).mapToDouble(i -> 30. * i * 2* Math.PI/360.).forEac
h(d -> System.out.println(Math.sin(d)));
0.0
0.49999999999999994
0.8660254037844386
1.0
```

Again, note how similar this snippet is to how a Java application achieving the same would look like. For convenience, such a Java application is shown in the following:

```
import java.util.stream.*;
public class JshellSin {
    public static void main(String[] args) {
        IntStream.range(0, 4)
            .mapToDouble(i -> 30. * i * 2* Math.PI/360.)
            .forEach(d -> System.out.println(Math.sin(d)));
    }
}
```

One of the great things about JShell is the integrated editor functionalities. We can use the arrow up/down to move to a previous/next statement and edit that statement.

For example, suppose we made a mistake in our algorithm. Instead of the sine, we wanted to print the cosine.

We can easily do this by pressing the arrow up key once, which will show the previous line again, and we can modify it so that we replace "Math.sin" with "Math.cos."

Pressing return immediately reevaluates the expression and prints the results:

```
jshell> IntStream.range(0, 4).mapToDouble(i -> 30. * i * 2* Math.PI/360.).forEac
h(d -> System.out.println(Math.cos(d)));
1.0
0.8660254037844387
0.5000000000000001
6.123233995736766E-17
```

As such, what JShell is allowing us here is to experiment with our statements or algorithm, by editing statements and immediately getting feedback about the results.

This approach is already more similar to how scientists work with Python and Matlab to create algorithms.

A huge advantage of JShell is that the code is 100% compatible with new or existing Java applications. The JShell code can easily be pasted in a Java class.

JShell contains a number of commands for saving and loading snippets. Those snippets can then be pasted in your applications.

Hence, the final resulting work, achieved by a scientist using JShell, can immediately be used by a Java developer who uses an IDE and works on integrating the scientific algorithms with other components in the project. The JShell snippet can be wrapped in a private method, submitted to an executor, surrounded with header parameters including security credentials and more.

While we touched some of the core concepts of JShell, we barely scratched the surface of what is possible. In the remainder of this chapter, we will focus on how JShell can be used in environments that combine scientific work and high-quality visualizations. If you want to learn more about JShell itself, you are recommended to have a look at the official JShell product page at https://docs.oracle.com/en/java/javase/17/jshell/introduction-jshell.html.

About ND4J

The ND4J linear algebra library, which was introduced in the previous chapter, allows for Java developers to access high-performant linear algebra functionality in a way that is very convenient to Java developers.

ND4J provides an abstraction layer on top of the platform-dependent libraries that provide linear algebra tools. The name ND4J refers to N-dimensional linear algebra for Java. Many platforms (e.g., Windows, macOS, Linux, iOS, Android) contain linear algebra libraries that are highly optimized for the specific platform. Moreover, the availability of specific hardware (e.g., GPUs) may lead to even more specific implementations of some functionality.

Since performance is very important in the data science area, it is crucial for Java developers to be able to leverage the functionality provided by those native libraries. However, it would be a pain for those developers if they have to write applications that only work for a specific hardware or operating system configuration.

This is where ND4J, and its dependencies, provides a solution. The top layer of ND4J provides APIs that users can interact with. These are Java APIs that are familiar to Java developers, but also to scientists as they provide the typical functionality one can expect from a linear algebra library. Under the hood, those APIs are mapped to the best available native library.

The ND4J library provides lots of value to Java developers who want to work with mathematical functionality, but also to researchers and scientists who want their work to be easily integrated in new or existing Java applications, whether they are running in a big enterprise or cloud environment or on embedded or mobile devices or anything between them.

Before we show how to use ND4J with JShell, we show a very simple application that uses ND4J for doing basic matrix manipulations.

Consider the following sample:

```java
import org.nd4j.linalg.api.ndarray.INDArray;
import org.nd4j.linalg.factory.Nd4j;
public class HelloNd4j {
    public static void main(String[] args) {
        INDArray a = Nd4j.zeros(3,5);
        System.out.println("Matrix a has 3 rows and 5 columns:\n"+a);
        System.out.println("++++++++++++++++++++++++++++++++++\n");
        INDArray b = Nd4j.create(new double[] {0.,1.,2.,3.,4.,5.},
        new int[] {2,3});
        INDArray c = Nd4j.create(new double[] {2.,-1.,3.}, new int[] {3,1});
        System.out.println("Matrix b has 2 rows and 3 columns:\n"+b);
        System.out.println("++++++++++++++++++++++++++++++++++\n");
        System.out.println("Vector c has 3 elements:\n"+c);
        System.out.println("++++++++++++++++++++++++++++++++++\n");
        INDArray d = b.mmul(c);
```

```
        System.out.println("matrix product of b x c  =\n"+d);
        System.out.println("+++++++++++++++++++++++++++++++++\n");
    }
}
```

The ND4J library requires other libraries to be available on the classpath. Since we don't want to be bothered about exactly what libraries we need, we delegate that part to a build tool, for example, Maven. In a pom.xm file, we declare what we need, and Maven will make sure all related dependencies are downloaded and put on the classpath.

The following pom.xml can be used to achieve this:

```xml
<project xmlns="http://maven.apache.org/POM/4.0.0"
xmlns:xsi="http://www.w3.org/2001/XMLSchema-instance"
  xsi:schemaLocation="http://maven.apache.org/POM/4.0.0
  http://maven.apache.org/maven-v4_0_0.xsd">
  <modelVersion>4.0.0</modelVersion>
  <packaging>jar</packaging>
  <groupId>org.modernclient</groupId>
  <artifactId>nd4jshell</artifactId>
  <version>1.0.0</version>
  <url>http://maven.apache.org</url>
  <dependencies>
    <dependency>
      <groupId>org.nd4j</groupId>
      <artifactId>nd4j-native-platform</artifactId>
      <version>1.0.0-M1</version>
    </dependency>
    <dependency>
      <groupId>org.openjfx</groupId>
      <artifactId>javafx-controls</artifactId>
      <version>17.0.1</version>
    </dependency>
  </dependencies>
  <build>
    <plugins>
      <plugin>
```

```
            <groupId>org.apache.maven.plugins</groupId>
            <artifactId>maven-compiler-plugin</artifactId>
            <version>3.8.0</version>
            <configuration>
              <release>11</release>
            </configuration>
          </plugin>
          <plugin>
            <groupId>org.codehaus.mojo</groupId>
            <artifactId>exec-maven-plugin</artifactId>
            <version>1.6.0</version>
            <executions>
              <execution>
                <goals>
                  <goal>java</goal>
                </goals>
              </execution>
            </executions>
            <configuration>
              <mainClass>org.modernclient.HelloNd4j</mainClass>
            </configuration>
          </plugin>
        </plugins>
      </build>
</project>
```

If we run this application using

```
mvn compile exec:java
```

we see the following output:

```
Matrix a has 3 rows and 5 columns:
[[         0,          0,          0,          0,          0],
 [         0,          0,          0,          0,          0],
 [         0,          0,          0,          0,          0]]
```

```
+++++++++++++++++++++++++++++++
Matrix b has 2 rows and 3 columns:
[[         0,    1.0000,    2.0000],
 [    3.0000,    4.0000,    5.0000]]
+++++++++++++++++++++++++++++++
Vector c has 3 elements:
[2.0000,
 -1.0000,
 3.0000]
+++++++++++++++++++++++++++++++
matrix product of b x c  =
[5.0000,
 17.0000]
+++++++++++++++++++++++++++++++
```

In this simple application, we created a few matrices and a vector, and we multiplied a matrix and a vector. While these are not extraordinary calculations, they show how ND4J works. If you want to read more about ND4J, and by extension about the projects that are related with it, we recommend to have a look at `https://deeplearning4j.org/docs/latest/nd4j-overview`. In the next section, we will explain how you can easily integrate applications based on ND4J in JShell.

Using ND4J in JShell

We can start JShell with the same classpath as the application that is hosted in the same directory by typing

```
mvn compile com.github.johnpoth:jshell-maven-plugin:1.3:run
```

Note that this requires the pom.xml file to be available in the same directory as where we type this command. The pom.xml file contains the dependencies for the application, and based on those dependencies (including transitive dependencies), the JShell-maven-plugin composes the classpath that is provided to JShell. The pom file used for this sample is shown in the following:

```
<project xmlns="http://maven.apache.org/POM/4.0.0"
xmlns:xsi="http://www.w3.org/2001/XMLSchema-instance"
  xsi:schemaLocation="http://maven.apache.org/POM/4.0.0
```

```xml
http://maven.apache.org/maven-v4_0_0.xsd">
<modelVersion>4.0.0</modelVersion>
<packaging>jar</packaging>
<groupId>org.modernclient</groupId>
<artifactId>plotjshell</artifactId>
<version>1.0.0</version>
<url>http://maven.apache.org</url>
<dependencies>
  <dependency>
    <groupId>org.openjfx</groupId>
    <artifactId>javafx-controls</artifactId>
    <version>17.0.1</version>
  </dependency>
</dependencies>
<build>
  <plugins>
    <plugin>
      <groupId>org.apache.maven.plugins</groupId>
      <artifactId>maven-compiler-plugin</artifactId>
      <version>3.8.0</version>
      <configuration>
        <release>11</release>
      </configuration>
    </plugin>
    <plugin>
      <groupId>org.codehaus.mojo</groupId>
      <artifactId>exec-maven-plugin</artifactId>
      <version>1.6.0</version>
      <executions>
        <execution>
          <goals>
            <goal>exec</goal>
          </goals>
        </execution>
      </executions>
```

```
<configuration>
    <executable>java</executable>
    <longModulepath>false</longModulepath>
    <arguments>
        <argument>--module-path</argument>
        <classpath />
        <argument>--add-modules</argument>
        <argument>javafx.controls</argument>
        <argument>-classpath</argument>
        <classpath />
        <argument>org.modernclient.Plot</argument>
    </arguments>
</configuration>
                </plugin>
            </plugins>
        </build>
</project>
```

As a result, the command shown in the preceding text will start JShell with the classpath that is also used in the application. First, we import the packages that we require in our application:

```
● ● ●   hellond4j — java ‹ java -Xmx2048m -classpath /opt/apache-maven-3.5.4/boot...
[INFO]
[INFO] ----------------------< org.modernclient:nd4jshell >----------------------
[INFO] Building nd4jshell 1.0.0
[INFO] --------------------------------[ jar ]---------------------------------
[INFO]
[INFO] --- maven-resources-plugin:2.6:resources (default-resources) @ nd4jshell
---
[WARNING] Using platform encoding (UTF-8 actually) to copy filtered resources, i
.e. build is platform dependent!
[INFO] skip non existing resourceDirectory /Users/johan/javafx/mcj-samples/ch14-
JavaFXScience/hellond4j/src/main/resources
[INFO]
[INFO] --- maven-compiler-plugin:3.8.0:compile (default-compile) @ nd4jshell ---
[INFO] Nothing to compile - all classes are up to date
[INFO]
[INFO] --- jshell-maven-plugin:1.3:run (default-cli) @ nd4jshell ---
|  Welcome to JShell -- Version 17-internal
|  For an introduction type: /help intro

[jshell> import org.nd4j.linalg.api.ndarray.INDArray;                         ]

[jshell> import org.nd4j.linalg.factory.Nd4j;                                 ]

 jshell> ▮
```

We now enter the commands from the preceding application one by one. JShell will give immediate output after a single line has been entered. The first command that uses the ND4J API will initialize the ND4J backend, during which the most optimal provider for linear algebraic functions is selected and initialized. The feedback for this is printed before the result of this first command.

In our case, the first command is the creation of a 3 × 5 matrix, which contains all zeroes. Entering this command generates the following output:

```
jshell> import org.nd4j.linalg.api.ndarray.INDArray;

jshell> import org.nd4j.linalg.factory.Nd4j;

jshell> INDArray a = Nd4j.zeros(3,5);
SLF4J: Failed to load class "org.slf4j.impl.StaticLoggerBinder".
SLF4J: Defaulting to no-operation (NOP) logger implementation
SLF4J: See http://www.slf4j.org/codes.html#StaticLoggerBinder for further details.
a ==> [[        0,        0,        0,        0,    ...  0,        0,        0]]
```

Note   The Nd4j library has a number of different implementations, based on a combination of parameters including operating system, CPU, and GPU. Some of these implementations give more (or different) logging output than others, so you might see different output than the one pasted previously. The important line is the last one, where the result of the command is being printed.

We can now continue entering commands and inspect the output. For example, after entering the first line where we declare the 2 × 3 matrix, we get the following output:

```
jshell> INDArray b = Nd4j.create(new double[] {0.,1.,2.,3.,4.,5.}, new int[] {2,3});
b ==> [[        0,   1.0000,   2.0000],
 [    3.0000,   4.0000,   5.0000]]
```

After entering the last command (ignoring the System.out.println), the output of the matrix-vector multiplication is shown:

```
jshell>            INDArray d = b.mmul(c);
d ==> [5.0000,
  17.0000]

jshell> ▊
```

This is the same result as we got from our application.

One of the nice things we can now do with JShell is to just build on top of this result. For example, if we want to multiply all elements in the resulting vector with a scalar 3, we enter the command d.mul(3) . The ND4J Javadoc explains that the mul command will multiply the matrix elements by a provided number – see https://deeplearning4j. org/api/latest/org/nd4j/linalg/api/ndarray/INDArray.html#mul-java.lang. Number-.

We do not have to rerun the existing code or recompile an application. We simply type the command, and the result is immediately shown:

```
[jshell> d.muli(3);
$7 ==> [15.0000,
   51.0000]
```

Finally, we will show some operations you can do using JShell. The examples we show have no scientific meaning, but they should illustrate the flexibility of the JShell tool, compared to the typical development cycle that involves modifying source code in an IDE, recompiling, and running from scratch.

After we executed the commands from the previous sample, we want to create a new function. In this new function, all elements of a matrix (or a vector) are multiplied by a number, and then another number is subtracted from the result.

The function, which we will name someOperation, that does this is defined as follows, in Java syntax:

```
INDArray someOperation(INDArray src, int m, int s) {
        return src.mul(m).add(-s);
}
```

Defining functions in JShell is very similar to defining functions in Java applications. We just enter the function definition. JShell will give confirmation about the created function, and from that moment on, we can use the function in all our operations:

```
jshell> INDArray someOperation(INDArray src, int m, int s) {
   ...> return src.mul(m).add(-s);
   ...> }
|  created method someOperation(INDArray,int,int)
```

For example, we can now use this new function on the b matrix that was created before. We will multiply all elements of b with 2 and then subtract 1 of each element. For clarity, we first print the current value of b, which is easily done by simply entering b; at the JShell prompt:

```
jshell> b;
b ==> [[           0,    1.0000,     2.0000],
   [    3.0000,    4.0000,     5.0000]]

jshell> someOperation(b,2,1);
$31 ==> [[   -1.0000,    1.0000,     3.0000],
   [    5.0000,    7.0000,     9.0000]]
```

Note the "$31" prefixing the result. When no result variable is used, JShell will automatically create a variable itself and assign the result to this variable. Those variables can later be used again, similar to how other variables are used.

USING JavaFX in JShell

Since JShell is built on top of the JVM, any library, framework, or application that runs on the JVM can run using JShell. It may sound overkill to use a REPL to create JavaFX applications, and in many cases it is indeed not recommended. However, the Java visualization technologies in JavaFX allow for rapid visualization of data, which can be very useful when developing a scientific application.

Before we show an example of this rapid visualization, we explain how a JavaFX application can be executed inside JShell. But first, we will show an alternative way of starting stand-alone JavaFX applications.

Starting Stand-Alone JavaFX Code

Typically, a JavaFX application extends javafx.application.Application. Its start method is called by the JavaFX runtime. The JavaFX launcher manages the bootstrap of the JavaFX runtime.

However, we can also directly start the JavaFX runtime and run JavaFX applications inside a single method. The following code snippet shows how to do this:

```
package org.modernclient;
import javafx.application.Application;
import javafx.application.Platform;
```

```
import javafx.scene.Scene;
import javafx.scene.control.Button;
import javafx.scene.control.Label;
import javafx.scene.layout.StackPane;
import javafx.stage.Stage;
public class StandAlone {
    public static void showHello() {
        Platform.startup(() -> {});
        Platform.setImplicitExit(false);
        Platform.runLater( () -> {
            Label label = new Label ("Hello, standalone JavaFX");
            Button button = new Button ("Click me");
            button.setOnAction(e -> {label.setText("Clicked");});
            button.setTranslateY(50);
            StackPane box = new StackPane();
            box.getChildren().addAll(label, button);
            Scene s = new Scene(box, 200, 200);
            Stage stage = new Stage();
            stage.setTitle("StandAlone Hello");
            stage.setScene(s);
            stage.show();
        });
    }
    public static void main(String[] args) {
        showHello();
    }
}
```

In this application, the main method calls a static method showHello(), which launches the JavaFX runtime manually by calling

```
Platform.startup(() -> {})
```

This method will start the JavaFX runtime and call the supplied Runnable when the startup has been completed successfully. In our case, we don't call a Runnable immediately; hence, we pass an empty Runnable. Once this method returns, the JavaFX

Application Thread is created, and we can use Platform.runLater() statements to create or modify the SceneGraph, similar to how we should do it with JavaFX applications where the runtime is started by the JavaFX launcher.

We first compile the class with Maven, using

```
mvn compile
```

If you prefer to use a command-line compilation, that is easily done by the following command:

```
javac -p /opt/javafx-sdk-17/lib --add-modules javafx.controls src/main/
java/org/modernclient/StandAlone.java
where /opt/javafx-sdk-17 should be replaced with the location where you
downloaded the JavaFX 17 SDK.
```

We run it with

```
mvn exec:exec
```

or, if you used the command-line compilation and have the classes compiled to the same directory as the sources

```
java -p /opt/javafx-sdk-17/lib --add-modules javafx.controls -cp src/main/
java/ org.modernclient.StandAlone
```

The result is shown in the following:

In order for Maven to correctly launch this application, we have to supply the module path and the required modules (javafx.controls) to the pom.xml. The relevant part of the pom.xml file is shown in the following:

```xml
<plugin>
        <groupId>org.codehaus.mojo</groupId>
        <artifactId>exec-maven-plugin</artifactId>
        <version>1.6.0</version>
        <executions>
          <execution>
            <goals>
              <goal>exec</goal>
            </goals>
          </execution>
        </executions>
        <configuration>
            <executable>java</executable>
            <longModulepath>false</longModulepath>
            <arguments>
                <argument>--module-path</argument>
                <classpath />
                <argument>--add-modules</argument>
                <argument>javafx.controls</argument>
                <argument>-classpath</argument>
                <classpath />
                <argument>org.modernclient.StandAlone</argument>
            </arguments>
        </configuration>
    </plugin>
```

In this snippet, we configured the exec task to call the Java command, but we don't use the default launcher that Maven would otherwise use. Instead, we manually tell Java that it should take the module path from the classpath (which includes the dependency javafx-controls) and add the javafx.controls module.

Running this application can also be done on the command line. For example, if the JavaFX SDK is installed at /opt/javafx-sdk-17, the following works:

```
java -p /opt/javafx-sdk-17/lib/ --add-modules javafx.controls -cp target/
classes org.modernclient.StandAlone
```

JavaFX Applications in JShell

We can now run the code in JShell. As we mentioned before, JShell is using a JVM for its execution. We can simply enter the same commands in JShell, and the output will immediately tell us what happened.

If we assume the JavaFX SDK is installed in /opt/javafx-sdk-11.0.12, the following command launches JShell, sets the module path correctly, and adds the javafx.controls module:

```
jshell --module-path /opt/javafx-sdk-11.0.12/lib/ --add-modules javafx.controls
```

We can now enter the commands that ultimately make a JavaFX application, starting with the imports:

```
|   Welcome to JShell -- Version 11
|   For an introduction type: /help intro

jshell> import javafx.application.Application;

jshell> import javafx.application.Platform;

jshell> import javafx.scene.Scene;

jshell> import javafx.scene.control.Button;

jshell> import javafx.scene.control.Label;

jshell> import javafx.scene.layout.StackPane;

jshell> import javafx.stage.Stage;

jshell> █
```

Note that we didn't add a package declaration. This touches on one of the few differences between regular Java applications and JShell code. Packages are created with the goal of exposing functionality and using that in other components, in other libraries. The JShell concept is to provide a stand-alone, interactive, and self-contained environment; hence, it does not make sense to expose packages.

Now that the imports are added, we can create the showHello() method. We will first use JShell in a less efficient way, but in the next section, we will show how this can be done in a much more productive way.

For now, we simply copy-paste the showHello method. This gives the following output:

```
jshell>     public static void showHello() {
   ...>           Platform.startup(() -> {});
   ...>           Platform.setImplicitExit(false);
   ...>           Platform.runLater( () -> {
   ...>               Label label = new Label ("Hello, standalone JavaFX");
   ...>               Button button = new Button ("Click me");
   ...>               button.setOnAction(e -> {label.setText("Clicked");});
   ...>               button.setTranslateY(50);
   ...>               StackPane box = new StackPane();
   ...>               box.getChildren().addAll(label, button);
   ...>               Scene s = new Scene(box, 200, 200);
   ...>               Stage stage = new Stage();
   ...>               stage.setTitle("StandAlone Hello");
   ...>               stage.setScene(s);
   ...>               stage.show();
   ...>           });
   ...>     }
|  Warning:
|  Modifier 'static'  not permitted in top-level declarations, ignored
|      public static void showHello() {
|      ^------------^
|  created method showHello()
```

The JShell editor allows for statements or declarations to be split over many lines. The parser recognizes that after the first line is entered, more content is needed. Hence, it will only process the method declaration after we complete it. It will detect the final closing curly bracket.

In earlier versions of JShell, a warning was shown, telling us that the static keyword was ignored. In JShell, all top-level declarations are static so that keyword is useless in this context. This is another difference between regular applications and code living in the JShell context.

Now that the method is declared, we can call it. This is simply done by calling showHello() from the JShell prompt:

```
jshell> showHello();

jshell>
```

The statement returns immediately, and it will render the same image as shown in the preceding screenshot.

593

JavaFX Libraries in JShell

While the example in the previous section works, it is very verbose, requires manual typing or copy-pasting, and does not really allow for fast prototyping. The real benefit for the combination of JavaFX and JShell comes from libraries and functions that provide simple things that can then be called from JShell statements. Typically, the functions are created in Java files, compiled, and made available to JShell. This is very similar to how the ND4J libraries are made available to JShell.

As an example, we create a simple function that creates a JavaFX chart containing some scattered data.

We write the function as a regular Java function, as shown in the code in the following:

```java
package org.modernclient;
import javafx.application.*;
import javafx.collections.FXCollections;
import javafx.collections.ObservableList;
import javafx.scene.Scene;
import javafx.scene.chart.NumberAxis;
import javafx.scene.chart.ScatterChart;
import javafx.scene.chart.XYChart;
import javafx.scene.chart.XYChart.Data;
import javafx.stage.Stage;
public class Plot {
    public static void scatter(double[] x, double[] y, String title) {
        Platform.startup(() -> {});
        Platform.setImplicitExit(false);
        Platform.runLater( () -> {
        NumberAxis xAxis = new NumberAxis();
        NumberAxis yAxis = new NumberAxis();
        ScatterChart chart = new ScatterChart(xAxis, yAxis);
        ObservableList<XYChart.Series> chartData =
         FXCollections.observableArrayList();
        XYChart.Series<Number, Number> series = new XYChart.Series<>();
        ObservableList<Data<Number, Number>> data =
         FXCollections.observableArrayList();
```

```
    for (int i = 0; i < x.length; i++) {
        Data<Number, Number> d = new Data<>(x[i],y[i]);
        data.add(d);
    }
    series.setData(data);
    chartData.setAll(series);
    chart.setData(chartData);
    Scene s = new Scene(chart, 400, 400);
    Stage stage = new Stage();
    stage.setTitle(title);
    stage.setScene(s);
    stage.show();
    });
  }
  public static void main(String[] args) {
      double[] x = new double[]{0.,1.,2.};
      double[] y = new double[]{0.,10.,16.};
      scatter(x, y, "plot");
  }
}
```

In this code, we defined a scatter function that takes three arguments: an array of doubles containing the x coordinates, an array of doubles containing the y coordinates, and a title for the chart. The scatter function initializes the JavaFX runtime, and then it creates a ScatterChart containing the data provided by the arguments. The chart is added to the Scene and rendered on the Stage.

We added a main function to this class so that we can test the function using regular Java invocations. In this main function, we pass three data points (hence three values for the x array and three values for the y array), and we supply the title "plot."

To get the UI in Figure 14-6, we will compile and run the application using the same approach as before:

```
Mvn compile exec:exec
```

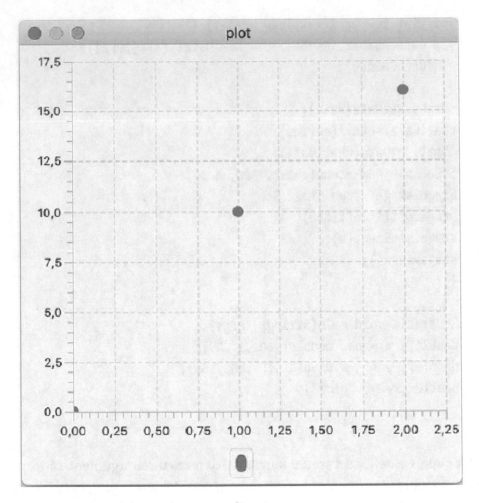

Figure 14-6. *Results of the running application*

We will now make this function available to JShell and call it from there.
We start JShell using the Maven plugin we used before:

```
mvn com.github.johnpoth:jshell-maven-plugin:1.1:run
```

Make sure to invoke this command in the directory that contains the pom.xml file for the plot code. This will add the compiled classes and dependencies to the class and module path.

When JShell is started, the following message is shown:

```
[INFO] Scanning for projects...
[INFO]
[INFO] ------------------------------------------------------------------------
[INFO] Building plotjshell 1.0.0
[INFO] ------------------------------------------------------------------------
[INFO]
[INFO] --- jshell-maven-plugin:1.1:run (default-cli) @ plotjshell ---
|  Welcome to JShell -- Version 11-ea
|  For an introduction type: /help intro
```

We first import the Plot class by entering

```
Import org.modernclient.Plot;
```

We also create two arrays containing the x and y values for the data points we want to visualize:

```
jshell> import org.modernclient.Plot;

jshell> double[] c = new double[]{0.0, 1.0, 2.5, 3.4, 4.8};
c ==> double[5] { 0.0, 1.0, 2.5, 3.4, 4.8 }

jshell> double[] d = new double[]{4.0, 5.2, 6.5, 5.4, 3.8};
d ==> double[5] { 4.0, 5.2, 6.5, 5.4, 3.8 }
```

Finally, to create the graph shown in Figure 14-7, we call the scatter function as follows:

```
Plot.scatter(c, d, "plot from jshell");
```

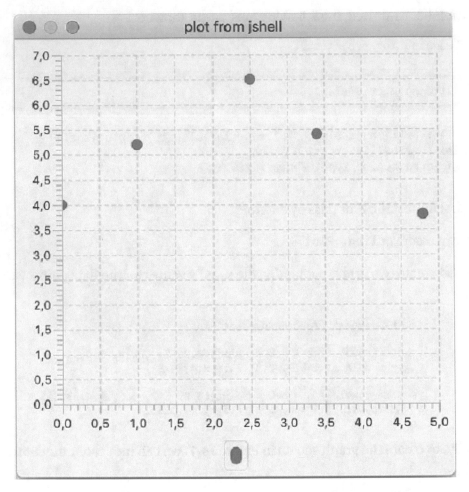

Figure 14-7. *The new plot graph, resulting from the preceding code*

One of the nice features of JShell is that there are a number of built-in commands that allow it to work more efficiently with the editor. The /list command, for example, shows the commands that have been executed in order. After we successfully applied the previous steps, the result of the /list command is shown in the following:

```
[jshell> /list

   1 : import org.modernclient.Plot;
   2 : double[] c = new double[]{0.0, 1.0, 2.5, 3.4, 4.8};
   3 : double[] d = new double[]{4.0, 5.2, 6.5, 5.4, 3.8};
   4 : Plot.scatter(c, d, "plot from jshell");

       —
```

This screenshot clearly shows that it is much easier to call predefined functions in JShell than to declare all functions manually in JShell. As a rule of thumb, if you expect your function to be modified very often, you can declare it in JShell. But if you mainly want to evaluate functions and inspect the results, declaring them in classes and importing them in the JShell environment is more appropriate.

Conclusion

The combination of Java and JavaFX provides a solid foundation for scientific work. Java itself is already very performant and highly scalable. Using JShell and ND4J, it becomes possible for (data) scientists to work on research projects that require flexible manipulation of data, using familiar linear algebra routines.

Often, interactive visualization during the design process shortens the development cycle and improves the quality of the result. Bringing the JavaFX visualization in the picture during the research phase allows for real-time visualization and highly interactive scientific applications.

Index

A

Accordion class, 157

addAll() method, 124

addListener(), 112

Advanced controls

    ListView (*see* ListView control)

    TableView (*see* TableView control)

    TreeTableView, 200–202

    TreeView control, 192, 193

Ahead Of Time (AOT), 395, 420

Alert class, 181, 182

AlertType, 182

AmbientLight, 334, 335

AnchorPane, 30, 31, 43

Animation, JavaFX, 50–52

Applets, 12

ArrayChangeListener interface, 112

ArrayChangeListener events, 124–126

Artificial neural networks, 541–544

asString() method, 57

B

Bidirectional binding, 52, 57, 88

BidirectionalBindingExample.java, 91, 92

bindBidirectional() method, 57, 88

bindContentBidirectional() method, 127

bindContent() method, 127

Binding interface, 92

Binding, JavaFX

    bidirectional, 57

    fluent and bindings APIs, 57, 58

    unidirectional, 56

Bindings creation

    by direct extension, 93, 95

    with Fluent API, 101–106

    JavaFX bindings, 92, 93

    observable collections, 127

Bindings utility class, 127

bind() method, 56, 88, 94

Blocking dialog, 182

BorderPane, 44

Bouncing balls, 245, 247

Bound property, 134

build.gradle file, 443

build() method, 137

ButtonBar control, 157

ButtonBar class, 158

Button class, 147

Button control, 169, 173

C

Canvas

    application

        bouncing balls, 245, 247

        GraphicApp abstract class, 243–245

    build geometric shapes, 239

    fillRect and fillOval, 237

© Stephen Chin, Johan Vos and James Weaver 2022
S. Chin et al., *The Definitive Guide to Modern Java Clients with JavaFX 17*,
https://doi.org/10.1007/978-1-4842-7268-8

U, V

Printed in the United States
by Baker & Taylor Publisher Services